Study Guide

Principles of Macroeconomics
Third Edition

N. Gregory Mankiw
Harvard University

Prepared by

David R. Hakes
University of Northern Iowa

THOMSON

SOUTH-WESTERN

2516

Australia · Canada · Mexico · Singapore · Spain · United Kingdom · United States

THOMSON
SOUTH-WESTERN

Study Guide to accompany

Principles of Macroeconomics, 3e

N. Gregory Mankiw

Prepared by

David R. Hakes

Vice President, Editorial Director:
Jack W. Calhoun

Vice President, Editor-in-Chief:
Michael P. Roche

Publisher of Economics:
Michael B. Mercier

Senior Acquisitions Editor:
Peter Adams

Developmental Editor:
Jane Tufts

Contributing Editors:
Jeff Gilbreath
Sarah K. Dorger
Susanna C. Smart

Senior Marketing Manager:
Janet Hennies

Senior Marketing Coordinator:
Jenny Fruechtenicht

Production Editor:
Daniel C. Plofchan

Manufacturing Coordinator:
Sandee Milewski

Senior Media Technology Editor:
Vicky True

Media Developmental Editor:
Peggy Buskey

Media Production Editor:
Pam Wallace

Compositor:
Graphic Arts Center Indianapolis

Project Management:
OffCenter Concept House
Soldotna, AK

Printer:
Globus Printing, Inc.
Minster, Ohio

Senior Design Project Manager:
Mike Stratton

Internal/Cover Designer:
Mike Stratton

Cover Illustration:
"Market Scene"
19th century French watercolor
Artist unknown
From a private collection

Cover Images:
PhotoDisc, Inc.

Book ISBN: 0-324-17465-9

One must learn by doing the thing;
For though you think you know it
You have no certainty, until you try.

Sophocles, c. 496–406 B.C.
Greek playwright
Trachiniae

Preface

This *Study Guide* accompanies N. Gregory Mankiw's *Principles of Macroeconomics*, Third Edition. It was written with only one audience in mind—you, the student.

Your time is scarce. To help you use it efficiently, this *Study Guide* focuses strictly on the material presented in Mankiw's *Principles of Macroeconomics*, Third Edition. It does not introduce extraneous material.

Objectives of the Study Guide

There are three broad objectives to the *Study Guide*. First, the *Study Guide* reinforces the text and improves your understanding of the material presented in the text. Second, it provides you with experience in using economic theories and tools to solve actual economic problems. That is, this *Study Guide* bridges the gap between economic concepts and economic problem solving. This may be the most important objective of the *Study Guide* because those students who find economics inherently logical often think that they are prepared for exams just by reading the text or attending lectures. However, it is one thing to watch an economist solve a problem in class and another thing altogether to solve a problem alone. There is simply no substitute for hands-on experience. Third, the *Study Guide* includes a self-test to validate areas of successful learning and to highlight areas needing improvement.

It is unlikely that you will truly enjoy any area of study if you fail to understand the material or if you lack confidence when taking tests over the material. It is my hope that this *Study Guide* improves your understanding of economics and improves your test performance so that you are able to enjoy economics as much as I do.

Organization of the Study Guide

Each chapter in the *Study Guide* corresponds to a chapter in Mankiw's *Principles of Macroeconomics*. Each chapter is divided into the following sections:

- The Chapter Overview begins with a description of the purpose of the chapter and how it fits into the larger framework of the text. Following this context and purpose section are learning objectives, a section-by-section Chapter Review, and some helpful hints for understanding the material. The Chapter Overview ends with terms and definitions. This part is particularly important because it is impossible for the text to communicate information to you or for you to communicate information to your instructor on your exams without the use of a common economic vocabulary.

- Problems and Short-Answer Questions provide hands-on experience with problems based on the material presented in the text. The practice problems are generally multiple-step problems while the short-answer questions are generally based on a single issue.

- The Self-Test is composed of 15 True/False questions and 20 Multiple-Choice questions.

- The Advanced Critical Thinking section is a real-world problem that employs the economic reasoning and tools developed in the chapter. It is an applied story problem.

- Solutions are provided for all questions in the *Study Guide*. Explanations are also provided for false responses to True/False questions in the Self-Test.

Use of the Study Guide

I hesitate to suggest a method for using this *Study Guide* because how one best uses a study guide is largely a personal matter. It depends on your preferences and talents and on your instructor's approach to the material. I will, however, discuss a few possible approaches, and trial and error may help you sort out an approach that best suits you.

Some students prefer to read an entire chapter in the text prior to reading the *Study Guide*. Others prefer to read a section in the text and then read the corresponding section in the Chapter Overview portion of the *Study Guide*. This second method may help you focus your attention on the most important aspects of each section in the text. Some students who feel particularly confident after reading the text may choose to take the Self-Test immediately. I do not generally support this approach. I suggest that you complete all of the Practice Problems and Short-Answer Questions before you attempt the Self-Test. You will receive more accurate feedback from the Self-Test if you are well prepared prior to taking it.

A study guide is not a substitute for a text any more than *Cliff Notes* is a substitute for a classic novel. Use this *Study Guide* in conjunction with Mankiw's *Principles of Macroeconomics*, not in place of it.

Final Thoughts

All of the problems and questions in this *Study Guide* have been checked by a number of accuracy reviewers. However, if you find a mistake, or if you have comments or suggestions for future editions, please feel free to contact me via e-mail at hakes@uni.edu.

Acknowledgments

I would like to thank Greg Mankiw for having written such a well thought-out text that it made writing the *Study Guide* a truly enjoyable task. I thank Sarah Dorger, the Developmental Editor, for keeping in close contact with me throughout the project. Our regular conversations kept me on schedule and made the entire project a pleasant experience. Sheryl Nelson and Greg Sallee copy-edited the manuscript and also offered many helpful suggestions. Daniel Flores-Guri reviewed the chapters that are new to this edition. Ken McCormick, a friend and colleague, provided constructive counsel throughout the project.

Finally, I would like to thank my family for being patient and understanding during the many months I spent working on this *Study Guide*.

David R. Hakes
University of Northern Iowa
March 2003

Comparative Table of Contents

Contents

TEN PRINCIPLES OF ECONOMICS

GOALS

⌐In this chapter you will

Learn that economics is about the allocation of scarce resources

Examine some of the tradeoffs that people face

Learn the meaning of opportunity cost

See how to use marginal reasoning when making decisions

Discuss how incentives affect people's behavior

Consider why trade among people or nations can be good for everyone

Discuss why markets are a good, but not perfect, way to allocate resources

Learn what determines some trends in the overall economy

OUTCOMES

⌐After accomplishing these goals, you should be able to

Define scarcity

Explain the classic tradeoff between "guns and butter"

Add up your particular opportunity cost of attending college

Compare the marginal costs and marginal benefits of continuing to attend school indefinitely

Consider how a quadrupling of your tuition payments would affect your decision to educate yourself

Explain why specialization and trade improve people's choices

Give an example of an externality

Explain the source of large and persistent inflation

CHAPTER OVERVIEW

Context and Purpose

Chapter 1 is the first chapter in a three-chapter section that serves as the introduction to the text. Chapter 1 introduces ten fundamental principles on which the study of economics is based. In a broad sense, the rest of the text is an elaboration on these ten principles. Chapter 2 will develop how economists approach problems while Chapter 3 will explain how individuals and countries gain from trade.

The purpose of Chapter 1 is to lay out ten economic principles that will serve as building blocks for the rest of the text. The ten principles can be grouped into three categories: how people make decisions, how people interact, and how the economy works as a whole. Throughout the text, references will be made repeatedly to these ten principles.

CHAPTER REVIEW

Introduction

Households and society face decisions about how to allocate scarce resources. Resources are **scarce** in that we have fewer resources than we wish. **Economics** is the study of how society manages its scarce resources. Economists study how people make decisions about buying and selling, and saving and investing. We study how people interact with one another in markets where prices are determined and quantities are exchanged. We also study the economy as a whole when we concern ourselves with total income, unemployment, and inflation.

This chapter addresses ten principles of economics. The text will refer to these principles throughout. The ten principles are grouped into three categories: how people make decisions, how people interact, and how the economy works as a whole.

How People Make Decisions

People face tradeoffs. Economists often say, "There is no such thing as a free lunch." This means that there are always tradeoffs—to get more of something we like, we have to give up something else that we like. For example, if you spend money on dinner and a movie, you won't be able to spend it on new clothes. Socially, we face tradeoffs as a group. For example, there is the classic tradeoff between "guns and butter." That is, if we decide to spend more on national defense (guns), then we will have less to spend on social programs (butter). There is also a social tradeoff between **efficiency** (getting the most from our scarce resources) and **equity** (benefits being distributed fairly across society). Policies such as taxes and welfare make incomes more equal but these policies reduce returns to hard work and, thus, the economy doesn't produce as much. As a result, when the government tries to cut the pie into more equal pieces, the pie gets smaller.

The cost of something is what you give up to get it. The **opportunity cost** of an item is what you give up to get that item. It is the true cost of the item. The opportunity cost of going to college obviously includes your tuition payment. It also includes the value of your time that you could have spent working, valued at your potential wage. It would exclude your room and board payment because you have to eat and sleep whether you are in school or not.

Rational people think at the margin. **Marginal changes** are incremental changes to an existing plan. Rational decision-makers only proceed with an action if the *marginal benefit* exceeds the *marginal cost*. For example, you should only go to another year of school if the benefits from that year of schooling exceed the cost of attending that year. A farmer should produce another bushel of corn only if the benefit (price received) exceeds the cost of producing it.

People respond to incentives. Since rational people weigh marginal costs and marginal benefits of activities, they will respond when these costs or benefits change. For example, when the price of automobiles rises, buyers have an incentive to buy fewer cars while automobile producers have an incentive to hire more workers and produce more autos. Public policy can alter the costs or benefits of activities. For example, a luxury tax on expensive boats raises the price and discourages purchases. Some policies have unintended consequences because they alter behavior in a manner that was not predicted.

How People Interact

Trade can make everyone better off. Trade is not a contest where one wins and one loses. Trade can make each trader better off. Trade allows each trader to specialize in what they do best, whether it be farming, building, or manufacturing, and trade their output for the output of other efficient producers. This is as true for countries as it is for individuals.

Markets are usually a good way to organize economic activity. In a **market economy,** the decisions about what goods and services to produce, how much to produce, and who gets to consume them, are made by millions of firms and households. Firms and households, guided by self-interest, interact in the marketplace where prices and quantities are determined. While this may appear like chaos, Adam Smith made the famous observation in the Wealth of Nations in 1776 that self-interested households and firms interact in markets and generate desirable social outcomes as if guided by an "invisible hand." These optimal social outcomes were not their original intent. The prices generated by their competitive activity signal the value of costs and benefits to producers and consumers, whose activities unknowingly maximize the welfare of society. Alternatively, the prices dictated by central planners contain no information on costs and benefits and, therefore, these prices fail to efficiently guide economic activity. Prices also fail to efficiently guide economic activity when governments distort prices with taxes or restrict price movements with price controls.

Governments can sometimes improve market outcomes. Government must first protect property rights in order for markets to work. In addition, government sometimes can intervene in the market to improve efficiency or equity. When markets fail to allocate resources efficiently, there has been **market failure.** There are many different sources of market failure. An **externality** is when the actions of one person affect the well-being of a bystander. Pollution is a standard example. **Market power** is when a single person or group can influence the price. In these cases, the government may be able to intervene and improve economic efficiency. The government may also intervene to improve equity with income taxes and welfare. Sometimes well-intentioned policy intervention has unintended consequences.

How the Economy as a Whole Works

A country's standard of living depends on its ability to produce goods and services. There is great variation in average incomes across countries at a point in time and within the same country over time. These differences in incomes and standards of living are largely attributable to differences in productivity. **Productivity** is the amount of goods and services produced by each hour of a worker's time. As a result, public policy intended to improve standards of living should improve education, generate more and better tools, and improve access to current technology.

Prices rise when the government prints too much money. Inflation is an increase in the overall level of prices in the economy. High inflation is costly to the economy. Large and persistent inflation is caused by rapid growth in the quantity of money. Policymakers wishing to keep inflation low should maintain slow growth in the quantity of money.

Society faces a short-run tradeoff between inflation and unemployment. An increase in inflation tends to reduce unemployment. The short-run tradeoff between inflation and unemployment is known as the **Phillips curve.** The tradeoff is temporary but can last for several years. Understanding this tradeoff is important for understanding the fluctuations in economic activity known as the **business cycle.** In the short run, policymakers may be able to affect the mix of inflation and unemployment by changing government spending, taxes, and the quantity of money.

HELPFUL HINTS

1. Place yourself in the story. Throughout the text, most economic situations will be composed of economic actors—buyers and sellers, borrowers and lenders, firms and workers, and so on. When you are asked to address how any economic actor would respond to economic incentives, place yourself in the story as the buyer or the seller, the borrower or the lender, the producer or the consumer. Don't think of yourself always as the buyer (a natural tendency) or always as the seller. You will find that your role-playing will usually produce the right response once you learn to think like an economist—which is the topic of the next chapter.

2. Trade is not a zero-sum game. Some people see an exchange in terms of winners and losers. Their reaction to trade is that, after the sale, if the seller is happy the buyer must be sad because the seller must have taken something from the buyer. That is, they view trade as a *zero-sum game* where what one gains the other must have lost. They fail to see that both parties to a voluntary transaction gain because each party is allowed to specialize in what it can produce most efficiently, and then trade for items that are produced more efficiently by others. Nobody loses, because trade is voluntary. Therefore, a government policy that limits trade reduces the potential gains from trade.

3. An externality can be positive. Because the classic example of an externality is pollution, it is easy to think of an externality as a cost that lands on a bystander. However, an externality can be positive in that it can be a benefit that lands on a bystander. For example, education is often cited as a product that emits a positive externality because when your neighbor educates herself, she is likely to be more reasonable, responsible, productive, and politically astute. In short, she is a better neighbor. Positive externalities, just as much as negative externalities, may be a reason for the government to intervene to promote efficiency.

TERMS AND DEFINITIONS

Choose a definition for each key term.

Key terms:

_____ Scarcity

_____ Economics

_____ Efficiency

_____ Equity

_____ Opportunity cost

_____ Marginal changes

_____ Market economy

_____ "Invisible hand"

_____ Market failure

_____ Externality

_____ Market power

_____ Monopoly

_____ Productivity

_____ Inflation

_____ Phillips curve

_____ Business cycle

Definitions:

1. The property of distributing output fairly among society's members

2. A situation in which the market fails to allocate resources efficiently

3. Limited resources and unlimited wants

4. The amount of goods and services produced per hour by a worker

5. The case in which there is only one seller in the market

6. The principle that self-interested market participants may unknowingly maximize the welfare of society as a whole

7. The property of society getting the most from its scarce resources

8. An economic system where interaction of households and firms in markets determine the allocation of resources

9. Fluctuations in economic activity

10. When one person's actions have an impact on a bystander

11. An increase in the overall level of prices

12. Incremental adjustments to an existing plan

13. Study of how society manages its scarce resources

14. Whatever is given up to get something else

15. The ability of an individual or group to substantially influence market prices

16. The short-run tradeoff between inflation and unemployment

PROBLEMS AND SHORT-ANSWER QUESTIONS

Practice Problems

1. People respond to incentives. Governments can alter incentives and, hence, behavior with public policy. However, sometimes public policy generates unintended consequences by producing results that were not anticipated. Try to find an unintended consequence of each of the following public policies.

   a. To help the "working poor," the government raises the minimum wage to $25 per hour.

   _____

   _____

   _____

   b. To help the homeless, the government places rent controls on apartments restricting rent to $10 per month.

   _____

   _____

   _____

   c. To reduce the deficit and limit consumption of gasoline, the government raises the tax on gasoline by $2.00 per gallon.

   _____

   _____

   _____

   d. To reduce the consumption of drugs, the government makes drugs illegal.

   _____

   _____

   _____

   e. To raise the population of wolves, the government prohibits the killing of wolves.

   _____

   _____

f. To improve the welfare of American sugar beet growers, the government bans imports of sugar from South America.

_____

_____

_____

2. Opportunity cost is what you give up to get an item. Since there is no such thing as a free lunch, what would likely be given up to obtain each of the items listed below?

a. Susan can work full time or go to college. She chooses college.

_____

_____

b. Susan can work full time or go to college. She chooses work.

_____

_____

c. Farmer Jones has 100 acres of land. He can plant corn, which yields 100 bushels per acre, or he can plant beans, which yield 40 bushels per acre. He chooses to plant corn.

_____

_____

d. Farmer Jones has 100 acres of land. He can plant corn, which yields 100 bushels per acre, or he can plant beans, which yield 40 bushels per acre. He chooses to plant beans.

_____

_____

e. In (a) and (b) above, and (c) and (d) above, which is the opportunity cost of which—college for work or work for college? Corn for beans or beans for corn?

_____

_____

Short-Answer Questions

1. Is air scarce? Is clean air scarce?

   _____

   _____

2. What is the opportunity cost of saving some of your paycheck?

   _____

   _____

3. Why is there a tradeoff between equity and efficiency?

   _____

   _____

   _____

4. Water is necessary for life. Diamonds are not. Is the marginal benefit of an additional glass of water greater or lesser than an additional one carat diamond? Why?

   _____

   _____

   _____

5. Your car needs to be repaired. You have already paid $500 to have the transmission fixed, but it still doesn't work properly. You can sell your car "as is" for $2000. If your car were fixed, you could sell it for $2500. Your car can be fixed with a guarantee for another $300. Should you repair your car? Why?

   _____

   _____

6. Why do you think air bags have reduced deaths from auto crashes less than we had hoped?

   _____

   _____

7. Suppose one country is better at producing agricultural products (because they have more fertile land) while another country is better at producing manufactured goods (because they have a better educational system and more engineers). If each country produced their specialty and traded, would

there be more or less total output than if each country produced all of their agricultural and manufacturing needs? Why?

_____

_____

_____

8. In the *Wealth of Nations* Adam Smith said, "It is not from the benevolence of the butcher, the brewer, or the baker that we expect our dinner, but from their regard to their own interest." What do you think he meant?

_____

_____

_____

9. If we save more and use it to build more physical capital, productivity will rise and we will have rising standards of living in the future. What is the opportunity cost of future growth?

_____

_____

10. If the government printed twice as much money, what do you think would happen to prices and output if the economy were already producing at maximum capacity?

_____

_____

_____

11. A goal for a society is to distribute resources equitably or fairly. How would you distribute resources if everyone were equally talented and worked equally hard? What if people had different talents and some people worked hard while others did not?

_____

_____

12. Who is more self-interested, the buyer or the seller?

_____

_____

SELF-TEST

True/False Questions

_____ 1. When the government redistributes income with taxes and welfare, the economy becomes more efficient.

_____ 2. When economists say, "There is no such thing as a free lunch," they mean that all economic decisions involve tradeoffs.

_____ 3. Adam Smith's "invisible hand" concept describes how corporate business reaches into the pockets of consumers like an "invisible hand."

_____ 4. Rational people act only when the marginal benefit of the action exceeds the marginal cost.

_____ 5. The United States will benefit economically if we eliminate trade with Asian countries because we will be forced to produce more of our own cars and clothes.

_____ 6. When a jet flies overhead, the noise it generates is an externality.

_____ 7. A tax on liquor raises the price of liquor and provides an incentive for consumers to drink more.

_____ 8. An unintended consequence of public support for higher education is that low tuition provides an incentive for many people to attend state universities even if they have no desire to learn anything.

_____ 9. Sue is better at cleaning and Bob is better at cooking. It will take fewer hours to eat and clean if Bob specializes in cooking and Sue specializes in cleaning than if they share the household duties evenly.

_____10. High and persistent inflation is caused by excessive growth in the quantity of money in the economy.

_____11. In the short run, a reduction in inflation tends to cause a reduction in unemployment.

_____12. An auto manufacturer should continue to produce additional autos as long as the firm is profitable, even if the cost of the additional units exceed the price received.

_____13. An individual farmer is likely to have market power in the market for wheat.

_____14. To a student, the opportunity cost of going to a basketball game would include the price of the ticket and the value of the time that could have been spent studying.

_____15. Workers in the United States have a relatively high standard of living because the United States has a relatively high minimum wage.

Multiple-Choice Questions

1. Which of the following involve a tradeoff?
   a. buying a new car
   b. going to college
   c. watching a football game on Saturday afternoon
   d. taking a nap
   e. All of the above involve tradeoffs.

2. Tradeoffs are required because wants are unlimited and resources are
   a. efficient.
   b. economical.
   c. scarce.
   d. unlimited.
   e. marginal.

3. Economics is the study of how
   a. to fully satisfy our unlimited wants.
   b. society manages its scarce resources.
   c. to reduce our wants until we are satisfied.
   d. to avoid making tradeoffs.
   e. society manages its unlimited resources.

4. A rational person does not act unless the action
   a. makes money for the person.
   b. is ethical.
   c. produces marginal costs that exceed marginal benefits.
   d. produces marginal benefits that exceed marginal costs.
   e. none of the above

5. Raising taxes and increasing welfare payments
   a. proves that there is such a thing as a free lunch.
   b. reduces market power.
   c. improves efficiency at the expense of equity.
   d. improves equity at the expense of efficiency.
   e. none of the above

6. Suppose you find $20. If you choose to use the $20 to go to the football game, your opportunity cost of going to the game is
   a. nothing, because you found the money.
   b. $20 (because you could have used the $20 to buy other things).
   c. $20 (because you could have used the $20 to buy other things) plus the value of your time spent at the game.
   d. $20 (because you could have used the $20 to buy other things) plus the value of your time spent at the game, plus the cost of the dinner you purchased at the game.
   e. none of the above

7. Foreign trade
   a. allows a country to have a greater variety of products at a lower cost than if it tried to produce everything at home.
   b. allows a country to avoid tradeoffs.
   c. makes a country more equitable.
   d. increases the scarcity of resources.
   e. none of the above

8. Since people respond to incentives, we would expect that, if the average salary of accountants increases by 50 percent while the average salary of teachers increases by 20 percent,
   a. students will shift majors from education to accounting.
   b. students will shift majors from accounting to education.
   c. fewer students will attend college.
   d. none of the above

9. Which of the following activities is most likely to produce an externality?
   a. A student sits at home and watches T.V.
   b. A student has a party in her dorm room.
   c. A student reads a novel for pleasure.
   d. A student eats a hamburger in the student union.

10. Which of the following products would be *least* capable of producing an externality?
    a. cigarettes
    b. stereo equipment
    c. inoculations against disease
    d. education
    e. food

11. Which of the following situations describes the greatest market power?
    a. a farmer's impact on the price of corn
    b. Volvo's impact on the price of autos
    c. Microsoft's impact on the price of desktop operating systems
    d. a student's impact on college tuition

12. Which of the following statements is true about a market economy?
    a. Market participants act as if guided by an "invisible hand" to produce outcomes that maximize social welfare.
    b. Taxes help prices communicate costs and benefits to producers and consumers.
    c. With a large enough computer, central planners could guide production more efficiently than markets.
    d. The strength of a market system is that it tends to distribute resources evenly across consumers.

13. Workers in the United States enjoy a high standard of living because
    a. unions in the United States keep the wage high.
    b. we have protected our industry from foreign competition.
    c. the United States has a high minimum wage.
    d. workers in the United States are highly productive.
    e. none of the above

14. High and persistent inflation is caused by
    a. unions increasing wages too much.
    b. OPEC raising the price of oil too much.
    c. governments increasing the quantity of money too much.
    d. regulations raising the cost of production too much.

15. The Phillips curve shows that
    a. an increase in inflation temporarily increases unemployment.
    b. a decrease in inflation temporarily increases unemployment.
    c. inflation and unemployment are unrelated in the short run.
    d. the business cycle has been eliminated.
    e. none of the above.

16. An increase in the price of beef provides information which
    a. tells consumers to buy more beef.
    b. tells consumers to buy less pork.
    c. tells producers to produce more beef.
    d. provides no information because prices in a market system are managed by planning boards.

17. You have spent $1000 building a hot dog stand based on estimates of sales of $2000. The hot dog stand is nearly completed but now you estimate total sales to be only $800. You can complete the hot dog stand for another $300. Should you complete the hot dog stand? (Assume that the hot dogs are cost-less to you.)
    a. Yes.
    b. No.
    c. There is not enough information to answer this question.

18. Referring to Question 17, your decision rule should be to complete the hot dog stand as long as the cost to complete the stand is less than
    a. $100.
    b. $300.
    c. $500.
    d. $800.
    e. none of the above.

19. Which of the following is *not* part of the opportunity cost of going on vacation?
    a. the money you could have made if you had stayed home and worked
    b. the money you spent on food
    c. the money you spent on airplane tickets
    d. the money you spent on a Broadway show

20. Productivity can be increased by
    a. raising minimum wages.
    b. raising union wages.
    c. improving the education of workers.
    d. restricting trade with foreign countries.

ADVANCED CRITICAL THINKING

Suppose your university decides to lower the cost of parking on campus by reducing the price of a parking permit from $200 per semester to $5 per semester.

1. What do you think would happen to the number of students desiring to park their cars on campus?

    _____

    _____

2. What do you think would happen to the amount of time it would take to find a parking place?

    _____

    _____

3. Thinking in terms of opportunity cost, would the lower price of a parking permit necessarily lower the true cost of parking?

    _____

    _____

4. Would the opportunity cost of parking be the same for students with no outside employment and students with jobs earning $15 per hour?

    _____

    _____

    _____

SOLUTIONS

Terms and Definitions

_3_ Scarcity

_13_ Economics

_7_ Efficiency

_1_ Equity

_14_ Opportunity cost

_12_ Marginal changes

_8_ Market economy

_6_ "Invisible hand"

_2_ Market failure

_10_ Externality

_15_ Market power

_5_ Monopoly

_4_ Productivity

_11_ Inflation

_16_ Phillips curve

_9_ Business cycle

Practice Problems

1. a. Many would want to work at $25/hour but few firms would want to hire low productivity workers at this wage; therefore it would simply create unemployment.
    b. Many renters would want to rent an apartment at $10/month, but few landlords could produce an apartment at this price, therefore this rent control would create more homelessness.
    c. Higher gas prices would reduce the miles driven. This would lower auto accidents, put less wear and tear on roads and cars, and reduce the demand for cars and road repairs.
    d. This raises the price of drugs and makes selling them more profitable. This creates more gangs and gang warfare.
    e. Restrictions on killing wolves reduces the population of animals upon which wolves may feed—rabbits, deer, etc.
    f. South American growers have difficulty repaying their bank loans to U.S. banks. They turn to more profitable crops such as coca leaves and marijuana.

2. a. She gives up income from work (and must pay tuition).
    b. She gives up a college degree and the increase in income through life that it would have brought her (but doesn't have to pay tuition).
    c. He gives up 4000 bushels of beans.
    d. He gives up 10,000 bushels of corn.
    e. Each is the opportunity cost of the other because each decision requires giving something up.

Short-Answer Questions

1. No, you don't have to give up anything to get it. Yes, you can't have as much as you want without giving up something to get it (pollution equipment on cars, etc.)

2. The items you could have enjoyed had you spent it (current consumption).

3. Taxes and welfare make us more equal but reduce incentives for hard work, lowering total output.

4. The marginal benefit of another glass of water is generally lower because we have so much water that one more glass is of little value. The opposite is true for diamonds.

5. Yes, because the marginal benefit of fixing the car is $2500 – $2000 = $500 and the marginal cost is $300. The original repair payment is not relevant.

6. The cost of an accident was lowered. This changed incentives so people drive faster and have more accidents.

7. There would be more total output if they specialize and trade because each is doing what it does most efficiently.

8. The butcher, brewer, and baker produce the best food possible, not out of kindness, but because it is in their best interest to do so. Self-interest can maximize social welfare.

9. We must give up consumption today.

10. Spending would double but since the quantity of output would remain the same, prices would double.

11. Fairness would require that everyone get an equal share. Fairness would require that people not get an equal share.

12. They are equally self-interested. The seller will sell to the highest bidder and the buyer will buy from the lowest offer.

True/False Questions

1. F; the economy becomes less efficient because it decreases the incentive to work hard.

2. T

3. F; the "invisible hand" refers to how markets guide self-interested people to create desirable social outcomes.

4. T

5. F; all countries gain from voluntary trade.

6. T

7. F; higher prices reduce the quantity demanded.

8. T

9. T

10. T

11. F; a reduction in inflation tends to raise unemployment.

12. F; a manufacturer should produce as long as the marginal benefit exceeds the marginal cost.

13. F; a single farmer is too small to influence the market.

14. T

15. F; workers in the United States have a high standard of living because they are productive.

Multiple-Choice Questions

1. e	5. d	9. b	13. d	17. a
2. c	6. c	10. e	14. c	18. d
3. b	7. a	11. c	15. b	19. b
4. d	8. a	12. a	16. c	20. c

Advanced Critical Thinking

1. More students would wish to park on campus.

2. It would take much longer to find a parking place.

3. No, because we would have to factor in the value of our time spent looking for a parking place.

4. No. Students who could be earning money working are giving up more while looking for a parking place. Therefore, their opportunity cost is higher.

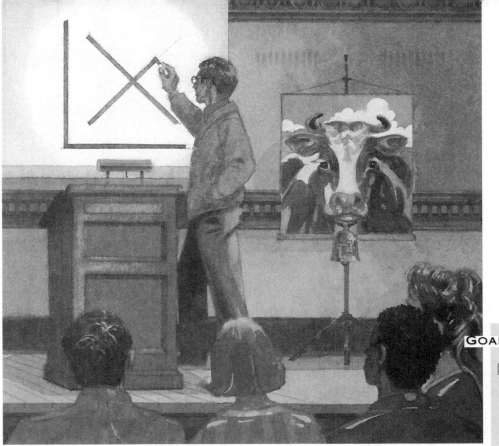

THINKING LIKE AN ECONOMIST

GOALS

⌐In this chapter you will

See how economists apply the methods of science

Consider how assumptions and models can shed light on the world

Learn two simple models—the circular-flow and the production possibilities frontier

Distinguish between microeconomics and macroeconomics

Learn the difference between positive and normative statements

Examine the role of economists in making policy

Consider why economists sometimes disagree with one another

OUTCOMES

⌐After accomplishing these goals, you should be able to

Describe the scientific method

Understand the art of making useful assumptions

Explain the slope of a production possibilities frontier

Place economic issues into the categories of microeconomics or macroeconomics

Place economic statements into the categories of normative or positive.

See the link between policymaking and normative statements

List two reasons why economists disagree

CHAPTER OVERVIEW

Context and Purpose

Chapter 2 is the second chapter in a three-chapter section that serves as the introduction of the text. Chapter 1 introduced ten principles of economics that will be revisited throughout the text. Chapter 2 develops how economists approach problems while Chapter 3 will explain how individuals and countries gain from trade.

The purpose of Chapter 2 is to familiarize you with how economists approach economic problems. With practice, you will learn how to approach similar problems in this dispassionate systematic way. You will see how economists employ the scientific method, the role of assumptions in model building, and the application of two specific economic models. You will also learn the important distinction between two roles economists can play: as scientists when we try to explain the economic world and as policymakers when we try to improve it.

CHAPTER REVIEW

Introduction

Like other fields of study, economics has its own jargon and way of thinking. It is necessary to learn the special language of economics because knowledge of the economic vocabulary will help you communicate with precision to others about economic issues. This chapter will also provide an overview of how economists look at the world.

The Economist as Scientist

While economists don't use test tubes or telescopes, they are scientists because they employ the *scientific method*—the dispassionate and objective development and testing of theories.

The scientific method: observation, theory, and more observation Just as in other sciences, an economist observes an event, develops a theory, and collects data to test the theory. An economist observes inflation, creates a theory that excessive growth in money causes inflation, and then collects data on money growth and inflation to see if there is a relationship. Collecting data to test economic theories is difficult, however, because economists usually cannot create data from experiments. That is, economists cannot manipulate the economy just to test a theory. Therefore, economists often use data gathered from historical economic events.

The role of assumptions Assumptions are made to make the world easier to understand. A physicist assumes an object is falling in a vacuum when measuring acceleration due to gravity. This assumption is reasonably accurate for a marble but not for a beachball. An economist may assume that prices are fixed (can't be changed) or may assume that prices are flexible (can move up or down in response to market pressures). Since prices often cannot be changed quickly (the menu in a restaurant is expensive to change) but can be changed easily over time, it is reasonable for economists to assume that prices are fixed in the short run but flexible in the long run. The art of scientific thinking is deciding which assumptions to make.

Economic models Biology teachers employ plastic models of the human body. They are simpler than the actual human body but that is what makes them useful. Economists use economic models that are composed of diagrams and equations. Economic models are based on assumptions and are simplifications of economic reality.

Our first model: the circular-flow diagram The **circular-flow diagram** shows the flow of goods and services, factors of production, and monetary payments between households and firms. Households sell the factors of production, such as land, labor, and capital to firms, in the market for factors of production. In exchange, the households receive wages, rent, and profit. Households use these dollars to buy goods and services from firms in the market for goods and services. The firms use this revenue to pay for the factors of production, and so on. This is a simplified model of the entire economy. This version of the circular flow diagram has been simplified because it excludes international trade and the government.

Our second model: the production possibilities frontier A **production possibilities frontier** is a graph that shows the combinations of output the economy can possibly produce given the available factors of production and the available production technology. It is drawn assuming the economy produces only two goods. This model demonstrates the following economic principles:

- If the economy is operating on the production possibilities frontier, it is operating *efficiently* because it is producing a mix of output that is the maximum possible from the resources available.

- Points inside the curve are therefore *inefficient*. Points outside the curve are currently unattainable.

- If the economy is operating on the production possibilities frontier, we can see the *tradeoffs* society faces. To produce more of one good, it must produce less of the other. The amount of one good given up when producing more of another good is the *opportunity cost* of the additional production.

- The production possibilities frontier is bowed outward because the opportunity cost of producing more of a good increases as we near maximum production of that good. This is because we use resources better suited toward production of the other good in order to continue to expand production of the first good.

- A technological advance in production shifts the production possibilities frontier outward. This is a demonstration of *economic growth*.

Microeconomics and macroeconomics Economics is studied on various levels. **Microeconomics** is the study of how households and firms make decisions and how they interact in specific markets. **Macroeconomics** is the study of economy-wide phenomena such as the federal deficit, the rate of unemployment, and policies to improve our standard of living. Microeconomics and macroeconomics are related because changes in the overall economy arise from decisions of millions of individuals. Although related, the methods employed in microeconomics and macroeconomics differ enough that they are often taught in separate courses.

The Economist as Policy Advisor

When economists attempt to explain the world as it is, they act as scientists. When economists attempt to improve the world, they act as policy advisors. Correspondingly, **positive statements** describe the world *as it is,* while **normative statements** prescribe how the world *ought to be.* Positive statements can be confirmed or refuted with evidence. Normative statements involve values (ethics, religion, political philosophy) as well as facts.

For example, "Money growth causes inflation" is a positive statement (of a scientist). "The government ought to reduce inflation" is a normative statement (of a policy advisor). The two statements are related because evidence about whether money causes inflation might help us decide what tool the government should use if it chooses to reduce inflation.

Economists act as policy advisors to the government in many different areas. The president is advised by economists on the Council of Economic Advisers, the Department of Treasury, the Department of Labor, and the Department of Justice. Congress is advised by economists from the Congressional Budget Office and the Federal Reserve.

Why Economists Disagree

There are two reasons why economists have a reputation for giving conflicting advice to policymakers.

- Economists may have different scientific judgments. That is, economists may disagree about the validity of alternative positive theories about how the world works. For example, economists differ in their views of the sensitivity of household saving to changes in the after-tax return to saving.

- Economists may have different values. That is, economists may have different normative views about what policy should try to accomplish. For example, economists differ in their views of whether taxes should be used to redistribute income.

In reality, although there are legitimate disagreements among economists on many issues, there is tremendous agreement on many basic principles of economics.

Let's Get Going

In the next chapter, we will begin to apply the ideas and methods of economics. As you begin to think like an economist, you will use a variety of skills—mathematics, history, politics, philosophy—with the objectivity of a scientist.

HELPFUL HINTS

1. Opportunity costs are usually not constant along a production possibilities frontier. Notice that the production possibilities frontier shown in Exhibit 1 is bowed outward. It shows the production tradeoffs for an economy that produces only paper and pencils.

   If we start at the point where the economy is using all of its resources to produce paper, producing 100 units of pencils only requires a tradeoff or an

EXHIBIT 1

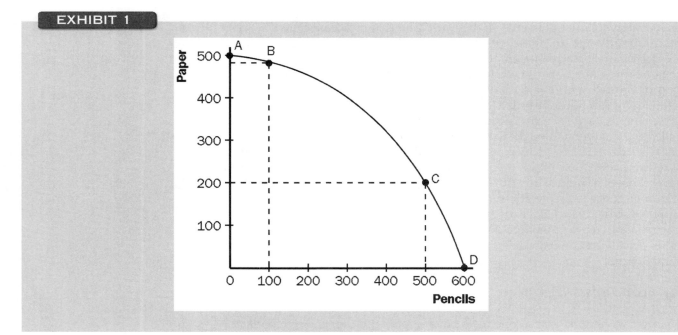

opportunity cost of 25 units of paper (point A to point B). This is because when we move resources from paper to pencil production, we first move those resources best suited for pencil production and poorly suited for paper production. Therefore, pencil production increases with very little decrease in paper production. However, if the economy were operating at point C, the opportunity cost of an additional 100 pencils (point C to D) is 200 units of paper. This is because we now move resources toward pencil production that were extremely well suited for paper production and are poorly suited for pencil production. Therefore, as we produce more and more of any particular good, the opportunity cost per unit tends to rise because resources are specialized. That is, resources are not equally well suited for producing each output.

The argument above applies when moving either direction on the production possibilities frontier. For example, if we start at point D (maximum production of pencils) a small reduction in pencil production (100 units) releases enough resources to increase production of paper by a large amount (200 units). However, moving from point B to point A only increases paper production by 25 units.

2. A production possibilities frontier only shows the choices available—not which point of production is best. A common mistake made by students when using production possibilities frontiers is to look at a production possibilities frontier and suggest that a point somewhere near the middle "looks best." Students make this subjective judgment because the middle point appears to provide the biggest total number of units of production of the two goods. However, ask yourself the following question. Using the production possibilities frontier in Exhibit 1, what production point would be best if paper were worth $10 per sheet and pencils were worth 1 cent per dozen? We would move our resources toward paper production. What if paper were worth 1 cent per sheet and pencils were worth $50 each? We would move our resources toward pencil production. Clearly, what we actually choose to produce depends on the price of each good. Therefore, a production possibilities frontier only provides the choices available; it alone cannot determine which choice is best.

3. Economic disagreement is interesting but economic consensus is more important. Economists have a reputation for disagreeing with one another because we tend to highlight our differences. While our disagreements are interesting to us, the matters on which we agree are more important to you. There are a great number of economic principles for which there is near unanimous support within the economics profession. The aim of this text is to concentrate on the areas of agreement within the profession as opposed to the areas of disagreement.

TERMS AND DEFINITIONS

Choose a definition for each key term.

Key terms:

_____Scientific method

_____Economic models

_____Circular-flow diagram

_____Factors of production

_____Production possibilities frontier

_____Opportunity cost

_____Efficiency

_____Microeconomics

_____Macroeconomics

_____Positive statements

_____Normative statements

Definitions:

1. Inputs such as land, labor, and capital

2. The study of economy-wide phenomena

3. Objective development and testing of theories

4. Whatever is given up to get something else

5. Prescription for how the world ought to be

6. Getting maximum output from the resources available

7. Descriptions of the world as it is

8. Simplifications of reality based on assumptions

9. A graph that shows the combinations of output the economy can possibly produce given the available factors of production and the available production technology

10. The study of how households and firms make decisions and how they interact in markets

11. A diagram of the economy that shows the flow of goods and services, factors of production, and monetary payments between households and firms.

PROBLEMS AND SHORT-ANSWER QUESTIONS
Practice Problems

1. Identify the parts of the circular-flow diagram immediately involved in the following transactions.
   a. Mary buys a car from General Motors for $20,000.

   _____

   _____

   _____

   _____

b. General Motors pays Joe $5,000/month for work on the assembly line.

_____

_____

_____

c. Joe gets a $15 hair cut.

_____

_____

_____

d. Mary receives $10,000 of dividends on her General Motors stock.

_____

_____

_____

2. The following table provides information about the production possibilities frontier of Athletic Country.

Bats	Rackets
0	420
100	400
200	360
300	300
400	200
500	0

a. In Exhibit 2, plot and connect these points to create Athletic Country's production possibilities frontier.

 EXHIBIT 2

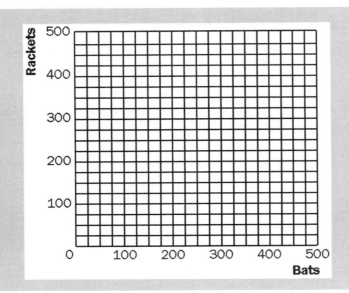

b. If Athletic Country currently produces 100 bats and 400 rackets, what is the opportunity cost of an additional 100 bats?

_____

_____

c. If Athletic Country currently produces 300 bats and 300 rackets, what is the opportunity cost of an additional 100 bats?

_____

_____

d. Why does the additional production of 100 bats in part (c) cause a greater tradeoff than the additional production of 100 bats in part (b)?

_____

_____

_____

e. Suppose Athletic Country is currently producing 200 bats and 200 rackets. How many additional bats could they produce without giving up any rackets? How many additional rackets could they produce without giving up any bats?

_____

_____

f. Is the production of 200 bats and 200 rackets efficient? Explain.

_____

_____

3. The production possibilities frontier in Exhibit 3 shows the available trade-offs between consumption goods and capital goods. Suppose two countries face this identical production possibilities frontier.

a. Suppose Party Country chooses to produce at point A while Parsimonious Country chooses to produce at point B. Which country will experience more growth in the future? Why?

_____

_____

EXHIBIT 3

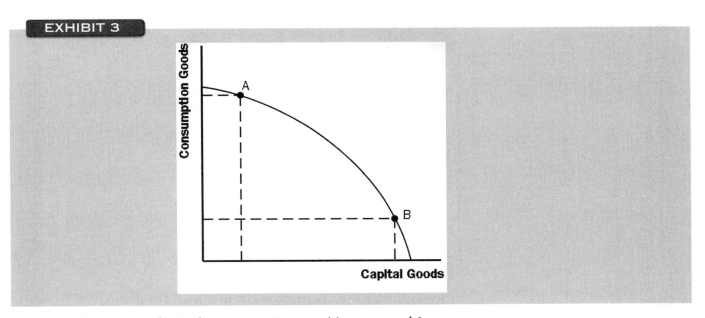

b. In this model, what is the opportunity cost of future growth?

_____

_____

c. Demonstrate in Exhibit 4 the impact of growth on a production possibilities frontier such as the one shown above. Would the production possibilities frontier for Parsimonious Country shift more or less than that for Party Country? Why?

_____

_____

EXHIBIT 4

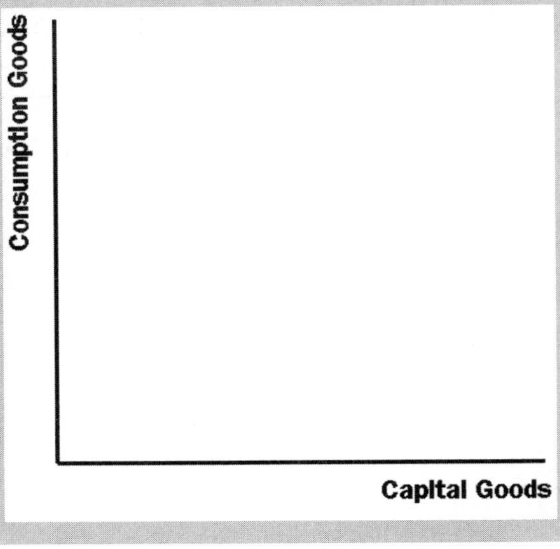

EXHIBIT 5

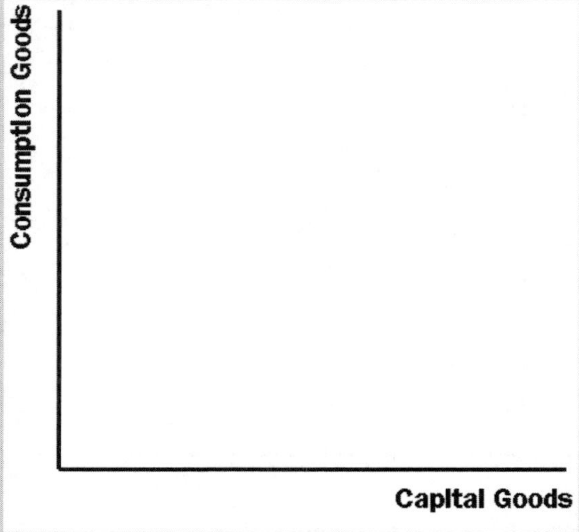

d. On the graph in Exhibit 5, show the shift in the production possibilities curve if there were an increase in technology that only affected the production of capital goods.

e. Does the shift in part (d) above imply that all additional production must be in the form of capital goods? Why?

_____

_____

Short-Answer Questions

1. Describe the scientific method.

_____

_____

2. What is the role of assumptions in any science?

_____

_____

3. Is a more realistic model always better?

_____

_____

_____

4. Why does a production possibilities frontier have a negative slope (slope down and to the right)?

_____

_____

5. Why is the production possibilities frontier bowed outward?

_____

_____

_____

6. What are the two subfields within economics? Which is more likely to be a building block of the other? Why?

_____

_____

_____

7. When an economist makes a normative statement, is she more likely to be acting as a scientist or a policy advisor? Why?

_____

_____

_____

8. Which statements are testable: positive statements or normative statements? Why?

_____

_____

9. Name two reasons why economists disagree.

_____

_____

10. Name two economic propositions for which more than 90 percent of economists agree.

_____

_____

_____

SELF-TEST

True/False Questions

_____ 1. Economic models must mirror reality or they are of no value.

_____ 2. Assumptions make the world easier to understand because they simplify reality and focus our attention.

_____ 3. It is reasonable to assume that the world is composed of only one person when modeling international trade.

_____ 4. When people act as scientists, they must try to be objective.

_____ 5. If an economy is operating on its production possibilities frontier, it must be using its resources efficiently.

_____ 6. If an economy is operating on its production possibilities frontier, it must produce less of one good if it produces more of another.

_____ 7. Points outside the production possibilities frontier are attainable but inefficient.

_____ 8. If an economy were experiencing substantial unemployment, the economy is producing inside the production possibilities frontier.

_____ 9. The production possibilities frontier is bowed outward because the tradeoffs between the production of any two goods are constant.

_____10. An advance in production technology would cause the production possibilities curve to shift outward.

_____11. Macroeconomics is concerned with the study of how households and firms make decisions and how they interact in specific markets.

_____12. The statement, "An increase in inflation tends to cause unemployment to fall in the short run," is normative.

_____13. When economists make positive statements, they are more likely to be acting as scientists.

_____14. Normative statements can be refuted with evidence.

_____15. Most economists believe that tariffs and import quotas usually reduce general economic welfare.

Multiple-Choice Questions

1. The scientific method requires that
   a. the scientist use test tubes and have a clean lab.
   b. the scientist be objective.
   c. the scientist use precision equipment.
   d. only incorrect theories are tested.
   e. only correct theories are tested.

2. Which of the following is most likely to produce scientific evidence about a theory?
   a. An economist employed by the AFL/CIO doing research on the impact of trade restrictions on workers' wages.
   b. A radio talk show host collecting data on how capital markets respond to taxation.
   c. A tenured economist employed at a leading university analyzing the impact of bank regulations on rural lending.
   d. A lawyer employed by General Motors addressing the impact of air bags on passenger safety.

3. Which of the following statements regarding the circular-flow diagram is true?
   a. The factors of production are owned by households.
   b. If Susan works for IBM and receives a paycheck, the transaction takes place in the market for goods and services.
   c. If IBM sells a computer, the transaction takes place in the market for factors of production.
   d. The factors of production are owned by firms.
   e. None of the above.

4. In which of the following cases is the assumption most reasonable?
   a. To estimate the speed at which a beach ball falls, a physicist assumes that it falls in a vacuum.
   b. To address the impact of money growth on inflation, an economist assumes that money is strictly coins.
   c. To address the impact of taxes on income distribution, an economist assumes that everyone earns the same income.
   d. To address the benefits of trade, an economist assumes that there are two people and two goods.

5. Economic models are
   a. created to duplicate reality.
   b. built with assumptions.
   c. usually made of wood and plastic.
   d. useless if they are simple.

6. Which of the following is not a factor of production?
   a. land
   b. labor
   c. capital
   d. money
   e. All of the above are factors of production.

7. Points on the production possibilities frontier are
   a. efficient.
   b. inefficient.
   c. unattainable.
   d. normative.
   e. none of the above.

8. Which of the following will not shift a country's production possibilities frontier outward?
   a. an increase in the capital stock
   b. an advance in technology
   c. a reduction in unemployment
   d. an increase in the labor force

9. Economic growth is depicted by
   a. a movement along a production possibilities frontier toward capital goods.
   b. a shift in the production possibilities frontier outward.
   c. a shift in the production possibilities frontier inward.
   d. a movement from inside the curve toward the curve.

Use Exhibit 6 to answer questions 10–13.

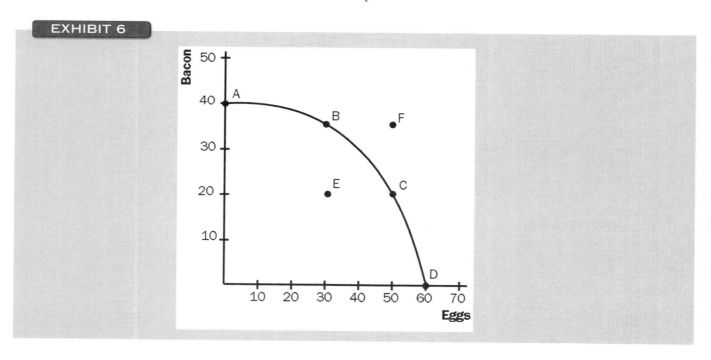

EXHIBIT 6

10. If the economy is operating at point C, the opportunity cost of producing an additional 15 units of bacon is
    a. 10 units of eggs.
    b. 20 units of eggs.
    c. 30 units of eggs.
    d. 40 units of eggs.
    e. 50 units of eggs.

11. If the economy were operating at point E,
    a. the opportunity cost of 20 additional units of eggs is 10 units of bacon.
    b. the opportunity cost of 20 additional units of eggs is 20 units of bacon.
    c. the opportunity cost of 20 additional units of eggs is 30 units of bacon.
    d. 20 additional units of eggs can be produced with no impact on bacon production.

12. Point F represents
    a. a combination of production that can be reached if we reduce the production of eggs by 20 units.
    b. a combination of production that is inefficient because there are unemployed resources.
    c. a combination of production that can be reached if there is a sufficient advance in technology.
    d. none of the above.

13. As we move from point A to point D,
    a. the opportunity cost of eggs in terms of bacon is constant.
    b. the opportunity cost of eggs in terms of bacon falls.
    c. the opportunity cost of eggs in terms of bacon rises.
    d. the economy becomes more efficient.
    e. the economy becomes less efficient.

14. Which of the following issues is related to microeconomics?
    a. the impact of money on inflation
    b. the impact of technology on economic growth
    c. the impact of the deficit on saving
    d. the impact of oil prices on auto production

15. Which of the following statements about microeconomics and macroeconomics is not true?
    a. The study of very large industries is a topic within macroeconomics.
    b. Macroeconomics is concerned with economy-wide phenomena.
    c. Microeconomics is a building block for macroeconomics.
    d. Microeconomics and macroeconomics cannot be entirely separated.

16. Which of the following statements is normative?
    a. Printing too much money causes inflation.
    b. People work harder if the wage is higher.
    c. The unemployment rate should be lower.
    d. Large government deficits cause an economy to grow more slowly.

17. In making which of the following statements is an economist acting more like a scientist?
    a. A reduction in unemployment benefits will reduce the unemployment rate.
    b. The unemployment rate should be reduced because unemployment robs individuals of their dignity.
    c. The rate of inflation should be reduced because it robs the elderly of their savings.
    d. The state should increase subsidies to universities because the future of our country depends on education.

18. Positive statements are
    a. microeconomic.
    b. macroeconomic.
    c. statements of prescription that involve value judgments.
    d. statements of description that can be tested.

19. Suppose two economists are arguing about policies that deal with unemployment. One economist says, "The government should fight unemployment because it is the greatest social evil." The other economists responds, "Hogwash. Inflation is the greatest social evil." These economists
    a. disagree because they have different scientific judgments.
    b. disagree because they have different values.
    c. really don't disagree at all. It just looks that way.
    d. none of the above

20. Suppose two economists are arguing about policies that deal with unemployment. One economist says, "The government could lower unemployment by one percentage point if it would just increase government spending by 50 billion dollars." The other economist responds, "Hogwash. If the government spent an additional 50 billion dollars, it would reduce unemployment by only one tenth of one percent, and that effect would only be temporary!" These economists
    a. disagree because they have different scientific judgments.
    b. disagree because they have different values.
    c. really don't disagree at all. It just looks that way.
    d. none of the above

ADVANCED CRITICAL THINKING

You are watching the McNeil News Hour on public television. The first focus segment is a discussion of the pros and cons of free trade (lack of obstructions to international trade). For balance, there are two economists present—one in support of free trade and one opposed. Your roommate says, "Those economists have no idea what's going on. They can't agree on anything. One says free trade makes us rich. The other says it will drive us into poverty. If the experts don't know, how is the average person ever going to know whether free trade is best?"

1. Can you give your roommate any insight into why economists might disagree on this issue?

_____

_____

_____

2. Suppose you discover that 93 percent of economists believe that free trade is generally best (which is the greatest agreement on any single issue). Could you now give a more precise answer as to why economists might disagree on this issue?

_____

_____

_____

3. What if you later discovered that the economist opposed to free trade worked for a labor union. Would that help you explain why there appears to be a difference of opinion on this issue?

_____

_____

_____

SOLUTIONS

Terms and Definitions

_3_ Scientific method   _6_ Efficiency

_8_ Economic models   _10_ Microeconomics

_11_ Circular-flow diagram   _2_ Macroeconomics

_1_ Factors of production   _7_ Positive Statements

_9_ Production possibilities frontier   _5_ Normative Statements

_4_ Opportunity cost

Practice Problems

1. a. $20,000 of spending from households to market for goods and services. Car moves from market for goods and services to household. $20,000 of revenue from market for goods and services to firms while car moves from firm to market for goods and services.
    b. $5,000 of wages from firms to market for factors of production. Inputs move from market for factors of production to firms. Labor moves from households to market for factors of production while $5,000 income moves from market for factors to households.
    c. $15 of spending from households to market for goods and services. Service moves from market for goods and services to household. Service moves from firms to market for goods and services in return for $15 revenue.
    d. $10,000 of profit from firms to market for factors of production. Inputs move from market for factors of production to firms. Capital services move from households to market for factors of production in return for $10,000 income.

2. a. See Exhibit 7.
    b. 40 rackets
    c. 100 rackets
    d. Because as we produce more bats, the resources best suited for making bats are already being used. Therefore it takes even more resources to produce 100 bats and greater reductions in racket production.
    e. 200 bats; 160 rackets
    f. No. Resources were not used efficiently if production can be increased with no opportunity cost.

3. a. Parsimonious country. Capital (plant and equipment) is a factor of production and producing more of it now will increase future production.
    b. Fewer consumption goods are produced now.
    c. See Exhibit 8. The production possibilities curve will shift more for Parsimonious Country because they have experienced a greater increase in factors of production (capital).
    d. See Exhibit 9.
    e. No, the outward shift improves choices available for both consumption and capital goods.

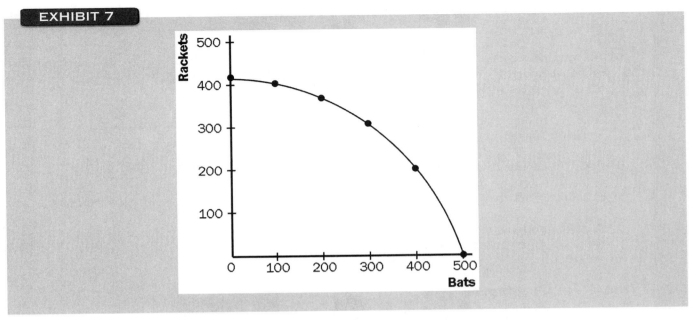

EXHIBIT 7

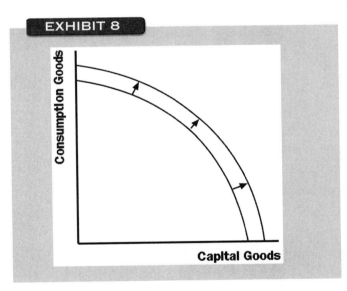

EXHIBIT 8

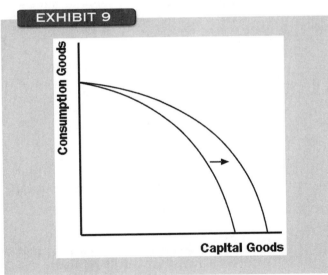

EXHIBIT 9

Short-Answer Questions

1. The dispassionate development and testing of theory by observing, testing, and observing again.

2. To simplify reality so that we can focus our thinking on what is actually important.

3. Not necessarily. Realistic models are more complex. They may be confusing and they may fail to focus on what is important.

4. Because if an economy is operating efficiently, production choices have opportunity costs. If we want more of one thing, we must have less of another.

5. Because resources are specialized and, thus, are not equally well-suited for producing different outputs.

6. Microeconomics and macroeconomics. Microeconomics is more of a building block of macro because when we address macro issues (say unemployment) we have to consider how individuals respond to work incentives such as wages and welfare.

7. As a policy advisor because normative statements are prescriptions about what ought to be and are somewhat based on value judgments.

8. Positive statements are statements of fact and are refutable by examining evidence.

9. Economists may have different scientific judgments. Economists may have different values.

10. A ceiling on rents reduces the quantity and quality of housing available. Tariffs and import quotas usually reduce general economic welfare.

True/False Questions

1. F; economic models are simplifications of reality.

2. T

3. F; there must be at least two individuals for trade.

4. T

5. T

6. T

7. F; points outside the production possibilities frontier cannot yet be attained.

8. T

9. F; it is bowed outward because the tradeoffs are not constant.

10. T

11. F; macroeconomics is the study of economy-wide phenomena.

12. F; this statement is positive.

13. T

14. F; normative statements cannot be refuted.

15. T

Multiple-Choice Questions

1. b	6. d	11.d	16. c
2. c	7. a	12. c	17. a
3. a	8. c	13. c	18. d
4. d	9. b	14. d	19. b
5. b	10. b	15. a	20. a

Advanced Critical Thinking

1. Economists may have different scientific judgments. Economists may have different values. There may not really be any real disagreement because the majority of economists may actually agree.

2. Those opposed to free trade are likely to have different values than the majority of economists. There is not much disagreement on this issue among the mainstream economics profession.

3. Yes. It suggests that impediments to international trade may benefit some groups (organized labor) but these impediments are unlikely to benefit the public in general. Supporters of these policies are promoting their own interests.

APPENDIX

Practice Problems

1. The following ordered pairs of price and quantity demanded describe Joe's demand for cups of gourmet coffee.

Price per Cup of Coffee	Quantity Demanded of Coffee
$5	2 cups
4	4 cups
3	6 cups
2	8 cups
1	10 cups

a. Plot and connect the ordered pairs on the graph in Exhibit 10.

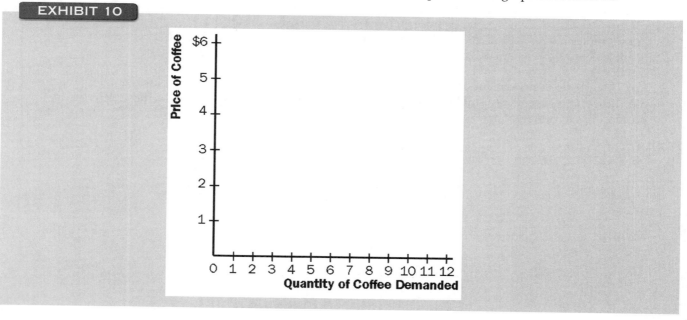

EXHIBIT 10

b. What is the slope of Joe's demand curve for coffee in the price range of $5 and $4?

_____

c. What is the slope of Joe's demand curve for coffee in the price range of $2 and $1?

_____

d. Are the price of coffee and Joe's quantity demanded of coffee positively correlated or negatively correlated? How can you tell?

_____

_____

e. If the price of coffee moves from $2 per cup to $4 per cup, what happens to the quantity demanded? Is this a movement along a curve or a shift in the curve?

_____

_____

f. Suppose Joe's income doubles from $20,000 per year to $40,000 per year. Now the following ordered pairs describe Joe's demand for gourmet coffee. Plot these ordered pairs on the graph provided in part (a) above.

Price per cup of coffee	Quantity demanded of coffee
$5	4 cups
4	6 cups
3	8 cups
2	10 cups
1	12 cups

g. Did the doubling of Joe's income cause a movement along his demand curve or a shift in his demand curve? Why?

_____

_____

2. An alien lands on earth and observes the following: on mornings when people carry umbrellas, it tends to rain later in the day. The alien concludes that umbrellas cause rain.
   a. What error has the alien committed?

_____

   b. What role did *expectations* play in the alien's error?

_____

_____

   c. If rain is truly caused by humidity, temperature, wind currents, and so on, what additional type of error has the alien committed when it decided that umbrellas cause rain?

_____

True/False Questions

_____ 1. When graphing in the coordinate system, the x-coordinate tells us the horizontal location while the y-coordinate tells us the vertical location of the point.

_____ 2. When a line slopes upward in the *x, y* coordinate system, the two variables measured on each axis are positively correlated.

_____ 3. Price and quantity demanded for most goods are positively related.

_____ 4. If three variables are related, one of them must be held constant when graphing the other two in the *x, y* coordinate system.

_____ 5. If three variables are related, a change in the variable not represented on the *x, y* coordinate system will cause a movement along the curve drawn in the *x, y* coordinate system.

_____ 6. The slope of a line is equal to the change in y divided by the change in x along the line.

_____ 7. When a line has negative slope, the two variables measured on each axis are positively correlated.

_____ 8. There is a positive correlation between lying down and death. If we conclude from this evidence that it is unsafe to lie down, we have an *omitted variable* problem because critically ill people tend to lie down.

_____ 9. Reverse causality means that while we think A causes B, B may actually cause A.

_____10. Since people carry umbrellas to work in the morning and it rains later in the afternoon, carrying umbrellas must cause rain.

SOLUTIONS FOR APPENDIX

Practice Problems

1. a. See Exhibit 11.
   b. −1/2
   c. −1/2
   d. Negatively correlated, because an increase in price is associated with a decrease in quantity demanded. That is, the demand curve slopes negatively.
   e. Decrease by 4 cups. Movement along curve.
   f. See Exhibit 12.
   g. Shift in curve because a variable changed (income) which is not measured on either axis.

2. a. Reverse causality.
   b. Since rain can be predicted, people's expectation of rain causes them to carry umbrellas *before* it rains, making it appear as if umbrellas cause rain.
   c. Omitted variables.

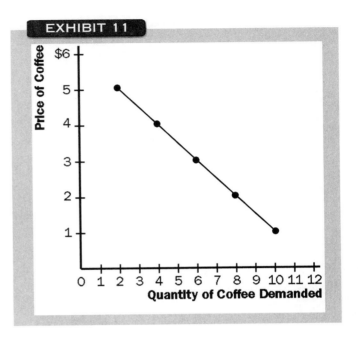

EXHIBIT 11

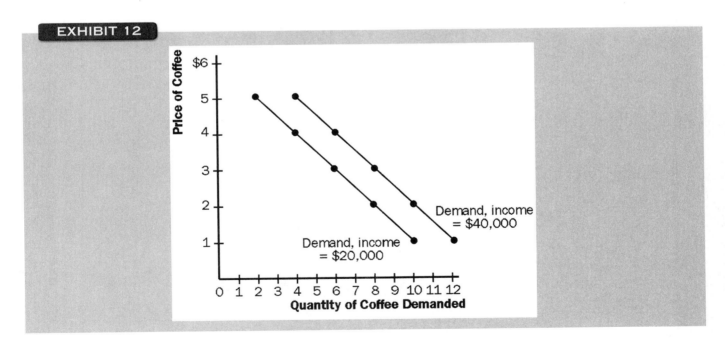

EXHIBIT 12

True/False Questions

1. T

2. T

3. F; they are negatively correlated.

4. T

5. F; a change in a variable not represented on the graph will cause a shift in the curve.

6. T

7. F; negative slope implies negative correlation.

8. T

9. T

10. F; this is an example of reverse causation.

GOALS

┌ In this chapter you will

Consider how everyone can benefit when people trade with one another

Learn the meaning of absolute advantage and comparative advantage

See how comparative advantage explains the gains from trade

Apply the theory of comparative advantage to everyday life and national policy

OUTCOMES

┌ After accomplishing these goals, you should be able to

Define scarcity

Show how total production rises when individuals specialize in the production of goods for which they have a comparative advantage

Explain why all people have a comparative advantage even if they have no absolute advantage

Demonstrate the link between comparative advantage and opportunity cost

Explain why people who are good at everything still tend to specialize

INTERDEPENDENCE AND THE GAINS FROM TRADE

CHAPTER OVERVIEW

Context and Purpose

Chapter 3 is the third chapter in the three-chapter section that serves as the introduction of the text. The first chapter introduced ten fundamental principles of economics. The second chapter developed how economists approach problems. This chapter shows how people and countries gain from trade (which is one of the ten principles discussed in Chapter 1).

The purpose of Chapter 3 is to demonstrate how everyone can gain from trade. Trade allows people to specialize in the production of goods for which they have a comparative advantage and then trade for goods other people produce. Because of specialization, total output rises and through trade we are all able to share in the bounty. This is as true for countries as it is for individuals. Since everyone can gain from trade, restrictions on trade tend to reduce welfare.

CHAPTER REVIEW

Introduction

Each of us consumes products every day that were produced in a number of different countries. Complex products contain components that were produced in many different countries so these products have no single country of origin.

Those who produce are neither generous nor ordered by government to produce. People produce because they wish to trade and get something in return. Hence, trade makes us interdependent.

A Parable for the Modern Economy

Imagine a simple economy. There are two people—a cattle rancher and a potato farmer. There are two goods—meat and potatoes.

- If each can produce only one product (the rancher can produce only meat and the farmer potatoes) they will trade just to increase the variety of products they consume. Each benefits because of increased variety.

- If each can produce both goods, but each is more efficient than the other at producing one good, then each will specialize in what he or she does best (again the rancher produces meat and the farmer produces potatoes), total output will rise, and they will trade. Trade allows each to benefit because trade allows for specialization, and specialization increases the total production available to share.

- If one producer is better than the other at producing *both* meat and potatoes, there are the same advantages to trade but it is more difficult to see. Again, trade allows each to benefit because trade allows for specialization, and specialization increases the total production available to share. To understand the source of the gains from trade when one producer is better at producing both products, we must understand the concept of comparative advantage.

The Principle of Comparative Advantage

To understand **comparative advantage,** we begin with the concept of **absolute advantage.** Absolute advantage compares the quantity of inputs required to produce a good. The producer that requires fewer resources (say fewer hours worked) to produce a good is said to have an absolute advantage in the production of that good. That is, the most efficient producer (the one with the highest productivity) has an absolute advantage.

While absolute advantage compares the actual cost of production for each producer, *comparative advantage* compares **opportunity costs** of production for each producer. The producer with the lower opportunity cost of production is said to have a comparative advantage. Regardless of absolute advantage, if producers have *different opportunity costs* of production for each good, each should specialize in the production of the good for which their opportunity cost of production is lower. That is, each producer should produce the item for which they have a comparative advantage. They can then trade some of their output for the other good. Trade makes both producers better off because trade allows for specialization, and specialization increases the total production available to be shared.

The decision to specialize and the resulting gains from trade are based on comparative advantage, not absolute advantage. Although a single producer can have an absolute advantage in the production of both goods, he/she cannot have a comparative advantage in the production of both goods because a low opportunity cost of producing one good implies a high opportunity cost of producing the other good.

In summary, trade allows producers to exploit the differences in their opportunity costs of production. Each specializes in the production of the good for which they have the lower opportunity cost of production and, thus, a comparative advantage. This increases total production and makes the economic pie larger. Everyone can benefit. The additional production generated by specialization is the gain from trade.

Adam Smith in his 1776 book, *An Inquiry into the Nature and Causes of the Wealth of Nations,* and David Ricardo in his 1817 book, *Principles of Political Economy and Taxation,* both recognized the gains from trade through specialization and the principle of comparative advantage. Current arguments for free trade are still based on their work.

Applications of Comparative Advantage

The principle of comparative advantage applies to individuals as well as countries.

Recall, absolute advantage does not determine specialization in production. For example, Tiger Woods may have an absolute advantage in both golf and lawn mowing. However, because he can earn $5,000/hour playing golf, he is better off paying someone to mow his lawn (even if they do it more slowly than he) as long as he can get someone to do it for less than $5,000/hour. This is because the opportunity cost of an hour of mowing for Tiger Woods is $5,000. Tiger Woods will likely specialize in golf and trade for other services. He does this because he has a comparative advantage in golf and a comparative disadvantage in lawn mowing even though he has an absolute advantage in both.

Trade between countries is subject to the same principle of comparative advantage. Goods produced abroad and sold domestically are called **imports.** Goods produced domestically and sold abroad are called **exports.** Even if the United States has an absolute advantage in the production of both cars and food, it should specialize in the production of the item for which it has a comparative advantage. Since the opportunity cost of food is low in the United States (better land) and high in Japan, the United States should produce more food and export it to Japan in exchange for imports of autos from Japan. While the U.S. gains from trade, the impact of trade on U.S. autoworkers is different from the impact of trade on U.S. farmers.

A reduction in barriers to free trade improves the welfare of the importing country *as a whole* but it does not improve the welfare of the domestic producers in the importing country. For this reason, domestic producers lobby their governments to maintain (or increase) barriers to free trade. For example, the American Sheep Industry Association has been able to maintain barriers to the importing of lamb to the detriment of the American consumer.

HELPFUL HINTS

1. A step by step example of comparative advantage will demonstrate most of the concepts discussed in Chapter 3. It will give you a pattern to follow when answering questions at the end of the chapter in your text and for the problems that follow in this Study Guide.

    Suppose we have the following information about the productivity of industry in Japan and Korea. The data are the units of output per hour of work.

	Steel	Televisions
Japan	6	3
Korea	8	2

EXHIBIT 1

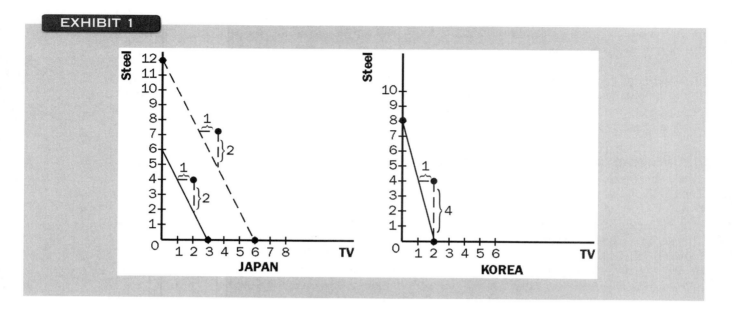

A Japanese worker can produce 6 units of steel or 3 TVs per hour. A Korean worker can produce 8 units of steel or 2 TVs per hour.

We can plot the production possibilities frontier for each country assuming each country has only one worker and the worker works only one hour. To plot the frontier, plot the end points and connect them with a line. For example, Japan can produce 6 units of steel with its worker or 3 TVs. It can also allocate one half hour to the production of each and get 3 units steel and 1 1/2 TVs. Any other proportion of the hour can be allocated to the two productive activities. The production possibilities frontier is linear in these cases because the labor resource can be moved from the production of one good to the other at a constant rate. We can do the same for Korea. Without trade, the production possibilities frontier is the consumption possibilities frontier, too.

Comparative advantage determines specialization and trade. The opportunity cost of a TV in Japan is 2 units of steel, which is shown by the slope of the production possibilities frontier in Exhibit 1. Alternatively, the opportunity cost of one unit of steel in Japan is 1/2 of a TV. In Korea, the opportunity cost of a TV is 4 units of steel and the cost of a unit of steel is 1/4 of a TV. Since the opportunity cost of a TV is lower in Japan, Japan has a comparative advantage in TV production and should specialize in TVs. Since the opportunity cost of steel is lower in Korea, Korea has a comparative advantage in steel production and should specialize in steel.

What is the range of prices at which each country would be willing to exchange? If Japan specializes in TV production and produces 3 televisions, it would be willing to trade TVs for steel as long as the price of steel is below 1/2 TV per unit of steel because that was the Japanese price for a unit of steel prior to trade. Korea would be willing to specialize in steel production and trade for TVs as long as the price of a TV is less than 4 units of steel because that was the Korean price of a TV prior to trade. In short, the final price must be between the original tradeoffs each faced in the absence of trade. One TV will cost between 2 and 4 of units of steel. One unit of steel will cost between 1/2 and 1/4 of a TV.

2.   Trade allows countries to consume outside their original production possibilities frontier. Suppose that Japan and Korea settle on a trading price of 3 units of steel for 1 TV (or 1/3 of a TV for 1 unit of steel). (I am giving you this price. There is nothing in the problem that would let you calculate the final trading price. You can only calculate the range in which it must lie.) This price is halfway between the two prices that each faces in the absence of trade. The range for the trading price is 4 units of steel for 1 TV to 2 units of steel for 1 TV.

     If Japan specializes in TV production, produces 3 televisions, and exports 1 TV for 3 units of steel, Japan will be able to consume 2 TVs and 3 units of steel. If we plot this point (2 TVs and 3 steel) on Japan's graph, we see that it lies outside its production possibilities frontier. If Korea specializes, produces 8 units of steel, and exports 3 units for 1 TV, Korea will be able to consume 5 units of steel and 1 TV. If we plot this point (5 steel and 1 TV) on Korea's graph, we see that it also lies outside its production possibilities frontier.

     This is the gain from trade. Trade allows countries (and people) to specialize. Specialization increases world output. After trading, countries consume outside their individual production possibilities frontiers. In this way, trade is like an improvement in technology. It allows countries to move beyond their current production possibilities frontiers.

3.   Only comparative advantage matters—absolute advantage is irrelevant. In the previous example, Japan had an absolute advantage in the production of TVs because it could produce 3 per hour while Korea could only produce 2. Korea had an absolute advantage in the production of steel because it could produce 8 units per hour compared to 6 for Japan.

     To demonstrate that comparative advantage, not absolute advantage, determines specialization and trade, we alter the previous example so that Japan has an absolute advantage in the production of both goods. To this end, suppose Japan becomes twice as productive as in the previous table. That is, a worker can now produce 12 units of steel or 6 TVs per hour.

	Steel	Televisions
Japan	12	6
Korea	8	2

     Now Japan has an absolute advantage in the production of both goods. Japan's new production possibilities frontier is the dashed line in Exhibit 1. Will this change the analysis? Not at all. The opportunity cost of each good within Japan is the same—2 units of steel per TV or 1/2 TV per unit of steel (and Korea is unaffected). For this reason, Japan still has the identical comparative advantage as before and it will specialize in TV production while Korea will specialize in steel. However, since productivity has doubled in Japan, its entire set of choices has improved and, thus, its material welfare has improved.

TERMS AND DEFINITIONS
Choose a definition for each key term.

Key terms:

_____Absolute advantage

_____Comparative advantage

_____Gains from trade

_____Opportunity cost

_____Imports

_____Exports

Definitions:

1. Whatever is given up to obtain some item

2. The comparison among producers of a good based on their opportunity cost

3. Goods produced domestically and sold abroad

4. Goods produced abroad and sold domestically

5. The comparison among producers of a good based on their productivity

6. The increase in total production due to specialization allowed by trade

PROBLEMS AND SHORT-ANSWER QUESTIONS

Practice Problems

1. Angela is a college student. She takes a full load of classes and has only 5 hours per week for her hobby. Angela is artistic and can make 2 clay pots per hour or 4 coffee mugs per hour.
   a. Draw Angela's production possibilities frontier for pots and mugs.

EXHIBIT 2

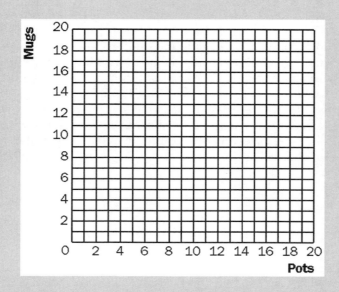

b. What is Angela's opportunity cost of 1 pot? 10 pots?

_____

c. What is Angela's opportunity cost of 1 mug? 10 mugs?

_____

d. Why is her production possibilities frontier a straight line instead of bowed out like those presented in Chapter 2?

_____

_____

2. Suppose a worker in Germany can produce 15 computers or 5 tons of grain per month. Suppose a worker in Poland can produce 4 computers or 4 tons of grain per month. For simplicity, assume that each country has only one worker.
   a. Fill out the following table:

	Computers	Grain
Germany	_____	_____
Poland	_____	_____

EXHIBIT 3

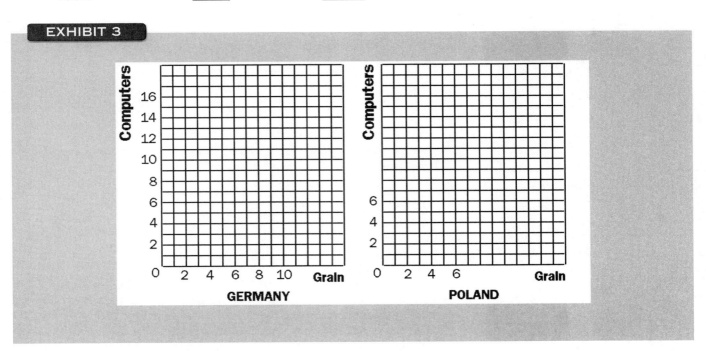

GERMANY   POLAND

b. Graph the production possibilities frontier for each country in Exhibit 3.
c. What is the opportunity cost of a computer in Germany? What is the opportunity cost of a ton of grain in Germany?

_____

_____

d. What is the opportunity cost of a computer in Poland? What is the opportunity cost of a ton of grain in Poland?

_____

_____

e. Which country has the absolute advantage in producing computers? Grain?

_____

_____

f. Which country has the comparative advantage in producing computers? Grain?

_____

_____

_____

_____

g. Each country should tend toward specialization in the production of which good? Why?

_____

_____

_____

_____

h. What is the range of prices for computers and grain for which both countries would benefit?

_____

_____

_____

i. Suppose Germany and Poland settle on a price of 2 computers for 1 ton of grain or 1/2 ton of grain for a computer. Suppose each country specializes in production and they trade 4 computers for 2 tons of grain. Plot the final consumption points on the graphs you made in part (b) above. Are these countries consuming inside or outside of their production possibilities frontier?

_____

_____

j. Suppose the productivity of a worker in Poland doubles so that a work-
    er can produce 8 computers or 8 tons of grain per month. Which country
    has the absolute advantage in producing computers? Grain?

    _____

    _____

k. After the doubling of productivity in Poland, which country has a com-
    parative advantage in producing computers? Grain? Has the comparative
    advantage changed? Has the material welfare of either country changed?

    _____

    _____

    _____

    _____

l. How would your analysis change if you assumed, more realistically, that
    each country had 10 million workers?

    _____

    _____

    _____

3. Suppose a worker in the United States can produce 4 cars or 20 computers
    per month while a worker in Russia can produce 1 car or 5 computers per
    month. Again, for simplicity, assume each country has only one worker.
    a. Fill out the following table:

	Cars	Computers
United States	_____	_____
Russia	_____	_____

b. Which country has the absolute advantage in the production of cars?
    Computers?

    _____

    _____

c. Which country has the comparative advantage in the production of cars?
    Computers?

    _____

    _____

    _____

d. Are there any gains to be made from trade? Why?

_____

_____

e. Does your answer in (d) above help you pinpoint a source for gains from trade?

_____

_____

_____

f. What might make two countries have different opportunity costs of production? (Use your imagination. This was not directly discussed in Chapter 3.)

_____

_____

_____

SHORT-ANSWER QUESTIONS

1. Why do people choose to become interdependent as opposed to self-sufficient?

_____

_____

_____

2. Why is comparative advantage important in determining trade instead of absolute advantage?

_____

_____

_____

3. What are the gains from trade?

_____

_____

_____

4. Why is a restriction of trade likely to reduce material welfare?

_____

_____

5. Suppose a lawyer that earns $200 per hour can also type at 200 words per minute. Should the lawyer hire a secretary who can only types 50 words per minute? Why?

_____

_____

_____

6. Evaluate this statement: A technologically advanced country, which is better than its neighbor at producing everything, would be better off if it closed its borders to trade because the less productive country is a burden to the advanced country.

_____

_____

_____

_____

SELF-TEST

True/False Questions

_____ 1. If Japan has an absolute advantage in the production of an item, it must also have a comparative advantage in the production of that item.

_____ 2. Comparative advantage, not absolute advantage, determines the decision to specialize in production.

_____ 3. Absolute advantage is a comparison based on productivity.

_____ 4. Self-sufficiency is the best way to increase one's material welfare.

_____ 5. Comparative advantage is a comparison based on opportunity cost.

_____ 6. If a producer is self-sufficient, the production possibilities frontier is also the consumption possibilities frontier.

_____ 7. If a country's workers can produce 5 hamburgers per hour or 10 bags of French fries per hour, absent trade, the price of 1 bag of fries is 2 hamburgers.

_____ 8. If producers have different opportunity costs of production, trade will allow them to consume outside their production possibilities frontiers.

_____ 9. If trade benefits one country, its trading partner must be worse off due to trade.

_____ 10. Talented people that are the best at everything have a comparative advantage in the production of everything.

_____ 11. The gains from trade can be measured by the increase in total production that comes from specialization.

_____ 12. When a country removes a specific import restriction, it always benefits every worker in that country.

_____ 13. If Germany's productivity doubles for everything it produces, this will not alter its prior pattern of specialization because it has not altered its comparative advantage.

_____ 14. If an advanced country has an absolute advantage in the production of everything, it will benefit if it eliminates trade with less developed countries and becomes completely self-sufficient.

_____ 15. If gains from trade are based solely on comparative advantage, and if all countries have the same opportunity costs of production, then there are no gains from trade.

Multiple-Choice Questions

1. If a nation has an absolute advantage in the production of a good,
   a. it can produce that good at a lower opportunity cost than its trading partner.
   b. it can produce that good using fewer resources than its trading partner.
   c. it can benefit by restricting imports of that good.
   d. it will specialize in the production of that good and export it.
   e. none of the above.

2. If a nation has a comparative advantage in the production of a good,
   a. it can produce that good at a lower opportunity cost than its trading partner.
   b. it can produce that good using fewer resources than its trading partner.
   c. it can benefit by restricting imports of that good.
   d. it must be the only country with the ability to produce that good.
   e. none of the above.

3. Which of the following statements about trade is true?
   a. Unrestricted international trade benefits every person in a country equally.
   b. People that are skilled at all activities cannot benefit from trade.
   c. Trade can benefit everyone in society because it allows people to specialize in activities in which they have an absolute advantage.
   d. Trade can benefit everyone in society because it allows people to specialize in activities in which they have a comparative advantage.

4. According to the principle of comparative advantage,
    a. countries with a comparative advantage in the production of every good need not specialize.
    b. countries should specialize in the production of goods that they enjoy consuming.
    c. countries should specialize in the production of goods for which they use fewer resources in production than their trading partners.
    d. countries should specialize in the production of goods for which they have a lower opportunity cost of production than their trading partners.

5. Which of the following statements is true?
    a. Self-sufficiency is the road to prosperity for most countries.
    b. A self-sufficient country consumes outside its production possibilities frontier.
    c. A self-sufficient country can, at best, consume on its production possibilities frontier.
    d. Only countries with an absolute advantage in the production of every good should strive to be self-sufficient.

6. Suppose a country's workers can produce 4 watches per hour or 12 rings per hour. If there is no trade,
    a. the domestic price of 1 ring is 3 watches.
    b. the domestic price of 1 ring is 1/3 of a watch.
    c. the domestic price of 1 ring is 4 watches.
    d. the domestic price of 1 ring is 1/4 of a watch.
    e. the domestic price of 1 ring is 12 watches.

7. Suppose a country's workers can produce 4 watches per hour or 12 rings per hour. If there is no trade,
    a. the opportunity cost of 1 watch is 3 rings.
    b. the opportunity cost of 1 watch is 1/3 of a ring.
    c. the opportunity cost of 1 watch is 4 rings.
    d. the opportunity cost of 1 watch is 1/4 of a ring.
    e. the opportunity cost of 1 watch is 12 rings.

The following table shows the units of output a worker can produce per month in Australia and Korea. Use this table for questions 8 through 15.

	Food	Electronics
Australia	20	5
Korea	8	4

8. Which of the following statements about absolute advantage is true?
    a. Australia has an absolute advantage in the production of food while Korea has an absolute advantage in the production of electronics.
    b. Korea has an absolute advantage in the production of food while Australia has an absolute advantage in the production of electronics.
    c. Australia has an absolute advantage in the production of both food and electronics.
    d. Korea has an absolute advantage in the production of both food and electronics.

9. The opportunity cost of 1 unit of electronics in Australia is
   a. 5 units of food.
   b. 1/5 of a unit of food.
   c. 4 units of food.
   d. 1/4 of a unit of food.

10. The opportunity cost of 1 unit of electronics in Korea is
    a. 2 units of food.
    b. 1/2 of a unit of food.
    c. 4 units of food.
    d. 1/4 units of food.

11. The opportunity cost of 1 unit of food in Australia is
    a. 5 units of electronics.
    b. 1/5 of a unit of electronics.
    c. 4 units of electronics.
    d. 1/4 of a unit of electronics.

12. The opportunity cost of 1 unit of food in Korea is
    a. 2 units of electronics.
    b. 1/2 of a unit of electronics.
    c. 4 units of electronics.
    d. 1/4 units of electronics.

13. Which of the following statements about comparative advantage is true?
    a. Australia has a comparative advantage in the production of food while Korea has a comparative advantage in the production of electronics.
    b. Korea has a comparative advantage in the production of food while Australia has a comparative advantage in the production of electronics.
    c. Australia has a comparative advantage in the production of both food and electronics.
    d. Korea has a comparative advantage in the production of both food and electronics.
    e. Neither country has a comparative advantage.

14. Korea should
    a. specialize in food production, export food, and import electronics.
    b. specialize in electronics production, export electronics, and import food.
    c. produce both goods because neither country has a comparative advantage.
    d. produce neither good because it has an absolute disadvantage in the production of both goods.

15. Prices of electronics can be stated in terms of units of food. What is the range of prices of electronics for which both countries could gain from trade?
    a. The price must be greater than 1/5 of a unit of food but less than 1/4 of a unit of food.
    b. The price must be greater than 4 units of food but less than 5 units of food.
    c. The price must be greater than 1/4 of a unit of food but less than 1/2 of a unit of food.
    d. The price must be greater than 2 units of food but less than 4 units of food.

16. Suppose the world consists of two countries—the U.S. and Mexico. Further, suppose there are only two goods—food and clothing. Which of the following statements is true?
    a. If the U.S. has an absolute advantage in the production of food, then Mexico must have an absolute advantage in the production of clothing.
    b. If the U.S. has a comparative advantage in the production of food, then Mexico must have a comparative advantage in the production of clothing.
    c. If the U.S. has a comparative advantage in the production of food, it must also have a comparative advantage in the production of clothing.
    d. If the U.S. has a comparative advantage in the production of food, Mexico might also have a comparative advantage in the production of food.
    e. none of the above.

EXHIBIT 4

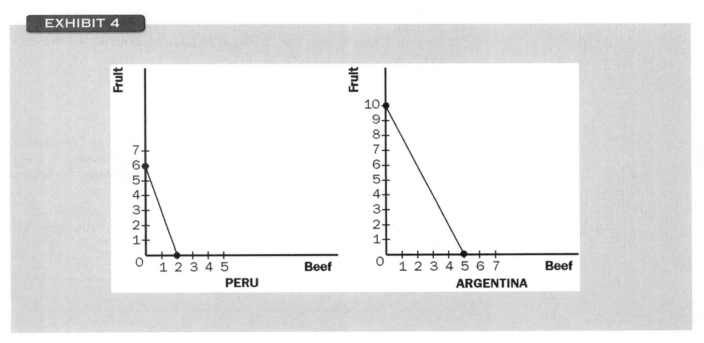

Use the production possibilities frontiers in Exhibit 4 to answer questions 17 through 19. Assume each country has the same number of workers, say 20 million, and that each axis is measured in metric tons per month.

17. Argentina has a comparative advantage in the production of
    a. both fruit and beef.
    b. fruit.
    c. beef.
    d. neither fruit nor beef.

18. Peru will export
    a. both fruit and beef.
    b. fruit.
    c. beef.
    d. neither fruit nor beef.

19. The opportunity cost of producing a metric ton of beef in Peru is
    a. 1/3 ton of fruit.
    b. 1 ton of fruit.
    c. 2 tons of fruit.
    d. 3 tons of fruit.
    e. 6 tons of fruit.

20. Joe is a tax accountant. He receives $100 per hour doing tax returns. He can type 10,000 characters per hour into spreadsheets. He can hire an assistant who types 2,500 characters per hour into spreadsheets. Which of the following statements is true?
    a. Joe should not hire an assistant because the assistant cannot type as fast as he.
    b. Joe should hire the assistant as long as he pays the assistant less than $100 per hour.
    c. Joe should hire the assistant as long as he pays the assistant less than $25 per hour.
    d. none of the above.

ADVANCED CRITICAL THINKING

You are watching an election debate on television. A candidate says, "We need to stop the flow of foreign automobiles into our country. If we limit the importation of autos, our domestic auto production will rise and the United States will be better off."

1. Is it likely that the *United States* will be better off if we limit auto imports? Explain.

_____

_____

_____

_____

2. Will anyone in the United States be better off if we limit auto imports? Explain.

_____

_____

_____

_____

3. In the real world, does every person in the country gain when restrictions on imports are reduced? Explain.

_____

_____

_____

_____

SOLUTIONS

Terms and Definitions

5 Absolute advantage

2 Comparative advantage

6 Gains from trade

1 Opportunity cost

4 Imports

3 Exports

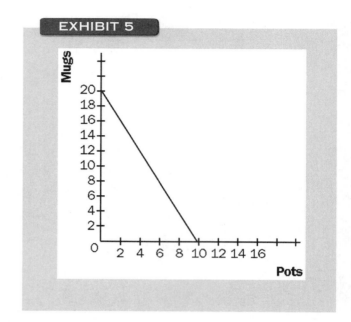

EXHIBIT 5

Practice Problems

1. a. See Exhibit 5.
   b. 2 mugs. 20 mugs.
   c. 1/2 pot. 5 pots.
   d. Because here resources can be moved from the production of one good to another at a constant rate.

2. a.

	Computers	Grain
Germany	15	5
Poland	4	4

   b. See Exhibit 6.
   c. 1/3 ton grain. 3 computers.

EXHIBIT 6

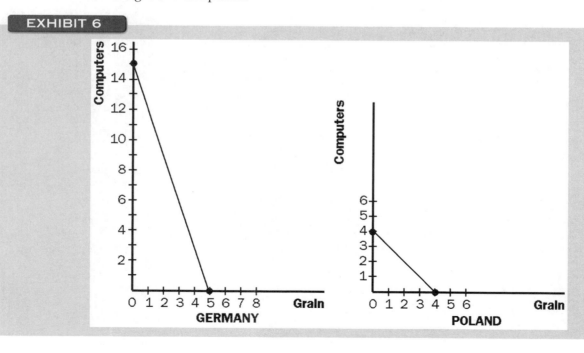

d. 1 ton grain. 1 computer.

e. Germany because one worker can produce 15 computers compared to 4. Germany because one worker can produce 5 tons of grain compared to 4.

f. Germany because a computer has the opportunity cost of only 1/3 ton of grain compared to 1 ton of grain in Poland. Poland because a ton of grain has the opportunity cost of only 1 computer compared to 3 computers in Germany.

g. Germany should produce computers while Poland should produce grain because the opportunity cost of computers is lower in Germany and the opportunity cost of grain is lower in Poland. That is, each has a comparative advantage in those goods.

h. Grain must cost less than 3 computers to Germany. Computers must cost less than 1 ton of grain to Poland.

i. See Exhibit 7. They are consuming outside their production possibilities frontier.

EXHIBIT 7

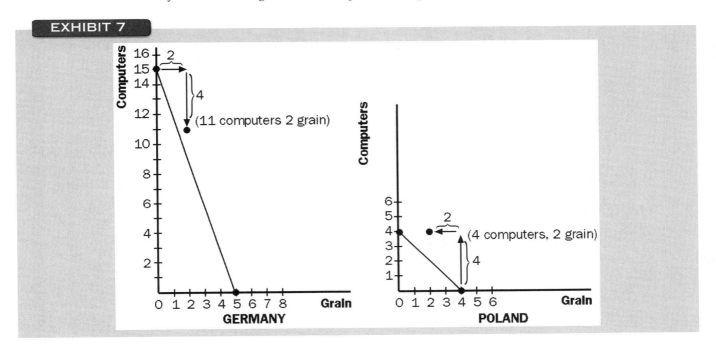

j. Germany because one worker can produce 15 compared to 8. Poland because one worker can produce 8 compared to 5.

k. Germany has comparative advantage in computers. Poland has comparative advantage in grain. No change in comparative advantage. Poland is better off, however, because it now has a larger set of choices.

l. It would not change absolute advantage or comparative advantage. It would change the scale in the previous two graphs by a factor of 10 million.

3. a.

	Cars	Computers
United States	4	20
Russia	1	5

b. United States because one worker can produce 4 cars compared to 1. The United States because one worker can produce 20 computers compared to 5.

c. In both, the opportunity cost of 1 car is 5 computers. In both, the opportunity cost of 1 computer is 1/5 of a car. Therefore, neither has a comparative advantage in either good.

d. No. Each can get the same tradeoff between goods domestically.

e. Yes. There needs to be differences in opportunity costs of producing goods across countries for there to be gains from trade.

f. The availability of resources or technology might be different across countries. That is, workers could have different levels of education, land could be of different quality, capital could be of different quality, or the available technology might be different.

Short-Answer Questions

1. Because a consumer gets a greater variety of goods at a much lower cost than they could produce by themselves. That is, there are gains from trade.

2. What is important in trade is how a country's costs without trade differ from each other. This is determined by the relative opportunity costs across countries.

3. The additional output that comes from countries with different opportunity costs of production specializing in the production of the item for which they have the lower domestic opportunity cost.

4. Because it forces people to produce at a higher cost than they pay when they trade.

5. Yes, as long as the secretary earns less than $50/hour, the lawyer is ahead.

6. This is not true. All countries can gain from trade if their opportunity costs of production differ. Even the least productive country will have a comparative advantage at producing something, and it can trade this good to the advanced country for less than the advanced country's opportunity cost.

True/False Questions

1. F; absolute advantage compares the quantities of inputs used in production while comparative advantage compares the opportunity costs.

2. T

3. T

4. F; restricting trade eliminates gains from trade.

5. T

6. T

7. F; the price of 1 bag of fries is 1/2 of a hamburger.

8. T

9. F; voluntary trade benefits both traders.

10. F; a low opportunity cost of producing one good implies a high opportunity cost of producing the other good.

11. T

12. F; it may harm those involved in that industry.

13. T

14. F; voluntary trade benefits all traders.

15. T

Multiple-Choice Questions

1. b	5. c	9. c	13. a	17. c
2. a	6. b	10. a	14. b	18. b
3. d	7. a	11. d	15. d	19. d
4. d	8. c	12. b	16. b	20. c

Advanced Critical Thinking

1. No. If we import autos, it is because the opportunity cost of producing them elsewhere is lower than in the United States.

2. Yes. Those associated with the domestic auto industry—stockholders of domestic auto producers and auto workers.

3. No. When we reduce restrictions on imports, the country gains from the increased trade but individuals in the affected domestic industry may lose.

THE MARKET FORCES OF SUPPLY AND DEMAND

GOALS

In this chapter you will

Learn what a competitive market is

Examine what determines the demand for a good in a competitive market

Examine what determines the supply of a good in a competitive market

See how supply and demand together set the price of a good and the quantity sold

Consider the key role of prices in allocating scarce resources in market economies

OUTCOMES

After accomplishing these goals, you should be able to

Define scarcity

List the two characteristics of a competitive market

List the factors that affect the amount that consumers wish to buy in a market

List the factors that affect the amount that producers wish to sell in a market

Draw a graph of supply and demand in a market and find the equilibrium price and quantity

Shift supply and demand in response to an economic event and find the new equilibrium price and quantity

CHAPTER OVERVIEW

Context and Purpose

Chapter 4 is the first chapter in a three-chapter sequence that deals with supply and demand and how markets work. Chapter 4 shows how supply and demand for a good determines both the quantity produced and the price at which the good sells. Chapter 5 will add precision to our discussion of supply and demand by addressing the concept of elasticity—the sensitivity of the quantity supplied and quantity demanded to changes in economic variables. Chapter 6 will address the impact of government policies on prices and quantities in markets.

The purpose of Chapter 4 is to establish the model of supply and demand. The model of supply and demand is the foundation for our discussion for the remainder of this text. For this reason, time spent studying the concepts in this chapter will return benefits to you throughout your study of economics. Many instructors would argue that this chapter is the most important chapter in the text.

CHAPTER REVIEW

Introduction

In a market economy, supply and demand determine both the quantity of each good produced and the price at which each good is sold. In this chapter, we develop the determinants of supply and demand. We also address how changes in supply and demand alter prices and change the allocation of the economy's resources.

Markets and Competition

A **market** is a group of buyers and sellers of a particular good or service. It can be highly organized like a stock market or less organized like the market for ice cream. A **competitive market** is a market in which there are many buyers and sellers so that each has a negligible impact on the market price.

A *perfectly competitive* market has two main characteristics:

* The goods offered for sale are all the same.

* The buyers and sellers are so numerous that no one buyer or seller can influence the price.

If a market is perfectly competitive, both buyers and sellers are said to be *price takers* because they cannot influence the price. The assumption of perfect competition applies well to agricultural markets because the product is similar and no individual buyer or seller can influence the price.

There are other types of markets. If a market has only one seller, the market is known as a *monopoly*. If there are only a few sellers, the market is known as an *oligopoly*. If there are many sellers but each product is slightly different so that each seller has some ability to set its own price, the market is called *monopolistically competitive*.

Demand

The behavior of buyers is captured by the concept of demand. The **quantity demanded** is the amount of a good that buyers are willing and able to purchase. While many things determine the quantity demanded of a good, the *price* of the good plays a central role. Other things equal, an increase in the price of a good reduces the quantity demanded. This negative relationship between the price of a good and the quantity demanded of a good is known as the **law of demand.**

The **demand schedule** is a table that shows the relationship between the price of a good and the quantity demanded. The **demand curve** is a graph of this relationship with the price on the vertical axis and the quantity demanded on the horizontal axis. The demand curve is downward sloping due to the law of demand.

Market demand is the sum of the quantities demanded for each individual buyer at each price. That is, the market demand curve is the horizontal sum of the individual demand curves. The market demand curve shows the total quantity demanded of a good at each price, while all other factors that affect how much buyers wish to buy are held constant.

Shifts in the demand curve When people change how much they wish to buy at each price, the demand curve shifts. If buyers increase the quantity demanded at each price, the demand curve shifts right which is called an *increase in demand*. Alternatively, if buyers decrease the quantity demanded at each price, the demand curve shifts left which is called a *decrease in demand*. The most important factors that shift demand curves are:

* *Income:* A **normal good** is a good for which an increase in income leads to an increase in demand. An **inferior good** is a good for which an increase in income leads to a decrease in demand.

- *Prices of Related Goods:* If two goods can be used in place of one another, they are known as **substitutes.** When two goods are substitutes, an increase in the price of one good leads to an increase in the demand for the other good. If two goods are used together, they are known as **complements.** When two goods are complements, an increase in the price of one good leads to a decrease in the demand for the other good.

- *Tastes:* If your preferences shift toward a good, it will lead to an increase in the demand for that good.

- *Expectations:* Expectations about future income or prices will affect the demand for a good today.

- *Number of Buyers:* An increase in the number of buyers will lead to an increase in the market demand for a good because there are more individual demand curves to horizontally sum.

A demand curve is drawn with price on the vertical axis and quantity demanded on the horizontal axis while holding other things equal. Therefore, a change in the price of a good represents a movement along the demand curve while a change in income, prices of related goods, tastes, expectations, and the number of buyers causes a shift in the demand curve.

Supply

The behavior of sellers is captured by the concept of supply. The **quantity supplied** is the amount of a good that sellers are willing and able to sell. While many things determine the quantity supplied of a good, the *price* of the good is central. Other things equal, an increase in the price makes production more profitable and increases the quantity supplied. This positive relationship between the price of a good and the quantity supplied is known as the **law of supply.**

The **supply schedule** is a table that shows the relationship between the price of a good and the quantity supplied. The **supply curve** is a graph of this relationship with the price on the vertical axis and the quantity supplied on the horizontal axis. The supply curve is upward sloping due to the law of supply.

Market supply is the sum of the quantity supplied for each individual seller at each price. That is, the market supply curve is the horizontal sum of the individual supply curves. The market supply curve shows the total quantity supplied of a good at each price, while all other factors that affect how much producers wish to sell are held constant.

Shifts in the supply curve When producers change how much they wish to sell at each price, the supply curve shifts. If producers increase the quantity supplied at each price, the supply curve shifts right, which is called an *increase in supply*. Alternatively, if producers decrease the quantity suppled at each price, the supply curve shifts left, which is called a *decrease in supply*. The most important factors that shift supply curves are:

- *Input Prices:* A decrease in the price of an input makes production more profitable and increases supply.

- *Technology:* An improvement in technology reduces costs, makes production more profitable, and increases supply.

- *Expectations:* Expectations about the future will affect the supply of a good today.

- *Number of Sellers:* An increase in the number of sellers will lead to an increase in the market supply for a good because there are more individual supply curves to horizontally sum.

A supply curve is drawn with price on the vertical axis and quantity supplied on the horizontal axis while holding other things equal. Therefore, a change in the price of a good represents a movement along the supply curve while a change in input prices, technology, expectations, and the number of sellers causes a shift in the supply curve.

Supply and Demand Together

When placed on the same graph, the intersection of supply and demand is called the market's **equilibrium.** Equilibrium is a situation in which the price has reached the level where quantity supplied equals quantity demanded. The **equilibrium price,** or the market-clearing price, is the price that balances the quantity demanded and the quantity supplied. When the quantity supplied equals the quantity demanded at the equilibrium price, we have determined the **equilibrium quantity.**

The market naturally moves toward its equilibrium. If the price is above the equilibrium price, the quantity supplied exceeds the quantity demanded and there is a **surplus,** or an excess supply of the good. A surplus causes the price to fall until it reaches equilibrium. If the price is below the equilibrium price, the quantity demanded exceeds the quantity supplied and there is a **shortage,** or an excess demand for the good. A shortage causes the price to rise until it reaches equilibrium. This natural adjustment of the price to bring the quantity supplied and the quantity demanded into balance is known as the **law of supply and demand.**

When an economic event shifts the supply or the demand curve, the equilibrium in the market changes. The analysis of this change is known as *comparative statics* because we are comparing the initial equilibrium to the new equilibrium. When analyzing the impact of some event on the market equilibrium, employ the following three steps:

- Decide whether the event shifts the supply curve or demand curve or both.

- Decide which direction the curve shifts.

- Use the supply-and-demand diagram to see how the shift changes the equilibrium price and quantity.

A shift in the demand curve is called a "change in demand." It is caused by a change in a variable that affects the amount people wish to purchase of a good *other than the price of the good.* A change in the price of a good causes a movement along a given demand curve and is called a "change in the quantity demanded." Likewise, a shift in the supply curve is called a "change in supply." It is caused by a change in a variable that affects the amount producers wish to supply of a good *other than the price of the good.* A change in the price of a good causes a movement along a supply curve and is called a "change in the quantity supplied."

For example, a frost that destroys much of the orange crop causes a decrease in the supply of oranges (supply of oranges shifts to the left). This increases the price of oranges and decreases the quantity demanded of oranges. In other words, a decrease in the supply of oranges increases the price of oranges and decreases the quantity of oranges purchased.

If both supply and demand shift at the same time, there may be more than one possible outcome for the changes in the equilibrium price and quantity. For example, if demand were to increase (shift right) while supply were to decrease (shift left), the price will certainly rise but the impact on the equilibrium quantity is ambiguous. In this case, the change in the equilibrium quantity depends on the magnitudes of the shifts in supply and demand.

Conclusion: How Prices Allocate Resources

Markets generate equilibrium prices. These prices are the signals that guide the allocation of scarce resources. Prices of products rise to the level necessary to allocate the products to those who are willing to pay for them. Prices of inputs (say labor) rise to the level necessary to induce people to do the jobs that need to get done. In this way, no jobs go undone, and there is no shortage of goods and services for those willing and able to pay for them.

HELPFUL HINTS

1. Equilibrium in a market is a static state. That is, once a market is in equilibrium, there are no further forces for change. That is why economists use the term *comparative statics* to describe the analysis of comparing an initial static equilibrium to a new static equilibrium.

2. By far, the greatest difficulty students have when studying supply and demand is distinguishing between a "change in demand" and a "change in the quantity demanded" and between a "change in supply" and a "change in the quantity supplied." It helps to remember that "demand" is the entire relationship between price and quantity demanded. That is, demand is the entire demand curve, not a point on a demand curve. Therefore, a change in demand is a shift in the entire demand curve, which can only be caused by a change in a determinant of demand other than the price of the good. A change in the quantity demanded is a movement along the demand curve and is caused by a change in the price of the good. Likewise, "supply" refers to the entire supply curve, not a point on the supply curve. Therefore, a change in supply is a shift in the entire supply curve, which can only be caused by a change in a determinant of supply other than the price of the good. A change in the quantity supplied is a movement along the supply curve and is caused by a change in the price of the good.

3. If both supply and demand shift at the same time and we do not know the magnitude of each shift, then the change in either the price or the quantity must be ambiguous. For example, if there is an increase in supply (supply shifts right) and an increase in demand (demand shifts right), the equilibrium quantity must certainly rise, but the change in the equilibrium price is ambiguous. Do this for all four possible combinations of changes in supply and demand. You will find that if you know the impact on the equilibrium price with certainty, then the impact on the equilibrium quantity must be ambiguous. If you know the impact on the equilibrium quantity with certainty, then the impact on the equilibrium price must be ambiguous.

TERMS AND DEFINITIONS

Choose a definition for each key term.

Key terms:

_____ Market

_____ Competitive market

_____ Monopoly

_____ Oligopoly

_____ Monopolistically competitive

_____ Quantity demanded

_____ Law of demand

_____ Demand schedule

_____ Demand curve

_____ Normal good

_____ Inferior good

_____ Substitutes

_____ Complements

_____ Quantity supplied

_____ Law of supply

_____ Supply schedule

_____ Supply curve

_____ Equilibrium

_____ Equilibrium price

_____ Equilibrium quantity

_____ Surplus

_____ Shortage

_____ The law of supply and demand

Definitions:

1. The quantity supplied and the quantity demanded at the equilibrium price
2. A table that shows the relationship between the price of a good and the quantity demanded
3. A table that shows the relationship between the price of a good and the quantity supplied
4. Market with sellers offering slightly different products
5. A group of buyers and sellers of a particular good or service
6. Market with only one seller
7. A good for which, other things equal, an increase in income leads to a decrease in demand
8. A situation in which quantity demanded is greater than quantity supplied
9. A situation in which quantity supplied is greater than quantity demanded
10. The amount of a good that buyers are willing and able to purchase
11. A situation in which the price has reached the level where quantity supplied equals quantity demanded
12. A market in which there are many buyers and sellers so that each has a negligible impact on the market price
13. The claim that, other things equal, the quantity demanded of a good falls when the price of the good rises
14. Market with only a few sellers
15. The price that balances quantity supplied and quantity demanded
16. The amount of a good that sellers are willing and able to sell
17. The claim that, other things equal, the quantity supplied of a good rises when the price of the good rises
18. The claim that the price of any good adjusts to bring the quantity supplied and quantity demanded for that good into balance
19. Two goods for which an increase in the price of one leads to a decrease in the demand for the other
20. A good for which, other things equal, an increase in income leads to an increase in demand
21. A graph of the relationship between the price of a good and the quantity supplied
22. Two goods for which an increase in the price of one leads to an increase in the demand for the other
23. A graph of the relationship between the price of a good and the quantity demanded

EXHIBIT 1

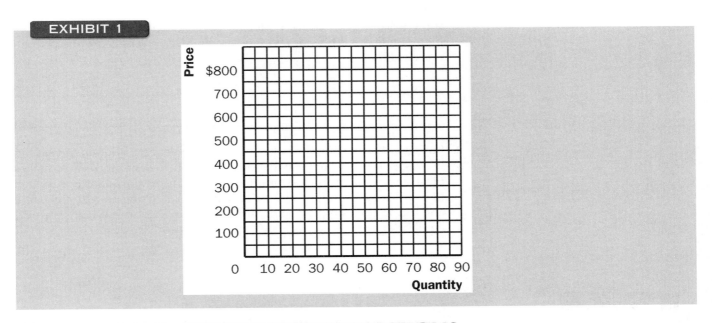

PROBLEMS AND SHORT-ANSWER QUESTIONS

Practice Problems

1. Suppose we have the following market supply and demand schedules for bicycles:

Price	Quantity Demanded	Quantity Supplied
$100	70	30
200	60	40
300	50	50
400	40	60
500	30	70
600	20	80

a. Plot the supply curve and the demand curve for bicycles in Exhibit 1.

b. What is the equilibrium price of bicycles?

_____

c. What is the equilibrium quantity of bicycles?

_____

d. If the price of bicycles were $100, is there a surplus or a shortage? How many units of surplus or shortage are there? Will this cause the price to rise or fall?

_____

_____

e. If the price of bicycles were $400, is there a surplus or a shortage? How many units of surplus or shortage are there? Will this cause the price to rise or fall?

_____

_____

f. Suppose that the bicycle maker's labor union bargains for an increase in its wages. Further, suppose this event raises the cost of production, makes bicycle manufacturing less profitable, and reduces the quantity supplied of bicycles by 20 units at each price of bicycles. Plot the new supply curve and the original supply and demand curves in Exhibit 2. What is the new equilibrium price and quantity in the market for bicycles?

_____

EXHIBIT 2

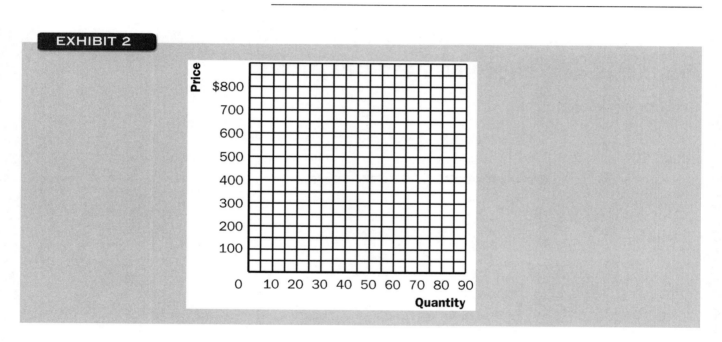

2. Each of the events listed below has an impact on the market for bicycles. For each event, which curve is affected (supply or demand for bicycles), what direction is it shifted, and what is the resulting impact on the equilibrium price and quantity of bicycles?

a. The price of automobiles increases.

_____

_____

b. Consumers' incomes decrease, and bicycles are a normal good.

_____

_____

c. The price of steel used to make bicycle frames increases.

_____

_____

d. An environmental movement shifts tastes toward bicycling.

_____

_____

e. *Consumers* expect the price of bicycles to fall in the future.

_____

_____

f. A technological advance in the manufacture of bicycles occurs.

_____

_____

g. The price of bicycle helmets and shoes falls.

_____

_____

h. Consumers' incomes decrease, and bicycles are an inferior good.

_____

_____

3. The following questions address a market when both supply and demand shift.
   a. What would happen to the equilibrium price and quantity in the bicycle market if there is an increase in both the supply and the demand for bicycles?

   _____

   _____

   b. What would happen to the equilibrium price and quantity in the bicycle market if the demand for bicycles increases more than the increase in the supply of bicycles?

   _____

   _____

Short-Answer Questions

1. What are the two main characteristics of a perfectly competitive market?

   _____

   _____

2. Explain the law of demand.

   _____

3. What are the variables that should affect the amount of a good that consumers wish to buy, other than its price?

   _____

4. What is the difference between a normal good and an inferior good?

   _____

   _____

5. Explain the law of supply.

   _____

6. What are the variables that should affect the amount of a good that producers wish to sell, other than its price?

   _____

7. Suppose *suppliers* of corn expect the price of corn to rise in the future. How would this affect the supply and demand for corn and the equilibrium price and quantity of corn?

   _____

   _____

   _____

8. If there is a surplus of a good, is the price above or below the equilibrium price for that good?

   _____

9. Suppose there is an increase in consumers' incomes. In the market for automobiles (a normal good), does this event cause an increase in demand or an increase in quantity demanded? Does this cause an increase in supply or an increase in quantity supplied? Explain.

_____

_____

_____

_____

_____

10. Suppose there is an advance in the technology employed to produce automobiles. In the market for automobiles, does this event cause an increase in supply or an increase in the quantity supplied? Does this cause an increase in demand or an increase in the quantity demanded? Explain.

_____

_____

_____

_____

_____

SELF-TEST

True/False Questions

_____ 1. A perfectly competitive market consists of products that are all slightly different from one another.

_____ 2. An oligopolistic market has only a few sellers.

_____ 3. The law of demand states that an increase in the price of a good decreases the demand for that good.

_____ 4. If apples and oranges are substitutes, an increase in the price of apples will decrease the demand for oranges.

_____ 5. If golf clubs and golf balls are complements, an increase in the price of golf clubs will decrease the demand for golf balls.

_____ 6. If consumers expect the price of shoes to rise, there will be an increase in the demand for shoes today.

_____ 7. The law of supply states that an increase in the price of a good increases the quantity supplied of that good.

_____ 8. An increase in the price of steel will shift the supply of automobiles to the right.

_____ 9. When the price of a good is below the equilibrium price, it causes a surplus.

_____10. The market supply curve is the horizontal summation of the individual supply curves.

_____11. If there is a shortage of a good, then the price of that good tends to fall.

_____12. If pencils and paper are complements, an increase in the price of pencils causes the demand for paper to decrease or shift to the left.

_____13. If Coke and Pepsi are substitutes, an increase in the price of Coke will cause an increase in the equilibrium price and quantity in the market for Pepsi.

_____14. An advance in the technology employed to manufacture roller blades will result in a decrease in the equilibrium price and an increase in the equilibrium quantity in the market for roller blades.

_____15. If there is an increase in supply accompanied by a decrease in demand for coffee, then there will be a decrease in both the equilibrium price and quantity in the market for coffee.

Multiple-Choice Questions

1. A perfectly competitive market has
   a. only one seller.
   b. at least a few sellers.
   c. many buyers and sellers.
   d. firms that set their own prices.
   e. none of the above.

2. If an increase in the price of blue jeans leads to an increase in the demand for tennis shoes, then blue jeans and tennis shoes are
   a. substitutes.
   b. complements.
   c. normal goods.
   d. inferior goods.
   e. none of the above.

3. The *law of demand* states that an increase in the price of a good
   a. decreases the demand for that good.
   b. decreases the quantity demanded for that good.
   c. increases the supply of that good.
   d. increases the quantity supplied of that good.
   e. none of the above.

4. The *law of supply* states that an increase in the price of a good
   a. decreases the demand for that good.
   b. decreases the quantity demanded for that good.
   c. increases the supply of that good.
   d. increases the quantity supplied of that good.
   e. none of the above.

5. If an increase in consumer incomes leads to a decrease in the demand for camping equipment, then camping equipment is
   a. a complementary good.
   b. a substitute good.
   c. a normal good.
   d. an inferior good.
   e. none of the above.

6. A monopolistic market has
   a. only one seller.
   b. at least a few sellers.
   c. many buyers and sellers.
   d. firms that are price takers.
   e. none of the above.

7. Which of the following shifts the demand for watches to the right?
   a. a decrease in the price of watches
   b. a decrease in consumer incomes if watches are a normal good
   c. a decrease in the price of watch batteries if watch batteries and watches are complements
   d. an increase in the price of watches
   e. none of the above

8. All of the following shift the supply of watches to the right except
   a. an increase in the price of watches.
   b. an advance in the technology used to manufacture watches.
   c. a decrease in the wage of workers employed to manufacture watches.
   d. manufacturers' expectation of lower watch prices in the future.
   e. All of the above cause an increase in the supply of watches.

9. If the price of a good is above the equilibrium price,
   a. there is a surplus and the price will rise.
   b. there is a surplus and the price will fall.
   c. there is a shortage and the price will rise.
   d. there is a shortage and the price will fall.
   e. the quantity demanded is equal to the quantity supplied and the price remains unchanged.

10. If the price of a good is below the equilibrium price,
    a. there is a surplus and the price will rise.
    b. there is a surplus and the price will fall.
    c. there is a shortage and the price will rise.
    d. there is a shortage and the price will fall.
    e. the quantity demanded is equal to the quantity supplied and the price remains unchanged.

11. If the price of a good is equal to the equilibrium price,
    a. there is a surplus and the price will rise.
    b. there is a surplus and the price will fall.
    c. there is a shortage and the price will rise.
    d. there is a shortage and the price will fall.
    e. the quantity demanded is equal to the quantity supplied and the price remains unchanged.

12. An increase (rightward shift) in the demand for a good will tend to cause
    a. an increase in the equilibrium price and quantity.
    b. a decrease in the equilibrium price and quantity.
    c. an increase in the equilibrium price and a decrease in the equilibrium quantity.
    d. a decrease in the equilibrium price and an increase in the equilibrium quantity.
    e. none of the above.

13. A decrease (leftward shift) in the supply for a good will tend to cause
    a. an increase in the equilibrium price and quantity.
    b. a decrease in the equilibrium price and quantity.
    c. an increase in the equilibrium price and a decrease in the equilibrium quantity.
    d. a decrease in the equilibrium price and an increase in the equilibrium quantity.
    e. none of the above.

14. Suppose there is an increase in both the supply and demand for personal computers. In the market for personal computers, we would expect
    a. the equilibrium quantity to rise and the equilibrium price to rise.
    b. the equilibrium quantity to rise and the equilibrium price to fall.
    c. the equilibrium quantity to rise and the equilibrium price to remain constant.
    d. the equilibrium quantity to rise and the change in the equilibrium price to be ambiguous.
    e. the change in the equilibrium quantity to be ambiguous and the equilibrium price to rise.

15. Suppose there is an increase in both the supply and demand for personal computers. Further, suppose the supply of personal computers increases more than demand for personal computers. In the market for personal computers, we would expect
    a. the equilibrium quantity to rise and the equilibrium price to rise.
    b. the equilibrium quantity to rise and the equilibrium price to fall.
    c. the equilibrium quantity to rise and the equilibrium price to remain constant.
    d. the equilibrium quantity to rise and the change in the equilibrium price to be ambiguous.
    e. the change in the equilibrium quantity to be ambiguous and the equilibrium price to fall.

16. Which of the following statements is true about the impact of an increase in the price of lettuce?
    a. The demand for lettuce will decrease.
    b. The supply of lettuce will decrease.
    c. The equilibrium price and quantity of salad dressing will rise.
    d. The equilibrium price and quantity of salad dressing will fall.
    e. Both (a) and (d).

17. Suppose a frost destroys much of the Florida orange crop. At the same time, suppose consumer tastes shift toward orange juice. What would we expect to happen to the equilibrium price and quantity in the market for orange juice?
    a. Price will increase; quantity is ambiguous.
    b. Price will increase; quantity will increase.
    c. Price will increase; quantity will decrease.
    d. Price will decrease; quantity is ambiguous.
    e. The impact on both price and quantity is ambiguous.

18. Suppose consumer tastes shift toward the consumption of apples. Which of the following statements is an accurate description of the impact of this event on the market for apples?
    a. There is an increase in the demand for apples and an increase in the quantity supplied of apples.
    b. There is an increase in the demand and supply of apples.
    c. There is an increase in the quantity demanded of apples and in the supply for apples.
    d. There is an increase in the demand for apples and a decrease in the supply of apples.
    e. There is a decrease in the quantity demanded of apples and an increase in the supply for apples.

19. Suppose both buyers and sellers of wheat expect the price of wheat to rise in the near future. What would we expect to happen to the equilibrium price and quantity in the market for wheat today?
    a. The impact on both price and quantity is ambiguous.
    b. Price will increase; quantity is ambiguous.
    c. Price will increase; quantity will increase.
    d. Price will increase; quantity will decrease.
    e. Price will decrease; quantity is ambiguous.

20. An inferior good is one for which an increase in income causes
    a. an increase in supply.
    b. a decrease in supply.
    c. an increase in demand.
    d. a decrease in demand.

ADVANCED CRITICAL THINKING

You are watching a national news broadcast. It is reported that a typhoon is heading for the Washington coast and that it will likely destroy much of this year's apple crop. Your roommate says, "If there are going to be fewer apples available, I'll bet that apple prices will rise. We should buy enormous quantities of apples now and put them in storage. Later we will sell them and make a killing."

1. If this information about the storm is publicly available so that all buyers and sellers in the apple market expect the price of apples to rise in the future, what will happen immediately to the supply and demand for apples and the equilibrium price and quantity of apples?

   _____

   _____

   _____

2. Can you "beat the market" with public information? That is, can you use publicly available information to help you buy something cheap and quickly sell it at a higher price? Why or why not?

   _____

   _____

   _____

3. Suppose a friend of yours works for the U.S. Weather Bureau. She calls you and provides you with inside information about the approaching storm—information not available to the public. Can you "beat the market" with inside information? Why?

   _____

   _____

   _____

SOLUTIONS

Terms and Definitions

_5_ Market

_12_ Competitive market

_6_ Monopoly

_14_ Oligopoly

_4_ Monopolistically competitive

_10_ Quantity demanded

_13_ Law of demand

_2_ Demand schedule

_23_ Demand curve

_20_ Normal good

_7_ Inferior good

_22_ Substitutes

_19_ Complements

_18_ The law of supply and demand

_16_ Quantity supplied

_17_ Law of supply

_3_ Supply schedule

_21_ Supply curve

_11_ Equilibrium

_15_ Equilibrium price

_1_ Equilibrium quantity

_9_ Surplus

_8_ Shortage

Practice Problems

1. a. See Exhibit 3.

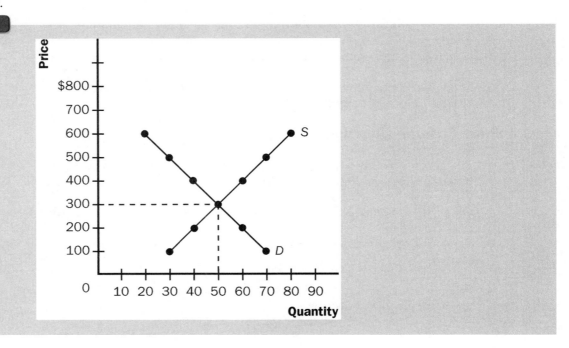

EXHIBIT 3

b. $300
c. 50 bicycles
d. Shortage, 70 – 30 = 40 units, the price will rise
e. Surplus, 60 – 40 = 20 units, the price will fall
f. See Exhibit 4. equilibrium price = $400, equilibrium quantity = 40 bicycles

EXHIBIT 4

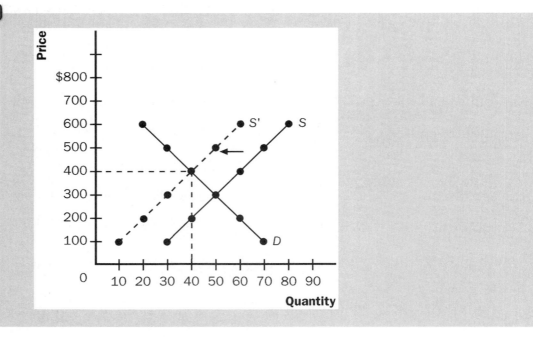

2. a. demand, shifts right, equilibrium price and quantity rise
   b. demand, shifts left, equilibrium price and quantity fall
   c. supply, shifts left, equilibrium price rises, equilibrium quantity falls
   d. demand, shifts right, equilibrium price and quantity rise
   e. demand, shifts left, equilibrium price and quantity fall
   f. supply, shifts right, equilibrium price falls, equilibrium quantity rises
   g. demand, shifts right, equilibrium price and quantity rise
   h. demand, shifts right, equilibrium price and quantity rise

3. a. equilibrium quantity will rise, equilibrium price is ambiguous
   b. equilibrium price and quantity will rise

Short-Answer Questions

1. The goods offered for sale are all the same and the buyers and sellers are so numerous that no one buyer or seller can influence the price.

2. Other things equal, price and quantity demanded of a good are negatively related.

3. The variables are income, prices of related goods, tastes, expectations, and number of buyers in the market.

4. When income rises, demand for a normal good increases or shifts right. When income rises, demand for an inferior good decreases or shifts left.

5. Other things equal, price and quantity supplied of a good are positively related.

6. The variables are input prices, technology, expectations, and number of sellers in the market.

7. The supply of corn in today's market would decrease (shift left) as sellers hold back their offerings in anticipation of greater profits if the price rises in the future. If only suppliers expect higher prices, demand would be unaffected. The equilibrium price would rise and the equilibrium quantity would fall.

8. The price must be above the equilibrium price.

9. There would be an *increase in the demand* for automobiles, which means that the entire demand curve shifts to the right. This implies a movement along the fixed supply curve as the price rises. The increase in price causes an *increase in the quantity supplied* of automobiles but there is no increase in the supply of automobiles.

10. There would be an *increase in the supply* of automobiles, which means that the entire supply curve shifts to the right. This implies a movement along the fixed demand curve as the price falls. The decrease in price causes an *increase in the quantity demanded* of automobiles but there is no increase in the demand for automobiles.

True/False Questions

1. F; a perfectly competitive market consists of goods offered for sale that are all the same.

2. T

3. F; the law of demand states that an increase in the price of a good decreases the *quantity demanded* of that good (a movement along the demand curve).

4. F; it will increase the demand for oranges.

5. T

6. T

7. T

8. F; an increase in the price of an input shifts the supply curve for the output to the left.

9. F; it causes an excess demand.

10. T

11. F; an excess demand causes the price to rise.

12. T

13. T

14. T

15. F; there will be a decrease in the equilibrium price, but the impact on the equilibrium quantity is ambiguous.

Multiple-Choice Questions

1. c	5. d	9. b	13. c	17. a
2. a	6. a	10. c	14. d	18. a
3. b	7. c	11. e	15. b	19. b
4. d	8. a	12. a	16. d	20. d

Advanced Critical Thinking

1. Sellers reduce supply (supply shifts left) in the hope of selling apples later at a higher price and buyers increase demand (demand shifts right) in the hope of buying apples now before the price goes up. The price will immediately rise and the quantity exchanged is ambiguous.

2. No. Usually the market immediately adjusts so that the price has already moved to its new equilibrium value before the amateur speculator can make his or her purchase.

3. Yes. In this case, you can make your purchase before the market responds to the information about the storm.

ELASTICITY AND ITS APPLICATION

GOALS

⌐In this chapter you will

Learn the meaning of the elasticity of demand

Examine what determines the elasticity of demand

Learn the meaning of the elasticity of supply

Examine what determines the elasticity of supply

Apply the concept of elasticity in three very different markets

OUTCOMES

⌐After accomplishing these goals, you should be able to

Define scarcity

Calculate the price and income elasticity of demand

Distinguish between the price elasticity of demand for necessities and luxuries

Calculate the price elasticity of supply

Distinguish between an inelastic and elastic supply curve

Demonstrate the impact of the price elasticity of demand on total revenue

CHAPTER OVERVIEW

Context and Purpose

Chapter 5 is the second chapter of a three-chapter sequence that deals with supply and demand and how markets work. Chapter 4 introduced supply and demand. Chapter 5 shows how much buyers and sellers respond to changes in market conditions. Chapter 6 will address the impact of government polices on competitive markets.

The purpose of Chapter 5 is to add precision to our supply and demand model. We introduce the concept of elasticity, which measures the responsiveness of buyers and sellers to changes in economic variables such as prices and income. The concept of elasticity allows us to make quantitative observations about the impact of changes in supply and demand on equilibrium prices and quantities.

CHAPTER REVIEW

Introduction

In Chapter 4, we learned that an increase in price reduces the quantity demanded and increases the quantity supplied in a market. In this chapter, we will develop the concept of elasticity so that we can address how much the quantity demanded and the quantity supplied responds to changes in market conditions such as price.

The Elasticity of Demand

To measure the response of demand to its determinants, we use the concept of **elasticity**. **Price elasticity of demand** measures how much the quantity demanded responds to a change in the price of that good, computed as the percentage change in quantity demanded divided by the percentage change in price.

If the quantity demanded changes substantially from a change in price, demand is *elastic*. If the quantity demanded changes little from a change in price, demand is *inelastic*. Whether a demand curve tends to be price elastic or inelastic depends on the following:

- *Availability of close substitutes:* The demand for goods with close substitutes is more sensitive to changes in prices and, thus, is more price elastic.

- *Necessities versus luxuries:* The demand for necessities is inelastic while the demand for luxuries is elastic. Since one cannot do without a necessity, an increase in the price has little impact on the quantity demanded. However, an increase in price greatly reduces the quantity demanded of a luxury.

- *Definition of the market:* The more narrowly we define the market, the more likely there are to be close substitutes and the more price elastic the demand curve.

- *Time horizon:* The longer the time period considered, the greater the availability of close substitutes and the more price elastic the demand curve.

The formula for computing the price elasticity of demand is:

$$\text{Price elasticity of demand} = \frac{\text{Percentage change in quantity demanded}}{\text{Percentage change in price}}$$

Since price elasticity of demand is always negative, it is customary to drop the negative sign.

When we compute price elasticity between any two points on a demand curve, we get a different answer depending on which point we choose to start and which point we choose to finish if we take the change in price and quantity as a percent of the starting value for each. To avoid this problem, economists often employ the *midpoint method* to calculate elasticities. With this method, the percentage changes in quantity and price are calculated by dividing the change in the variable by the *average* or midpoint value of the two points on the curve, not the starting point on the curve. Thus, the formula for the price elasticity of demand using the midpoint method is:

$$\text{Price elasticity of demand} = \frac{(Q_2 - Q_1)/[(Q_2 + Q_1)/2]}{(P_2 - P_1)/[(P_2 + P_1)/2]}$$

If price elasticity of demand is greater than one, demand is elastic. If elasticity is less than one, demand is inelastic. If elasticity is equal to one, demand is said to have unit elasticity. If elasticity is zero, demand is perfectly inelastic (vertical). If elasticity is infinite, demand is perfectly elastic (horizontal). In general, the flatter the demand curve, the more elastic. The steeper the demand curve, the more inelastic.

Total revenue is the amount paid by buyers and received by sellers, computed simply as price times quantity. The elasticity of demand determines the impact of a change in price on total revenue:

- If demand is price inelastic (less than 1) an increase in price increases total revenue because the price increase is proportionately larger than the reduction in quantity demanded.

- If demand is price elastic (greater than 1) an increase in price decreases total revenue because the decrease in the quantity demanded is proportionately larger than the increase in price.

- If demand is unit price elastic (exactly equal to 1) a change in price has no impact on total revenue because the increase in price is proportionately equal to the decrease in quantity.

Along a linear demand curve, price elasticity is not constant. When price is high and quantity low, price elasticity is large because a change in price causes a larger *percentage* change in quantity. When price is low and quantity high, price elasticity is small because a change in price causes a smaller *percentage* change in quantity.

There are additional demand elasticities. The **income elasticity of demand** is a measure of how much the quantity demanded responds to a change in consumers' income, computed as the percentage change in quantity demanded divided by the percentage change in income or:

$$\text{Income elasticity of demand} = \frac{\text{Percentage change in quantity demanded}}{\text{Percentage change in income}}$$

For *normal goods*, income elasticity is positive. For *inferior goods*, income elasticity is negative. Within the group of normal goods, necessities like food have small income elasticities because the quantity demanded changes little when income changes. Luxuries have larger income elasticities.

The **cross-price elasticity of demand** is a measure of the response of the quantity demanded of one good to a change in the price of another good, computed as the percentage change in the quantity demanded of one good divided by the percentage change in the price of another good or:

$$\text{Cross-price elasticity of demand} = \frac{\text{Percentage change in quantity demanded of good 1}}{\text{Percentage change in the price of good 2}}$$

The cross-price elasticity of demand is positive for *substitutes* and *negative* for complements.

The Elasticity of Supply

Price elasticity of supply measures how much the quantity supplied responds to a change in the price of that good, computed as the percentage change in quantity supplied divided by the percentage change in price.

If the quantity supplied changes substantially from a change in price, supply is *elastic*. If the quantity supplied changes little from a change in price, supply is *inelastic*. Supply is more elastic when the sellers have greater flexibility to change the amount of a good they produce in response to a change in price. Generally, the shorter the time period considered, the less flexibility the seller has in choosing how much to produce, and the more inelastic the supply curve.

The formula for computing the price elasticity of supply is:

$$\text{Price elasticity of supply} = \frac{\text{Percentage change in quantity supplied}}{\text{Percentage change in price.}}$$

If price elasticity of supply is greater than one, supply is elastic. If elasticity is less than one, supply is inelastic. If elasticity is equal to one, supply is said to have unit elasticity. If elasticity is zero, supply is perfectly inelastic (vertical). If elasticity is infinite, supply is perfectly elastic (horizontal). In general, the flatter the supply curve, the more elastic. The steeper the supply curve, the more inelastic.

Price elasticity of supply may not be constant along a given supply curve. At low quantities, a small increase in price may stimulate a large increase in quantity supplied because there is excess capacity in the production facility. Therefore, price elasticity is large. At high quantities, a large increase in price may cause only a small increase in quantity supplied because the production facility is at full capacity. Therefore, price elasticity is small.

Three Applications of Supply, Demand, and Elasticity

- *The market for agricultural products:* Advances in technology have shifted the supply curve for agricultural products to the right. The demand for food, however, is generally inelastic (steep) because food is inexpensive and a necessity. As a result, the rightward shift in supply has caused a great reduction in the equilibrium price and a small increase in the equilibrium quantity. Thus, ironically, technological advances in agriculture reduce total revenue paid to farmers as a group.

- *The market for oil:* In the 1970s, the Organization of Petroleum Exporting Countries (OPEC) reduced the supply of oil in order to raise its price. In the short run, the demand for oil tends to be inelastic (steep) because consumers cannot easily find substitutes. Thus, the decrease in supply raised the price substantially and increased total revenue to the producers. In the long run, however, consumers found substitutes and drove more fuel efficient cars causing the demand for oil to become more elastic, and producers searched for more oil causing supply to become more elastic. As a result, while the price of oil rose a great deal in the short run, it did not rise much in the long run.

- *The market for illegal drugs:* In the short run, the demand for illegal addictive drugs is relatively inelastic. As a result, drug interdiction policies that reduce the supply of drugs tend to greatly increase the price of drugs while reducing the quantity consumed very little and, thus, total revenue paid by drug users increases. This need for additional funds by drug users may cause drug-related crime to rise. This increase in total revenue and in crime is likely to be smaller in the long run because the demand for illegal drugs becomes more elastic as time passes. Alternatively, policies aimed at reducing the demand for drugs reduce total revenue in the drug market and reduce drug-related crime.

Conclusion

The tools of supply and demand allow you to analyze the most important events and policies that shape the economy.

HELPFUL HINTS

1. An easy way to remember the difference between the terms elastic and inelastic is to substitute the word *sensitivity* for elasticity. For example, price elasticity of demand becomes price *sensitivity* of demand. If the quantity demanded is sensitive to a change in price (demand is relatively flat), demand is elastic. If the quantity demanded is insensitive to a change in price (demand is relatively steep), demand is inelastic. The same is true for

the price elasticity of supply. If the quantity supplied is sensitive to a change in price, supply is elastic. If the quantity supplied is insensitive to a change in price, supply is inelastic.

2. While elasticity and slope are similar, they are not the same. Along a straight line, slope is constant. Slope (rise over run) is the same anywhere on the line and is measured as the change in the dependent variable divided by the change in the independent variable. Elasticity, however, is measured as the *percent* change in the dependent variable divided by the *percent* change in the independent variable. This value changes as we move along a line because a one-unit change in a variable is a larger percentage change when the initial values are small as opposed to when they are large. In practice, however, it is still reasonable to suggest that flatter curves tend to be more elastic and steeper curves tend to be more inelastic.

3. The term "elasticity" is used to describe how much the quantity stretches (or changes) in response to some economic event such as a change in price or income. If the quantity stretches a great deal in response to a change in price or income, it is considered elastic. This mental picture should also help you to remember how to calculate an elasticity—in the numerator you will always find the percent change in quantity and in the denominator you will always find the percent change in the variable that is the source of the change in quantity.

TERMS AND DEFINITIONS
Choose a definition for each key term.

Key terms:

_____ Elasticity

_____ Price elasticity of demand

_____ Elastic

_____ Inelastic

_____ Total revenue

_____ Income elasticity of demand

_____ Cross-price elasticity of demand

_____ Price elasticity of supply

_____ Normal good

_____ Inferior good

Definitions:

1. A measure of how much the quantity demanded of a good responds to a change in consumers' income.

2. When the quantity demanded or supplied responds substantially to a change in one of its determinants.

3. A good characterized by a negative income elasticity.

4. A measure of the responsiveness of the quantity demanded or quantity supplied to one of its determinants.

5. A good characterized by a positive income elasticity.

6. A measure of how much the quantity supplied of a good responds to a change in the price of that good.

7. When the quantity demanded or supplied responds only slightly to a change in one of its determinants.

8. The amount paid by buyers and received by sellers of a good computed as P ¥ Q.

9. A measure of how much the quantity demanded of a good responds to a change in the price of that good.

10. A measure of how much the quantity demanded of one good responds to a change in the price of another good.

PROBLEMS AND SHORT-ANSWER QUESTIONS

Practice Problems

1. For each pair of goods listed below, which good would you expect to have the more elastic demand? Why?
   a. cigarettes; a trip to Florida over spring break

   _____

   _____

   b. an AIDS vaccine over the next month; an AIDS vaccine over the next five years

   _____

   _____

   c. beer; Budweiser

   _____

   _____

   d. insulin; aspirin

   _____

   _____

2. Suppose the *Daily Newspaper* estimates that if it raises the price of its newspaper from $1.00 to $1.50 then the number of subscribers will fall from 50,000 to 40,000.
   a. What is the price elasticity of demand for the *Daily Newspaper* when elasticity is calculated using the midpoint method?

   _____

   _____

   b. What is the advantage of using the midpoint method?

   _____

   _____

c. If the *Daily Newspaper*'s only concern is to maximize total revenue, should it raise the price of a newspaper from $1.00 to $1.50? Why or why not?

_____

_____

3. The table below provides the demand schedule for motel rooms at Small Town Motel. Use the information provided to complete the table. Answer the following questions based on your responses in the table. Use the midpoint method to calculate the percentage changes used to generate the elasticities.

Price	Quantity Demanded	Total Revenue	% Change in Price	% Change in Quantity	Elasticity
$20	24	_____			
			_____	_____	_____
40	20	_____			
			_____	_____	_____
60	16	_____			
			_____	_____	_____
80	12	_____			
			_____	_____	_____
100	8	_____			
			_____	_____	_____
120	4	_____			

a. Over what range of prices is the demand for motel rooms elastic? To maximize total revenue, should Small Town Motel raise or lower the price within this range?

_____

_____

b. Over what range of prices is the demand for motel rooms inelastic? To maximize total revenue, should Small Town Motel raise or lower the price within this range?

_____

_____

c. Over what range of prices is the demand for motel rooms unit elastic? To maximize total revenue, should Small Town Motel raise or lower the price within this range?

_____

_____

4. The demand schedule from question 3 above is reproduced below along with another demand schedule when consumer incomes have risen to $60,000 from $50,000. Use this information to answer the following questions. Use the midpoint method to calculate the percentage changes used to generate the elasticities.

Price	Quantity Demanded When Income is $50,000	Quantity Demanded When Income is $60,000
$ 20	24	34
40	20	30
60	16	26
80	12	22
100	8	18
120	4	14

a. What is the income elasticity of demand when motel rooms rent for $40?

_____

_____

b. What is the income elasticity of demand when motel rooms rent for $100?

_____

_____

c. Are motel rooms normal or inferior goods? Why?

_____

_____

d. Are motel rooms likely to be necessities or luxuries? Why?

_____

_____

5. For each pair of goods listed below, which good would you expect to have the more elastic supply? Why?
a. televisions; beach front property

_____

_____

b. crude oil over the next week; crude oil over the next year

_____

_____

c. a painting by van Gogh; a print of the same painting by van Gogh

_____

_____

Short-Answer Questions

1. What are the four major determinants of the price elasticity of demand?

   _____

   _____

   _____

2. If demand is inelastic, will an increase in price raise or lower total revenue? Why?

   _____

   _____

3. If the price of soda doubles from $1.00 per can to $2.00 per can and you buy the same amount, what is your price elasticity of demand for soda and is it considered elastic or inelastic?

   _____

   _____

4. If the price of Pepsi increases by one cent and this induces you to stop buying Pepsi altogether and to switch to Coke, what is your price elasticity of demand for Pepsi and is it considered elastic or inelastic?

   _____

   _____

5. Suppose your income rises by 20 percent and your quantity demanded of eggs falls by 10 percent. What is the value of your income elasticity of demand for eggs? Are eggs normal or inferior goods to you?

   _____

6. Suppose a firm is operating at half capacity. Is its supply curve for output likely to be relatively elastic or inelastic? Why?

   _____

   _____

7. Is the price elasticity of supply for fresh fish likely to be elastic or inelastic when measured over the time period of one day? Why?

_____

_____

8. If a demand curve is linear, is the elasticity constant along the demand curve? Which part tends to be elastic and which part tends to be inelastic? Why?

_____

_____

_____

_____

9. Suppose that at a price of $2.00 per bushel, the quantity supplied of corn is 25 million metric tons. At a price of $3.00 per bushel, the quantity supplied is 30 million metric tons. What is the elasticity of supply for corn? Is supply elastic or inelastic?

_____

_____

10. Suppose that when the price of apples rises by 20 percent, the quantity demanded of oranges rises by 6 percent. What is the cross-price elasticity of demand between apples and oranges? Are these two goods substitutes or complements?

_____

_____

SELF-TEST

True/False Questions

_____ 1. If the quantity demanded of a good is sensitive to a change in the price of that good, demand is said to be price inelastic.

_____ 2. Using the midpoint method to calculate elasticity, if an increase in the price of pencils from 10 cents to 20 cents reduces the quantity demanded from 1000 pencils to 500 pencils, then the demand for pencils is unit price elastic.

_____ 3. The demand for tires should be more inelastic than the demand for Goodyear brand tires.

_____ 4. The demand for aspirin this month should be more elastic than the demand for aspirin this year.

_____ 5. The price elasticity of demand is defined as the percentage change in the price of that good divided by the percentage change in quantity demanded of that good.

_____ 6. If the cross-price elasticity of demand between two goods is positive, the goods are likely to be complements.

_____ 7. If the demand for a good is price inelastic, an increase in its price will increase total revenue in that market.

_____ 8. The demand for a necessity such as insulin tends to be elastic.

_____ 9. If a demand curve is linear, the price elasticity of demand is constant along it.

_____10. If the income elasticity of demand for a bus ride is negative, then a bus ride is an inferior good.

_____11. The supply of automobiles for this week is likely to be more price inelastic than the supply of automobiles for this year.

_____12. If the price elasticity of supply for blue jeans is 1.3, an increase in the price of blue jeans of 10 percent would increase the quantity supplied of blue jeans by 13 percent.

_____13. The price elasticity of supply tends to be more inelastic as the firm's production facility reaches maximum capacity.

_____14. An advance in technology that shifts the market supply curve to the right always increases total revenue received by producers.

_____15. The income elasticity of demand for luxury items, such as diamonds, tends to be large (greater than 1).

Multiple-Choice Questions

1. If a small percentage increase in the price of a good greatly reduces the quantity demanded for that good, the demand for that good is
   a. price inelastic.
   b. price elastic.
   c. unit price elastic.
   d. income inelastic.
   e. income elastic.

2. The price elasticity of demand is defined as
   a. the percentage change in price of a good divided by the percentage change in the quantity demanded of that good.
   b. the percentage change in income divided by the percentage change in the quantity demanded.
   c. the percentage change in the quantity demanded of a good divided by the percentage change in the price of that good.
   d. the percentage change in the quantity demanded divided by the percentage change in income.
   e. none of the above.

3. In general, a flatter demand curve is more likely to be
   a. price elastic.
   b. price inelastic.
   c. unit price elastic.
   d. none of the above.

4. In general, a steeper supply curve is more likely to be
   a. price elastic.
   b. price inelastic.
   c. unit price elastic.
   d. none of the above.

5. Which of the following would cause a demand curve for a good to be price inelastic?
   a. There are a great number of substitutes for the good.
   b. The good is inferior.
   c. The good is a luxury.
   d. The good is a necessity.

6. The demand for which of the following is likely to be the most price inelastic?
   a. airline tickets
   b. bus tickets
   c. taxi rides
   d. transportation

7. If the cross-price elasticity between two goods is negative, the two goods are likely to be
   a. luxuries.
   b. necessities.
   c. complements.
   d. substitutes.

8. If a supply curve for a good is price elastic, then
   a. the quantity supplied is sensitive to changes in the price of that good.
   b. the quantity supplied is insensitive to changes in the price of that good.
   c. the quantity demanded is sensitive to changes in the price of that good.
   d. the quantity demanded is insensitive to changes in the price of that good.
   e. none of the above.

9. If a fisherman must sell all of his daily catch before it spoils for whatever price he is offered, once the fish are caught the fisherman's price elasticity of supply for fresh fish is
   a. zero.
   b. one.
   c. infinite.
   d. unable to be determined from this information.

10. A decrease in supply (shift to the left) will increase total revenue in that market if
   a. supply is price elastic.
   b. supply is price inelastic.
   c. demand is price elastic.
   d. demand is price inelastic.

11. If an increase in the price of a good has no impact on the total revenue in that market, demand must be
   a. price inelastic.
   b. price elastic.
   c. unit price elastic.
   d. all of the above.

12. If consumers always spend 15 percent of their income on food, then the income elasticity of demand for food is
   a. 0.15.
   b. 1.00.
   c. 1.15.
   d. 1.50.
   e. none of the above.

13. Technological improvements in agriculture that shift the supply of agricultural commodities to the right tend to
   a. reduce total revenue to farmers as a whole because the demand for food is inelastic.
   b. reduce total revenue to farmers as a whole because the demand for food is elastic.
   c. increase total revenue to farmers as a whole because the demand for food is inelastic.
   d. increase total revenue to farmers as a whole because the demand for food is elastic.

14. If supply is price inelastic, the value of the price elasticity of supply must be
   a. zero.
   b. less than 1.
   c. greater than 1.
   d. infinite.
   e. none of the above.

15. If there is excess capacity in a production facility, it is likely that the firm's supply curve is
   a. price inelastic.
   b. price elastic.
   c. unit price elastic.
   d. none of the above.

Use the following information to answer the next two questions. Suppose that at a price of $30 per month, there are 30,000 subscribers to cable television in Small Town. If Small Town Cablevision raises its price to $40 per month, the number of subscribers will fall to 20,000.

16. Using the midpoint method for calculating the elasticity, what is the price elasticity of demand for cable TV in Small Town?
    a. 0.66
    b. 0.75
    c. 1.0
    d. 1.4
    e. 2.0

17. At which of the following prices does Small Town Cablevision earn the greatest total revenue?
    a. Either $30 or $40 per month because the price elasticity of demand is 1.0.
    b. $30 per month
    c. $40 per month
    d. $0 per month

18. If demand is linear (a straight line), then price elasticity of demand is
    a. constant along the demand curve.
    b. inelastic in the upper portion and elastic in the lower portion.
    c. elastic in the upper portion and inelastic in the lower portion.
    d. elastic throughout.
    e. inelastic throughout.

19. If the income elasticity of demand for a good is negative, it must be
    a. a luxury good.
    b. a normal good.
    c. an inferior good.
    d. an elastic good.

20. If consumers think that there are very few substitutes for a good, then
    a. supply would tend to be price elastic.
    b. supply would tend to be price inelastic.
    c. demand would tend to be price elastic.
    d. demand would tend to be price inelastic.
    e. none of the above.

ADVANCED CRITICAL THINKING

In order to reduce teen smoking, the government places a $2 per pack tax on cigarettes. After one month, while the price to the consumer has increased a great deal, the quantity demanded of cigarettes has been reduced only slightly.

1. Is the demand for cigarettes over the period of one month elastic or inelastic?

_____

_____

2. Suppose you are in charge of pricing for a tobacco firm. The president of your firm suggests that the evidence received over the last month demonstrates that the cigarette industry should get together and raise the price of cigarettes further because total revenue to the tobacco industry will certainly rise. Is the president of your firm correct? Why?

_____

_____

_____

3. As an alternative, suppose the president of your tobacco firm suggests that your firm should raise the price of your cigarettes independent of the other tobacco firms because the evidence clearly shows that smokers are insensitive to changes in the price of cigarettes. Is the president of your firm correct if it is his/her desire to maximize total revenue? Why?

_____

_____

_____

SOLUTIONS

Terms and Definitions

_4_   Elasticity

_9_   Price elasticity of demand

_2_   Elastic

_7_   Inelastic

_8_   Total revenue

_1_   Income elasticity of demand

_10_   Cross-price elasticity of demand

_6_   Price elasticity of supply

_5_   Normal good

_3_   Inferior good

Practice Problems

1. a. a trip to Florida because it is a luxury while cigarettes are a necessity (to smokers)
    b. an AIDS vaccine over the next five years because there are likely to be more substitutes (alternative medications) developed over this time period and consumers' behavior may be modified over longer time periods
    c. Budweiser because it is a more narrowly defined market than beer so there are more substitutes for Budweiser than for beer
    d. aspirin because there are many substitutes for aspirin but few substitutes for insulin

2. a. $(10,000/45,000)/(\$.50/\$1.25) = 0.56$
    b. With the midpoint method, the value of the elasticity is the same whether you begin at a price of $1.00 and raise it to $1.50 or begin at a price of $1.50 and reduce it to $1.00.
    c. Yes. Since the price elasticity of demand is less than one (inelastic), an increase in price will increase total revenue.

3.

Price	Quantity Demanded	Total Revenue	% Change In Price	% Change In Quantity	Elasticity
$ 20	24	480			
			0.67	0.18	0.27
40	20	800			
			0.40	0.22	0.55
60	16	960			
			0.29	0.29	1.00
80	12	960			
			0.22	0.40	1.82
100	8	800			
			0.18	0.67	3.72
120	4	480			

a. $80 to $120; lower its prices
b. $20 to $60; raise its prices
c. $60 to $80; it doesn't matter. For these prices, a change in price proportionately changes the quantity demanded so total revenue is unchanged.

4. a. $(10/25)/(\$10{,}000/\$55{,}000) = 2.2$
    b. $(10/13)/(\$10{,}000/\$55{,}000) = 4.2$
    c. Normal goods, because the income elasticity of demand is positive.
    d. Luxuries, because the income elasticity of demand is large (greater than 1). In each case, an 18 percent increase in income caused a much larger increase in quantity demanded.

5. a. Televisions because the production of televisions can be increased in response to an increase in the price of televisions while the quantity of beach front property is fixed.
    b. Crude oil over the next year because production of oil over the next year can more easily be increased than the production of oil over the next week.
    c. A van Gogh print because more of them can be created in response to an increase in price while the quantity of an original work is fixed.

Short-Answer Questions

1. Whether the good is a necessity or a luxury, the availability of close substitutes, the definition of the market, and the time horizon over which demand is measured.

2. It will increase total revenue because a large increase in price will be accompanied by only a small reduction in the quantity demanded if demand is inelastic.

3. Zero, therefore it is considered perfectly inelastic.

4. Infinite, therefore it is considered perfectly elastic.

5. $-0.10/0.20 = -1/2$. Eggs are inferior goods.

6. Elastic because a small increase in price will induce the firm to increase production a large amount.

7. Inelastic (nearly vertical) because once the fish are caught, the quantity offered for sale is fixed and must be sold before it spoils, regardless of the price.

8. No. The upper part tends to be elastic while the lower part tends to be inelastic. This is because on the upper part, for example, a one unit change in the price is a small percentage change while a one unit

change in quantity is a large percentage change. This effect is reversed on the lower part of the demand curve.

9. $\dfrac{(30 - 25)/[(25 + 30)/2]}{(3 - 2)/[(2 + 3)/2]} = 0.45$, therefore supply is inelastic.

10. $0.06/0.20 = 0.30$, apples and oranges are substitutes because the cross-price elasticity is positive (an increase in the price of apples increases the quantity demanded of oranges).

True/False Questions

1. F; demand would be price elastic.

2. T

3. T

4. F; the longer the time period considered, the more price elastic the demand curve because consumers have an opportunity to substitute or change their behavior.

5. F; the price elasticity of demand is defined as the percentage change in the quantity demanded of a good divided by the percentage change in the price of that good.

6. F; the two goods are likely to be substitutes.

7. T

8. F; the demand for necessities tends to be inelastic.

9. F; demand will be price elastic in its upper portion and price inelastic in its lower portion.

10. T

11. T

12. T

13. T

14. F; it will increase total revenue only if demand is price elastic.

15. T

Multiple-Choice Questions

1. b	5. d	9. a	13. a	17. b
2. c	6. d	10. d	14. b	18. c
3. a	7. c	11. c	15. b	19. c
4. b	8. a	12. b	16. d	20. d

Advanced Critical Thinking

1. Inelastic.

2. Not necessarily. Demand tends to be more elastic over longer periods. In the case of cigarettes, some consumers will substitute toward cigars and pipes. Others may quit or never start to smoke.

3. No. While the demand for cigarettes (the market broadly defined) may be inelastic, the demand for any one brand (market narrowly defined) is likely to be much more elastic because consumers can substitute toward other lower priced brands.

SUPPLY, DEMAND, AND GOVERNMENT POLICIES

GOALS

⌈In this chapter you will

Examine the effects of government policies that place a ceiling on prices

Examine the effects of government policies that put a floor under prices

Consider how a tax on a good affects the price of the good and the quantity sold

Learn that taxes levied on buyers and taxes levied on sellers are equivalent

See how the burden of a tax is split between buyers and sellers

CHAPTER OVERVIEW

Context and Purpose

Chapter 6 is the third chapter in a three-chapter sequence that deals with supply and demand and how markets work. Chapter 4 developed the model of supply and demand. Chapter 5 added precision to the model of supply and demand by developing the concept of elasticity—the sensitivity of the quantity supplied and quantity demanded to changes in economic conditions. Chapter 6 addresses the impact of government policies on competitive markets using the tools of supply and demand that you learned in Chapters 4 and 5.

The purpose of Chapter 6 is to consider two types of government policies—price controls and taxes. Price controls set the maximum or minimum price at which a good can be sold while a tax creates a wedge between what the buyer pays and the seller receives. These policies can be analyzed within the model of supply and demand. We will find that government policies sometimes produce unintended consequences.

OUTCOMES

⌈After accomplishing these goals, you should be able to

Describe the conditions necessary for a price ceiling to be a binding constraint

Explain why a binding price floor creates a surplus

Demonstrate why a tax placed on a good generally reduces the quantity of the good sold

Demonstrate why the results are the same when a tax is placed on the buyers or sellers of a good

Show whether the buyers or sellers of a good bear the burden of the tax when demand is inelastic and supply is elastic

CHAPTER REVIEW

Introduction

In Chapters 4 and 5, we acted as scientists because we built the model of supply and demand to describe the world as it is. In Chapter 6, we act as policy advisors because we address how government policies are used to try to improve the world. We address two policies—price controls and taxes. Sometimes these policies produce unintended consequences.

Controls on Prices

There are two types of controls on prices: price ceilings and price floors. A **price ceiling** sets a legal maximum on the price at which a good can be sold. A **price floor** sets a legal minimum on the price at which a good can be sold.

Price ceilings   Suppose the government is persuaded by buyers to set a price ceiling. If the price ceiling is set above the equilibrium price, it is *not binding*. That is, it has no impact on the market because the price can move to equilibrium without restriction. If the price ceiling is set below the equilibrium price, it is a *binding constraint* because it does not allow the market to reach equilibrium. A binding price ceiling causes the quantity demanded to exceed the quantity supplied, or a shortage. Since there is a shortage, methods develop to ration the small quantity supplied across a large number of buyers. Buyers willing to wait in long lines might get the good, or sellers could sell only to their friends, family, or same race. Lines are inefficient and discrimination is both inefficient and unfair. Free markets are impersonal and ration goods with prices.

Price ceilings are commonly found in the markets for gasoline and apartments. When OPEC restricted the quantity of petroleum in 1973, the supply of gasoline was reduced and the equilibrium price rose above the price ceiling and the price ceiling became binding. This caused a shortage of gas and long lines at the pump. In response, the price ceilings were later repealed. Price ceilings on apartments are known as rent controls. Binding rent controls create a shortage of housing. Both the demand and supply of housing are inelastic in the short run so the initial shortage is small. In the long run, however, the supply and demand for housing become more elastic and the shortage is more apparent. This causes waiting lists for apartments, bribes to landlords, unclean and unsafe buildings, and lower quality housing.

When the government does not allow the price of water to rise during a drought, it acts as a price ceiling and a water shortage develops.

Price floors   Suppose the government is persuaded by sellers to set a price floor. If the price floor is set below the equilibrium price, it is *not binding*. That is, it has no impact on the market because the price can move to equilibrium without restriction. If the price floor is set above the equilibrium price, it is a *binding constraint* because it does not allow the market to reach equilibrium. A binding price floor causes the quantity supplied to exceed the quantity demanded, or a surplus. In order to eliminate the surplus, sellers may appeal to the biases of the buyers and sell to family or same race buyers. Free markets are impersonal and ration goods with prices.

An important example of a price floor is the minimum wage. The minimum wage is a binding constraint in the market for young and unskilled workers. When the wage is set above the market equilibrium wage, the quantity supplied of labor exceeds the quantity demanded. The result is unemployment. Studies show that a 10 percent increase in the minimum wage depresses teenage employ-ment by 1 to 3 percent. The minimum wage also causes teenagers to look for work and drop out of school.

Price controls often hurt those they are trying to help—usually the poor. The minimum wage may help those who find work at the minimum wage but harm those who become unemployed as a result of the minimum wage. Rent controls reduce the quality and availability of housing.

Taxes

Governments use taxes to raise revenue. A tax on a good will affect the quantity sold and both the price paid by buyers and the price received by sellers. If the tax is collected from the buyers, demand shifts downward by the size of the tax per unit. As a result of the decrease in demand, the quantity sold decreases, the price paid by the buyer increases, and the price received by the seller decreases. If the tax is collected from the sellers, supply shifts upward by the size of the tax per unit. As a result of the decrease in supply, the quantity sold decreases, the price paid by the buyer increases, and the price received by the seller decreases. Therefore, a tax collected from buyers has the same effect as a tax collected from sellers. After a tax has been placed on a good, the difference between what the buyer pays and the seller receives is the tax per unit and is known as the *tax wedge*. In summary:

- A tax discourages market activity. That is, the quantity sold is reduced.

- Buyers and sellers share the burden of a tax because the price paid by the buyers increases while the price received by the sellers decreases.

- The effect of a tax collected from buyers is equivalent to a tax collected from sellers.

- The government cannot legislate the relative burden of the tax between buyers and sellers. The relative burden of a tax is determined by the elasticity of supply and demand in that market.

Tax incidence is the manner in which the burden of a tax is shared among par-ticipants in a market. When a tax wedge is placed between buyers and sellers, the tax burden falls more heavily on the side of the market that is less elastic. That is, the tax burden falls more heavily on the side of the market that is less willing to leave the market when price movements are unfavorable to them. For example, in the market for cigarettes, since cigarettes are addictive, demand is likely to be less elastic than supply. Therefore, a tax on cigarettes tends to raise the price paid by buyers more than it reduces the price received by sellers and, as a result, the burden of a cigarette tax falls more heavily on the buyers of cigarettes. With regard to the payroll tax (Social Security and Medicare tax), since labor supply is less elastic than labor demand, most of the tax burden is born by the workers as opposed to the 50-50 split intended by lawmakers.

Conclusion

Supply and demand can be utilized to analyze the impact of government policies such as price controls and taxes.

HELPFUL HINTS

1. Price ceilings and price floors only matter if they are binding constraints. Price ceilings do not automatically cause a shortage. A price ceiling only causes a shortage if the price ceiling is set below the equilibrium price. In a similar manner, a price floor only causes a surplus if the price floor is set above the equilibrium price.

2. It is useful to think of taxes as causing vertical shifts in demand and supply. Since demand is the maximum buyers are willing to pay for each quantity, a tax imposed on the buyers in a market reduces or shifts downward the demand *faced by sellers* by precisely the size of the tax per unit. That is, the buyers now offer the sellers an amount that has been reduced by precisely the size of the tax per unit. Alternatively, since supply is the minimum sellers are willing to accept for each quantity, a tax imposed on the sellers in a market reduces or shifts upward the supply *faced by buyers* by precisely the size of the tax per unit. This is because the sellers now require an additional amount from the buyers that is precisely the size of the tax per unit.

TERMS AND DEFINITIONS

Choose a definition for each key term.

Key terms:

_____ Price ceiling

_____ Price floor

_____ Tax incidence

_____ Tax wedge

Definitions:

1. The manner in which the burden of a tax is shared among participants in a market

2. A legal maximum on the price at which a good can be sold

3. The difference between what the buyer pays and the seller receives after a tax has been imposed

4. A legal minimum on the price at which a good can be sold

PROBLEMS AND SHORT-ANSWER QUESTIONS

Practice Problems

1. Use the following supply and demand schedules for bicycles to answer the questions below.

Price	Quantity demanded	Quantity supplied
$300	60	30
400	55	40
500	50	50
600	45	60
700	40	70
800	35	80

a. In response to lobbying by the Bicycle Riders Association, Congress places a price ceiling of $700 on bicycles. What effect will this have on the market for bicycles? Why?

_____

_____

_____

_____

b. In response to lobbying by the Bicycle Riders Association, Congress places a price ceiling of $400 on bicycles. Use the information provided above to plot the supply and demand curves for bicycles in Exhibit 1. Impose the price ceiling. What is the result of a price ceiling of $400 on bicycles?

_____

_____

_____

_____

EXHIBIT 1

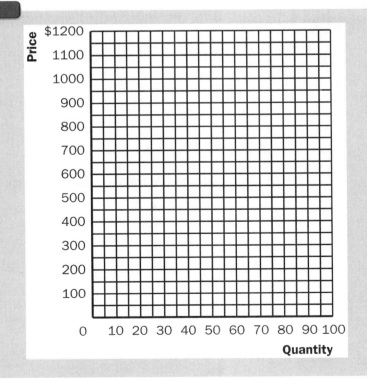

c. Does a price ceiling of $400 on bicycles make all bicycle buyers better off? Why or why not?

_____

_____

_____

_____

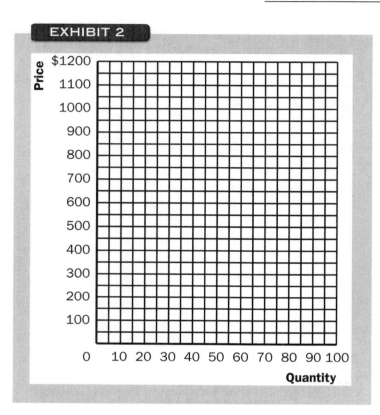

EXHIBIT 2

d. Suppose instead, in response to lobbying by the Bicycle Manufactures Association, Congress imposes a price floor on bicycles of $700. Use the information provided above to plot the supply and demand curves for bicycles in Exhibit 2. Impose the $700 price floor. What is the result of the $700 price floor?

_____

_____

_____

_____

_____

_____

_____

_____

_____

2. Use the following supply and demand schedules for bicycles to answer the questions below.

Price	Quantity demanded	Quantity supplied
$300	60	30
400	55	40
500	50	50
600	45	60
700	40	70
800	35	80

a. Plot the supply and demand curves for bicycles in Exhibit 3. On the graph, impose a tax of $300 per bicycle to be collected from the sellers. After the tax, what has happened to the price paid by the buyers, the price received by the sellers, and the quantity sold when compared to the free market equilibrium?

_____

_____

_____

_____

_____

_____

_____

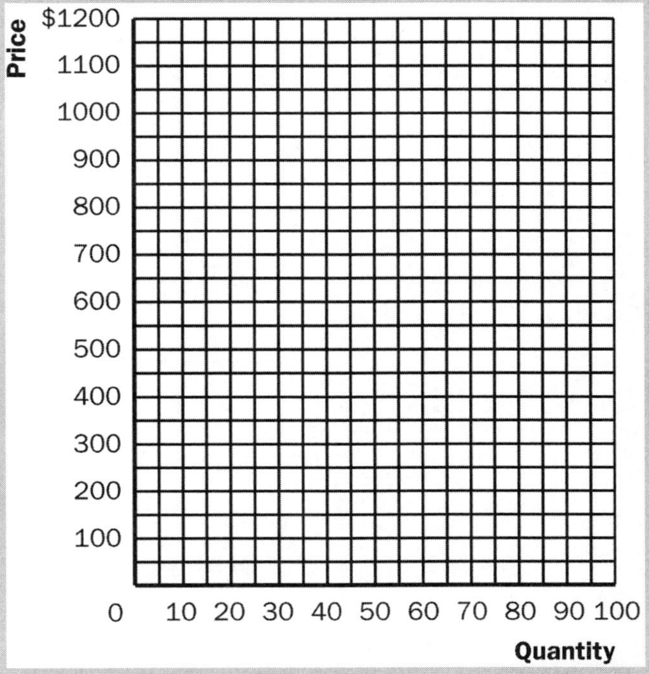

b. Again, plot the supply and demand curves for bicycles in Exhibit 4. On the graph, impose a tax of $300 per bicycle to be collected from the buyers. After the tax, what has happened to the price paid by the buyers, the price received by the sellers, and the quantity sold when compared to the free market equilibrium?

_____

_____

_____

_____

_____

_____

c. Compare your answers to questions (a) and (b) above. What conclusion do you draw from this comparison?

_____

_____

_____

_____

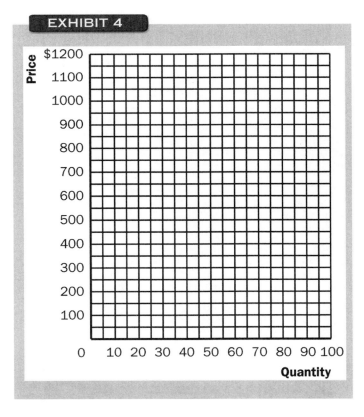

EXHIBIT 3

EXHIBIT 4

d. Who bears the greater burden of this tax, the buyers or the sellers? Why?

_____

_____

_____

_____

Short-Answer Questions

1. What is the impact on the price and quantity in a market if a price ceiling is set above the equilibrium price? Why?

   _____

   _____

2. What is the impact on the price and quantity in a market if a price ceiling is set below the equilibrium price?

   _____

3. What are some of the problems created by a binding price ceiling?

   _____

   _____

   _____

4. Is the impact of a binding price ceiling greater in the short run or the long run? Why?

   _____

   _____

   _____

5. What is the impact on the price and quantity in a market if a price floor is set below the equilibrium price? Why?

   _____

   _____

6. What is the impact on the price and quantity in a market if a price floor is set above the equilibrium price?

   _____

7. When we use the model of supply and demand to analyze a tax that is collected from the buyers, which way do we shift the demand curve? Why?

_____

_____

_____

8. When we use the model of supply and demand to analyze a tax that is collected from the sellers, which way do we shift the supply curve? Why?

_____

_____

_____

9. Why is a tax collected from the buyers equivalent to a tax collected from the sellers?

_____

_____

_____

10. Suppose a gas-guzzler tax is placed on luxury automobiles. Who will likely bear the greater burden of the tax, the buyers of luxury autos or the sellers? Why?

_____

_____

_____

_____

SELF-TEST

True/False Questions

_____ 1. If the equilibrium price of gasoline is $1.00 per gallon and the government places a price ceiling on gasoline of $1.50 per gallon, the result will be a shortage of gasoline.

_____ 2. A price ceiling set below the equilibrium price causes a surplus.

_____ 3. A price floor set above the equilibrium price is a binding constraint.

_____ 4. The shortage of housing caused by a binding rent control is likely to be more severe in the long run when compared to the short run.

_____ 5. The minimum wage helps all teenagers because they receive higher wages than they would otherwise.

_____ 6. A 10 percent increase in the minimum wage causes a 10 percent reduction in teenage employment.

_____ 7. A price ceiling that is not a binding constraint today could cause a shortage in the future if demand were to increase and raise the equilibrium price above the fixed price ceiling.

_____ 8. A price floor in a market always creates a surplus in that market.

_____ 9. A $10 tax on baseball gloves will always raise the price that the buyers pay for baseball gloves by $10.

_____10. The ultimate burden of a tax lands most heavily on the side of the market that is less elastic.

_____11. If medicine is a necessity, the burden of a tax on medicine will likely land more heavily on the buyers of medicine.

_____12. When we use the model of supply and demand to analyze a tax collected from the buyers, we shift the demand curve upward by the size of the tax.

_____13. A tax collected from buyers has an equivalent impact to a same size tax collected from sellers.

_____14. A tax creates a tax wedge between a buyer and a seller. This causes the price paid by the buyer to rise, the price received by the seller to fall, and the quantity sold to fall.

_____15. The government can choose to place the burden of a tax on the buyers in a market by collecting the tax from the buyers rather than the sellers.

Multiple-Choice Questions

1. For a price ceiling to be a binding constraint on the market, the government must set it
   a. above the equilibrium price.
   b. below the equilibrium price.
   c. precisely at the equilibrium price.
   d. at any price because all price ceilings are binding constraints.

2. A binding price ceiling creates
   a. a shortage.
   b. a surplus.
   c. an equilibrium.
   d. a shortage or a surplus depending on whether the price ceiling is set above or below the equilibrium price.

3. Suppose the equilibrium price for apartments is $500 per month and the government imposes rent controls of $250. Which of the following is *unlikely* to occur as a result of the rent controls?
   a. There will be a shortage of housing.
   b. Landlords may discriminate among apartment renters.
   c. Landlords may be offered bribes to rent apartments.
   d. The quality of apartments will improve.
   e. There may be long lines of buyers waiting for apartments.

4. A price floor
   a. sets a legal maximum on the price at which a good can be sold.
   b. sets a legal minimum on the price at which a good can be sold.
   c. always determines the price at which a good must be sold.
   d. is not a binding constraint if it is set above the equilibrium price.

5. Which of the following statements about a binding price ceiling is true?
   a. The surplus created by the price ceiling is greater in the short run than in the long run.
   b. The surplus created by the price ceiling is greater in the long run than in the short run.
   c. The shortage created by the price ceiling is greater in the short run than in the long run.
   d. The shortage created by the price ceiling is greater in the long run than in the short run.

6. Which side of the market is more likely to lobby government for a price floor?
   a. Neither buyers or sellers desire a price floor.
   b. Both buyers and sellers desire a price floor.
   c. the sellers
   d. the buyers

7. The surplus caused by a binding price floor will be greatest if
   a. both supply and demand are elastic.
   b. both supply and demand are inelastic.
   c. supply is inelastic and demand is elastic.
   d. demand is inelastic and supply is elastic.

8. Which of the following is an example of a price floor?
   a. rent controls
   b. restricting gasoline prices to $1.00 per gallon when the equilibrium price is $1.50 per gallon
   c. the minimum wage
   d. All of the above are price floors.

9. Which of the following statements is true if the government places a price ceiling on gasoline at $1.50 per gallon and the equilibrium price is $1.00 per gallon?
   a. There will be a shortage of gasoline.
   b. There will be a surplus of gasoline.
   c. A significant increase in the supply of gasoline could cause the price ceiling to become a binding constraint.
   d. A significant increase in the demand for gasoline could cause the price ceiling to become a binding constraint.

10. Studies show that a 10 percent increase in the minimum wage
    a. decreases teenage employment by about 10 to 15 percent.
    b. increases teenage employment by about 10 to 15 percent.
    c. decreases teenage employment by about 1 to 3 percent.
    d. increases teenage employment by about 1 to 3 percent.

11. Within the supply and demand model, a tax collected from the buyers of a good shifts the
    a. demand curve upward by the size of the tax per unit.
    b. demand curve downward by the size of the tax per unit.
    c. supply curve upward by the size of the tax per unit.
    d. supply curve downward by the size of the tax per unit.

12. Within the supply and demand model, a tax collected from the sellers of a good shifts the
    a. demand curve upward by the size of the tax per unit.
    b. demand curve downward by the size of the tax per unit.
    c. supply curve upward by the size of the tax per unit.
    d. supply curve downward by the size of the tax per unit.

13. Which of the following takes place when a tax is placed a good?
    a. an increase in the price buyers pay, a decrease in the price sellers receive, and a decrease in the quantity sold
    b. an increase in the price buyers pay, a decrease in the price sellers receive, and an increase in the quantity sold
    c. a decrease in the price buyers pay, an increase in the price sellers receive, and a decrease in the quantity sold
    d. a decrease in the price buyers pay, an increase in the price sellers receive, and an increase in the quantity sold

14. When a tax is collected from the buyers in a market,
    a. the buyers bear the burden of the tax.
    b. the sellers bear the burden of the tax.
    c. the tax burden on the buyers and sellers is the same as an equivalent tax collected from the sellers.
    d. the tax burden falls most heavily on the buyers.

15. A tax of $1.00 per gallon on gasoline
    a. increases the price the buyers pay by $1.00 per gallon.
    b. decreases the price the sellers receive by $1.00 per gallon.
    c. increases the price the buyers pay by precisely $.50 and reduces the price received by sellers by precisely $.50.
    d. places a tax wedge of $1.00 between the price the buyers pay and the price the sellers receive.

16. The burden of a tax falls more heavily on the sellers in a market when
    a. demand is inelastic and supply is elastic.
    b. demand is elastic and supply is inelastic.
    c. both supply and demand are elastic.
    d. both supply and demand are inelastic.

17. A tax placed on a good that is a necessity for consumers will likely generate a tax burden that
    a. falls more heavily on buyers.
    b. falls more heavily on sellers.
    c. is evenly distributed between buyers and sellers.
    d. falls entirely on sellers.

18. The burden of a tax falls more heavily on the buyers in a market when
    a. demand is inelastic and supply is elastic.
    b. demand is elastic and supply is inelastic.
    c. both supply and demand are elastic.
    d. both supply and demand are inelastic.

19. Which of the following statements about the burden of a tax is correct?
    a. The tax burden generated from a tax placed on a good consumers perceive to be a necessity will fall most heavily on the sellers of the good.
    b. The tax burden falls most heavily on the side of the market (buyers or sellers) that is most willing to leave the market when price movements are unfavorable to them.
    c. The burden of a tax lands on the side of the market (buyers or sellers) from which it is collected.
    d. The distribution of the burden of a tax is determined by the relative elasticities of supply and demand and is not determined by legislation.

20. For which of the following products would the burden of a tax likely fall more heavily on the sellers?
    a. food
    b. entertainment
    c. clothing
    d. housing

ADVANCED CRITICAL THINKING

Suppose that the government needs to raise tax revenue. A politician suggests that the government place a tax on food because everyone must eat and, thus, a food tax would surely raise a great deal of tax revenue. However, since the poor spend a large proportion of their income on food, the tax should be collected only from the sellers of food (grocery stores) and not from the buyers of food. The politician argues that this type of tax would place the burden of the tax on corporate grocery store chains and not on poor consumers.

1. Can the government legislate that the burden of a food tax will fall only on the sellers of food? Why or why not?

_____

_____

_____

_____

2. Do you think the burden of a food tax will tend to fall on the sellers of food or the buyers of food. Why?

_____

_____

_____

_____

SOLUTIONS

Terms and Definitions

_2_ Price ceiling

_4_ Price floor

_1_ Tax incidence

_3_ Tax wedge

Practice Problems

1. a. It will have no effect. The price ceiling is not binding because the equilibrium price is $500 and the price ceiling is set at $700.
    b. See Exhibit 5. The quantity demanded rises to 55 units, the quantity supplied falls to 40 units, and there is a shortage of 15 units.
    c. No. It may make those bicycle buyers better off that actually get a bicycle. However, some buyers are unable to get a bike, must wait in line, pay a bribe, or accept a lower quality bicycle.
    d. See Exhibit 6. The quantity supplied rises to 70 units, the quantity demanded falls to 40 units, and there is a surplus of 30 units.

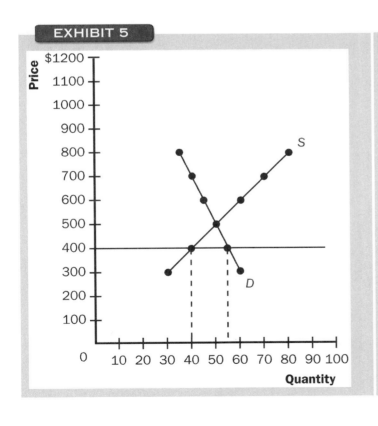

EXHIBIT 5

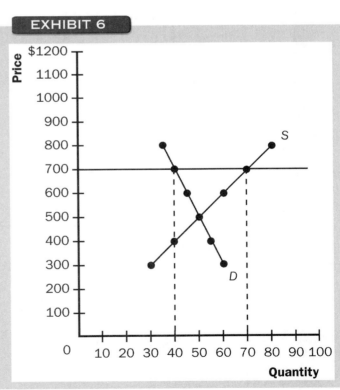

EXHIBIT 6

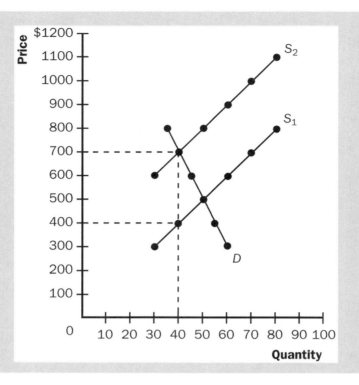

EXHIBIT 7

2. a. See Exhibit 7. The price buyers pay rises to $700, the price sellers receive falls to $400, and the quantity sold falls to 40 units.
    b. See Exhibit 8. The price buyers pay rises to $700, the price sellers receive falls to $400, and the quantity sold falls to 40 units.

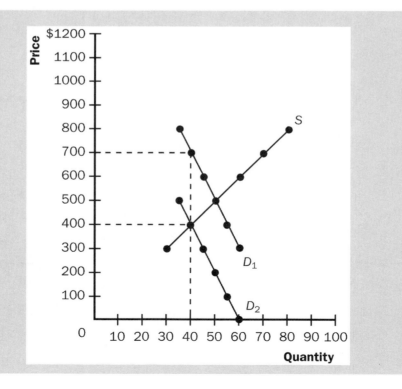

EXHIBIT 8

c. The impact of a tax collected from sellers is equivalent to the impact of a tax collected from buyers.
d. The greater burden of the tax has fallen on the buyers. The free market equilibrium price was $500. After the tax, the price the buyers pay has risen $200 while the price the sellers receive has fallen $100. This is because demand is less elastic than supply.

Short-Answer Questions

1. There is no impact because the price can move to equilibrium without restriction. That is, the price ceiling is not a binding constraint.

2. The quantity supplied decreases and the quantity demanded increases, causing a shortage.

3. There will be a shortage, buyers may wait in lines, sellers may be able to discriminate among buyers, the quality of the product may be reduced, and bribes may be paid to sellers.

4. The impact is greater in the long run because both supply and demand tend to be more elastic in the long run. As a result, the shortage becomes more severe in the long run.

5. There is no impact because the price can move to equilibrium without restriction. That is, the price floor is not a binding constraint.

6. The quantity supplied increases and the quantity demanded decreases, causing a surplus.

7. The demand curve is shifted downward by the size of the tax because the amount the buyer is willing to offer the seller has been reduced precisely by the size of the tax.

8. The supply curve is shifted upward by the size of the tax because the amount the seller requires from the buyer has been increased by precisely the size of the tax.

9. A tax places a wedge between what the buyer pays and the seller receives. Whether the buyer or the seller actually hands the tax to the government makes no difference whatsoever.

10. The sellers will bear the greater burden because the demand for luxuries tends to be highly elastic. That is, when the price buyers pay rises due to the tax, wealthy buyers can easily shift their purchases toward alternative items while producers cannot quickly reduce production when the price they receive falls. The burden falls on side of the market that is less elastic.

True/False Questions

1. F; a price ceiling set above the equilibrium price is not binding.

2. F; it causes a shortage.

3. T

4. T

5. F; some may be helped but others become unemployed and still others quit school to earn what appears to a teenager to be a good wage.

6. F; it causes a 1 to 3 percent reduction in employment.

7. T

8. F; it creates a surplus only if the floor is set above the equilibrium price.

9. F; the difference between what the sellers receive and the buyers pay will be $10 but the price received by the sellers usually will fall some so the price paid by the buyers will rise by less than $10.

10. T

11. T

12. F; we shift the demand curve downward by the size of the tax.

13. T

14. T

15. F; the burden of a tax is determined by the relative elasticities of supply and demand.

Multiple-Choice Questions

1. b	5. d	9. d	13. a	17. a
2. a	6. c	10. c	14. c	18. a
3. d	7. a	11. b	15. d	19. d
4. b	8. c	12. c	16. b	20. b

Advanced Critical Thinking

1. No. The tax burden is determined by the elasticity of supply and demand. The burden of a tax falls most heavily on the side of the market that is less elastic. That is, the burden is on the side of the market least willing to leave the market when the price moves unfavorably.

2. The burden will fall most heavily on the buyers of food regardless of whether the tax is collected from the buyers or the sellers. Food is a necessity and therefore the demand for food is relatively inelastic. When the price rises due to the tax, people still must eat. Grocery chains can sell another product line when the price they receive for food falls due to the tax.

CONSUMERS, PRODUCERS, AND THE EFFICIENCY OF MARKETS

GOALS

⌈In this chapter you will

Examine the link between buyers' willingness to pay for a good and the demand curve

Learn how to define and measure consumer surplus

Examine the link between sellers' costs of producing a good and the supply curve

Learn how to define and measure producer surplus

See that the equilibrium of supply and demand maximizes total surplus in a market

CHAPTER OVERVIEW

Context and Purpose

Chapter 7 is the first chapter in a three-chapter sequence on welfare economics and market efficiency. Chapter 7 employs the supply and demand model to develop consumer surplus and producer surplus as a measure of welfare and market efficiency. These concepts are then utilized in Chapters 8 and 9 to determine the winners and losers from taxation and restrictions on international trade.

The purpose of Chapter 7 is to develop *welfare economics*—the study of how the allocation of resources affects economic well-being. Chapters 4 through 6 employed supply and demand in a positive framework when we asked the question, "What is the equilibrium price and quantity in a market?" We now address the normative question, "Is the equilibrium price and quantity in a market the best possible solution to the resource allocation problem or is it simply the price and quantity that balance supply and demand?" We will discover that under most circumstances the equilibrium price and quantity is also the one that maximizes welfare.

OUTCOMES

⌈After accomplishing these goals, you should be able to

Derive a demand curve from a group of individual buyers' willingness to pay schedules

Locate consumer surplus on a supply and demand graph

Derive a supply curve from a group of individual sellers' cost of production schedules

Locate producer surplus on a supply and demand graph

Demonstrate why all other quantities other than the equilibrium quantity fail to maximize total surplus in a market

CHAPTER REVIEW

Introduction

In this chapter we address **welfare economics**—the study of how the allocation of resources affects economic well-being. We measure the benefits that buyers and sellers receive from taking part in a market and we discover that the equilibrium price and quantity in a market maximizes the total benefits received by buyers and sellers.

Consumer Surplus

Consumer surplus measures the benefits received by buyers from participating in a market. Each potential buyer in a market has some **willingness to pay** for a good. This willingness to pay is the maximum amount that a buyer will pay for the good. If we plot the value of the greatest willingness to pay for the first unit followed by the next greatest willingness to pay for the second unit and so on (on a price and quantity graph) we have plotted the market demand curve for the good. That is, the height of the demand curve is the marginal buyers' willingness to pay. Since some buyers value a good more than other buyers, the demand curve is downward sloping.

Consumer surplus is a buyer's willingness to pay minus the amount the buyer actually pays. For example, if you are willing to pay $20 for a new CD by your favorite music artist and you are able to purchase it for $15, you receive consumer surplus on that CD of $5. In general, since the height of the demand curve measures the value buyers place on a good measured by the buyer's willingness to pay, *consumer surplus is the area below the demand curve and above the price*.

When the price of a good falls, consumer surplus increases for two reasons. First, existing buyers receive greater surplus because they are allowed to pay less for the quantities they were already going to purchase and, second, new buyers are brought into the market because the price is now lower than their willingness to pay.

Note that since the height of the demand curve is the value buyers place on a good measured by their willingness to pay, consumer surplus measures the benefits received by buyers *as the buyers themselves perceive it*. Therefore, consumer surplus is an appropriate measure of buyers' benefits if policymakers respect the preferences of buyers. Economists generally believe that buyers are rational and that buyer preferences should be respected except possibly in cases of drug addiction, and so on.

Producer Surplus

Producer surplus measures the benefits received by sellers from participating in a market. Each potential seller in a market has some *cost* of production. This **cost** is the value of everything a seller must give up to produce a good and it should be interpreted as the producers' opportunity cost of production—actual out-of-pocket expenses plus the value of the producers' time. The cost of production is the minimum amount a seller is willing to accept in order to produce the good. If we plot the cost of the least cost producer of the first unit, then the next least cost producer of the second unit, and so on (on a price and quantity graph), we have plotted the market supply curve for the good. That is, the height of the supply curve is the marginal sellers' cost of production. Since some sellers have a lower cost than other sellers, the supply curve is upward sloping.

Producer surplus is the amount a seller is paid for a good minus the seller's cost. For example, if a musician can produce a CD for a cost of $10 and sell it for

$15, the musician receives a producer surplus of $5 on that CD. In general, since the height of the supply curve measures the sellers' costs, *producer surplus is the area below the price and above the supply curve.*

When the price of a good rises, producer surplus increases for two reasons. First, existing sellers receive greater surplus because they receive more for the quantities they were already going to sell and, second, new sellers are brought into the market because the price is now higher than their cost.

Market Efficiency

We measure economic well-being with *total surplus*—the sum of consumer and producer surplus.

Total surplus = (value to buyers – amount paid by buyers) +
(amount received by sellers – cost to sellers)

Total surplus = value to buyers – cost to sellers.

Graphically, total surplus is the area below the demand curve and above the supply curve. Resource allocation is said to exhibit **efficiency** if it maximizes the total surplus received by all members of society. Free market equilibrium is efficient because it maximizes total surplus. This efficiency is demonstrated by the following observations:

- Free markets allocate output to the buyers who value it the most—those with a willingness to pay greater than or equal to the equilibrium price. Therefore consumer surplus cannot be increased by moving consumption from a current buyer to any other non-buyer.

- Free markets allocate buyers for goods to the sellers who can produce at least cost—those with a cost of production less than or equal to the equilibrium price. Therefore producer surplus cannot be increased by moving production from a current seller to any other non-seller.

- Free markets produce the quantity of goods that maximizes the sum of consumer and producer surplus or total surplus. If we produce less than the equilibrium quantity, we fail to produce units where the value to buyers exceeds the cost to producers. If we produce more than the equilibrium quantity, we produce units where the cost to producers exceeds the value to buyers.

Economists generally advocate free markets because they are efficient. Since markets are efficient, many believe that government policy should be *laissez-faire* which means "allow them to do." Adam Smith's "invisible hand" of the marketplace guides buyers and sellers to an allocation of resources that maximizes total surplus. Many economists argue that free markets for scalped tickets (and possibly even markets for organs for transplant) maximize total surplus. The recognition that free markets are efficient is not new. Prior to Adam Smith, the Pilgrims discovered that when they practiced "farming in common" (socialized farming) there was famine, but when they allowed each to till their own soil and trade, there was plenty.

In addition to efficiency, policymakers may also be concerned with **equity**—the fairness of the distribution of well-being among the members of society. The issue of equity involves normative judgements that go beyond the realm of economics.

Conclusion: Market Efficiency and Market Failure

There are two main reasons a free market may not be efficient:

- A market may not be perfectly competitive. If individual buyers or sellers (or small groups of them) can influence the price, they have *market power* and they may be able to keep the price and quantity away from equilibrium.

- A market may generate side effects, or *externalities*, which affect people who are not participants in the market at all. These side effects, such as pollution, are not taken into account by buyers and sellers in a market so the market equilibrium may not be efficient for society as a whole.

Market power and externalities are the two main types of *market failure*—the inability of some unregulated markets to allocate resources efficiently.

HELPFUL HINTS

1. To better understand "willingness to pay" for the buyer and "cost" to seller, read both demand and supply "backward." That is, read both demand and supply from the quantity axis to the price or dollar axis. When we read demand from quantity to price, we find that the potential buyer for the first unit has a very high willingness to pay because that buyer places a great value on the good. As we move farther out along the quantity axis, the buyers for those quantities have a somewhat lower willingness to pay and, thus, the demand curve slopes negatively. When we read supply from quantity to price, we find that the potential seller for the first unit is extremely efficient and, accordingly, has a very low cost of production. As we move farther out along the quantity axis, the sellers for those quantities have somewhat higher costs and, thus, the supply curve slopes upward. At equilibrium between supply and demand, only those units are produced which generate a value to buyers that exceeds the cost to the sellers.

2. Consumer surplus exists, in part, because in a competitive market there is one price and all participants are price takers. With a single market price determined by the interactions of many buyers and sellers, individual buyers may have a willingness to pay that exceeds the price and, as a result, some buyers receive consumer surplus. If, however, sellers are aware of the buyers' willingness to pay and the sellers engage in price discrimination, that is, charge each buyer their willingness to pay, there would be no consumer surplus. Each buyer would be forced to pay their individual willingness to pay. This issue will be addressed in later chapters.

TERMS AND DEFINITIONS

Choose a definition for each key term.

Key terms:

_____ Welfare economics

_____ Willingness to pay

_____ Consumer surplus

_____ Cost

_____ Producer surplus

_____ Efficiency

_____ Equity

_____ Market failure

Definitions:

1. A buyer's willingness to pay minus the amount the buyer actually pays

2. The property of a resource allocation of maximizing the total surplus received by all members of society

3. The study of how the allocation of resources affects economic well-being

4. The inability of some unregulated markets to allocate resources efficiently

5. The fairness of the distribution of well-being among the members of society

6. The amount a seller is paid for a good minus the seller's cost

7. The maximum amount that a buyer will pay for a good

8. The value of everything a seller must give up to produce a good

PROBLEMS AND SHORT-ANSWER QUESTIONS

Practice Problems

1. The following information describes the value Lori Landlord places on having her five apartment houses repainted. She values the repainting of each apartment house at a different amount depending on how badly it needs repainting.

Value of new paint on first apartment house	$5,000
Value of new paint on second apartment house	4,000
Value of new paint on third apartment house	3,000
Value of new paint on fourth apartment house	2,000
Value of new paint on fifth apartment house	1,000

a. Plot Lori Landlord's willingness to pay in Exhibit 1.

b. If the price to repaint her apartments is $5,000 each, how many will she repaint? What is the value of her consumer surplus?

_____

_____

_____

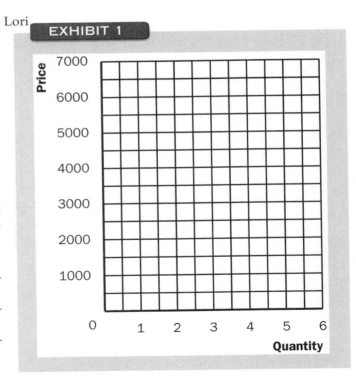

EXHIBIT 1

c. Suppose the price to repaint her apartments falls to $2,000 each. How many apartments will Lori choose to have repainted? What is the value of her consumer surplus?

_____

_____

d. What happened to Ms. Landlord's consumer surplus when the price of having her apartments repainted fell? Why?

_____

_____

_____

2. The following information shows the costs incurred by Peter Painter when he paints apartments. Because painting is backbreaking work, the more he paints, the higher the costs he incurs in both pain and chiropractic bills.

Cost of painting first apartment house	$1,000
Cost of painting second apartment house	2,000
Cost of painting third apartment house	3,000
Cost of painting fourth apartment house	4,000
Cost of painting fifth apartment house	5,000

EXHIBIT 2

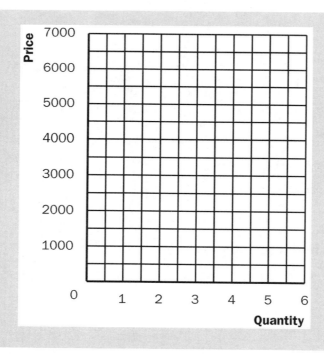

a. Plot Peter Painter's cost in Exhibit 2.

b. If the price of painting apartment houses is $2000 each, how many will he paint? What is the value of his producer surplus?

_____

_____

c. Suppose the price to paint apartments rises to $4000 each. How many apartments will Peter choose to repaint? What is the value of his producer surplus?

_____

_____

d. What happened to Mr. Painter's producer surplus when the price to paint apartments rose? Why?

_____

_____

_____

3. Use the information about willingness to pay and cost from (1) and (2) above to answer the following questions.

a. If a benevolent social planner sets the price for painting apartment houses at $5,000, what is the value of consumer surplus? Producer surplus? Total surplus?

_____

_____

b. If a benevolent social planner sets the price for painting apartment houses at $1,000, what is the value of consumer surplus? Producer surplus? Total surplus?

_____

_____

c. If the price for painting apartment houses is allowed to move to its free market equilibrium price of $3,000, what is the value of consumer surplus, producer surplus, and total surplus in the market? How does total surplus in the free market compare to the total surplus generated by the social planner?

_____

_____

_____

_____

EXHIBIT 3

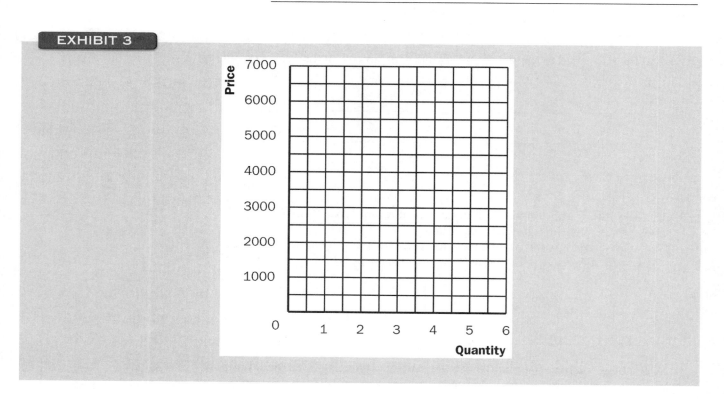

4. In Exhibit 3, plot the linear supply and demand curves for painting apartments implied by the information in questions (1) and (2) above (draw them so that they contact the vertical axis). Show consumer and producer surplus for the free market equilibrium price and quantity. Is this allocation of resources efficient? Why?

_____

_____

_____

_____

EXHIBIT 4

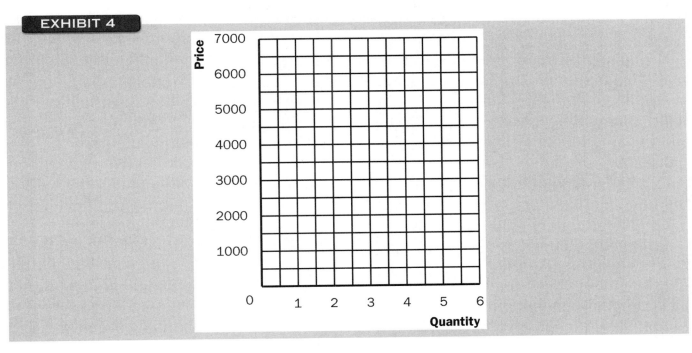

5. Suppose Lori Landlord has difficulty renting her dilapidated apartments so she increases her willingness to pay for painting by $2,000 per apartment. Plot Lori's new willingness to pay along with Peter's cost in Exhibit 4. If the equilibrium price rises to $4,000, what is the value of consumer surplus, producer surplus, and total surplus? Show consumer and producer surplus on the graph. Compare your answer to the answer you found in 3 (c) above.

_____

_____

_____

_____

_____

Short-Answer Questions

1. What is the relationship between the buyers' willingness to pay for a good and the demand curve for that good?

_____

_____

2. What is consumer surplus and how is it measured?

_____

_____

3. What is the value of consumer surplus for the marginal buyer? Why?

    _____

    _____

4. If the cost for Moe to mow a lawn is $5, for Larry to mow a lawn is $7, and for Curly to mow a lawn is $9, what is the value of their producer surplus if each mow a lawn and the price for lawn mowing is $10?

    _____

    _____

5. What is the relationship between the sellers' cost to produce a good and the supply curve for that good?

    _____

    _____

6. What is producer surplus and how is it measured?

    _____

    _____

7. When the price of a good rises, what happens to producer surplus? Why?

    _____

    _____

    _____

8. Can a benevolent social planner choose a quantity that provides greater economic welfare than the equilibrium quantity generated in a competitive market? Why?

    _____

    _____

    _____

9. What does an economist mean by "efficiency?"

    _____

    _____

10. Is a competitive market efficient? Why?

_____

_____

11. How does a competitive market choose which producers will produce and sell a product?

_____

_____

_____

SELF-TEST

True/False Questions

_____ 1. Consumer surplus is the buyer's willingness to pay minus the seller's cost.

_____ 2. If the demand curve in a market is stationary, consumer surplus decreases when the price in that market increases.

_____ 3. If your willingness to pay for a hamburger is $3.00 and the price is $2.00, your consumer surplus is $5.00.

_____ 4. Producer surplus is a measure of the unsold inventories of suppliers in a market.

_____ 5. Consumer surplus is a good measure of buyers' benefits if buyers are rational.

_____ 6.   Cost to the seller includes the opportunity cost of the seller's time.

_____ 7. The height of the supply curve is the marginal seller's cost.

_____ 8. Total surplus is the seller's cost minus the buyer's willingness to pay.

_____ 9. Free markets are efficient because they allocate output to buyers who have a willingness to pay that is below the price.

_____10. Producer surplus is the area above the supply curve and below the price.

_____11. The major advantage of allowing free markets to allocate resources is that the outcome of the allocation is efficient.

_____12. Equilibrium in a competitive market maximizes total surplus.

_____13. The two main types of market failure are market power and externalities.

_____ 14. Externalities are side effects, such as pollution, that are not taken into account by the buyers and sellers in a market.

_____ 15. Producing more of a product always adds to total surplus.

Multiple-Choice Questions

1. Consumer surplus is the area
   a. above the supply curve and below the price.
   b. below the supply curve and above the price.
   c. above the demand curve and below the price.
   d. below the demand curve and above the price.
   e. below the demand curve and above the supply curve.

2. A buyer's willingness to pay is that buyer's
   a. consumer surplus.
   b. producer surplus.
   c. maximum amount they are willing to pay for a good.
   d. minimum amount they are willing to pay for a good.
   e. none of the above.

3. If a buyer's willingness to pay for a new Honda is $20,000 and she is able to actually buy it for $18,000, her consumer surplus is
   a. $0.
   b. $2,000.
   c. $18,000.
   d. $20,000.
   e. $38,000.

4. An increase in the price of a good along a stationary demand curve
   a. increases consumer surplus.
   b. decreases consumer surplus.
   c. improves the material welfare of the buyers.
   d. improves market efficiency.

5. Suppose there are three identical vases available to be purchased. Buyer 1 is willing to pay $30 for one, buyer 2 is willing to pay $25 for one, and buyer 3 is willing to pay $20 for one. If the price is $25, how many vases will be sold and what is the value of consumer surplus in this market?
   a. One vase will be sold and consumer surplus is $30.
   b. One vase will be sold and consumer surplus is $5.
   c. Two vases will be sold and consumer surplus is $5.
   d. Three vases will be sold and consumer surplus is $0.
   e. Three vases will be sold and consumer surplus is $80.

6. Producer surplus is the area
   a. above the supply curve and below the price.
   b. below the supply curve and above the price.
   c. above the demand curve and below the price.
   d. below the demand curve and above the price.
   e. below the demand curve and above the supply curve.

7. If a benevolent social planner chooses to produce less than the equilibrium quantity of a good, then
   a. producer surplus is maximized.
   b. consumer surplus is maximized.
   c. total surplus is maximized.
   d. the value placed on the last unit of production by buyers exceeds the cost of production.
   e. the cost of production on the last unit produced exceeds the value placed on it by buyers.

8. If a benevolent social planner chooses to produce more than the equilibrium quantity of a good, then
   a. producer surplus is maximized.
   b. consumer surplus is maximized.
   c. total surplus is maximized.
   d. the value placed on the last unit of production by buyers exceeds the cost of production.
   e. the cost of production on the last unit produced exceeds the value placed on it by buyers.

9. The seller's cost of production is
   a. the seller's consumer surplus.
   b. the seller's producer surplus.
   c. the maximum amount the seller is willing to accept for a good.
   d. the minimum amount the seller is willing to accept for a good.
   e. none of the above.

10. Total surplus is the area
    a. above the supply curve and below the price.
    b. below the supply curve and above the price.
    c. above the demand curve and below the price.
    d. below the demand curve and above the price.
    e. below the demand curve and above the supply curve.

11. An increase in the price of a good along a stationary supply curve
    a. increases producer surplus.
    b. decreases producer surplus.
    c. improves market equity.
    d. does all of the above.

12. Adam Smith's "invisible hand" concept suggests that a competitive market outcome
    a. minimizes total surplus.
    b. maximizes total surplus.
    c. generates equality among the members of society.
    d. both (b) and (c).

13. In general, if a benevolent social planner wanted to maximize the total benefits received by buyers and sellers in a market, the planner should
    a. choose a price above the market equilibrium price.
    b. choose a price below the market equilibrium price.
    c. allow the market to seek equilibrium on its own.
    d. choose any price the planner wants because the losses to the sellers (buyers) from any change in price are exactly offset by the gains to the buyers (sellers).

14. If buyers are rational and there is no market failure,
    a. free market solutions are efficient.
    b. free market solutions are equitable.
    c. free market solutions maximize total surplus.
    d. all of the above.
    e. (a) and (c) are correct.

15. If a producer has market power (can influence the price of the product in the market) then free market solutions
    a. are equitable.
    b. are efficient.
    c. are inefficient.
    d. maximize consumer surplus.

16. If a market is efficient, then
    a. the market allocates output to the buyers that value it the most.
    b. the market allocates buyers to the sellers who can produce the good at least cost.
    c. the quantity produced in the market maximizes the sum of consumer and producer surplus.
    d. all of the above.
    e. none of the above.

17. If a market generates a side effect or externality, then free market solutions
    a. are equitable.
    b. are efficient.
    c. are inefficient.
    d. maximize producer surplus.

18. Medical care clearly enhances peoples lives. Therefore, we should consume medical care until
    a. everyone has as much as they would like.
    b. the benefit buyers place on medical care is equal to the cost of producing it.
    c. buyers receive no benefit from another unit of medical care.
    d. we must cut back on the consumption of other goods.

19. Joe has ten baseball gloves and Sue has none. A baseball glove costs $50 to produce. If Joe values an additional baseball glove at $100 and Sue values a baseball glove at $40, then to maximize
    a. efficiency Joe should receive the glove.
    b. efficiency Sue should receive the glove.
    c. consumer surplus both should receive a glove.
    d. equity, Joe should receive the glove.

20. Suppose that the price of a new bicycle is $300. Sue values a new bicycle at $400. It costs $200 for the seller to produce the new bicycle. What is the value of total surplus if Sue buys a new bike?
    a. $100
    b. $200
    c. $300
    d. $400
    e. $500

ADVANCED CRITICAL THINKING

Suppose you are having an argument with your roommate about whether the Federal Government should subsidize the production of food. Your roommate argues that since food is something that is unambiguously good (unlike liquor, guns, and drugs which may be considered inherently evil by some members of society) we simply cannot have too much of it. That is, since food is clearly good, having more of it must always improve our economic well-being.

1. Is it true that you cannot have too much of a good thing? Conversely, is it possible to overproduce unambiguously good things such as food, clothing, and shelter? Why?

   _____

   _____

   _____

   _____

   _____

2. In Exhibit 5, demonstrate your answer to question (1) above with a supply and demand graph for food by showing the impact on economic well-being of producing quantities in excess of the equilibrium quantity.

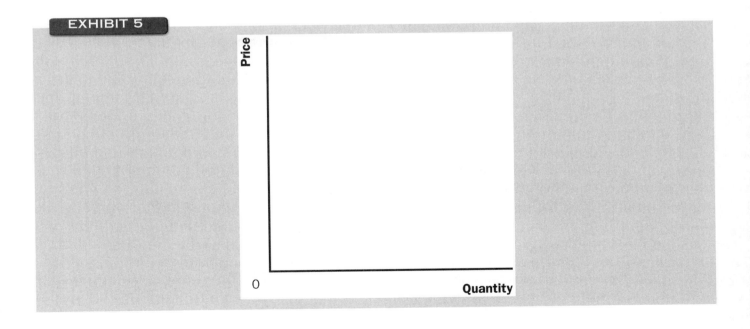

SOLUTIONS

Terms and Definitions

_3_ Welfare economics

_7_ Willingness to pay

_1_ Consumer surplus

_8_ Cost

_6_ Producer surplus

_2_ Efficiency

_5_ Equity

_4_ Market failure

Practice Problems

1. a. See Exhibit 6.
   b. One apartment painted. $5000 – $5000 = 0, therefore she has no consumer surplus.
   c. Four apartments painted. ($5000 – $2000) + ($4000 – $2000) + ($3000 – $2000) + ($2000 – $2000) = $6000 of consumer surplus.
   d. Her consumer surplus rose because she gains surplus on the unit she would have already purchased at the old price plus she gains surplus on the new units she now purchases due to the lower price.

2. a. See Exhibit 7.
   b. Two. ($2000 – $1000) + ($2000 – $2000) = $1000 of producer surplus.
   c. Four apartments. ($4000 – $1000) + ($4000 – $2000) + ($4000 – $3000) + ($4000 – $4000) = $6000 of producer surplus.
   d. He received greater producer surplus on the unit he would have produced anyway plus additional surplus on the units he now chooses to produce due to the increase in price.

3. a. Only one unit will be purchased so consumer surplus = ($5000 – $5000)

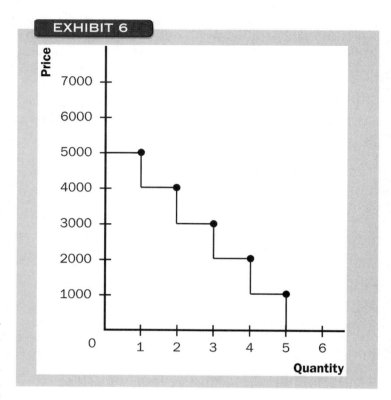

EXHIBIT 6

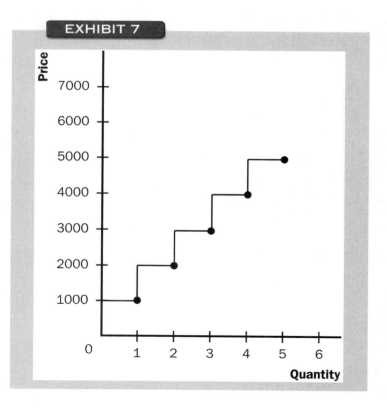

EXHIBIT 7

= $0, producer surplus = ($5000 – $1000) = $4000, and total surplus = $0 + $4000 = $4000.

b. Only one unit will be produced so consumer surplus = ($5000 – $1000) = $4000, producer surplus = ($1000 – $1000) = $0, and total surplus = $4000 + $0 = $4000.

c. Consumer surplus = ($5000 – $3000) + ($4000 – $3000) + ($3000 – $3000) = $3000. Producer surplus = ($3000 – $1000) + ($3000 – $2000) + ($3000 – $3000) = $3000. Total surplus = $3000 + $3000 = $6000. Free market total surplus is greater than social planner total surplus.

4. See Exhibit 8. Yes, it is efficient because at a quantity that is less than the equilibrium quantity we fail to produce units that buyers value more than their cost. At a quantity above the equilibrium quantity, we produce units that cost more than the buyers value them. At equilibrium we produce all possible units that are valued in excess of what they cost, which maximizes total surplus.

5. See Exhibit 9. Consumer surplus = $3000 + $2000 + $1000 + $0 = $6000.

Producer surplus = $3000 + $2000 + $1000 + $0 = $6000.

Total surplus = $6000 + $6000 = $12000.

Consumer surplus, producer surplus, and total surplus have all increased.

Short-Answer Questions

1. The height of the demand curve at any quantity is the marginal buyer's willingness to pay. Therefore, a plot of buyers' willingness to pay for each quantity is a plot of the demand curve.

2. Consumer surplus is a buyer's willingness to pay minus the amount the buyer actually pays. It is measured as the area below the demand curve and above the price.

3. Zero, because the marginal buyer is the buyer who would leave the market if the price were any higher. Therefore, they are paying their willingness to pay and are receiving no surplus.

4. ($10 – $5) + ($10 – $7) + ($10 – $9) = $9

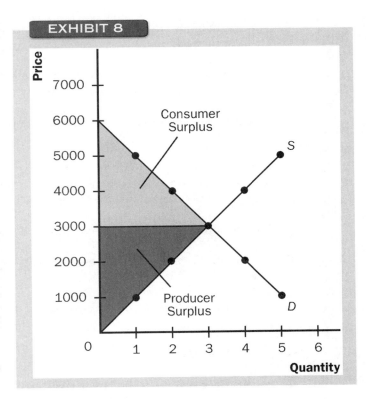

EXHIBIT 8

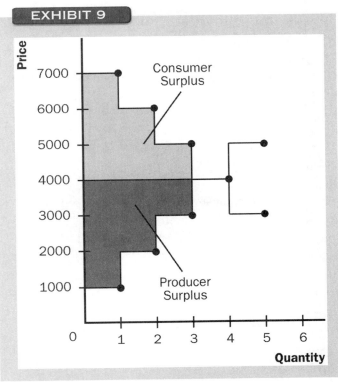

EXHIBIT 9

5. The height of the supply curve at any quantity is the marginal seller's cost. Therefore, a plot of the sellers' cost for each quantity is a plot of the supply curve.

6. Producer surplus is the amount a seller is paid for a good minus the seller's cost. It is measured as the area below the price and above the supply curve.

7. Producer surplus increases because existing sellers receive a greater surplus on the units they were already going to sell and new sellers enter the market because the price is now above their cost.

8. Generally, no. At any quantity below the equilibrium quantity, the market fails to produce units where the value to the buyers exceeds the cost. At any quantity above the equilibrium quantity, the market produces units where the cost exceeds the value to the buyers.

9. It is a resource allocation that maximizes the total surplus received by all members of society.

10. Yes, because it maximizes the area below the demand curve and above the supply curve, or total surplus.

11. Only those producers who have costs at or below the market price will be able to produce and sell that good.

True/False Questions

1. F; consumer surplus is the buyer's willingness to pay minus the amount the buyer actually pays.

2. T

3. F; $3.00 – $2.00 = $1.00.

4. F; it is a measure of the benefits of market participation to the sellers in a market.

5. T

6. T

7. T

8. F; total surplus is the buyer's willingness to pay minus the seller's cost.

9. F; free markets allocate output to buyers who have a willingness to pay that is above the price.

10. T

11. T

12. T

13. T

14. T

15. F; producing above the equilibrium quantity reduces total surplus because units are produced for which cost exceeds the value to buyers.

Multiple-Choice Questions

1. d	5. c	9. d	13. c	17. c
2. c	6. a	10. e	14. e	18. b
3. b	7. d	11. a	15. c	19. a
4. b	8. e	12. b	16. d	20. b

Advanced Critical Thinking

1. You can have too much of a good thing. Yes, any good with a positive cost and a declining willingness to pay from the consumer can be overproduced. This is because at some point of production, the cost per unit will exceed the value to the buyer and there will be a loss to total surplus associated with additional production.

2. See Exhibit 10.

EXHIBIT 10

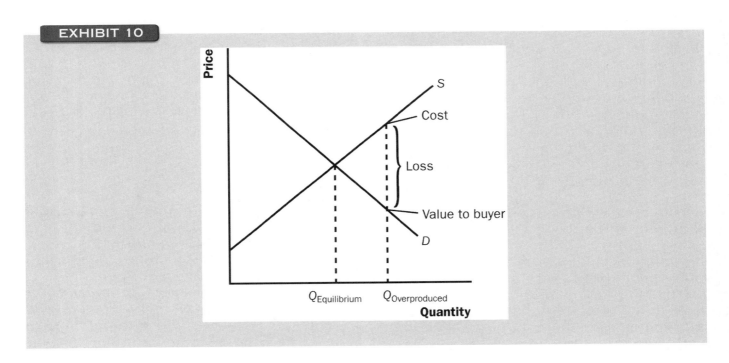

APPLICATION:
THE COSTS OF TAXATION

8

GOALS

In this chapter you will

Examine how taxes reduce consumer and producer surplus

Learn the meaning and causes of the deadweight loss of a tax

Consider why some taxes have larger deadweight losses than others

Examine how tax revenue and deadweight loss vary with the size of a tax

OUTCOMES

After accomplishing these goals, you should be able to

Place a tax wedge in a supply and demand graph and determine the tax revenue and the levels of consumer and producer surplus

Place a tax wedge in a supply and demand graph and determine the value of the deadweight loss

Show why a given tax will generate a greater deadweight loss if supply and demand are elastic than if they are inelastic

Demonstrate why some very large taxes generate little tax revenue but a great deal of deadweight loss

CHAPTER OVERVIEW

Context and Purpose

Chapter 8 is the second chapter in a three-chapter sequence dealing with welfare economics. In the previous section on supply and demand, Chapter 6 introduced taxes and demonstrated how a tax affects the price and quantity sold in a market. Chapter 6 also described the factors that determine how the burden of the tax is divided between the buyers and sellers in a market. Chapter 7 developed welfare economics—the study of how the allocation of resources affects economic well-being. Chapter 8 combines the lessons learned in Chapters 6 and 7 and addresses the effects of taxation on welfare. Chapter 9 will address the effects of trade restrictions on welfare.

The purpose of Chapter 8 is to apply the lessons learned about welfare economics in Chapter 7 to the issue of taxation which we addressed in Chapter 6. We will learn that the cost of a tax to buyers and sellers in a market exceeds the revenue collected by the government. We will also learn about the factors that determine the degree by which the cost of a tax exceeds the revenue collected by the government.

CHAPTER REVIEW

Introduction

Taxes raise the price buyers pay, reduce the price sellers receive, and reduce the quantity exchanged. Clearly, the welfare of the buyers and sellers is reduced and the welfare of the government is increased. However, overall welfare is reduced because the cost of a tax to buyers and sellers exceeds the revenue raised by the government.

The Deadweight Loss of Taxation

Recall from Chapter 6 that a tax places a wedge between what a buyer pays and a seller receives and reduces the quantity sold regardless of whether the tax is collected from the buyer or the seller. With regard to welfare, recall from Chapter 7 that consumer surplus is the amount buyers are willing to pay minus the price they actually pay, while producer surplus is the price sellers actually receive minus their costs. The welfare or benefit to the government from a tax is the revenue it collects from the tax, which is the quantity of the good sold *after the tax is placed on the good* multiplied by the tax per unit. This benefit actually accrues to those on whom the tax revenue is spent.

Referring to Exhibit 1, without a tax the price is P_0 and the quantity is Q_0. Thus, consumer surplus is the area A + B + C and producer surplus is D + E + F. Tax revenue is zero. Total surplus is A + B + C + D + E + F.

With a tax, the price to buyers rises to P_B, the price to sellers falls to P_S, and the quantity falls to Q_1. Consumer surplus is now A, producer surplus is now F, and tax revenue is B + D. Total surplus is now A + B + D + F. Consumer surplus and producer surplus have both been reduced and tax revenue has been increased. However, consumer and producer surplus have been reduced by B + C + D + E and government revenue has been increased by only B + D. Therefore, losses to buyers and sellers from a tax exceed the revenue raised by the government. The

EXHIBIT 1

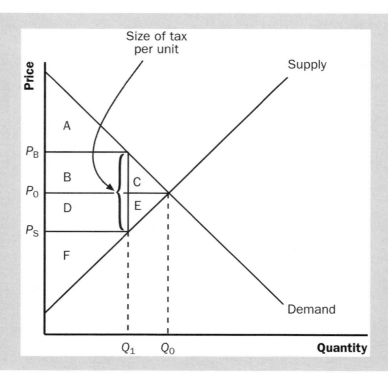

reduction in total surplus that results from a tax is known as **deadweight loss** and is equal to C + E.

Taxes cause deadweight losses because taxes prevent buyers and sellers from realizing some of the gains from trade. That is, taxes distort incentives because taxes raise the price paid by buyers, which reduces the quantity demanded, and lowers the price received by sellers, which reduces the quantity supplied. The size of the market is reduced below its optimum and sellers fail to produce and sell goods for which the benefits to buyers exceed the costs of the producers. Deadweight loss is a loss of potential gains from trade.

The Determinants of the Deadweight Loss

The size of the deadweight loss from a tax depends on the elasticities of supply and demand. Deadweight loss from a tax is caused by the distortion in the price faced by buyers and sellers. The more sensitive buyers are to an increase in the price of the good (more elastic demand), the more they reduce their quantity demanded when a tax is placed on a good. The more sensitive sellers are to a decrease in the price of a good (more elastic supply), the more they reduce their quantity supplied when a tax is placed on a good. A greater reduction in the quantity exchanged in the market causes a greater deadweight loss. As a result, *the greater the elasticities of supply and demand, the greater the deadweight loss of a tax*.

The most important tax in the U.S. economy is the tax on labor—federal and state income taxes and Social Security taxes. Taxes on labor encourage workers to work fewer hours, second earners to stay home, the elderly to retire early, and the unscrupulous to enter the underground economy. The more elastic the supply of labor, the greater the deadweight loss of taxation and, thus, the greater the cost of any government program that relies on income tax revenue for funding. Economists and politicians argue about how elastic the supply of labor is and, thus, how large these effects are.

Henry George, a 19th century economist, suggested that there should be a single tax on land because the supply of land is inelastic. Therefore, the burden of the tax would be entirely on the owners of land and the tax would have no deadweight loss. Few modern economists support a single tax on land because it would not raise enough revenue and because it would need to be a tax on unimproved land (which would be difficult to implement). A tax on improved land would cause landowners to devote fewer resources toward improving their land and would create a deadweight loss.

Deadweight Loss and Tax Revenue as Taxes Vary

Deadweight loss increases as a tax increases. Indeed, deadweight loss increases at an increasing rate as a tax increases. It increases as the square of the factor of increase in the tax. For example, if a tax is doubled, the deadweight loss rises by a factor of 4. If a tax is tripled, the deadweight loss rises by a factor of 9, and so on.

Tax revenue first increases and then decreases as a tax increases. This is because, at first, an increase in a tax increases the taxes collected per unit more than it reduces the units sold. At some point, however, an ever increasing tax reduces the size of the market (the quantity sold and taxed) to such a degree that the government begins to collect a large tax on such a small quantity that tax revenue begins to fall.

The idea that a high tax rate could so shrink the market that it reduces tax revenue was expressed by Arthur Laffer in 1974. The *Laffer curve* is a diagram that shows that as the size of a tax on a good is increased, revenue first rises and then falls. The implication is that if tax rates are already extremely high, a reduction in tax rates could increase tax revenue. This is a part of what has come to be called supply-side economics. Evidence has shown that this may be true for individuals who are taxed at extremely high rates, but it is unlikely to be true for an entire economy. A possible exception is Sweden in the 1980s because its tax rates were about 80 percent for the typical worker.

Conclusion

Taxes place a cost on market participants in two ways:

- Resources are diverted from buyers and sellers to the government.

- Taxes distort incentives so fewer goods are produced and sold than otherwise. That is, taxes cause society to lose some of the benefits of efficient markets.

HELPFUL HINTS

1. As a tax increases, it reduces the size of the market more and more. At some point, the tax is so high that it is greater than or equal to the potential surplus even from the first unit. At that point, the tax has become a *prohibitive tax* because it eliminates the market altogether. Note that when a tax is prohibitive, the government collects no revenue at all from the tax because no units are sold. The market has reached the far side of the Laffer curve.

2. As a tax increases, the deadweight loss increases *at an increasing rate* because there are two sources to the deadweight loss and both sources are generating an increase in deadweight loss as a tax increases. First, an increase in a tax reduces the quantity exchanged and that increases deadweight loss. Second, as quantity exchanged decreases due to the tax, each successive unit that is not produced and sold *has a higher total surplus associated with it*. This further increases the deadweight loss from a tax.

TERMS AND DEFINITIONS

Choose a definition for each key term.

Key terms:

_____ Tax wedge

_____ Deadweight loss

_____ Laffer curve

Definitions:

1. The reduction in total surplus that results from a tax

2. A graph showing the relationship between the size of a tax and the tax revenue collected

3. The difference between what the buyer pays and the seller receives when a tax is placed in a market

PROBLEMS AND SHORT-ANSWER QUESTIONS

Practice Problems

1. Exhibit 2 shows the market for tires. Suppose that a $12 road-use tax is placed on each tire sold.
   a. In Exhibit 2, locate consumer surplus, producer surplus, tax revenue, and the deadweight loss.

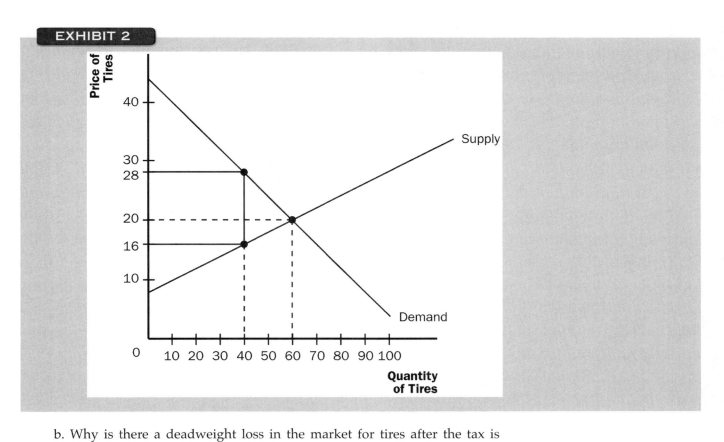

EXHIBIT 2

b. Why is there a deadweight loss in the market for tires after the tax is imposed?

_____

_____

_____

_____

_____

c. What is the value of the tax revenue collected by the government? Why wasn't the government able to collect $12 per tire on 60 tires sold (the original equilibrium quantity)?

_____

_____

_____

d. What is the value of the tax revenue collected from the buyers? What is the value of the tax revenue collected from the sellers? Did the burden of the tax fall more heavily on the buyers or the sellers? Why?

_____

_____

_____

_____

e. Suppose over time, buyers of tires are able to substitute away from auto tires (they walk and ride bicycles). Because of this, their demand for tires becomes more elastic. What will happen to the size of the deadweight loss in the market for tires? Why?

_____

_____

_____

_____

_____

2. Use Exhibit 3, which shows the market for music CDs, to answer the following questions.
   a. Complete the table. (Note: to calculate deadweight loss, the area of a triangle is 1/2 base × height).

Tax per unit	Tax revenue collected	Deadweight loss
$ 0	_____	_____
3	_____	_____
6	_____	_____
9	_____	_____
12	_____	_____
15	_____	_____
18	_____	_____

EXHIBIT 3

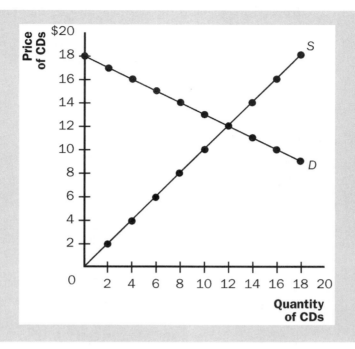

b. As the tax is increased, what happens to the amount of tax revenue collected? Why?

_____

_____

_____

_____

c. At a tax of $18 per CD, how much tax revenue is collected? Why?

_____

_____

_____

d. If the government wanted to maximize tax revenue, what tax per unit should it impose?

_____

_____

e. If the government wanted to maximize efficiency (total surplus) what tax per unit should it impose?

_____

f. What happens to the deadweight loss due to the tax as the tax is increased? Why?

_____

_____

_____

_____

Short-Answer Questions

1. Why does a tax reduce consumer surplus?

_____

_____

2. Why does a tax reduce producer surplus?

_____

_____

3. Why does a tax generally produce a deadweight loss?

_____

_____

_____

4. Under what conditions would a tax fail to produce a deadweight loss?

_____

_____

5. When a tax is placed on a good, does the government collect revenue equal to the loss in total surplus due to the tax? Why?

_____

_____

_____

_____

_____

_____

6. Suppose Rachel values having her house painted at $1,000. The cost for Paul
    to paint her house is $700. What is the value of the total surplus or the gains
    from trade on this transaction? What is the size of the tax that would elimi-
    nate this trade? What is the deadweight loss from this tax? What general-
    ization can you make from this exercise?

    _____

    _____

    _____

7. Would you expect a tax on gasoline to have a greater deadweight loss in the
    short run or the long run? Why?

    _____

    _____

    _____

    _____

    _____

8. Would a tax on unimproved land generate a large deadweight loss? Why?
    Who would bear the burden of the tax, the renter or the landlord? Why?

    _____

    _____

    _____

    _____

9. As a tax on a good increases, what happens to tax revenue? Why?

    _____

    _____

    _____

    _____

10. As a tax on a good increases, what happens to the deadweight loss from the
    tax? Why?

    _____

    _____

    _____

SELF-TEST

True/False Questions

_____1. In general, a tax raises the price the buyers pay, lowers the price the sellers receive, and reduces the quantity sold.

_____2. If a tax is placed on a good and it reduces the quantity sold, there must be a deadweight loss from the tax.

_____3. Deadweight loss is the reduction in consumer surplus that results from a tax.

_____4. When a tax is placed on a good, the revenue the government collects is exactly equal to the loss of consumer and producer surplus from the tax.

_____5. If John values having his hair cut at $20 and Mary's cost of providing the hair cut is $10, any tax on hair cuts larger than $10 will eliminate the gains from trade and cause a $20 loss of total surplus.

_____6. If a tax is placed on a good in a market where supply is perfectly inelastic, there is no deadweight loss and the sellers bear the entire burden of the tax.

_____7. A tax on cigarettes would likely generate a larger deadweight loss than a tax on luxury boats.

_____8. A tax will generate a greater deadweight loss if supply and demand are inelastic.

_____9. A tax causes a deadweight loss because it eliminates some of the potential gains from trade.

_____10. A larger tax always generates more tax revenue.

_____11. A larger tax always generates a larger deadweight loss.

_____12. If an income tax rate is high enough, a reduction in the tax rate could increase tax revenue.

_____13. A tax collected from buyers generates a smaller deadweight loss than a tax collected from sellers.

_____14. If a tax is doubled, the deadweight loss from the tax more than doubles.

_____15. A deadweight loss results when a tax causes market participants to fail to produce and consume units on which the benefits to the buyers exceeded the costs to the sellers.

Multiple-Choice Questions

Use Exhibit 4 for questions 1 through10.

EXHIBIT 4

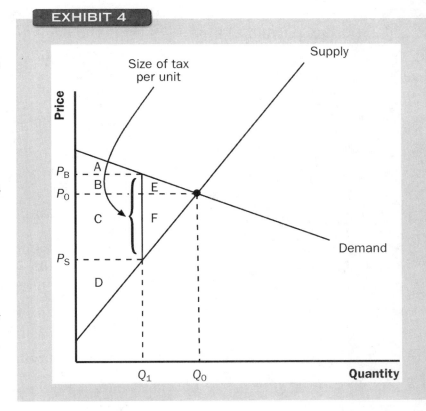

1. If there is no tax placed on the product in this market, consumer surplus is the area
   a. A + B + C.
   b. D + C + B.
   c. A + B + E.
   d. C + D + F.
   e. A.

2. If there is no tax placed on the product in this market, producer surplus is the area
   a. A + B + C + D.
   b. C + D + F.
   c. D.
   d. C + F.
   e. A + B + E.

3. If a tax is placed on the product in this market, consumer surplus is the area
   a. A.
   b. A + B.
   c. A + B + E.
   d. A + B + C + D.
   e. D.

4. If a tax is placed on the product in this market, producer surplus is the area
   a. A.
   b. A + B + E.
   c. C + D + F.
   d. D.
   e. A + B + C + D.

5. If a tax is placed on the product in this market, tax revenue paid by the buyers is the area
   a. A.
   b. B.
   c. C.
   d. B + C.
   e. B + C + E + F.

6. If a tax is placed on the product in this market, tax revenue paid by the sellers is the area
   a. A.
   b. B.
   c. C.
   d. C + F.
   e. B + C + E + F.

7. If there is no tax placed on the product in this market, total surplus is the area
   a. A + B + C + D.
   b. A + B + C + D + E + F.
   c. B + C + E + F.
   d. E + F.
   e. A + D + E + F.

8. If a tax is placed on the product in this market, total surplus is the area
   a. A + B + C + D.
   b. A + B + C + D + E + F.
   c. B + C + E + F.
   d. E + F.
   e. A + D.

9. If a tax is placed on the product in this market, deadweight loss is the area
   a. B + C.
   b. B + C + E + F.
   c. A + B + C + D.
   d. E + F.
   e. A + D.

10. Which of the following is true with regard to the burden of the tax in Exhibit 4?
    a. The buyers pay a larger portion of the tax because demand is more inelastic than supply.
    b. The buyers pay a larger portion of the tax because demand is more elastic than supply.
    c. The sellers pay a larger portion of the tax because supply is more elastic than demand.
    d. The sellers pay a larger portion of the tax because supply is more inelastic than demand.

11. Which of the following would likely cause the greatest deadweight loss?
    a. a tax on cigarettes
    b. a tax on salt
    c. a tax on cruise line tickets
    d. a tax on gasoline

12. A tax on gasoline is likely to
    a. cause a greater deadweight loss in the long run when compared to the short run.
    b. cause a greater deadweight loss in the short run when compared to the long run.
    c. generate a deadweight loss that is unaffected by the time period over which it is measured.
    d. none of the above

13. Deadweight loss is greatest when
    a. both supply and demand are relatively inelastic.
    b. both supply and demand are relatively elastic.
    e. supply is elastic and demand is perfectly inelastic.
    d. demand is elastic and supply is perfectly inelastic.

14. Since the supply of unimproved land is relatively inelastic, a tax on unimproved land would generate
    a. a large deadweight loss and the burden of the tax would fall on the renter.
    b. a small deadweight loss and the burden of the tax would fall on the renter.
    c. a large deadweight loss and the burden of the tax would fall on the landlord.
    d. a small deadweight loss and the burden of the tax would fall on the landlord.

15. Which of the following is true with regard to a tax on labor income? Taxes on labor income tend to encourage
    a. workers to work fewer hours.
    b. second earners to stay home.
    c. the elderly to retire early.
    d. the unscrupulous to enter the underground economy.
    e. all of the above.

16. When a tax on a good starts small and is gradually increased, tax revenue
    a. will rise.
    b. will fall.
    c. will first rise and then fall.
    d. will first fall and then rise.
    e. none of the above

17. The graph that shows the relationship between the size of a tax and the tax revenue collected by the government is known as a
    a. Keynesian curve.
    b. Henry George curve.
    c. Laffer curve.
    d. Reagan curve.
    e. none of the above

18. If a tax on a good is doubled, the deadweight loss from the tax
    a. stays the same.
    b. doubles.
    c. increases by a factor of four.
    d. could rise or fall.

19. The reduction of a tax
    a. could increase tax revenue if the tax had been extremely high.
    b. will always reduce tax revenue regardless of the prior size of the tax.
    c. will have no impact on tax revenue.
    d. causes a market to become less efficient.

20. When a tax distorts incentives to buyers and sellers so that fewer goods are produced and sold than otherwise, the tax has
    a. increased efficiency.
    b. decreased equity.
    c. generated no tax revenue.
    d. caused a deadweight loss.

ADVANCED CRITICAL THINKING

You are watching the local news report on television with your roommate. The news anchor reports that the state budget has a deficit of $100 million. Since the state currently collects exactly $100 million from its 5 percent sales tax, your roommate says, "I can tell them how to fix their deficit. They should simply double the sales tax to 10 percent. That will double their tax revenue from $100 million to $200 million and provide the needed $100 million."

1. Is it true that doubling a tax will always double tax revenue? Why?

    _____

    _____

    _____

    _____

    _____

2. Will doubling the sales tax affect the tax revenue and the deadweight loss in all markets to the same degree? Explain?

    _____

    _____

    _____

    _____

    _____

    _____

SOLUTIONS

Terms and Definitions

_3_ Tax wedge

_1_ Deadweight loss

_2_ Laffer curve

Practice Problems

1. a. See Exhibit 5.
    b. The tax raises the price paid by buyers and lowers the price received by sellers causing them to reduce their quantities demanded and supplied. Therefore, they fail to produce and exchange units where the value to buyers exceeds the cost to sellers.

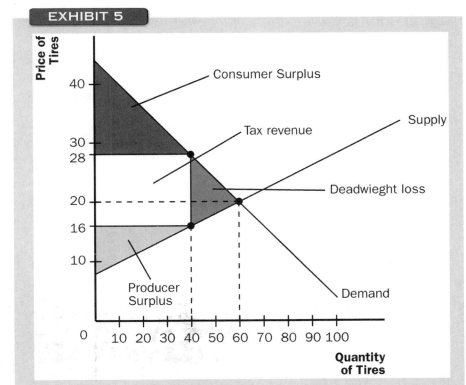

EXHIBIT 5

    c. $12 × 40 = $480. The tax distorted prices to the buyers and sellers so that the quantity supplied and demanded with the tax is reduced to 40 units from 60 units.
    d. $8 × 40 = $320 from buyers. $4 × 40 = $160 from sellers. The burden fell more heavily on the buyers because the demand for tires was less elastic than the supply of tires.
    e. Deadweight loss will increase because when buyers are more sensitive to an increase in price (due to the tax) they will reduce their quantity demanded even more and shrink the market more. Thus, even fewer units that are valued by buyers in excess of their cost will be sold.

2. a.

Tax per unit	Tax revenue collected	Deadweight loss
$0	$0	$0
3	30	($3 × 2)/2 = $3
6	48	($6 × 4)/2 = $12
9	54	($9 × 6)/2 = $27
12	48	($12 × 8)/2 = $48
15	30	($15 × 10)/2 = $75
18	0	($18 × 12)/2 = $108

    b. It first rises, then falls. At first, as the tax is increased tax revenue rises. At some point, the tax reduces the size of the market to such a degree that the government is collecting a large tax on such a small quantity that tax revenue begins to fall.
    c. No tax revenue is collected because the tax is as large as the total surplus on the first unit. Therefore, there is no incentive to produce and consume even one unit and the entire market is eliminated.
    d. $9 per unit.
    e. $0 per unit which causes the market to return to its free market equilibrium.
    f. It increases. Indeed, it increases at an increasing rate. This is because as the tax increases it causes the quantity exchanged to be reduced on units that have an ever larger potential surplus attached to them.

Short-Answer Questions

1. Consumer surplus is what the buyer is willing to pay for a good minus what the buyer actually pays and a tax raises the price the buyer actually pays.

2. Producer surplus is the amount the seller receives for a good minus the seller's cost and a tax reduces what the seller receives for a good.

3. A tax raises the price buyers pay and lowers the price sellers receive. This price distortion reduces the quantity demanded and supplied so we fail to produce and consume units where the benefits to the buyers exceeds the cost to the sellers.

4. If either supply or demand were perfectly inelastic (insensitive to a change in price), then a tax would fail to reduce the quantity exchanged and the market would not shrink.

5. No. The tax distorts prices to buyers and sellers and causes them to reduce their quantities demanded and supplied. Taxes are collected only on the units sold after the tax is imposed. Those units that are no longer produced and sold generate no tax revenue but those units would have added to total surplus because they were valued by buyers in excess of their cost to sellers. The reduction in total surplus is the deadweight loss.

6. Total surplus = $300. Any tax larger than $300. Deadweight loss would be $300. A tax that is greater than the potential gains from trade will eliminate trade and create a deadweight loss equal to the lost gains from trade.

7. There would be a greater deadweight loss in the long run. This is because both demand and supply tend to be more elastic in the long run as consumers and producers are able to substitute away from this market when prices move in an adverse direction. The more a market shrinks from a tax the greater the deadweight loss.

8. No, because the supply of unimproved land is highly inelastic so the quantity supplied is not responsive to a decrease in the price received by the seller. The landlord would bear the burden of the tax for the same reason—supply of unimproved land is highly inelastic.

9. First tax revenue increases. At some point tax revenue decreases as the distortion in prices to buyers and sellers causes the market to shrink and large taxes are collected on a small number of units exchanged.

10. Deadweight loss increases continuously because as a tax increases the distortion in prices caused by the tax causes the market to shrink continuously. Thus, we fail to produce more and more units where the benefits to buyers exceeded the costs to sellers.

True/False Questions

1. T

2. T

3. F; deadweight loss is the reduction in *total surplus* that results from a tax.

4. F; the loss of producer and consumer surplus exceeds the revenue from the tax. The difference is deadweight loss.

5. F; the loss in total surplus is the buyer's value minus the seller's cost or $20 – $10 = $10.

6. T

7. F; the more elastic the demand curve the greater the deadweight loss and the demand for cigarettes (a necessity) should be more inelastic than the demand for luxury boats (a luxury).

8. F; a tax generates a greater deadweight loss when supply and demand are more elastic.

9. T

10. F; as a tax increases, revenue first rises and then falls as the tax shrinks the market to a point where all trades are eliminated and tax revenue is zero.

11. T

12. T

13. F; taxes collected from the either the buyers or the sellers are equivalent. That is why economists simply use a tax wedge when analyzing a tax and avoid the issue altogether.

14. T

15. T

Multiple-Choice Questions

1. c	5. b	9. d	13. b	17. c
2. b	6. c	10. d	14. d	18. c
3. a	7. b	11. c	15. e	19. a
4. d	8. a	12. a	16. c	20. d

Advanced Critical Thinking

1. No. Usually an increase in a tax will reduce the size of the market because the tax will increase the price to buyers causing them to reduce their quantity demanded and decrease the price to sellers causing them to reduce their quantity supplied. Therefore, when taxes double, the government collects twice as mucsh per unit on many fewer units so tax revenue will increase by less than double and tax revenue could, in some extreme cases, even go down.

2. No. Some markets may have extremely elastic supply and demand curves. In these markets, an increase in a tax causes market participants to leave the market and little revenue is generated from the tax increase but deadweight loss increases a great deal. Other markets may have inelastic supply and demand curves. In these markets, an increase in a tax fails to cause market participants to leave the market and a great deal of additional tax revenue is generated with little increase in deadweight loss.

APPLICATION: INTERNATIONAL TRADE

GOALS

⌈In this chapter you will

Consider what determines whether a country imports or exports a good

Examine who wins and who loses from international trade

Learn that the gains to winners from international trade exceed the losses to losers

Analyze the welfare effects of tariffs and import quotas

Examine the arguments people use to advocate trade restrictions

OUTCOMES

⌈After accomplishing these goals, you should be able to

Determine whether a country imports or exports a good if the world price is greater than the before-trade domestic price

Show that the consumer wins and the producer loses when a country imports a good

Use consumer and producer surplus to show that the gains of the consumer exceed the losses of the producer when a country imports a good

Show the deadweight loss associated with a tariff or a quota

Defeat the arguments made in support of trade restrictions

CHAPTER OVERVIEW

Context and Purpose

Chapter 9 is the third chapter in a three-chapter sequence dealing with welfare economics. Chapter 7 introduced welfare economics—the study of how the allocation of resources affects economic well-being. Chapter 8 applied the lessons of welfare economics to taxation. Chapter 9 applies the tools of welfare economics from Chapter 7 to the study of international trade, a topic that was first introduced in Chapter 3.

The purpose of Chapter 9 is to use our knowledge of welfare economics to address the gains from trade more precisely than we did in Chapter 3 when we studied comparative advantage and the gains from trade. We will develop the conditions that determine whether a country imports or exports a good and discover who wins and who loses when a country imports or exports a good. We will find that when free trade is allowed, the gains of the winners exceed the losses of the losers. Since there are gains from trade, we will see that restrictions on free trade reduce the gains from trade and cause deadweight losses similar to those generated by a tax.

CHAPTER REVIEW

Introduction

This chapter employs welfare economics to address the following questions:

- How does international trade affect economic well-being?

- Who gains and who loses from free international trade?

- How do the gains from trade compare to the losses from trade?

The Determinants of Trade

In the absence of international trade, a market generates a domestic price that equates the domestic quantity supplied and domestic quantity demanded in that market. The **world price** is the price of the good that prevails in the world market for that good. Prices represent opportunity costs. Therefore, comparing the world price and the domestic price of a good before trade indicates whether a country has the lower opportunity cost of production and, thus, a comparative advantage in the production of a good, or if other countries have a comparative advantage in the production of the good.

- If the world price is above the domestic price for a good, the country has a comparative advantage in the production of that good and that good should be exported if trade is allowed.

- If the world price is below the domestic price for a good, foreign countries have a comparative advantage in the production of that good and that good should be imported if trade is allowed.

The Winners and Losers from Trade

Assume that the country being analyzed is a small country and is therefore a *price taker* on world markets. This means that the country takes the world price as given and cannot influence the world price.

Exhibit 1 depicts a situation where the world price is higher than the before-trade domestic price. This country has a comparative advantage in the production of this good. If free trade is allowed, the domestic price will rise to the world price and it will export the difference between the domestic quantity supplied and the domestic quantity demanded.

With regard to gains and losses to an exporting country from trade, before trade consumer surplus was A + B and producer surplus was C so total surplus was A + B + C. After trade, consumer surplus is A and producer surplus is B + C + D (the area below the price and above the supply curve). Total surplus is now A + B + C + D for a gain of area D. This analysis generates two conclusions:

- When a country allows trade and becomes an exporter of a good, domestic producers are better off and domestic consumers are worse off.

- Trade increases the economic well-being of a nation because the gains of the winners exceed the losses of the losers.

Exhibit 2 depicts a situation where the world price is lower than the before-trade domestic price. Other countries have a comparative advantage in the production of this good. If free trade is allowed, the domestic price will fall to the

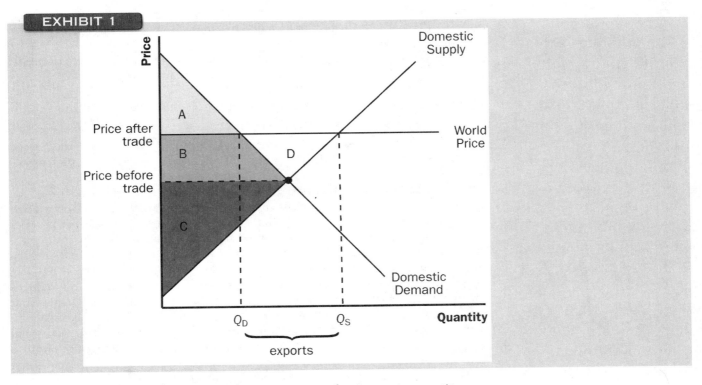

EXHIBIT 1

world price and it will import the difference between the domestic quantity supplied and the domestic quantity demanded.

With regard to gains and losses to an importing country from trade, before trade consumer surplus was A and producer surplus was B + C so total surplus was A + B + C. After trade, consumer surplus is A + B + D (the area below the

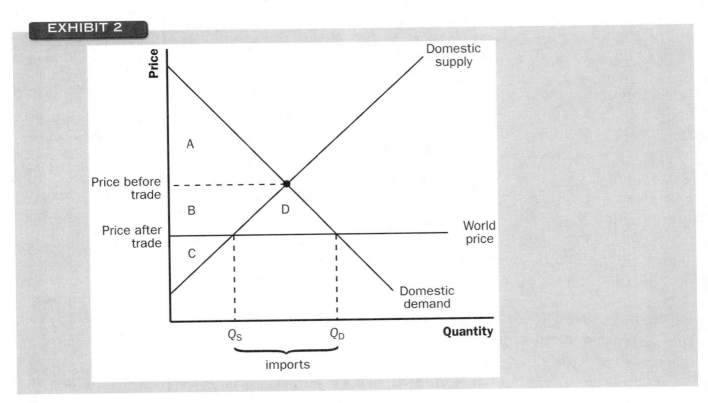

EXHIBIT 2

demand curve and above the price) and producer surplus is C. Total surplus is now A + B + C + D for a gain of area D. This analysis generates two conclusions:

- When a country allows trade and becomes an importer of a good, domestic consumers are better off and domestic producers are worse off.

- Trade increases the economic well-being of a nation because the gains of the winners exceed the losses of the losers.

Trade can make everyone better off if the winners compensate the losers. Compensation is rarely paid so the losers lobby for trade restrictions, such as tariffs and import quotas.

Tariffs and import quotas restrict international trade. A **tariff** is a tax on goods produced abroad and sold domestically. Therefore, a tariff is placed on a good only if the country is an importer of that good. A tariff raises the price of the good, reduces the domestic quantity demanded, increases the domestic quantity supplied, and, thus, reduces the quantity of imports. A tariff moves the market closer to the no-trade equilibrium.

A tariff increases producer surplus, increases government revenue, but reduces consumer surplus by a greater amount than the increase in producer surplus and government revenue. Therefore, a tariff creates a deadweight loss because total surplus is reduced. The deadweight loss comes from two sources. The increase in the price due to the tariff causes the production of units that cost more to produce than the world price (overproduction) and causes consumers to fail to consume units where the value to the consumer is greater than world price (underconsumption).

An **import quota** sets a limit on the quantity of a good that can be produced abroad and sold domestically. To accomplish this, a government can distribute a limited number of import licenses. An import quota shifts the portion of the domestic supply curve above the world price to the right by the size of the quota. An import quota raises the price of the good, reduces the domestic quantity demanded, increases the domestic quantity supplied, and, thus reduces the quantity of imports. It moves the market closer to the no-trade equilibrium.

An import quota increases producer surplus, increases license holder surplus, but reduces consumer surplus by a greater amount than the increase in producer and license holder surplus. Therefore, an import quota also creates a deadweight loss in a manner similar to a tariff.

Note that the results of a tariff and an import quota are nearly the same. If the government sells the import licenses, it will collect revenue equal to the tariff revenue and a tariff and a quota become identical. If quotas are "voluntary" in the sense that they are imposed by the exporting country, the revenue from the quota accrues to the foreign firms or governments.

Tariffs and import quotas cause deadweight losses. Therefore, if economic efficiency is a policy goal, countries should allow free trade and avoid using tariffs and import quotas.

Free trade offers benefits beyond efficiency. Free trade increases variety for consumers, allows firms to take advantage of economies of scale, makes markets more competitive, and facilitates the spread of technology.

The Arguments for Restricting Trade

Opponents of free trade (often producers hurt by free trade) offer the following arguments in support of trade restrictions:

The jobs argument   Opponents of free trade argue that trade destroys domestic jobs. However, while free trade does destroy inefficient jobs in the importing sector, it creates more efficient jobs in the export sector, industries where the country has a comparative advantage. This is always true because each country has a comparative advantage in the production of something.

The national-security argument   Some industries argue that their product is vital for national security so it should be protected from international competition. The danger of this argument is that it runs the risk of being overused.

The infant-industry argument   New industries argue that they need temporary protection from international competition until they become mature enough to compete. However, there is a problem choosing which new industries to protect and, once protected, temporary protection often becomes permanent. In addition, industries truly expected to be competitive in the future don't need protection because the owners will accept short-term losses.

The unfair-competition argument   Opponents of free trade argue that other countries provide their industries with unfair advantages such as subsidies, tax breaks, and lower environmental restrictions. However, the gains of consumers in the importing country will exceed the losses of the producers in that country, and the country will gain when importing subsidized production.

The protection-as-a-bargaining-chip argument   Opponents of free trade argue that the threat of trade restrictions may result in other countries lowering their trade restrictions. However, if this does not work, the threatening country must back down or reduce trade—neither of which is desirable.

When countries choose to reduce trade restrictions, they can take a *unilateral* approach and remove trade restrictions on their own. Alternatively, they can take a *multilateral* approach and reduce trade restrictions along with other countries. Examples of the multilateral approach are NAFTA and GATT. The rules of GATT are enforced by the WTO. The multilateral approach has advantages in that it provides freer overall trade because many countries do it together and thus it is sometimes more easily accomplished politically. However, it may fail if negotiations between countries break down. Many economists suggest a unilateral approach because there will be gains to the domestic economy and this will cause other countries to emulate it.

Globalization is blamed by the uninformed for low wages and poor working conditions in less-developed countries. Economists argue, however, that low wages in poor countries are due to such things as low productivity. Attempts to increase wages in poor countries by restricting trade causes workers in poor countries to lose their jobs, which makes the poor even poorer.

Conclusion

Economists overwhelmingly support free trade. Free trade between states in the United States improves welfare by allowing each area of the country to specialize in the production of goods for which they have a comparative advantage. In the same manner, free trade between countries allows each country to enjoy the benefits of comparative advantage and the gains from trade.

HELPFUL HINTS

1. Countries that restrict trade usually restrict imports rather than exports. This is because producers lose from imports and gain from exports and producers are better organized to lobby the government to protect their interests. For example, when a country imports a product, consumers win and producers lose. Consumers are less likely to be able to organize and lobby

the government than the affected producers so imports may be restricted. When a country exports a product, producers win and consumers lose. But again, consumers are less likely to organize and lobby the government to restrict exports so exports are rarely restricted.

2. The overwhelming majority of economists find no sound *economic* argument in opposition to free trade. The only argument against free trade that may not be defeated on economic grounds is the "national-security argument." This is because it is the only argument against free trade that is not based on economics but rather is based on other strategic objectives.

3. A *prohibitive* tariff or import quota is one that is so restrictive that it returns the market to its original no-trade equilibrium. This occurs if the tariff is greater than or equal to the difference between the world price and the no-trade domestic price or if the import quota is set at zero.

TERMS AND DEFINITIONS

Choose a definition for each key term.

Key terms:

_____ World price

_____ Price takers

_____ Tariff

_____ Import quota

Definitions:

1. A limit on the quantity of a good that can be produced abroad and sold domestically

2. Market participants that cannot influence the price so they view the price as given

3. The price of a good that prevails in the world market for that good

4. A tax on goods produced abroad and sold domestically

PROBLEMS AND SHORT-ANSWER QUESTIONS

Practice Problems

1. Use Exhibit 3 to answer the following questions.
    a. If trade is not allowed, what is the equilibrium price and quantity in this market?

    _____

    _____

    b. If trade is allowed, will this country import or export this commodity? Why?

    _____

    _____

EXHIBIT 3

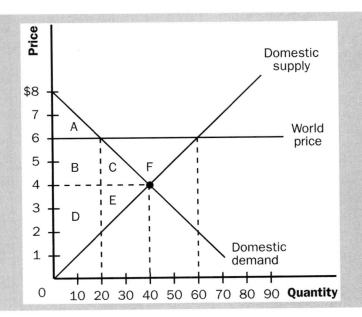

c. If trade is allowed, what is the price at which the good is sold, the domestic quantity supplied and demanded, and the quantity imported or exported?

_____

_____

d. What area corresponds to consumer surplus if no trade is allowed?

_____

e. What area corresponds to consumer surplus if trade is allowed?

_____

f. What area corresponds to producer surplus if no trade is allowed?

_____

g. What area corresponds to producer surplus if trade is allowed?

_____

h. If free trade is allowed, who gains and who loses, the consumers or the producers, and what area corresponds to their gain or loss?

_____

_____

i. What area corresponds to the gains from trade?

_____

2. Use Exhibit 4 to answer the following questions.

a. If trade is not allowed, what is the equilibrium price and quantity in this market?

_____

_____

- -

b. If trade is allowed, will this country import or export this commodity? Why?

_____

_____

- -

c. If trade is allowed, what is the price at which the good is sold, the domestic quantity supplied and demanded, and the quantity imported or exported?

_____

_____

- -

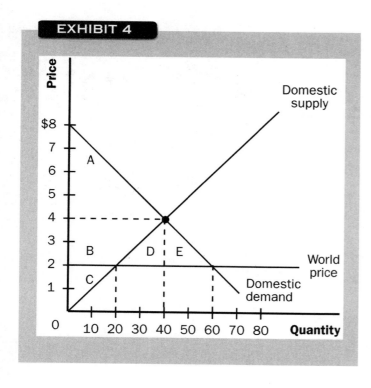

EXHIBIT 4

d. What area corresponds to consumer surplus if no trade is allowed?

_____

e. What area corresponds to consumer surplus if trade is allowed?

_____

f. What area corresponds to producer surplus if no trade is allowed?

_____

g. What area corresponds to producer surplus if trade is allowed?

_____

h. If free trade is allowed, who gains and who loses, the consumers or the producers, and what area corresponds to their gain or loss?

_____

_____

i. What area corresponds to the gains from trade?

_____

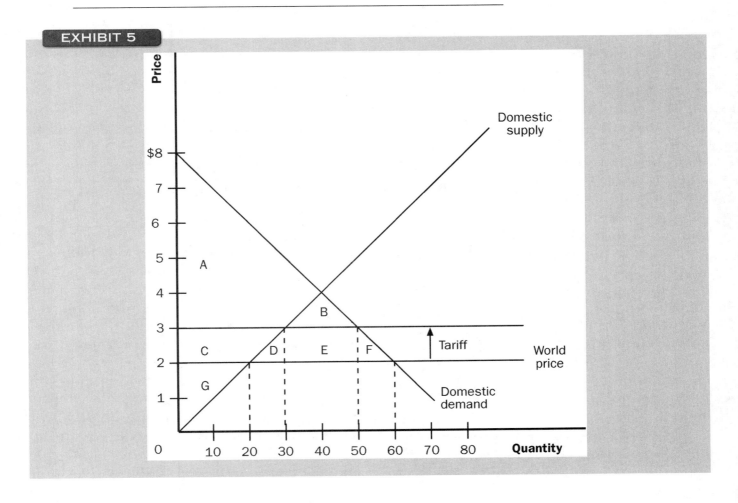

EXHIBIT 5

3. Use Exhibit 5 to answer the following questions.
   a. If free trade is allowed, what is the domestic quantity supplied, domestic quantity demanded, and the quantity imported?

   _____

   _____

   b. If a $1 tariff is placed on this good, what is the domestic quantity supplied, domestic quantity demanded, and the quantity imported?

   _____

   _____

c. What area corresponds to consumer and producer surplus before the tariff is applied?

_____

_____

d. What area corresponds to consumer surplus, producer surplus, and government revenue after the tariff is applied?

_____

_____

e. What area corresponds to the deadweight loss associated with the tariff?

_____

f. Describe in words the sources of the deadweight loss from a tariff.

_____

_____

g. What is the size of the import quota that would generate results most similar to this $1 tariff?

_____

h. What is the size of the tariff that would eliminate trade altogether (i.e. that would return the market to its no-trade domestic solution)?

_____

Short-Answer Questions

The following table shows the amount of output a worker can produce per hour in Partyland and Laborland.

	Beer	Pizza
Partyland	2	4
Laborland	4	12

1. If free trade is allowed, which good will each country export to the other? Why? (Explain in terms of each country's opportunity cost of production.)

_____

_____

_____

_____

2. If the world price for a good is above a country's before-trade domestic price, will this country import or export this good? Why?

_____

_____

3. If residents of a country are allowed to import a good, who gains and who loses when compared to the before-trade equilibrium, the producers or the consumers? Why?

_____

_____

4. Describe in words the source of the gains from trade (the additional total surplus) received by an exporting country.

_____

_____

5. Describe in words the source of the gains from trade (the additional total surplus) received by an importing country.

_____

_____

6. Describe in words the source of the deadweight loss from restricting trade.

_____

_____

_____

7. For every tariff there is an import quota that will generate a similar result. What are the short-comings of using an import quota to restrict trade versus using a tariff?

_____

_____

_____

_____

8. What arguments are made to support trade restrictions?

_____

_____

_____

_____

9. Present the free-trade response to the argument that imports should be restricted on goods that a country needs for national security.

_____

_____

10. If tariffs and quotas reduce total surplus and, therefore, total economic well-being, why do governments employ them?

_____

_____

_____

11. List other benefits of free trade beyond those suggested by our standard analysis.

_____

_____

_____

SELF-TEST

True/False Questions

_____1. If the world price for a good exceeds a country's before-trade domestic price for that good, the country should import that good.

_____2. Countries should import products for which they have a comparative advantage in production.

_____3. If a worker in Brazil can produce 6 oranges or 2 apples in an hour while a worker in Mexico can produce 2 oranges or 1 apple in an hour, then Brazil should export oranges and Mexico should export apples.

_____4. If free trade is allowed and a country imports wheat, domestic buyers of bread are better off and domestic farmers are worse off when compared to the before-trade domestic equilibrium.

_____5. If free trade is allowed and a country exports a good, domestic producers of the good are worse off and domestic consumers of the good are better off when compared to the before-trade domestic equilibrium.

_____6. If free trade is allowed and a country exports a good, the gains of domestic producers exceed the losses of domestic consumers and total surplus rises.

_____7. Trade makes everyone better off.

_____8. Trade can make everyone better off if the winners from trade compensate the losers from trade.

_____9. Trade increases the economic well-being of a nation because the gains of the winners exceed the losses of the losers.

_____10. Tariffs tend to benefit consumers.

_____11. A tariff raises the price of a good, reduces the domestic quantity demanded, increases the domestic quantity supplied, and increases the quantity imported.

_____12. An import quota that restricts imports to the same degree as a tariff raises more government revenue than the equivalent tariff.

_____13. Opponents of free trade often argue that free trade destroys domestic jobs.

_____14. If a foreign country subsidizes its export industries, its tax payers are paying to improve the welfare of consumers in the importing countries.

_____15. Tariffs and quotas cause deadweight losses because they raise the price of the imported good and cause overproduction and underconsumption of the good in the importing country.

Multiple-Choice Questions

1. If free trade is allowed, a country will export a good if the world price is
   a. below the before-trade domestic price of the good.
   b. above the before-trade domestic price of the good.
   c. equal to the before-trade domestic price of the good.
   d. none of the above

2. Suppose the world price is below the before-trade domestic price for a good. If a country allows free trade in this good,
   a. consumers will gain and producers will lose.
   b. producers will gain and consumers will lose.
   c. both producers and consumers will gain.
   d. both producers and consumers will lose.

The following table shows the amount of output a worker can produce per hour in the United States and Canada.

	Pens	Pencils
United States	8	4
Canada	8	2

3. Which of the following statements about free trade between the United States and Canada is true?
   a. The United States will export pencils but there will be no trade in pens because neither country has a comparative advantage in the production of pens.
   b. The United States will export pens and Canada will export pencils.
   c. The United States will export pencils and Canada will export pens.
   d. The United States will export both pens and pencils.

4. If the world price for a good exceeds the before-trade domestic price for a good, then that country must have
   a. an absolute advantage in the production of the good.
   b. an absolute disadvantage in the production of the good.
   c. a comparative advantage in the production of the good.
   d. a comparative disadvantage in the production of the good.

EXHIBIT 6

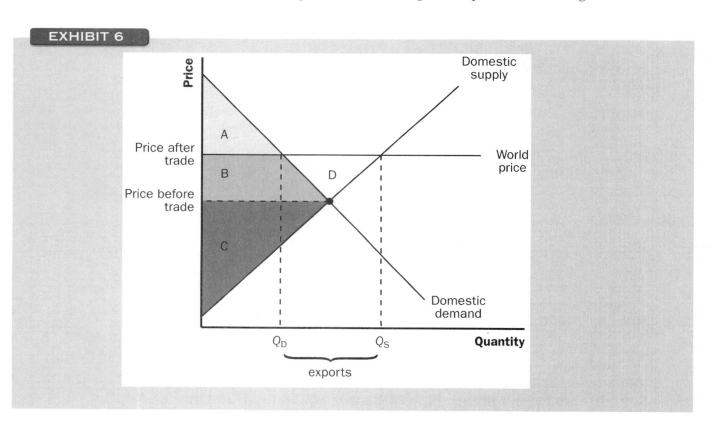

Use Exhibit 6 for questions 5 through 9.

5. If trade is not allowed, consumer surplus is the area
   a. A.
   b. A + B.
   c. A + B + C.
   d. A + B + D.
   e. A + B + C + D.

6. If free trade is allowed, consumer surplus is the area
   a. A.
   b. A + B.
   c. A + B + C.
   d. A + B + D.
   e. A + B + C + D.

7. If trade is not allowed, producer surplus is the area
   a. C.
   b. B + C.
   c. B + C + D.
   d. A + B + C.
   e. A + B + C + D.

8. If free trade is allowed, producer surplus is the area
   a. C.
   b. B + C.
   c. B + C + D.
   d. A + B + C.
   e. A + B + C + D.

9. The gains from trade correspond to the area
   a. A.
   b. B.
   c. C.
   d. D.
   e. B + D.

10. When a country allows trade and exports a good,
    a. domestic consumers are better off, domestic producers are worse off, and the nation is worse off because the losses of the losers exceed the gains of the winners.
    b. domestic consumers are better off, domestic producers are worse off, and the nation is better off because the gains of the winners exceed the losses of the losers.
    c. domestic producers are better off, domestic consumers are worse off, and the nation is worse off because the losses of the losers exceed the gains of the winners.
    d. domestic producers are better off, domestic consumers are worse off, and the nation is better off because the gains of the winners exceed the losses of the losers.

EXHIBIT 7

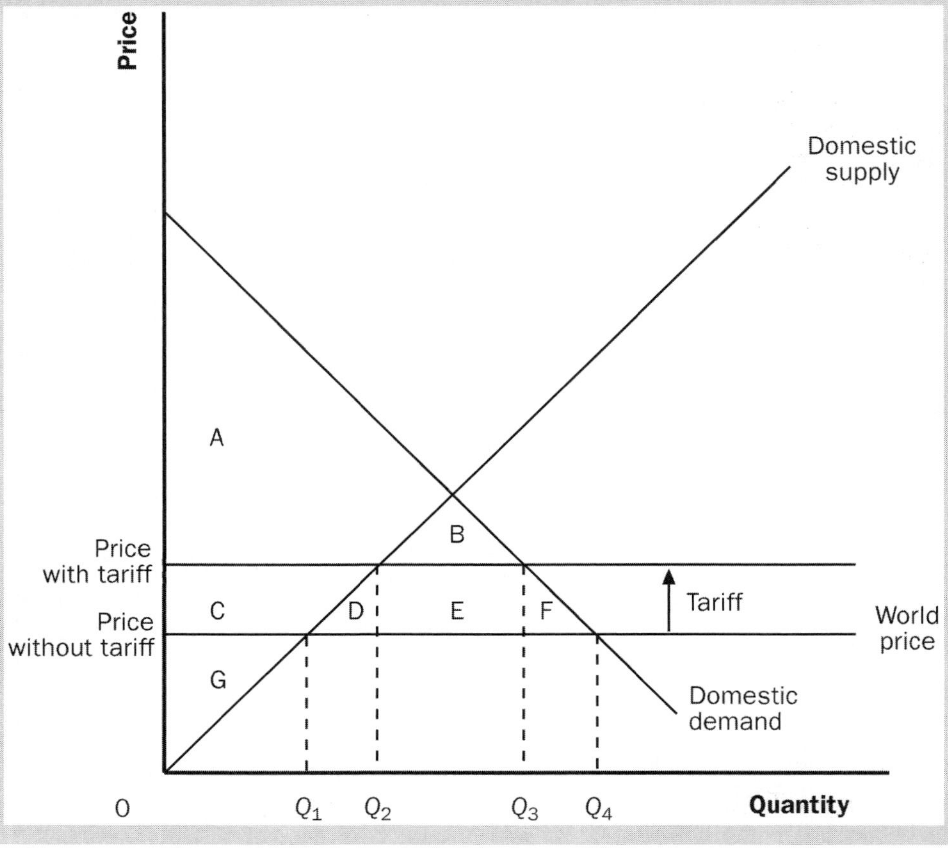

Use Exhibit 7 for questions 11 through 16.

11. If free trade is allowed, consumer surplus is the area
    a. A.
    b. A + B.
    c. A + B + C.
    d. A + B + C + D + E + F.
    e. A + B + C + D + E + F + G.

12. If a tariff is placed on this good, consumer surplus is the area
    a. A.
    b. A + B.
    c. A + B + C.
    d. A + B + C + D + E + F.
    e. A + B + C + D + E + F + G.

13. Government revenue from the tariff is the area
    a. C + D + E + F.
    b. D + E + F.
    c. D + F.
    d. G.
    e. E.

14. If a tariff is placed on this good, producer surplus is the area
    a. G.
    b. G + C.
    c. G + C + D + E + F.
    d. G + C + D + E + F + B.
    e. G + C + E.

15. The deadweight loss from the tariff is the area
    a. B + D + E + F.
    b. B.
    c. D + E + F.
    d. D + F.
    e. E.

16. What is the size of the import quota that would have the same impact on trade as the tariff?
    a. $Q_2 - Q_1$
    b. $Q_3 - Q_2$
    c. $Q_4 - Q_3$
    d. $Q_4 - Q_1$
    e. none of the above

17. Which of the following statements about a tariff is true?
    a. A tariff increases producer surplus, decreases consumer surplus, increases revenue to the government, and reduces total surplus.
    b. A tariff increases consumer surplus, decreases producer surplus, increases revenue to the government, and reduces total surplus.
    c. A tariff increases producer surplus, decreases consumer surplus, increases revenue to the government, and increases total surplus.
    d. A tariff increases consumer surplus, decreases producer surplus, increases revenue to the government, and increases total surplus.

18. Which of the following statements about import quotas is true?
    a. Import quotas are preferred to tariffs because they raise more revenue for the imposing government.
    b. Voluntary quotas established by the exporting country reduce the importing country's deadweight loss from the trade restriction.
    c. For every tariff, there is an import quota that could have generated a similar result.
    d. An import quota reduces the price to the domestic consumers.

19. Which of the following is not employed as an argument in support of trade restrictions?
    a. Free trade destroys domestic jobs.
    b. Free trade harms the national security if vital products are imported.
    c. Free trade is harmful to importing countries if foreign countries subsidize their exporting industries.
    d. Free trade harms both domestic producers and domestic consumers and therefore reduces total surplus.
    e. Free trade harms infant industries in an importing country.

20. Because producers are better able to organize than consumers, we would expect there to be political pressure to create
    a. free trade.
    b. import restrictions.
    c. export restrictions.
    d. none of the above.

ADVANCED CRITICAL THINKING

You are watching the nightly news. A political candidate being interviewed says, "I'm for free trade, but it must be fair trade. If our foreign competitors will not raise their environmental regulations, reduce subsidies to their export industries, and lower tariffs on their imports of our goods, we should retaliate with tariffs and import quotas on their goods to show them that we won't be played for fools!"

1. If a foreign country artificially lowers the cost of production for its producers with lax environmental regulations and direct subsidies and then exports the products to us, who gains and who loses in our country, producers or consumers?

   _____

   _____

2. Continuing from question 1 above, does our country gain or lose? Why?

   _____

   _____

3. If a foreign country subsidizes the production of a good exported to the United States, who bears the burden of their mistaken policy?

   _____

4. What happens to our overall economic well-being if we restrict trade with a country that subsidizes its export industries? Explain.

   _____

   _____

   _____

5. Is there any difference in the analysis of our importation of a good sold at the cost of production or sold at a subsidized price? Why?

_____

_____

_____

_____

6. Is it a good policy to threaten trade restrictions in the hope that foreign governments will reduce their trade restrictions? Explain.

_____

_____

_____

SOLUTIONS

Terms and Definitions

__3__ World price

__2__ Price takers

__4__ Tariff

__1__ Import quota

Practice Problems

1. a. Price = $4, quantity = 40 units.
    b. Export because the world price is above the domestic price which implies that this country has a comparative advantage in the production of this good.
    c. Price = $6, quantity supplied = 60 units, quantity demanded = 20 units, quantity exported = 40 units.
    d. A + B + C
    e. A
    f. D + E
    g. B + C + D + E + F
    h. Consumers lose B + C, producers gain B + C + F
    i. F

2. a. Price = $4, quantity = 40 units.
    b. Import because the world price is below the domestic price, which implies that other countries have a comparative advantage in the production of this good.
    c. Price = $2, quantity supplied = 20 units, quantity demanded = 60 units, quantity imported = 40 units.
    d. A
    e. A + B + D + E
    f. B + C
    g. C
    h. Consumers gain B + D + E, producers lose B
    i. D + E

3. a. Quantity supplied = 20 units, quantity demanded = 60 units, quantity imported = 40 units.
    b. Quantity supplied = 30 units, quantity demanded = 50 units, quantity imported = 20 units.
    c. Consumer surplus = A + B + C + D + E + F, producer surplus = G
    d. Consumer surplus = A + B, producer surplus = C + G, government revenue = E
    e. D + F
    f. First, the rise in the price due to the tariff causes *overproduction* because units are produced that cost more than the world price. Second, the rise in price causes *underconsumption* because consumers fail to consume units where the value to consumers is greater than the world price.
    g. Import quota of 20 units—the same number of units imported with the $1 tariff.
    h. A $2 tariff would raise the price to $4 (the no-trade domestic price) and eliminate trade.

Short-Answer Questions

1. In Partyland, the opportunity cost of 1 beer is 2 pizzas. In Laborland, the opportunity cost of 1 beer is 3 pizzas. Partyland has the lower opportunity cost of beer and, thus, a comparative advantage in beer

production, and it will export beer. In Laborland, the opportunity cost of 1 pizza is 1/3 of a beer. In Partyland, the opportunity cost of 1 pizza is 1/2 of a beer. Laborland has the lower opportunity cost of pizza and, thus, a comparative advantage in pizza production, and it will export pizza. The fact that Laborland is more efficient at both is irrelevant.

2. Export, because the domestic opportunity cost of production is lower than the opportunity cost of production in other countries.

3. Consumers gain and producers lose because, if trade is allowed, the domestic price falls to the world price.

4. The gains are the additional value placed on the exported units by buyers in the rest of the world in excess of the domestic cost of production.

5. The gains are the additional value placed by domestic buyers on the imported units in excess of their cost of production in the rest of the world.

6. The rise in price from restricting trade causes overproduction of the good (production of units that cost more than the world price) and underconsumption of the good (failure to consume units valued more than the world price).

7. The revenue from an import quota will accrue to the license holders or foreign firms and governments unless the domestic government sells the import licenses for the maximum possible amount. In addition, expenditures incurred while lobbying the government to obtain import licenses add to the deadweight loss from the import quota.

8. Free trade will destroy domestic jobs, reduce national security, harm infant industries, force domestic producers to compete with foreign companies that have unfair advantages, and allow other countries to have trade restrictions while our country does not.

9. The danger is that nearly any good (far beyond standard military items) can be argued to be necessary for national security, including watches, clothing, shoes . . .

10. Tariffs and quotas harm domestic consumers while helping domestic producers. Producers are better able to organize than are consumers and, thus, they are better able to lobby the government on their behalf.

11. Free trade increases the variety of goods for consumers, allows firms to take advantage of economies of scale, makes markets more competitive, and facilitates the spread of technology.

True/False Questions

1. F; the country should export that good.

2. F; countries should export goods for which they have a comparative advantage in production.

3. T

4. T

5. F; producers gain, consumers lose.

6. T

7. F; Some gain and some lose but the gains of the winners outweigh the losses of the losers.

8. T

9. T

10. F; tariffs benefit producers.

11. F; tariffs decrease imports.

12. F; at most, a quota can raise the same revenue if the government sells the import licenses for the maximum amount possible.

13. T

14. T

15. T

Multiple-Choice Questions

1. b	5. b	9. d	13. e	17. a
2. a	6. a	10. d	14. b	18. c
3. c	7. a	11. d	15. d	19. d
4. c	8. c	12. b	16. b	20. b

Advanced Critical Thinking

1. Consumers gain, producers lose.

2. Our country gains because the gains of the consumers exceed the losses of the producers.

3. The taxpayers of the foreign country.

4. Producers gain, consumers lose, but consumers lose more than producers gain so total surplus is reduced and there is a deadweight loss. The result is no different than restricting trade when the foreign producer has no unfair advantage.

5. No. In either case, the world price is lower than the before-trade domestic price, causing consumers to gain and producers to lose from trade. Also, restrictions on trade cause consumers to lose more than producers gain whether the production of the good was subsidized or not.

6. Usually not. If the other country fails to give in to the threat, the threatening country has to choose between backing down and reducing trade—neither of which is desirable.

10

MEASURING A NATION'S INCOME

⌈In this chapter you will

Consider why an economy's total income equals its total expenditure

Learn how gross domestic product (GDP) is defined and calculated

See the breakdown of GDP into its four major components

Learn the distinction between real GDP and nominal GDP

Consider whether GDP is a good measure of economic well-being

OUTCOMES

⌈After accomplishing these goals, you should be able to

Demonstrate why income equals expenditure equals output

Explain the key words and phrases in the definition of GDP

Define consumption, investment, government purchases, and net exports

Calculate real and nominal GDP using base year and current year prices

List a number of welfare-enhancing activities that are not captured by GDP

CHAPTER OVERVIEW

Context and Purpose

Chapter 10 is the first chapter in the macroeconomic section of the text. It is the first of a two-chapter sequence that introduces you to two vital statistics that economists use to monitor the macroeconomy—GDP and the consumer price index. Chapter 10 develops how economists measure production and income in the macroeconomy. Chapter 11 develops how economists measure the level of prices in the macroeconomy. Taken together, Chapter 10 concentrates on the *quantity* of output in the macroeconomy while Chapter 11 concentrates on the *price* of output in the macroeconomy.

The purpose of this chapter is to provide you with an understanding of the measurement and the use of gross domestic product (GDP). GDP is the single most important measure of the health of the macroeconomy. Indeed, it is the most widely reported statistic in every developed economy.

CHAPTER REVIEW

Introduction

Microeconomics is the study of individual markets and the decisionmaking of individual firms and households that meet in those markets. **Macroeconomics** is the study of the entire economy as a whole. This chapter, and the remainder of this text, deals with macroeconomics.

The Economy's Income and Expenditure

In a nation's macroeconomy, income must equal expenditure. This is true because, in every transaction, the income of the seller must be equal to the expenditure of the buyer. Gross Domestic Product (GDP) is a measure of the total income or total output in the economy. Since income equals expenditure, GDP can be measured by adding up the income earned in the economy (wages, rent, and profit) or the expenditure on goods and services produced in the economy. That is, income equals expenditure equals GDP.

The Measurement of Gross Domestic Product

GDP is defined as the market value of all final goods and services produced within a country in a given period of time.

- "Market value" means that production is valued at the price paid for the output. Hence, items sold at higher prices are more heavily weighted in GDP.

- "Of all" means that GDP attempts to measure all production in the economy that is legally sold in markets. For example, GDP excludes the production and sale of illegal drugs and household production such as when homeowners clean their own houses. However, in an attempt to be comprehensive, GDP does include the estimated rental value of owner-occupied housing as production of housing services.

- "Final" means that GDP includes only goods and services that are sold to the end user. Thus, GDP counts the sale of a Ford Taurus when it is sold at retail, but it excludes Ford's purchases of intermediate goods such as glass, steel, and tires used up during the production of the car. *Intermediate goods* are goods that are produced by one firm to be further processed by another firm. Counting only final goods and services avoids double counting intermediate production.

- "Goods and services" means that while GDP clearly includes tangible manufactured items such as cars and trucks, it also includes intangible items such as lawyers' and doctors' services.

- "Produced" means that we exclude the sale of used items which were produced (and counted) in a previous period. Again, this avoids double counting.

- "Within a country" means that GDP measures the value of production within the geographic borders of a country.

- "In a given period of time" means that we measure GDP per year or per quarter.

GDP data is statistically "seasonally adjusted" to eliminate the systematic variations in the data which are caused by seasonal events such as Christmas and crop harvest.

Other measures of income besides GDP are listed below, from largest to smallest.

- *Gross National Product (GNP):* GNP measures the income or production of a nation's permanent residents or "nationals" (both people and their factories) no matter where they are located.

- *Net National Product (NNP):* NNP is the total income of a nation's residents (GNP) minus depreciation. Depreciation is the value of the wear and tear on the economy's capital stock.

- *National income:* national income is the total income earned by a nation's residents. It is NNP less indirect business taxes plus business subsidies.

- *Personal income:* personal income is the income of households and non-corporate businesses. It excludes retained earnings (corporate income not paid out as dividends) but includes interest income households receive from government debt and government transfer payments (welfare and social security).

- *Disposable personal income:* this is income of households and non-incorporated businesses after they pay their obligations to the government (taxes, traffic tickets).

The Components of GDP

GDP can be measured by adding up the value of the expenditures on final goods and services. Economists divide expenditures into four components: consumption (C), investment (I), government purchases (G), and net exports (NX).

- *Consumption* is spending by households on goods and services, with the exception of new housing.

- *Investment* is spending on capital equipment, inventories, and structures such as new housing. Investment does not include spending on stocks and bonds.

- *Government purchases* is spending on goods and services by all levels of government (federal, state, and local). Government purchases do not include *transfer payments* such as government payments for Social Security, welfare, and unemployment benefits because the government does not receive any product or service in return.

- *Net exports* is the value of foreign purchases of U.S. domestic production (exports) minus U.S. domestic purchases of foreign production (imports). Imports must be subtracted because consumption, investment, and government purchases include expenditures on all goods, foreign and domestic, and the foreign component must be removed so that only spending on domestic production remains.

   Denoting GDP as Y, we can say that $Y = C + I + G + NX$. The variables are defined in such a way that this equation is an identity.

Real Versus Nominal GDP

Nominal GDP is the value of output measured in the prices that existed during the year in which the output was produced (current prices). Real GDP is the value of output measured in the prices that prevailed in some arbitrary (but fixed) base year (constant prices). If we observe that nominal GDP has risen from one year to the next, we are unable to determine whether the quantity of goods and services has risen or whether the prices of goods and services have risen. However, if we observe that real GDP has risen, we are certain that the quantity of goods and services has risen because the output from each year is valued in terms of the same base year prices. Thus, real GDP is the better measure of production in the economy.

The GDP deflator = (nominal GDP / real GDP) × 100. It is a measure of the level of prices in the current year relative to the level of prices in the base year.

In the United States, real GDP tends to grow at a rate of about 3 percent per year. Occasional periods of decline in real GDP are known as *recessions*.

GDP and Economic Well-Being

Real GDP is a strong indicator of the economic well-being of a society because countries with a large real GDP per person tend to have better educational systems, better health care systems, more literate citizens, better housing, a better diet, a longer life expectancy, and so on. A country with a larger GDP even wins more Olympic medals. That is, a larger real GDP per person generally indicates a larger consumption per person. However, GDP is not a perfect measure of material well-being because it excludes leisure, the quality of the environment, and goods and services produced at home and not sold in markets such as child-rearing, housework, and volunteer work. In addition, GDP says nothing about the *distribution* of income. GDP also fails to capture the underground or shadow economy—the portion of the economy that does not report its economic activity. For example, GDP does not measure illegal drug sales or income that is unreported to avoid taxation.

HELPFUL HINTS

1. GDP measures production. When we set out to measure GDP, we must first remember that we are measuring *production* (and the income earned from producing it) over a period of time. If we can remember that, we will generally account for unusual types of production correctly. Examples:

   - How should we handle the measurement of the production of a cruise ship that takes three years to build and is sold at the end of the third year? Logically, we should count the portion of the ship that was completed during each year and apply it to that year's GDP. In fact, that is what economists do. If we had accounted for the entire ship in the year in which it was sold, we would have overestimated GDP in the third year and underestimated GDP in the previous two years.

   - Similarly, if a new house were built during one year but sold for the first time during the next year, we should account for it during the first year because that is when it was produced. That is, the builder "purchased" the finished home during the first year and added it to his or her inventory of homes.

   While in general we only wish to count final goods and services, we do count the production of intermediate goods that were not used during the period but were added to a firm's inventory because this production will not be captured by counting all of the final goods.

2. GDP does not include all expenditures. We have learned that we can measure GDP by adding the expenditures on final goods and services ($Y = C + I + G + NX$). Once we have learned the expenditure approach, however, we must not forget the words "on final goods and services" and mistakenly count all expenditures. When we include expenditures on used items, intermediate goods, stocks and bonds, or government transfer payments, we get

a very large dollar value, but it has nothing to do with GDP. The dollar value of total transactions in the economy is enormous and many times that of GDP.

3. Intermediate goods and final goods are distinct. It should be helpful to clarify the distinction between intermediate goods and final goods with an example. Recall:

    - Intermediate goods are goods that are produced by one firm to be further processed by another firm.

    - Final goods are sold to the end user.

    GDP only includes the value of the final goods and services because the value of the intermediate goods used in the production of a final good or service is fully captured in the price of the final good or service. If we include the value of intermediate production in GDP, we would double count the intermediate goods.

    If we understand this distinction, can we list the *items* in the economy that are intermediate or final? For example, is a tire an intermediate good or a final good? The answer is: it depends on who bought it. When General Motors buys a tire from Goodyear, the tire is an intermediate good because General Motors will attach it to a car and sell it. When you buy a tire from your Goodyear dealer, it is a final good and should be counted in GDP. Thus, it is difficult to list items in the economy that are intermediate or final without knowledge of the buyer.

4. Comparisons of GDP across countries and time can be biased. We should be cautious when we compare GDP across nations of different levels of market development and when we compare GDP across long periods of time within a single nation. This is because GDP excludes most non-market activities. Clearly, a greater proportion of the output of lesser-developed nations is likely to be household production such as when someone does their own farming, cleaning, sewing, and maybe even home construction. Since these activities are not captured by a market transaction, they are not recorded in lesser-developed nations or in earlier periods of industrialized nations when market development was less extensive. This results in an even lower estimate of their GDP.

TERMS AND DEFINITIONS

Choose a definition for each key term.

Key terms:

_7_ Inflation

_13_ Unemployment

_16_ Macroeconomics

_14_ Microeconomics

_6_ Total income

_19_ Total expenditure

_5 ~~8~~_ Gross Domestic Product

_15_ Intermediate production

_18_ Final production

_8_ Gross National Product

_21_ Depreciation

_2_ Consumption

_9_ Investment

_10_ Government purchases

_3_ Net exports

_12_ Transfer payment

_17_ Real GDP

_1_ Nominal GDP

_20_ Base year

_11_ GDP deflator

_4_ Recession

NO

Definitions:

1. The production of goods and services valued at current year prices

2. Spending by households on goods and services, excluding new housing

3. Spending on domestically produced goods by foreigners (exports) minus spending on foreign goods by domestic residents (imports)

4. Period of decline in GDP.

5. Market value of all final goods and services produced within a country in a given period of time

6. Wages, rent, and profit

7. The rate at which prices are rising

8. Market value of all final goods and services produced by a nation's residents in a given period of time

9. Spending on capital equipment, inventories, and structures, including household purchases of new housing

10. Spending on goods and services by all levels of government

11. A measure of the price level calculated as the ratio of nominal GDP to real GDP, then multiplied by 100

12. Expenditures by government for which they receive no goods or services

13. Percent of the labor force that is out of work

14. The study of how households and firms make decisions and how they interact in markets

15. Goods that are produced by one firm to be further processed by another firm

16. The study of economy-wide phenomena

17. The production of goods and services valued at base year prices

18. Finished products sold to the end user

19. Consumption, investment, government purchases, and net exports

20. The year from which prices are used to measure real GDP

21. Value of worn out equipment and structures

PROBLEMS AND SHORT-ANSWER QUESTIONS

Practice Problems

1. a. Complete the following table.

	Year 1	Year 2	Year 3
Gross Domestic Product	4532	4804	
Consumption		3320	3544
Investment	589	629	673
Government Purchases	861		977
Net Exports	−45	−58	−54

   b. What is the largest expenditure component of GDP?

   _____

   c. Does investment include the purchase of stocks and bonds? Why?

   _____

   _____

   d. Do government purchases include government spending on unemployment checks? Why?

   _____

   _____

   _____

   e. What does it mean to say that net exports are negative?

   _____

   _____

2. Suppose the base year in the following table is 2000.

Year	Production of X	Price per Unit of X
2000	20 units	$5
2001	20 units	10
2002	20 units	20

   a. What is nominal GDP for 2000, 2001, and 2002?

   _____

   b. What is real GDP for 2000, 2001, and 2002?

   _____

3. Suppose the following table records the total output and prices for an entire economy. Further, suppose the base year in the following table is 2000.

Year	Price of Soda	Quantity of Soda	Price of Jeans	Quantity of Jeans
2000	$1.00	200	$10.00	50
2001	1.00	220	11.00	50

a. What is the value of nominal GDP in 2000?

_____

b. What is the value of real GDP in 2000?

_____

c. What is the value of nominal GDP in 2001?

_____

d. What is the value of real GDP in 2001?

_____

e. What is the value of the GDP deflator in 2000?

_____

f. What is the value of the GDP deflator in 2001?

_____

g. From 2000 to 2001, prices rose approximately what percentage?

_____

h. Was the increase in nominal GDP from 2000 to 2001 mostly due to an increase in real output or due to an increase in prices?

_____

_____

4. Complete the following table.

Year	Nominal GDP	Real GDP	GDP deflator
1		$100	100
2	$120		120
3	150	125	

a. What year is the base year? How can you tell?

_____

_____

b. From year 1 to year 2, did real output rise or did prices rise? Explain?

_____

_____

c. From year 2 to year 3, did real output rise or did prices rise? Explain?

_____

_____

Short-Answer Questions

1. Why does income = expenditure = GDP?

_____

_____

_____

2. Define GDP and explain the important terms in the definition.

_____

_____

_____

_____

_____

_____

3. What are the components of expenditure? Provide an example of each.

_____

_____

_____

4. Provide an example of a transfer payment. Do we include it in GDP? Why?

_____

_____

5. If nominal GDP in 2002 exceeds nominal GDP in 2001, did real output rise? Did prices rise?

_____

_____

6. If real GDP in 2002 exceeds real GDP in 2001, did real output rise? Did prices rise?

_____

_____

7. If you buy a $20,000 Toyota that was produced entirely in Japan, does this affect U.S. GDP? Show how this transaction would affect the appropriate expenditure categories that make up GDP.

_____

_____

_____

8. Explain the difference between GDP and GNP. If the residents of the United States generate as much production in the rest of the world as the rest of the world produces in the United States, what should be true about U.S. GDP and GNP?

_____

_____

_____

9. Which contributes more when measuring GDP, a new diamond necklace purchased by a wealthy person or a soda purchased by a thirsty person? Why?

_____

_____

_____

10. If your neighbor hires you to mow her lawn instead of doing it herself, what will happen to GDP? Why? Did output change?

_____

_____

SELF-TEST

True/False Questions

_T_ 1. For an economy as a whole, income equals expenditure because the income of the seller must be equal to the expenditure of the buyer.

_F_ 2. The production of an apple contributes more to GDP than the production of a gold ring because food is necessary for life itself.

_F_ 3. If the lumberyard sells $1,000 of lumber to a carpenter and the carpenter uses the lumber to build a garage which he sells for $5,000, the contribution to GDP is $6,000.

_T_ 4. A country with a larger GDP per person generally has a greater standard of living or quality of life than a country with a smaller GDP per person.

_F_ 5. If nominal GDP in 2003 exceeds nominal GDP in 2002, real output must have risen. _prices or_

_T_ 6. If U.S. GDP exceeds U.S. GNP, then foreigners produce more in the United States than U.S. citizens produce in the rest of the world.

_F_ 7. Wages are an example of a transfer payment because there is a transfer of payment from the firm to the worker.

_F_ 8. In the United States, investment is the largest component of GDP.

_T_ 9. Nominal GDP employs current prices to value output while real GDP employs constant base-year prices to value output.

_F_ 10. A new car produced in 2002, but first sold in 2003, should be counted in 2003 GDP because that is when it was first sold as a final good.

_F_ 11. When the city of Chicago purchases a new school building, the investment component of GDP increases. _gov't spending_

_T_ 12. A recession occurs when real GDP declines.

_T_ 13. Depreciation is the value of the wear and tear on the economy's equipment and structures.

_T_ 14. Cigarettes should be valued in GDP at $3.50 per pack even though $1.00 of that price is tax because the buyers paid $3.50 per pack.

_F_ 15. Net National Product always exceeds a nation's total income because of depreciation and taxes.

Multiple-Choice Questions

1. An example of a transfer payment is
   a. wages.
   b. profit.
   c. rent.
   d. government purchases.
   e. unemployment benefits.

2. The value of plant and equipment worn out in the process of manufacturing goods and services is measured by
   a. consumption.
   b. depreciation.
   c. Net National Product.
   d. investment.
   e. intermediate production.

3. Which of the following would be excluded from 1989 GDP? The sale of
   a. a 1989 Honda made in Tennessee.
   b. a haircut.
   c. a realtor's services.
   d. a home built in 1988 and first sold in 1989.
   e. All of the above should be counted in 1989 GDP.

4. Gross Domestic Product can be measured as the sum of
   a. consumption, investment, government purchases, and net exports.
   b. consumption, transfer payments, wages, and profits.
   c. investment, wages, profits, and intermediate production.
   d. final goods and services, intermediate goods, transfer payments, and rent.
   e. Net National Product, Gross National Product, and Disposable personal income.

5. U.S. Gross Domestic Product (in contrast to Gross National Product) measures the production and income of
   a. Americans and their factories no matter where they are located in the world.
   b. people and factories located within the borders of the United States.
   c. the domestic service sector only.
   d. the domestic manufacturing sector only.
   e. none of the above.

6. Gross Domestic Product is the sum of the market value of the
   a. intermediate goods.
   b. manufactured goods.
   c. normal goods and services.
   d. inferior goods and services.
   e. final goods and services.

7. If nominal GDP in 2002 exceeds nominal GDP in 2001, then the production of output must have
   a. risen.
   b. fallen.
   c. stayed the same.
   d. risen or fallen because there is not enough information to determine what happened to real output.

8. If a cobbler buys leather for $100 and thread for $50 and uses them to produce and sell $500 worth of shoes to consumers, the contribution to GDP is
   a. $50.
   b. $100.
   c. $500.
   d. $600.
   e. $650.

9. GDP would include which of the following?
   a. housework
   b. illegal drug sales
   c. intermediate sales
   d. consulting services
   e. the value of taking a day off from work

10. Real GDP is measured in _____ prices while nominal GDP is measured in _____ prices.
    a. current year; base year
    b. base year; current year
    c. intermediate; final
    d. domestic; foreign
    e. foreign; domestic

The following table contains information about an economy that produces only pens and books. The base year is 1999. Use this information for questions 11 through 16.

Year	Price of Pens	Quantity of Pens	Price of Books	Quantity of Books
1999	$3	100	$10	50
2000	3	120	12	70
2001	4	120	14	70

11. What is the value of nominal GDP for 2000?
    a. $800
    b. $1,060
    c. $1,200
    d. $1,460
    e. none of the above

12. What is the value of real GDP for 2000?
    3·120 + 10·70 = 1060
    a. $800
    b. $1,060
    c. $1,200
    d. $1,460
    e. none of the above

13. What is the value of the GDP deflator in 2000?
    a. 100
    b. 113
    c. 116
    d. 119
    e. 138

14. What is the percentage increase in prices from 1999 to 2000?
    a. 0 percent
    b. 13 percent
    c. 16 percent
    d. 22 percent
    e. 38 percent

15. What is the approximate percentage increase in prices from 2000 to 2001?
    a. 0 percent
    b. 13 percent
    c. 16 percent
    d. 22 percent
    e. 38 percent

16. What is the percentage increase in real GDP from 2000 to 2001?
    a. 0 percent
    b. 7 percent
    c. 22 percent
    d. 27 percent
    e. 32 percent

17. If U.S. GDP exceeds U.S. GNP, then
    a. foreigners are producing more in the United States than Americans are producing in foreign countries.
    b. Americans are producing more in foreign countries than foreigners are producing in the United States.
    c. real GDP exceeds nominal GDP.
    d. real GNP exceeds nominal GNP.
    e. intermediate production exceeds final production.

18. U.S. GDP would exclude which of the following?
    a. lawyer services purchased by a home buyer
    b. lawn care services purchased by a home owner
    c. a new bridge purchased by the state of Texas
    d. cotton purchased by Lee Jeans
    e. the purchase of a new Mazda produced in Illinois

19. How is your purchase of a $40,000 BMW automobile that was produced entirely in Germany recorded in the U.S. GDP accounts?
    a. Investment increases by $40,000 and net exports increases by $40,000.
    b. Consumption increases by $40,000 and net exports decreases by $40,000.
    c. Net exports decreases by $40,000.
    d. Net exports increases by $40,000.
    e. There is no impact because this transaction does not involve domestic production.

20. If your grandparents buy a new retirement home, this transaction would affect
   a. consumption.
   b. investment.
   c. government purchases.
   d. net exports.
   e. none of the above.

ADVANCED CRITICAL THINKING

You are watching a news report with your father. The news anchor points out that a certain troubled Caribbean nation generates a GDP per capita of only $350 per year. Since your father knows that U.S. GDP per capita is approximately $35,000, he suggests that we are materially 100 times better off in the United States than in the Caribbean nation.

1. Is your father's statement accurate?

   _____

2. What general category of production is not captured by GDP in both the United States and the Caribbean nation?

   _____

   _____

3. Provide some examples of this type of activity.

   _____

   _____

4. Why would the exclusion of this type of production affect the measurement of Caribbean output more than U.S. output?

   _____

   _____

   _____

5. Does this mean that residents of the Caribbean nation are actually as well off materially as residents in the United States?

   _____

   _____

   _____

SOLUTIONS

Terms and Definitions

_7_ Inflation

_13_ Unemployment_

_16_ Macroeconomics

_14_ Microeconomics

_6_ Total income

_19_ Total expenditure

_5_ Gross Domestic Product

_15_ Intermediate production

_18_ Final production

_8_ Gross National Product

_21_ Depreciation

_2_ Consumption

_9_ Investment

_10_ Government purchases

_3_ Net exports

_12_ Transfer payment

_17_ Real GDP

_1_ Nominal GDP

_20_ Base year

_11_ GDP deflator

_4_ Recession

Practice Problems

1. a.

	Year 1	Year 2	Year 3
Gross Domestic Product	4,532	4,804	5,140
Consumption	3,127	3,320	3,544
Investment	589	629	673
Government Purchases	861	913	977
Net Exports	−45	−58	−54

b. consumption

c. No, because that transaction is a purchase of an asset, not a purchase of currently produced capital goods.

d. No, because unemployment benefits are expenditures for which the government receives no production in return.

e. It means that imports exceed exports.

2. a. $100, $200, $400
   b. $100, $100, $100

3. a. $700
   b. $700
   c. $770
   d. $720
   e. 100
   f. 107
   g. $(107 - 100)/100 = 0.07 = 7\%$

h. Percent increase in nominal = ($770 – $700)/700 = 0.10 = 10%. Percent increase in prices = 7%, therefore most of the increase was due to prices.

4.

Year	Nominal GDP	Real GDP	GDP deflator
1	$100	$100	100
2	120	100	120
3	150	125	120

a. Year 1, because the deflator = 100.
b. Prices rose 20 percent and real output stayed the same.
c. Prices stayed the same and real output rose 25 percent.

Short-Answer Questions

1. Because the income of the seller equals the expenditure of the buyer and GDP can be measured with either one.

2. Market value of all final goods and services produced within a country in a given period of time. "Market value" = price paid, "of all" = all legal production, "final" = to end users, "goods and services" = includes services, "produced" = no used items, "within a country" = inside borders, "in a given period" = per quarter or year.

3. Consumption (food), investment (factory), government purchases (military equipment), net exports (sale of a Ford to France minus purchase of a Toyota from Japan).

4. Social Security payments. No, because the government received no good or service in return.

5. We can't be certain which rose, prices or real output, because an increase in either prices or real output will cause nominal output to rise.

6. Real output rose because the value of output in each year is measured in constant base year prices. We have no information on prices.

7. No. Consumption would increase by $20,000 and net exports would decrease by $20,000. As a result, U.S. GDP is unaffected.

8. GDP is the production within the borders of the U.S. GNP is the production of Americans no matter where the production takes place. They should be equal.

9. A diamond necklace because GDP measures market value.

10. GDP will rise because the mowing of the lawn was a market transaction. However, output didn't really rise.

True/False Questions

1. T

2. F; contribution is based on market value.

3. F; the garage is the final good, valued at $5,000.

4. T

5. F; prices or real output could have risen.

6. T

7. F; transfer payments are expenditures for which no good or service is received in return.

8. F; consumption is the largest component of GDP.

9. T

10. F; goods are counted in the year produced.

11. F; the purchase is included in government purchases.

12. T

13. T

14. T

15. F; total income – depreciation = NNP.

Multiple-Choice Questions

1. e	5. b	9. d	13. b	17. a
2. b	6. e	10. b	14. b	18. d
3. d	7. d	11. c	15. d	19. b
4. a	8. c	12. b	16. a	20. b

Advanced Critical Thinking

1. No.

2. Nonmarket activities such as household production.

3. Household production done by an individual without pay such as gardening, cleaning, sewing, home improvement or construction, child supervision, etc.

4. A greater proportion of the output produced by less-developed nations is nonmarket output. That is, it is not sold and recorded as a market transaction.

5. No. It just means that quantitative comparisons between nations of greatly different levels of development are very difficult to do and are often inaccurate.

MEASURING THE COST OF LIVING

GOALS

In this chapter you will

Learn how the consumer price index (CPI) is constructed

Consider why the CPI is an imperfect measure of the cost of living

Compare the CPI and the GDP deflator as a measure of the overall price level

See how to use a price index to compare dollar amounts from different times

Learn the distinction between real and nominal interest rates

CHAPTER OVERVIEW

Context and Purpose

Chapter 11 is the second chapter of a two-chapter sequence that deals with how economists measure output and prices in the macroeconomy. Chapter 10 addressed how economists measure output. Chapter 11 develops how economists measure the overall price level in the macroeconomy.

The purpose of Chapter 11 is twofold: first, to show you how to generate a price index and, second, to teach you how to employ a price index to compare dollar figures from different points in time and to adjust interest rates for inflation. In addition, you will learn some of the shortcomings of using the consumer price index as a measure of the cost of living.

OUTCOMES

After accomplishing these goals, you should be able to

List the five steps necessary to calculate the inflation rate

Discuss three reasons why the CPI may be biased

Describe two differences between the CPI and GDP deflator

Convert a value measured in 1965 dollars to its value measured in 1990 dollars

Explain the relationship between the real interest rate, the nominal interest rate, and the inflation rate

CHAPTER REVIEW

Introduction

To compare the income of a worker in, say, 1930, to the income of a worker today, we must first convert the dollar amount of each of their incomes into a comparable measure of purchasing power because there has been inflation over this time period. This chapter explains how economists correct economic variables for the effects of inflation. Inflation is generally measured by the consumer price index (CPI).

The Consumer Price Index

The **consumer price index** is a measure of the overall cost of the goods and services bought by a typical consumer. It is calculated by the Bureau of Labor Statistics.

There are five steps to calculating a CPI:

- *Fix the basket.* Estimate the *quantities* of the products purchased by the typical consumer (i.e. the basket of goods and services).

- *Find the prices.* Locate the prices of each item in the basket for each point in time (each year for an annual CPI).

- *Compute the basket's cost.* Use the prices and quantities to calculate the cost of the basket for each year.

- *Choose a base year and compute the index.* Choose a year as the benchmark against which the other years can be compared (i.e. the base year). *(This must be the same year you surveyed consumers and fixed the quantities in the consumption basket.)* Make a ratio of the cost of the basket for each year to the cost in the base year. Multiply each ratio times 100. Each resulting number is the value of the index for that year.

- *Compute inflation.* Inflation is the percentage change in the price index from the preceding year. For example:

$$\text{Inflation rate in 2001} = \frac{(\text{CPI in year 2001} - \text{CPI in year 2000})}{\text{CPI in year 2000}} \times 100$$

The actual CPI is calculated both monthly and annually. In addition, the Bureau of Labor Statistics calculates a **producer price index** (PPI), which measures the cost of a basket of goods and services purchased by firms. Changes in the PPI usually precede changes in the CPI because firms often pass on higher costs in the form of higher consumer prices.

The major categories in the CPI basket are housing (41 percent), transportation (17 percent), food and beverages (16 percent), education and communication (6 percent), medical care (6 percent), recreation (6 percent), apparel (4 percent), and other goods and services (4 percent).

The *cost of living* is the amount by which incomes must rise in order to maintain a constant standard of living. There are three problems with using the CPI to measure changes in the cost of living:

- *Substitution bias:* Over time, some prices rise more than others. Consumers will substitute toward goods that have become relatively less expensive. The CPI, however, is based on a fixed basket of purchases. Because the CPI fails to acknowledge the consumer's substitution of less expensive products for more expensive products, the CPI overstates the increase in the cost of living.

- *Introduction of new goods:* When new goods are introduced, a dollar has increased in value because it can buy a greater variety of products. Because the CPI is based on a fixed consumer basket, it does not reflect this increase in the purchasing power of the dollar (equivalent to a reduction in prices). Thus, again, the CPI overstates the increase in the cost of living.

- *Unmeasured quality change:* If the quality of a good rises from year to year, as with tires and computers, then the value of a dollar is rising even if actual prices are constant. This is equivalent to a reduction in prices. To the degree that an increase in quality is not accounted for by the Bureau of Labor Statistics, the CPI overstates the increase in the cost of living. The opposite is true for a deterioration of quality.

Economists believe that these three factors have caused the CPI to overestimate inflation by about one percent each year. This small overestimation of inflation may cause overpayment of Social Security benefits because Social Security benefits are tied to the CPI. Recent technical changes to the CPI may have reduced the upward bias in the CPI by about half.

Recall that the GDP deflator is the ratio of nominal GDP (current output valued at current prices) to real GDP (current output valued at base year prices). Thus, the GDP deflator is a price index, too. It differs from the CPI in two ways:

- First, the basket of goods is different. The GDP deflator utilizes the prices of all goods and services produced domestically. The CPI utilizes the prices of goods and services *bought by consumers* only, regardless of where the goods were produced. Therefore, a change in the price of foreign oil which raises the price of gasoline is captured by the CPI but not by the GDP deflator, while a change in the price of a domestically produced nuclear missile is captured by the GDP deflator but not by the CPI.

- Second, the GDP deflator utilizes the quantities of goods and services in *current* output, so the "basket" changes each year. The CPI utilizes the quantities in a *fixed* basket, so the basket changes only when the Bureau of Labor Statistics chooses. Although the CPI and GDP deflator should track each other very closely, the CPI may tend to rise slightly faster due to its inherent substitution bias and the bias associated with the introduction of new goods.

Correcting Economic Variables for the Effects of Inflation

Economists use the CPI to correct *income* and *interest rates* for the effects of inflation.

We correct income for inflation so that we can compare income from different years. The general formula for comparing dollar values from different years is:

Value in year X dollars = Value in year Y dollars × (CPI in year X/CPI in year Y)

In words, to make the above conversion, multiply the dollar value you wish to adjust by the ratio of the ending price level to the starting price level. Your value will now be measured in dollars consistent with the ending price level.

For example, suppose your aunt earned $17,000 in 1969 and earned $55,000 in 1994. Over those 25 years, has her standard of living increased?

CPI in 1969 = 36.7

CPI in 1994 = 148.2

$17,000 × (148.2/36.7) = $68,649 > $55,000

A $17,000 salary in 1969 would buy as much as a $68,649 salary in 1994. Since your aunt only earned $55,000 in 1994, her real income fell and her standard of living actually decreased.

When a dollar amount, for example a Social Security payment, is automatically adjusted for inflation, we say that it has been **indexed** for inflation. A contract with this provision is said to contain a *COLA* or cost-of-living-allowance.

We also correct interest rates for inflation. A correction is necessary because, if prices have risen during the term of a loan, the dollars used for repayment will not buy as much as the dollars originally borrowed.

The **nominal interest rate** is the interest rate uncorrected for the effects of inflation. The **real interest rate** is the interest rate corrected for the effects of inflation. The formula for correcting the nominal interest rate for inflation is:

$$\text{real interest rate} = \text{nominal interest rate} - \text{inflation rate}$$

For example, if the bank paid you a nominal interest rate of 4 percent on your account, and the inflation rate were 3 percent, the real interest rate on your account would be only 1 percent: $4\% - 3\% = 1\%$.

HELPFUL HINTS

1. The year we choose to determine the typical consumption basket must also be chosen as the base year. When we construct the CPI, we choose a year to survey consumers and *fix the basket*. The year we choose to fix the basket must also be chosen as the base year. That is, we also use that year as the benchmark year against which other years are to be compared.

2. Your particular consumption basket may not be typical. Since the GDP deflator and the CPI are based on different baskets of goods and services, each will provide a slightly different measurement of the cost of living. Continuing in this same line of thinking, your particular consumption basket may differ from the typical consumption basket used by the Bureau of Labor Statistics when they calculate the CPI. For example, when you are a young adult, your basket may be more heavily weighted toward electronics and clothing. If clothing prices are rising faster than average, young people may have a greater increase in the cost of living than is suggested by the CPI. In like manner, when you become old, your consumption basket may be more heavily weighted toward medicine and travel. Exceptional increases in these prices may cause the cost of living for the elderly to rise more quickly than suggested by the CPI.

3. Dollar values can be adjusted backward in time as well as forward. In the earlier section, there is a numerical example that converts $17,000 of income in 1969 into the amount of income that would be necessary in 1994 to generate the same purchasing power. We discovered that it would take $68,649 for your aunt to have the same standard of living in 1994 as she had in 1969. Because she only made $55,000 in 1994, we argued that her standard of living actually fell over the 25 year period.

    Alternatively, we can convert her 1994 salary of $55,000 into its equivalent purchasing power measured in 1969 dollars and compare the resulting figure with her $17,000 income in 1969. We arrive at the same conclusion— she was better off in 1969.

$$\$55,000 \times (36.7 / 148.2) = \$13,630 < \$17,000$$

Her $55,000 income in 1994 is equivalent to (or generates the same standard of living as) a $13,620 income in 1969. Since she actually made $17,000 in 1969, she had a higher standard of living in 1969.

4. When correcting interest rates for inflation, think like a lender. If you loan someone $100 for one year, and you charge them 7 percent interest, you will receive $107 at the end of the year. Did you receive 7 additional dollars of purchasing power? Suppose inflation was 4 percent. You would need to receive $104 at the end of the year just to break even. That is, you would need $104 just to be able to buy the same set of goods and services that you could have purchased for $100 at the time you granted the loan. In this sense, you received only 3 additional dollars of purchasing power for having made the $100 loan, or a 3 percent real return. Thus, the *real interest rate* on the loan is 3 percent. Using your formula:

$$7\% - 4\% = 3\%$$

Although not explicitly stated, the interest rate example in your text is also approached from the lender's perspective. That is, when you deposit money in a bank and receive interest, the deposit is actually a loan from you to the bank.

TERMS AND DEFINITIONS

Choose a definition for each key term.

Key terms:

___3___ Consumer price index

___6___ Inflation rate

___13___ GDP deflator

___4___ Basket (of goods and services)

___15___ Base year

___16___ Bureau of Labor Statistics

___5___ Producer price index

___1___ Cost of living

___10___ Standard of living

___9___ Substitution bias

___12___ Nominal GDP

___11___ Real GDP

___2___ Indexed contract

___8___ Cost-of-living-allowance (COLA)

___14___ Nominal interest rate

___7___ Real interest rate

Definitions:

1. The income necessary to maintain a constant standard of living

2. A contract that requires that a dollar amount be automatically corrected for inflation

3. The ratio of the value of the fixed basket purchased by the typical consumer to the basket's value in the base year, multiplied by 100

4. The quantities of each item purchased by the typical consumer

5. The ratio of the value of a fixed basket of goods and services purchased by firms to the basket's value in the base year, multiplied by 100

6. The percent change in a price index

7. The interest rate corrected for the effects of inflation

8. An automatic increase in income in order to maintain a constant standard of living

9. The inability of the CPI to account for consumers' substitution toward relatively cheaper goods and services

10. Material well-being

11. Output valued at base year prices

12. Output valued at current prices

13. The ratio of nominal GDP to real GDP, multiplied by 100

14. The interest rate uncorrected for the effects of inflation

15. The benchmark year against which other years are compared

16. The government agency responsible for tracking prices

PROBLEMS AND SHORT-ANSWER QUESTIONS

Practice Problems

1. The following table shows the prices and the quantities consumed in the country known as the University States. Suppose the base year is 1999. *This is the year the typical consumption basket was determined so the quantities consumed during 1999 are the only quantities needed to calculate the CPI in every year.*

Year	Price of Books	Quantity of Books	Price of Pencils	Quantity of Pencils	Price of Pens	Quantity of Pens
1999	$50	10	$1	100	$ 5	100
2000	50	12	1	200	10	50
2001	60	12	1.50	250	20	20

a. What is the value of the CPI in 1999?

_____

b. What is the value of the CPI in 2000?

_____

c. What is the value of the CPI in 2001?

_____

d. What is the inflation rate in 2000?

_____

e. What is the inflation rate in 2001?

_____

f. What type of bias do you observe in the CPI and corresponding inflation rates you generated above? Explain.

_____

_____

g. If you had a COLA clause in your wage contract based on the CPI calculated above, would your standard of living likely increase, decrease, or stay the same over the years 1999–2001? Why?

_____

_____

h. Again, suppose you had a COLA clause in your wage contract based on the CPI calculated above. If you personally only consume pens (no paper or pencils), would your standard of living likely increase, decrease, or stay the same over the years 1999–2001? Why?

_____

_____

_____

2. The following table contains the CPI and the Federal Minimum Hourly Wage Rates for the period 1965 through 2000.

Year	CPI	Minimum Wage
1965	31.5	$1.25
1966	32.4	1.25
1967	33.4	1.40
1968	34.8	1.60
1969	36.7	1.60
1970	38.8	1.60
1971	40.5	1.60
1972	41.8	1.60
1973	44.4	1.60
1974	49.3	2.00
1975	53.8	2.10
1976	56.9	2.30
1977	60.6	2.30
1978	65.2	2.65
1979	72.6	2.90
1980	82.4	3.10
1981	90.9	3.35
1982	96.5	3.35
1983	99.6	3.35
1984	103.9	3.35
1985	107.6	3.35
1986	109.6	3.35
1987	113.6	3.35
1988	118.3	3.35
1989	124.0	3.35
1990	130.7	3.80
1991	136.2	4.25
1992	140.3	4.25
1993	144.5	4.25
1994	148.2	4.25
1995	152.4	4.25
1996	156.9	4.75
1997	160.5	5.15
1998	163.0	5.15
1999	166.6	5.15
2000	172.2	5.15

a. Inflate the 1965 minimum wage to its equivalent value measured in 1990 prices.

_____

_____

b. What happened to the standard of living of minimum-wage workers over this 25 year period?

_____

_____

c. Deflate the 1990 minimum wage to its equivalent value measured in 1965 prices.

_____

_____

d. Do these two methods give you consistent results with regard to the standard of living of minimum-wage workers over time?

_____

_____

e. The minimum wage did not change over the eight year period from 1981 to 1989. By what percentage did the purchasing power of the minimum wage decline over this period? (Hint: inflate the value of the minimum wage in 1981 to its equivalent in 1989. Then generate the percent change).

_____

_____

f. What happened to the standard of living of minimum-wage workers over the period from 1990 to 2000? (Inflate the 1990 minimum wage and compare it to the 2000 minimum wage.)

_____

_____

3. Suppose that you lend your roommate $100 for one year at 9 percent nominal interest.
   a. How many dollars of interest will your roommate pay you at the end of the year?

_____

_____

   b. Suppose at the time you both agreed to the terms of the loan, you both expected the inflation rate to be 5 percent during the year of the loan. What do you both expect the real interest rate to be on the loan?

_____

_____

c. Suppose at the end of the year, you are surprised to discover that the actual inflation rate over the year was 8 percent. What was the actual real interest rate generated by this loan?

_____

d. In the case described above, actual inflation turned out to be higher than expected. Which of the two of you had the unexpected gain or loss? Your roommate (the borrower), or you (the lender)? Why?

_____

_____

e. What would the real interest rate on the loan have been if the actual inflation rate had turned out to be a whopping 11 percent?

_____

_____

f. Explain what it means to have a negative real interest rate.

_____

_____

_____

_____

Short-Answer Questions

1. What does the consumer price index attempt to measure?

_____

2. What are the steps that one must go through in order to construct a consumer price index?

_____

_____

_____

3. Which would have a greater impact on the CPI: a 20 percent increase in the price of Rolex watches or a 20 percent increase in the price of new cars? Why?

_____

_____

4. Suppose there is an increase in the price of imported BMW automobiles (which are produced in Germany). Would this have a larger impact on the CPI or the GDP deflator? Why?

_____

_____

_____

5. If the Bureau of Labor Statistics failed to recognize the increase in memory, power, and speed of newer model computers, in which direction would the CPI be biased? What do we call this type of bias?

_____

_____

6. From 1978 to 1979, the minimum wage increased 25 cents. Did minimum-wage workers see an increase in their standard of living? (Use the data from question 2 in the Practice Problems above.)

_____

_____

7. What does the real interest rate measure?

_____

_____

8. Suppose you lend money to your sister at a nominal interest rate of 10 percent because you both expect the inflation rate to be 6 percent. Further, suppose that after the loan has been repaid, you discover that the actual inflation rate over the life of the loan was only 2 percent. Who gained at the other's expense: you or your sister? Why?

_____

_____

_____

9. Paying close attention to question 8, make a general statement with regard to who gains or loses (the borrower or the lender) on a loan contract when inflation turns out to be either higher or lower than expected.

_____

_____

_____

10. If workers and firms negotiate a wage increase based on their expectation of inflation, who gains or loses (the workers or the firms) if actual inflation turns out to be higher than expected? Why?

_____

_____

SELF-TEST

True/False Questions

F 1. An increase in the price of imported cameras is captured by the CPI but not by the GDP deflator.

F 2. An increase in the price of helicopters purchased by the U.S. military is captured by the CPI.

F 3. Because an increase in gasoline prices causes consumers to ride their bikes more and drive their cars less, the CPI tends to underestimate the cost of living.

F 4. An increase in the price of diamonds will have a greater impact on the CPI than an equal percentage increase in the price of food because diamonds are so much more expensive.

T 5. The "base year" in a price index is the benchmark year against which other years are compared.

F 6. If the CPI rises at 5 percent per year, then every individual in the country needs exactly a 5 percent increase in their income for their standard of living to remain constant. *CPI tends to overstate the effects of inflation.*

F 7. The producer price index (PPI) is constructed to measure the change in price of total production.

T 8. If the Bureau of Labor Statistics fails to recognize that recently produced automobiles can be driven for many more miles than older models, then the CPI tends to overestimate the cost of living.

T 9. If your wage rises from $5.00 to $6.25 while the CPI rises from 112 to 121, you should feel an increase in your standard of living.   *5 · 121/112*

F 10. The largest category of goods and services in the CPI is medical care.

F 11. It is impossible for real interest rates to be negative.

T 12. If the nominal interest rate is 12 percent and the rate of inflation is 7 percent, then the real rate of interest is 5 percent.

_T_ 13. If lenders demand a real rate of return of 4 percent and they expect inflation to be 5 percent, then they should charge 9 percent interest when they extend loans.

_F_ 14. If borrowers and lenders agree on a nominal interest rate and inflation turns out to be greater than they had anticipated, lenders will gain at the expense of borrowers.

_T_ 15. If workers and firms agree on an increase in wages based on their expectations of inflation and inflation turns out to be less than they expected, workers will gain at the expense of firms.

Multiple-Choice Questions

1. Inflation can be measured by all of the following except the
   a. GDP deflator.
   b. consumer price index.
   c. producer price index.
   d. finished goods price index.
   e. All of the above are used to measure inflation.

2. The CPI will be most influenced by a 10 percent increase in the price of which of the following consumption categories?
   a. housing
   b. transportation
   c. medical care
   d. food and beverages
   e. All of the above would produce the same impact.

3. In 1989, the CPI was 124.0. In 1990, it was 130.7. What was the rate of inflation over this period?
   a. 5.1 percent
   b. 5.4 percent
   c. 6.7 percent
   d. 30.7 percent
   e. You can't tell without knowing the base year.

4. Which of the following would likely cause the CPI to rise more than the GDP deflator?
   a. an increase in the price of Fords
   b. an increase in the price of tanks purchased by the military
   c. an increase in the price of domestically produced fighter planes sold exclusively to Israel
   d. an increase in the price of Hondas produced in Japan and sold in the United States
   e. an increase in the price of John Deere tractors

5. The "basket" on which the CPI is based is composed of
   a. raw materials purchased by firms.
   b. total current production.
   c. products purchased by the typical consumer.
   d. consumer production.
   e. none of the above.

6. If there is an increase in the price of apples which causes consumers to purchase fewer pounds of apples and more pounds of oranges, the CPI will suffer from
   a. substitution bias.
   b. bias due to the introduction of new goods.
   c. bias due to unmeasured quality change.
   d. base year bias.
   e. none of the above.

Use the following table for questions 7 through 12. The table shows the prices and the quantities consumed in Carnivore Country. The base year is 2000. *This means that 2000 is the year the typical consumption basket was determined so the quantities consumed in 2000 are the only quantities needed to calculate the CPI in each year.*

Year	Price of Beef	Quantity of Beef	Price of Pork	Quantity of Pork
2000	$2.00	100	$1.00	100
2001	2.50	90	0.90	120
2002	2.75	105	1.00	130

7. What is the value of the basket in the base year?
   a. $300
   b. $333
   c. $418.75
   d. $459.25
   e. none of the above

8. What are the values of the CPI in 2000, 2001, and 2002, respectively?
   a. 100, 111, 139.6
   b. 100, 109.2, 116
   c. 100, 113.3, 125
   d. 83.5, 94.2, 100
   e. none of the above

9. What is the inflation rate for 2001?
   a. 0 percent
   b. 9.2 percent
   c. 11 percent
   d. 13.3 percent
   e. none of the above

10. What is the inflation rate for 2002?
    a. 0 percent
    b. 10.3 percent
    c. 11 percent
    d. 13.3 percent
    e. none of the above

11. The table shows that the 2001 inflation rate is biased upward because of
    a. bias due to the introduction of new goods.
    b. bias due to unmeasured quality change.
    c. substitution bias.
    d. base year bias.
    e. none of the above.

12. Suppose the base year is changed in the table from 2000 to 2002 (now use the 2002 consumption basket). What is the new value of the CPI in 2001?
    a. 90.6
    b. 100.0
    c. 114.7
    d. 134.3
    e. none of the above

13. Suppose your income rises from $19,000 to $31,000 while the CPI rises from 122 to 169. Your standard of living has likely
    a. fallen.
    b. risen.
    c. stayed the same.
    d. You can't tell without knowing the base year.

14. If the nominal interest rate is 7 percent and the inflation rate is 3 percent, then the real interest rate is
    a. –4 percent.
    b. 3 percent.
    c. 4 percent.
    d. 10 percent.
    e. 21 percent.

15. Which of the following statements is correct?
    a. The real interest rate is the sum of the nominal interest rate and the inflation rate.
    b. The real interest rate is the nominal interest rate minus the inflation rate.
    c. The nominal interest rate is the inflation rate minus the real interest rate.
    d. The nominal interest rate is the real interest rate minus the inflation rate.
    e. none of the above

16. If inflation is 8 percent and the real interest rate is 3 percent, then the nominal interest rate should be
    a. 3/8 percent.
    b. 5 percent.
    c. 11 percent.
    d. 24 percent.
    e. –5 percent.

17. Under which of the following conditions would you prefer to be the lender?
    a. The nominal rate of interest is 20 percent and the inflation rate is 25 percent.
    b. The nominal rate of interest is 15 percent and the inflation rate is 14 percent.
    c. The nominal rate of interest is 12 percent and the inflation rate is 9 percent.
    d. The nominal rate of interest is 5 percent and the inflation rate is 1 percent.

18. Under which of the following conditions would you prefer to be the borrower?
    a. The nominal rate of interest is 20 percent and the inflation rate is 25 percent.
    b. The nominal rate of interest is 15 percent and the inflation rate is 14 percent.
    c. The nominal rate of interest is 12 percent and the inflation rate is 9 percent.
    d. The nominal rate of interest is 5 percent and the inflation rate is 1 percent.

19. If borrowers and lenders agree on a nominal interest rate and inflation turns out to be less than they had expected,
    a. borrowers will gain at the expense of lenders.
    b. lenders will gain at the expense of borrowers.
    c. neither borrowers nor lenders will gain because the nominal interest rate has been fixed by contract.
    d. none of the above

20. If workers and firms agree on an increase in wages based on their expectations of inflation and inflation turns out to be more than they expected,
    a. firms will gain at the expense of workers.
    b. workers will gain at the expense of firms.
    c. neither workers nor firms will gain because the increase in wages is fixed in the labor agreement.
    d. none of the above

ADVANCED CRITICAL THINKING

Your father quit smoking cigarettes in 1995. When you ask him why he quit, you get a surprising answer. Instead of reciting the health benefits of quitting smoking, he says, "I quit because it was just getting too expensive. I started smoking in 1965 in Vietnam and cigarettes were only 45 cents a pack. The last pack I bought was $2.00 and I just couldn't justify spending more than four times as much on cigarettes as I used to."

1. In 1965, the CPI was 31.5. In 1995 the CPI was 152.4. While it is commendable that your father quit smoking, what is wrong with his explanation?

_____

_____

2. What is the equivalent cost of a 1965 pack of cigarettes measured in 1995 prices?

_____

_____

3. What is the equivalent cost of a 1995 pack of cigarettes measured in 1965 prices?

    _____

    _____

4. Do both methods give you the same conclusion?

    _____

    _____

5. The preceding example demonstrates what economists refer to as "money illusion." Why do you think economists might choose the phrase "money illusion" to describe this behavior?

    _____

    _____

    _____

SOLUTIONS

Terms and Definitions

_3_ Consumer price index

_6_ Inflation rate

_13_ GDP deflator

_4_ Basket (of goods and services)

_15_ Base year

_16_ Bureau of Labor Statistics

_5_ Producer price index

_1_ Cost of living

_10_ Standard of living

_9_ Substitution bias

_12_ Nominal GDP

_11_ Real GDP

_2_ Indexed contract

_8_ Cost-of-living-adjustment (COLA)

_14_ Nominal interest rate

_7_ Real interest rate

Practice Problems

1. a. ($1,100/$1,100) × 100 = 100
    b. ($1,600/$1,100) × 100 = 145.5
    c. ($2,750/$1,100) × 100 = 250
    d. [(145.5 − 100)/100] × 100 = 45.5 percent
    e. [(250 − 145.5)/145.5] × 100 = 71.8 percent
    f. Substitution bias, because as the price of pens increased, the quantity consumed declined significantly.
    g. Increase, because this CPI overstates the increase in the cost of living.
    h. Decrease, because the price of pens has increased a greater percentage than the CPI.

2. a. $1.25 × (130.7/31.5) = $5.19
    b. It went down because $5.19 > $3.80
    c. $3.80 × (31.5/130.7) = $0.92
    d. Yes, because $0.92 < $1.25. Minimum-wage workers were better off in 1965.
    e. $3.35 × (124.0/90.9) = $4.57

Further, ($3.35-$4.57)/$4.57 = –27%

Alternatively, you can deflate the minimum wage from 1989 to 1981 and get the same result.

   f. $3.80 × (172.2/130.7) = $5.01 < $5.15, so the standard of living of a worker earning the minimum wage improved slightly during the 1990s.

3. a. $9

   b. 9 percent – 5 percent = 4 percent

   c. 9 percent – 8 percent = 1 percent

   d. Your roommate (the borrower) gained; you lost because the borrower repaid the loan with dollars of surprisingly little value.

   e. 9% – 11% = –2%

   f. Because of inflation, the interest payment is not large enough to allow the lender to break even (maintain constant purchasing power compared to the day the loan was made).

Short-Answer Questions

1. The overall cost of the goods and services purchased by the typical consumer.

2. Fix the basket, find the prices, compute the basket's cost, choose a base year and compute the index.

3. New cars, because there are a greater number of new cars in the typical consumption basket.

4. The CPI, because BMWs are in the typical consumption basket, but BMWs are not included in U.S. GDP.

5. Upward, unmeasured quality change.

6. No, $2.65 × (72.6/65.2) = $2.95 which is greater than $2.90.

7. The interest rate adjusted for the effects of inflation.

8. Expected real interest rate = 4 percent. Actual real interest rate = 8 percent. You gained and your sister lost.

9. When inflation is higher than expected, borrowers gain. When inflation is lower than expected, lenders gain.

10. Firms gain, workers lose, because wages didn't rise as much as the cost of living.

True/False Questions

1. T

2. F; military helicopters are not consumer goods.

3. F; the CPI tends to overstate the cost of living because people substitute toward cheaper goods.

4. F; prices in the CPI are weighted according to how much consumers buy of each and food is a larger portion of the consumption basket.

5. T

6. F; the CPI tends to overstate the effects of inflation.

7. F; the PPI measures the price of raw materials.

8. T

9. T

10. F; the largest category is housing.

11. F; if inflation exceeds the nominal interest rate, the real interest rate is negative.

12. T

13. T

14. F; borrowers will gain at the expense of lenders.

15. T

Multiple-Choice Questions

1. d	5. c	9. d	13. b	17. d
2. a	6. a	10. b	14. c	18. a
3. b	7. a	11. c	15. b	19. b
4. d	8. c	12. a	16. c	20. a

Advanced Critical Thinking

1. He is only looking at the cost of cigarettes uncorrected for inflation. It is likely that the real cost has not risen as much as first appears or maybe even gone down.

2. $\$0.45 \times (152.4/31.5) = \$2.18 > \$2.00$

3. $\$2.00 \times (31.5/152.4) = \$0.41 < \$0.45$

4. Yes, each method suggests that, after correcting for inflation, cigarettes were actually more expensive in 1965.

5. When people base decisions on values uncorrected for inflation, there may be an illusion that the cost of living has risen.

PRODUCTION AND GROWTH

GOALS

⌈In this chapter you will

See how much economic growth differs around the world

Consider why productivity is the key determinant of a country's standard of living

Analyze the factors that determine a country's productivity

Examine how a country's policies influence its productivity growth

OUTCOMES

⌈After accomplishing these goals, you should be able to

List the countries with the highest GDP per person and the countries whose GDP per person is growing the fastest

Explain why production limits consumption in the long run

List and explain the factors of production

Explain seven areas of policy action that may influence a country's productivity and growth

CHAPTER OVERVIEW

Context and Purpose

Chapter 12 is the first chapter in a four-chapter sequence on the production of output in the long run. Chapter 12 addresses the determinants of the level and growth rate of output. We find that capital and labor are among the primary determinants of output. In Chapter 13, we address how saving and investment in capital goods affect the production of output, and in Chapter 14, we learn about some of the tools people and firms use when choosing capital projects in which to invest. In Chapter 15, we address the market for labor.

The purpose of Chapter 12 is to examine the long-run determinants of both the level and the growth rate of real GDP per person. Along the way, we will discover the factors that determine the productivity of workers and address what governments might do to improve the productivity of their citizens.

CHAPTER REVIEW

Introduction

There is great variation in the standard of living across countries at a point in time and within a country across time—for example, between the United States and

India today, and between the United States of today and the United States of 100 years ago. Growth rates also vary from country to country with East Asia growing quickly and Africa growing slowly. This chapter examines the long-run determinants of both the *level* and the *growth rate* of real GDP per person.

Economic Growth around the World

There is great variation across countries in both the *level* of real GDP per person and the *growth rate* of real GDP per person.

- At present, the *level* of real GDP per person in the United States is about 14 times that of India and 9 times that of China.

- However, since the *growth rate* of real GDP per person also varies across countries, the ranking of countries by real GDP per person changes over time. For example, over the past 100 years, the ranking of Japan and Brazil has risen relative to others because they have had an above average growth rate while the ranking of the United Kingdom has fallen due to its below average growth rate.

Due to economic growth, the average American today enjoys conveniences, such as television, air conditioning, cars, telephones, and medicines, that the richest American didn't have 150 years ago. Since out measures of inflation and output fail to fully capture the introduction of new goods, we overestimate inflation and underestimate economic growth.

Productivity: Its Role and Determinants

A country's standard of living depends directly on the productivity of its citizens because an economy's income is equal to an economy's output. **Productivity** refers to the quantity of goods and services that a worker can produce per hour. The productivity of a worker is determined by the available physical capital, human capital, natural resources, and technological knowledge. These inputs or *factors of production* are explained below:

- **Physical capital** (or just capital): the stock of equipment and structures that are used to produce goods and services. Note that these tools and machines are themselves the output from prior human production.

- **Human capital:** the knowledge and skills that workers acquire through education, training, and experience. Note that human capital, like physical capital, is a human-made or produced factor of production.

- **Natural resources:** inputs provided by nature's bounty, such as land, rivers, and mineral deposits. Natural resources come in two forms: renewable and non-renewable.

- **Technological knowledge:** the understanding about the best ways to produce goods and services. Examples of advances in technology are the discovery and application of herbicides and pesticides in agriculture and of the assembly line in manufacturing.

Technological knowledge differs from human capital in that technological knowledge is society's understanding of the best production methods, while human capital is the amount of understanding of these methods that has been transmitted to the labor force.

A *production function* establishes the relationship between the quantity of inputs used in production and the quantity of output from production. If a production function has *constant returns to scale,* then doubling all of the inputs doubles output.

In summary, output per worker depends on physical capital per worker, human capital per worker, natural resources per worker, and the state of technology.

The only factor of production that is not a produced factor is natural resources. Since there is a fixed supply of nonrenewable natural resources, many people have argued that there is a limit to how much the world's economies can grow. So far, however, technological advances have found ways around these limits. Evidence of stable or falling prices of natural resources suggests that we are continuing to succeed at stretching our limited resources.

Economic Growth and Public Policy

Physical capital, human capital, natural resources, and technological knowledge determine productivity. Productivity determines living standards. If a government wishes to raise the productivity and standard of living of its citizens, it should pursue policies that:

- *encourage saving and investment.* If society consumes less and saves more, it has more resources available to invest in the production of capital. Additional capital increases productivity and living standards. This additional growth has an opportunity cost—society must give up current consumption in order to attain more growth. Investment in capital may be subject to **diminishing returns:** As the stock of capital rises, the extra output produced by an additional unit of capital declines. Thus, an additional increment of capital in a poor country increases growth more than the same increment in an already rich country. This is known as the **catch-up-effect** because it is easier for a relatively poor country to grow quickly. However, because of diminishing returns to capital, higher saving and investment in a poor country will lead to higher growth only for a period of time, with growth slowing down again as the economy accumulates a higher level of capital stock.

- *encourage investment from abroad,* by removing restrictions on the ownership of domestic capital and by providing a stable political environment. In addition to using domestic saving to invest in capital, countries can attract investment by foreigners. There are two categories of foreign investment. *Foreign direct investment* is capital investment that is owned and operated by a foreign entity. *Foreign portfolio investment* is capital investment that is financed with foreign money but is operated by domestic residents. Investment from abroad increases a country's GDP more than its GNP because the investing country earns the profits from the investment. The World Bank and the International Monetary Fund help channel foreign investment toward poor countries.

- *encourage education.* Education is investment in human capital. Education not only increases the productivity of the recipient, it may provide a positive *externality.* An externality occurs when the actions of one person affect the well-being of a bystander. An educated individual may generate ideas that become useful to others. This is an argument for public education. Poor counties may suffer from *brain drain* when their educated workers emigrate to rich counties. Children in very poor countries may work instead of going to school because the opportunity cost of going to school is too great. Paying parents for sending their children to school may both reduce child labor and increase the education of very poor children.

- *protect property rights and establish political stability. Property rights* refer to the ability of people to exercise control over their resources. For individuals to be willing to work, save and invest, and trade with others by contract, they must be confident that their production and capital will not be stolen and that their agreements will be enforced. Even a remote possibility of political instability creates uncertainty with regard to property rights because a revolutionary government might confiscate property—particularly capital.

- *encourage free trade.* Free trade is like a technological advance. It allows a country to transform the output from its production into products that another country produces more efficiently. The *infant-industry argument* suggests that developing countries should pursue *inward-oriented policies* by restricting international trade to protect fledgling domestic industry from foreign competition. Most economists disagree with the infant industry argument and promote *outward-oriented policies* that reduce or eliminate trade barriers.

- *encourage research and development.* Most of the increase in the standard of living is due to an increase in technological knowledge that comes from research and development. After a time, knowledge is a *public good* in that we all can use it at the same time without diminishing another's benefits. Research and development might be encouraged with grants, tax breaks, and patents to establish temporary property rights to an invention. Alternatively, it might be encouraged by simply maintaining property rights and political stability.

- *address population growth.* Population growth may affect productivity in both positive and negative ways. Rapid population growth may *stretch natural resources* across more people. Thomas Malthus (1766–1834) argued that population growth will always rise to the limit imposed by the food supply, causing mankind to live forever in poverty. Any attempt to alleviate poverty will simply cause the poor to have more children, returning them to subsistence living. Malthus' predictions have not come true because he underestimated the ability of technological progress to expand the food supply. Rapid population growth *dilutes the capital stock* (both physical and human capital) by spreading it across more workers. Educated women tend to have fewer children because the opportunity cost of having children increases as opportunities grow. However, a larger population may *promote technological progress.* Throughout history, most technological progress has come from larger population centers where there are more people able to discover things and exchange ideas.

The rate of productivity growth is not steady. Productivity grew quickly during the 1950s and 60s, slowly from 1970–1995, and then quickly again from 1995 to the present. Many economists attribute the changes in productivity to changes in the growth of technology. Others argue that growth during the period 1950–1970 was unusually high and that we have just returned to normal.

HELPFUL HINTS

1. A simple example more clearly defines the factors of production. The simpler the production process, the easier it is to separate and analyze the factors of production. For example, suppose output is "holes dug in the ground." Then the production function is:

$$Y = A\,F(L,\,K,\,H,\,N)$$

where Y is the number of holes dug, A is technological knowledge, L is labor, K is physical capital, H is human capital, and N is natural resources. If we have more workers, there is an increase in L and Y would increase. If we have more shovels, there is an increase in K and Y would increase. If workers are educated so that more of them dig with the spaded end of the shovel as opposed to digging with the handle, there is an increase in H and Y would increase (note, the number of workers and the number of shovels is unchanged). If our country has softer soil so that digging is easier here, N is larger and therefore Y is larger. Finally, if we discover that it is more productive to dig after it rains rather than during a drought, there is an increase in A and Y should increase.

TERMS AND DEFINITIONS

Choose a definition for each key term.

Key terms:

_6_ Real GDP per person

_14_ Growth rate

20 _8_ Productivity

_7_ Physical capital

_15_ Factors of production

_1_ Human capital

_21_ Natural resources

_10_ Renewable resource

_16_ Nonrenewable resource

_19_ Technological Knowledge

3 _22_ Production function

_9_ Constant returns to scale

_8_ Diminishing returns

_13_ Catch-up effect

_2_ Foreign direct investment

_22_ Foreign portfolio investment

_17_ Externality

_5_ Property rights

_11_ Infant-industry argument

_18_ Inward-oriented policies

_12_ Outward-oriented policies

_4_ Public good

Definitions:

1. The knowledge and skills that workers acquire through education, training, and experience

2. Capital investment owned and operated by foreigners

3. The relationship between inputs and output from production

4. A good that we may all use at the same time without diminishing another's benefits

5. The ability of people to exercise control over their resources

6. The quantity of goods and services available for the average individual in the economy

7. The stock of equipment and structures used to produce output

8. When the incremental increase in output declines as equal increments of an input are added to production

9. A production process where doubling all of the inputs doubles the output

10. Natural resource that can be reproduced

11. Restricting international trade to protect fledgling domestic industry from foreign competition

12. Policies that decrease international trade restrictions

13. The property that poorer countries tend to grow more rapidly than richer countries

14. The annual percentage change in output

15. Inputs used in production, such as labor, capital, and natural resources

16. Natural resource that is limited in supply

17. When the actions of one person affect the well-being of a bystander

18. Policies that increase international trade restrictions

19. A society's understanding about the best ways to produce goods and services

20. The quantity of goods and services that a worker can produce per hour

21. Inputs into production provided by nature

22. Capital investment financed with foreign money but operated by domestic residents

PROBLEMS AND SHORT-ANSWER QUESTIONS

Practice Problems

1.

Country	Current real GDP/person	Current Growth Rate
Northcountry	$15,468	1.98%
Southcountry	13,690	2.03
Eastcountry	6,343	3.12
Westcountry	1,098	0.61

a. Which country is richest? How do you know?

_____

b. Which country is advancing most quickly? How do you know?

_____

_____

c. Which country would likely see the greatest benefit from an increase in capital investment? Why?

_____

_____

_____

d. Referring to (c): Would this country continue to see the same degree of benefits from an increase in capital investment forever? Why?

_____

_____

e. Referring to (d): Why might investment in human capital and research and development fail to exhibit the same degree of diminishing returns as investment in physical capital?

_____

_____

f. Which country has the potential to grow most quickly? List some reasons why it may not be living up to potential.

_____

_____

_____

_____

g. If real GDP per person in Northcountry next year is $15,918, what is its annual growth rate?

_____

_____

2. Imagine a kitchen. It contains a cook, the cook's diploma, a recipe book, a stove and utensils, and some venison harvested from the open range.
   a. Link each object in the kitchen to a general category within the factors of production.

   _____

   _____

   _____

   b. While the different factors of production exhibit different levels of durability, which one is special in that it does not wear out?

   _____

   _____

   _____

3. a. List the policies governments might pursue to increase the productivity of their citizens.

   _____

   _____

   _____

   _____

   b. Which one is, at the very least, fundamentally necessary as a background in which the other policies may operate? Why?

   _____

   _____

   _____

c. Does a growing population enhance or inhibit growth in productivity? Explain.

_____

_____

_____

_____

Short-Answer Questions

1. Economists measure both the level of real GDP per person and the growth rate of real GDP per person. What different concept does each statistic capture?

_____

_____

_____

2. Must poor countries stay relatively poor forever and must rich countries stay relatively rich forever? Why?

_____

_____

_____

3. What factors determine productivity? Which ones are human produced?

_____

_____

4. How does human capital differ from physical capital?

_____

_____

_____

5. Explain the opportunity cost of investing in capital. Is there any difference in the opportunity cost of investing in human capital versus physical capital?

_____

_____

_____

6. Why does an increase in the rate of saving and investment only increase the rate of growth temporarily?

_____

_____

7. If foreigners buy newly issued stock in General Motors, and General Motors uses the proceeds to expand capacity by building new plants and equipment, which will rise more in the future: GDP or GNP? Why? What do we call this type of investment?

_____

_____

_____

_____

8. Some economists argue for lengthening patent protection while some economists argue for shortening it. Why might patents increase productivity? Why might they decrease productivity?

_____

_____

_____

SELF-TEST

True/False Questions

___F___ 1. The United States should grow faster than Japan because the United States has a larger economy.

___F___ 2. Evidence of rising prices for natural resources demonstrates that non-renewable resources will become so scarce that economic growth will be limited.

___T___ 3. The rate of economic growth is probably underestimated.

___F___ 4. Human capital refers to human-made capital such as tools and machinery, as opposed to natural capital such as rivers and timber.

___T___ 5. If a production function exhibits constant returns to scale, then doubling all of the inputs doubles output.

___T___ 6. In very poor countries, paying parents to send their children to school may increase the education of poor children and decrease the use of child labor.

_T_ 7. An increase in capital should cause the growth rate of a relatively poor country to increase more than that of a rich country.

_F_ 8. An increase in the rate of saving and investment permanently increases a country's rate of growth.

_F_ 9. A country can only increase its level of investment by increasing its saving.

_T_ 10. The only factor of production that is not "produced" is natural resources.

_T_ 11. Investment in human capital and technology may be particularly productive because of positive spillover effects.

_T_ 12. If Germans invest in the U.S. economy by building a new Mercedes factory, in the future U.S. GDP will rise by more than U.S. GNP.

_F_ 13. Most economists believe that inward-oriented policies that protect infant industries improve the growth rates of developing nations.

_F_ 14. Economic evidence supports the predictions of Thomas Malthus regarding the effects of population growth and the food supply on the standard of living.

_T_ 15. The opportunity cost of additional growth is that someone must forgo current consumption.

Multiple-Choice Questions

1. A reasonable measure of the standard of living in a country is
   a. real GDP per person.
   b. real GDP.
   c. nominal GDP per person.
   d. nominal GDP.
   e. the growth rate of nominal GDP per person.

2. Many East Asian countries are growing very quickly because
   a. they have enormous natural resources.
   b. they are imperialists and have collected wealth from previous victories in war.
   c. they save and invest an unusually high percentage of their GDP.
   d. they have always been wealthy and will continue to be wealthy, which is known as the "snowball effect."

3. When a nation has very little GDP per person,
   a. it is doomed to being relatively poor forever.
   b. it must be a small nation.
   c. it has the potential to grow relatively quickly due to the "catch-up-effect."
   d. an increase in capital will likely have little impact on output.
   e. none of the above

4. Once a country is wealthy,
    a. it is nearly impossible for it to become relatively poorer.
    b. it may be harder for it to grow quickly because of the diminishing returns to capital.
    c. capital becomes more productive due to the "catch-up effect."
    d. it no longer needs any human capital.
    e. none of the above

5. The opportunity cost of growth is
    a. a reduction in current investment.
    b. a reduction in current saving.
    c. a reduction in current consumption.
    d. a reduction in taxes.

6. *For a given level of technology,* we should expect an increase in productivity within a nation when there is an increase in each of the following *except*
    a. human capital/worker.
    b. physical capital/worker.
    c. natural resources/worker.
    d. labor.

7. Which of the following statements is true?
    a. Countries may have a different level of GDP/person but they all grow at the same rate.
    b. Countries may have a different growth rate but they all have the same level of GDP/person.
    c. Countries all have the same growth rate and level of output because any country can obtain the same factors of production.
    d. Countries have great variance in both the level and growth rate of GDP/person; thus, poor countries can become relatively rich over time.

8. If a production function exhibits constant returns to scale,
    a. doubling all of the inputs has absolutely no impact on output because output is constant.
    b. doubling all of the inputs doubles output.
    c. doubling all of the inputs more than doubles output due to the catch-up effect.
    d. doubling all of the inputs less than doubles output due to diminishing returns.

9. Copper is an example of
    a. human capital.
    b. physical capital.
    c. a renewable natural resource.
    d. a non-renewable natural resource.
    e. technology.

10. Which of the following statements regarding the impact of population growth on productivity is true?
    a. There is no evidence, yet, that rapid population growth stretches natural resources to the point that it limits growth in productivity.
    b. Rapid population growth may dilute the capital stock, lowering productivity.
    c. Rapid population growth may promote technological progress, increasing productivity.
    d. all of the above

11. Thomas Malthus argued that
    a. technological progress will continuously generate improvements in productivity and living standards.
    b. labor is the only true factor of production.
    c. an ever increasing population is constrained only by the food supply, resulting in chronic famines.
    d. private charities and government aid will improve the welfare of the poor.
    e. none of the above

12. Which of the following best describes the rate of growth in productivity in the United States over the last fifty years?
    a. Productivity grew quickly in the 1950s and 1960s, more slowly from the early 1970s through 1995, and then quickly again.
    b. Productivity has been growing more slowly every decade since World War II.
    c. Productivity has been growing more quickly every decade since World War II.
    d. Productivity growth has been steady over the last 50 years.
    e. Productivity grew slowly from the 1950s through the 1970s, and then began to accelerate, probably due to advances in computer technology.

13. Which of the following describes an increase in technological knowledge?
    a. A farmer discovers that it is better to plant in the spring rather than in the fall.
    b. A farmer buys another tractor.
    c. A farmer hires another day laborer.
    d. A farmer sends his child to agricultural college and the child returns to work on the farm.

14. Our standard of living is most closely related to
    a. how hard we work.
    b. our supply of capital, because everything of value is produced by machinery.
    c. our supply of natural resources, because they limit production.
    d. our productivity, because our income is equal to what we produce.

15. Which of the following is an example of foreign portfolio investment?
    a. A naturalized U.S. citizen, who was originally born in Germany, buys stock in Ford and Ford uses the proceeds to buy a new plant.
    b. Toyota builds a new plant in Tennessee.
    c. Toyota buys stock in Ford, and Ford uses the proceeds to build a new plant in Michigan.
    d. Ford builds a new plant in Michigan.
    e. none of the above

16. Which of the following government policies is *least* likely to increase growth in Africa?
    a. increase expenditures on public education
    b. increase restrictions on the importing of Japanese automobiles and electronics
    c. eliminate civil war
    d. reduce restrictions on foreign capital investment
    e. All of the above would increase growth.

17. If Mazda builds a new plant in Illinois,
    a. in the future U.S. GDP will rise more than U.S. GNP.
    b. in the future U.S. GDP will rise less than U.S. GNP.
    c. in the future U.S. GDP and GNP will both fall because some income from this investment will accrue to foreigners.
    d. there has been an increase in foreign portfolio investment in the United States.
    e. none of the above

18. If real GDP/person in 2000 is $18,073 and real GDP/person in 2001 is $18,635, what is the growth rate of real output over this period?
    a. 3.0 percent
    b. 3.1 percent
    c. 5.62 percent
    d. 18.0 percent
    e. 18.6 percent

19. Which of the following expenditures to enhance productivity is most likely to emit a positive externality?
    a. Megabank buys a new computer.
    b. Susan pays her college tuition.
    c. Exxon leases a new oil field.
    d. General Motors buys a new drill press.

20. To increase growth, governments should do all of the following except
    a. promote free trade.
    b. encourage saving and investment.
    c. encourage foreigners to investment in your country.
    d. encourage research and development.
    e. nationalize major industries.

ADVANCED CRITICAL THINKING

You are having a discussion with other Generation X-ers. The conversation turns to a supposed lack of growth and opportunity in the United States when compared to some Asian countries such as Japan, South Korea, Taiwan, and Singapore. Your roommate says, "These Asian countries must have cheated somehow. That's the only way they could have possibly grown so quickly."

1. Have you learned anything in this chapter that would make you question your roommate's assertion?

   _____

   _____

   _____

2. The phenomenal growth rate of Japan since World War II has often been referred to as the "Japanese miracle." Is it a miracle or is it explainable?

   _____

   _____

   _____

3. Are the high growth rates found in these Asian countries without cost?

   _____

   _____

SOLUTIONS

Terms and Definitions

_6_ Real GDP per person

_14_ Growth rate

_20_ Productivity

_7_ Physical capital

_15_ Factors of production

_1_ Human capital

_21_ Natural resources

_10_ Renewable resource

_16_ Nonrenewable resource

_19_ Technological knowledge

_3_ Production function

_9_ Constant returns to scale

_8_ Diminishing returns

_13_ Catch-up effect

_2_ Foreign direct investment

_22_ Foreign portfolio investment

_17_ Externality

_5_ Property rights

_11_ Infant-industry argument

_18_ Inward-oriented policies

_12_ Outward-oriented policies

_4_ Public good

Practice Problems

1. a. Northcountry, because it has the largest real GDP per person.
   b. Eastcountry, because it has the largest growth rate.
   c. Westcountry is the poorest and likely has the least capital. Since capital exhibits diminishing returns, it is most productive when it is relatively scarce.
   d. No. Because of diminishing returns to capital, the additional growth from increasing capital declines as a country has more capital.
   e. Human capital emits a positive externality. Research and development is a public good after dissemination.
   f. Westcountry, because it is currently the poorest and could easily benefit from additional capital. It may have trade restrictions (inward oriented policies), a corrupt or unstable government, few courts and a lack of established property rights, etc.
   g. ($15,918 − $15,468)/$15,468 = 0.029 = 2.9%

2. a. cook = labor, diploma = human capital, recipes = technological knowledge, stove and utensils = capital, venison = natural resource.
   b. Recipes (technological knowledge) never wear out. Labor and human capital die, the stove and utensils wear out slowly, and the venison is used up (although it is probably renewable).

3. a. Encourage saving and investment, investment from abroad, education, free trade, research and development, protect property rights and establish political stability.
   b. Property rights and political stability are necessary for there to be any incentive to save, invest, trade, or educate.
   c. The answer is uncertain. A rapidly growing population may reduce productivity by stretching natural resources across more people and by diluting the capital stock across more workers. However, there is evidence that more technological progress takes place in areas with large populations.

Short-Answer Questions

1. Level of real GDP/person measures standard of living. Growth rate measures rate of advance of the standard of living.

2. No. Since growth rates vary widely across countries, rich can become relatively poorer and poor can become relatively richer.

3. Physical capital per worker, human capital per worker, natural resources per worker, and technological knowledge. All except natural resources.

4. Human capital is the knowledge and skills of the worker. Physical capital is the stock of equipment and structures.

5. Someone must forgo current consumption. No, someone must save instead of consume regardless of whether education or machines are purchased with the saving.

6. Because there are diminishing returns to physical capital.

7. GDP. GNP measures only the income of Americans while GDP measures income generated inside the United States. Therefore, GDP will rise more than GNP because some of the profits from the capital investment will accrue to foreigners in the form of dividends. Foreign portfolio investment.

8. Patents provide a property right to an idea; therefore people are willing to invest in research and development because it is more profitable. Research and development is a public good once the information is disseminated.

True/False Questions

1. F; growth depends on the rate of increase in productivity.

2. F; the prices of natural resources, adjusted for inflation, are stable or falling, so our ability to conserve these resources is growing more rapidly than their supplies are dwindling.

3. T

4. F; human capital is the knowledge and skills of workers.

5. T

6. T

7. T

8. F; due to diminishing returns to capital, growth rises temporarily.

9. F; it can attract foreign investment.

10. T

11. T

12. T

13. F; most economists believe that outward-oriented policies improve growth.

14. F; Malthus underestimated technological improvements in food production. Thus, people are not doomed to live at subsistence.

15. T

Multiple-Choice Questions

1. a	5. c	9. d	13. a	17. a
2. c	6. d	10. d	14. d	18. b
3. c	7. d	11. c	15. c	19. b
4. b	8. b	12. a	16. b	20. e

Advanced Critical Thinking

1. Yes. There are many sources of growth and a country can influence all of them except natural resources.

2. Japan's growth is explainable. Indeed, all of the high growth Asian countries have extremely high investment as a percent of GDP.

3. No. The opportunity cost of investment is that someone must forgo current consumption in order to save and invest.

13

Learn about some of the important financial institutions in the U.S. economy

Consider how the financial system is related to key macroeconomic variables

Develop a model of the supply and demand for loanable funds in financial markets

Use the loanable funds model to analyze various government policies

Consider how government budget deficits affect the U.S. economy

OUTCOMES

⌈After accomplishing these goals, you should be able to

List and describe four important types of financial institutions

Describe the relationship between national saving, government deficits, and investment

Explain the slope of the supply and demand for loanable funds

Shift supply and demand in the loanable funds market in response to a change in taxes on interest or investment

Shift supply and demand in the loanable funds market in response to a change in the government's budget deficit

SAVING, INVESTMENT, AND THE FINANCIAL SYSTEM

CHAPTER OVERVIEW

Context and Purpose

Chapter 13 is the second chapter in a four-chapter sequence on the production of output in the long run. In Chapter 12, we found that capital and labor are among the primary determinants of output. For this reason, Chapter 13 addresses the market for saving and investment in capital, and Chapter 14 addresses the tools people and firms use when choosing capital projects in which to invest. Chapter 15 will address the market for labor.

The purpose of Chapter 13 is to show how saving and investment are coordinated by the loanable funds market. Within the framework of the loanable funds market, we are able to see the effects of taxes and government deficits on saving, investment, the accumulation of capital, and ultimately, the growth rate of output.

CHAPTER REVIEW

Introduction

Some people save some of their income and have funds that are available to loan. Some people wish to invest in capital equipment and thus need to borrow. The **financial system** consists of those institutions that help match, or balance, the

241

lending of savers to the borrowing of investors. This is important because investment in capital contributes to economic growth.

Financial Institutions in the U.S. Economy

The financial system is made up of financial institutions that match borrowers and lenders. Financial institutions can be grouped into two categories: financial markets and financial intermediaries.

Financial markets allow firms to borrow *directly* from those that wish to lend. The two most important financial markets are the bond market and the stock market.

- The *bond market* allows large borrowers to borrow directly from the public. The borrower sells a **bond** (a certificate of indebtedness or IOU) which specifies the *date of maturity* (the date the loan will be repaid), the amount of interest that will be paid periodically, and the *principal* (the amount borrowed and to be repaid at maturity). The buyer of the bond is the lender.

  Bond issues differ in three main ways.

  (1) Bonds are of different *term* (time to maturity). Longer term bonds are riskier and, thus, usually pay higher interest because the owner of the bond may need to sell it before maturity at a depressed price.

  (2) Bonds have different *credit risk* (probability of default). Higher risk bonds pay higher interest. *Junk bonds* are exceptionally risky bonds.

  (3) Bonds have different *tax treatment*. The interest received from owning a *municipal bond* (bond issued by state or local government) is tax exempt. Thus, municipal bonds pay lower interest.

- The *stock market* allows large firms to raise funds for expansion by taking on additional "partners" or owners of the firm. The sale of **stock** is called *equity finance* while the sale of bonds is called *debt finance.* Owners of stock share in the profits or losses of the firm while owners of bonds receive fixed interest payments as creditors. The stockholder accepts more risk than the bondholder but has a higher potential return. Stocks don't mature or expire and are traded on stock exchanges such as the New York Stock Exchange and NASDAQ. Stock prices are determined by supply and demand and reflect expectations of the firm's future profitability. A *stock index*, such as the Dow Jones Industrial Average, is an average of an important group of stock prices.

Financial intermediaries are financial institutions through which savers (lenders) can *indirectly* loan funds to borrowers. That is, financial intermediaries are middlepersons between borrowers and lenders. The two most important financial intermediaries are banks and mutual funds.

- **Banks** collect deposits from people and businesses (savers) and lend them to other people and businesses (borrowers). Banks pay interest on deposits and charge a slightly higher rate on their loans. Small businesses usually borrow from banks because they are too small to sell stock or bonds. Banks create a *medium of exchange* when they accept a deposit because individuals can write checks against the deposit to engage in transactions. Other intermediaries only offer savers a *store of value* because their saving is not as accessible.

- **Mutual funds** are institutions that sell shares to the public and use the proceeds to buy a group of stocks and/or bonds. This allows small savers to *diversify* their asset *portfolios* (own a variety of assets). It also allows small savers access to professional money managers. However, few money managers can beat *index funds,* which buy all of the stocks in a stock index without the aid of active management. There are two reasons why index funds outperform actively managed funds. First, it is hard to pick stocks whose prices will rise because the market price of a stock is already a good reflection of a company's true value. Second, index funds keep costs low by rarely buying and selling, and by not having to pay the salaries of professional money managers.

Although there are many differences among these financial institutions, the overriding similarity is that they all direct resources from lenders to borrowers.

China has lacked free financial markets resulting in inefficient capital investment. China is moving slowly toward freer capital markets.

Saving and Investment in the National Income Accounts

In order to truly appreciate the role of the financial system in directing saving into investment, we must begin to understand saving and investment from a macroeconomic perspective. The national income accounts record the relationship between income, output, saving, investment, expenditures, taxes, and so on. There are a number of national income *identities* (equations that are true by definition) that expose relationships between these variables.

Recall, GDP is the value of output, the value of income earned from producing it, and *the value of expenditures* on it. Therefore,

$$Y = C + I + G + NX$$

where Y = GDP, C = consumption expenditures, I = investment expenditures, G = government purchases, and NX = net exports. To simplify, we assume there is no international sector which means that we have a *closed economy.* (An *open economy* includes a foreign sector.) Therefore, for our example

$$Y = C + I + G$$

National saving or just **saving** is the income left over after paying for consumption and government purchases. To find saving, subtract C and G from both sides.

$$Y - C - G = I$$

$$\text{or } S = I$$

which says, saving = investment.

To appreciate the impact of the government's purchases and taxes on saving, we need to define saving as above:

$$S = Y - C - G$$

which says again that saving is income left over after consumption and government purchases. Now add and subtract T (taxes) from the right side:

$$S = (Y - T - C) + (T - G).$$

This says that saving is equal to **private saving** $(Y - T - C)$ which is income left over after paying taxes and consumption, and **public saving** $(T - G)$ which is the government's **budget surplus.** Often G is greater than T, and the government runs a negative surplus or a **budget deficit.**

In summary, $S = I$ for the economy as a whole and the amount of saving available for investment is the sum of private saving and public saving. Although $S =$

I for the entire economy, it is not true for each individual. That is, some people invest less than they save and have funds to lend while others invest more than they save and need to borrow funds. These groups meet in the **market for loanable funds.** Note that saving is the income that remains after paying for consumption and government purchases while investment is the purchase of new capital.

The Market for Loanable Funds

For simplicity, imagine that there is one loanable funds market where all savers take their funds to be loaned and where all investors go to borrow funds.

- The *supply* of loanable funds comes from national saving. A higher real interest rate increases the incentive to save and increases the quantity supplied of loanable funds.

- The *demand* for loanable funds comes from households and firms that wish to borrow to invest. A higher real interest rate increases the cost of borrowing and reduces the quantity demanded of loanable funds.

The supply and demand for loanable funds combine to generate a market for loanable funds. This market determines the equilibrium real interest rate and the equilibrium quantity of funds loaned and borrowed. Since the funds that are loaned are national saving and the funds that are borrowed are used for investment, the loanable funds market also determines the equilibrium level of saving and investment.

The following three policies increase saving, investment, and capital accumulation and, hence, these policies increase economic growth.

Reduced taxation on interest and dividends increases the return to saving for any real interest rate and, thus, increases the desire to save and loan at each real interest rate. Graphically, this policy will shift the supply of loanable funds to the right, lower the real interest rate, and raise the quantity demanded of funds for investment. Real interest rates fall while saving and investment rise.

Reduced taxation if one invests, for example an investment tax credit, will increase the return to investment in capital for any real interest rate and, thus, increase the desire to borrow and invest at each real interest rate. Graphically, this policy will shift the demand for loanable funds to the right, raise the real interest rate, and increase the quantity supplied of funds. Real interest rates, saving, and investment rises.

A reduction in government debt and deficits (or an increase in a budget surplus) increases public saving $(T - G)$ so more national saving is available at each real interest rate. Graphically, this policy will shift the supply of loanable funds to the right, decrease the real interest rate, and increase the quantity demanded of funds for investment. Real interest rates fall, and saving and investment rise.

Note that a *budget deficit* is an excess of government spending over tax revenue. The accumulation of past government borrowing is called the *government debt*. A *budget surplus* is an excess of tax revenue over government spending. When government spending equals tax revenue, there is a *balanced budget*. An increase in the deficit reduces national saving, shifts the supply of loanable funds to the left, raises the real interest rate and reduces the quantity demanded of funds for investment. When private borrowing and investment are reduced due to government borrowing, we say that government is **crowding out** investment. Government surpluses do just the opposite of budget deficits.

The debt–GDP ratio usually rises during wars and this is considered appropriate. However, it rose during the 1980s. Policymakers from both parties viewed this with alarm and deficits were reduced during the 1990s and a surplus arose. In 2001, the budget returned to deficit for a number of reasons, some of which are viewed as temporary. Therefore, the debt–GDP ratio is projected to continue to decline.

HELPFUL HINTS

1. A financial intermediary is a middleperson. An intermediary is someone who gets between two groups and negotiates a solution. For example, we have intermediaries in labor negotiations that sit between a firm and a union. In like manner, a bank is a financial intermediary in that it sits between the ultimate lender (the depositor) and the ultimate borrower (the firm or home builder) and "negotiates" the terms of the loan contracts. Banks don't lend their own money. They lend the depositor's money.

2. Investment is not the purchase of stocks and bonds. In casual conversation, people use the word "investment" to mean the purchase of stocks and bonds. For example, "I just invested in ten shares of IBM." (Even an economist might say this.) However, when speaking in economic terms, *investment* is the actual purchase of capital equipment and structures. In this technical framework, when I buy ten shares of newly issued IBM stock, there has been only an exchange of assets—IBM has my money and I have their stock certificates. If IBM takes my money and buys new equipment with it, their purchase of the equipment is economic *investment*.

3. Don't include consumption loans in the supply of loanable funds. In casual conversation, people use the word "saving" to refer to their new deposit in a bank. For example, "I just saved $100 this week." (An economist might say this, too.) However, if that deposit were loaned out to a consumer who used the funds to purchase airline tickets for a vacation, there has been no increase in *national saving* (or just *saving*) in a macroeconomic sense. This is because saving, in a macroeconomic sense, is income (GDP) that remains after *national* consumption expenditures and government purchases ($S = Y - C - G$). No national saving took place if your personal saving was loaned and used for consumption expenditures by another person. Since national saving is the source of the supply of loanable funds, consumption loans do not affect the supply of loanable funds.

4. Demand for loanable funds is private demand for investment funds. The demand for loanable funds only includes private (households and firms) demand for funds to invest in capital structures and equipment. When the government runs a deficit, it does absorb national saving but it does not buy capital equipment with the funds. Therefore, when the government runs a deficit, we consider it a reduction in the supply of loanable funds, not an increase in the demand for loanable funds.

TERMS AND DEFINITIONS

Choose a definition for each key term.

Key terms:

_____ Financial system

_____ Financial markets

_____ Financial intermediaries

_____ Bank

_____ Medium of exchange

_____ Bond

_____ Stock

_____ Mutual fund

_____ Closed economy

_____ National saving (saving)

_____ Private saving

_____ Budget surplus

_____ Budget deficit

_____ Government debt

_____ Investment

_____ Demand for loanable funds

_____ Supply of loanable funds

_____ Crowding out

Definitions:

1. Spendable asset such as a checking deposit

2. A shortfall of tax revenue relative to government spending causing public saving to be negative

3. An economy with no international transactions

4. Financial institutions through which savers can indirectly lend to borrowers

5. The group of institutions in the economy that help match borrowers and lenders

6. The amount of borrowing for investment desired at each real interest rate

7. The income that remains after consumption expenditures and taxes

8. The accumulation of past budget deficits

9. The amount of saving made available for lending at each real interest rate

10. Institution that collects deposits and makes loans

11. Institution that sells shares and uses the proceeds to buy a diversified portfolio

12. Financial institutions through which savers can directly lend to borrowers

13. Certificate of ownership of a small portion of a large firm

14. An excess of tax revenue over government spending causing public saving to be positive

15. The income that remains after consumption expenditures and government purchases

16. A decrease in investment as a result of government borrowing

17. Expenditures on capital equipment and structures

18. Certificate of indebtedness or IOU

PROBLEMS AND SHORT-ANSWER QUESTIONS

Practice Problems

1. Fly-by-night Corporation is in need of capital funds to expand its production capacity. It is selling short- and long-term bonds and is issuing stock. You are considering the prospect of helping finance their expansion.

   a. If you are to buy both short- and long-term bonds from Fly-by-night, from which bond would you demand a higher rate of return: short or long term? Why?

   _____

   _____

   b. If Standard and Poor's lowered the credit worthiness of Fly-by-night, would this affect the rate of return you would demand when buying their bonds? Why?

   _____

   _____

   c. If Fly-by-night has exactly the same credit worthiness as Deadbeat City and each is issuing the same term to maturity bonds, which issuer must pay the higher interest rate on its bonds? Why?

   _____

   _____

   d. If Fly-by-night is issuing both stocks and bonds, from which would you expect to earn the higher rate of return over the long run? Why?

   _____

   _____

   e. Which would be safer: putting all of your personal saving into Fly-by-night stock, or putting all of your personal saving into a mutual fund that has some Fly-by-night stock in its portfolio? Why?

   _____

   _____

2. Use the saving and investment identities from the National Income Accounts to answer the following questions. Suppose the following values are from the national income accounts of a country with a closed economy (all values are in billions).

$$Y = \$6,000$$
$$T = \$1,000$$
$$C = \$4,000$$
$$G = \$1,200$$

a. What is the value of saving and investment in this country?

_____

_____

b. What is the value of private saving?

_____

_____

c. What is the value of public saving?

_____

_____

d. Is the government's budget policy contributing to growth in this country or harming it? Why?

_____

_____

3. The following information describes a loanable funds market. Values are in billions.

Real Interest Rate	Quantity of Loanable Funds Supplied	Quantity of Loanable Funds Demanded
6%	$1,300	$ 700
5	1,200	800
4	1,000	1,000
3	800	1,200
2	600	1,500

a. Plot the supply and demand for loanable funds in Exhibit 1. What is the equilibrium real interest rate and the equilibrium level of saving and investment?

_____

_____

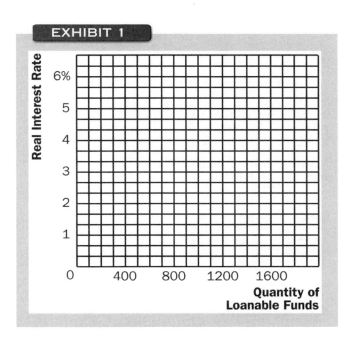

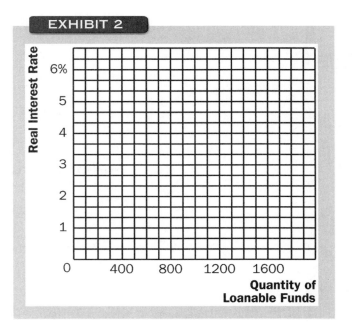

b. What "market forces" will not allow 2 percent to be the real interest rate?

_____

_____

c. Suppose the government suddenly increases its budget deficit by $400 billion. What is the new equilibrium real interest rate and equilibrium level of saving and investment? (Show graphically in Exhibit 2.)

_____

_____

d. Starting at the original equilibrium, suppose the government enacts an investment tax credit that stimulates the demand for loanable funds for capital investment by $400 billion at any real interest rate. What is the new equilibrium real interest rate and equilibrium level of saving and investment? (Show graphically in Exhibit 3.)

_____

_____

_____

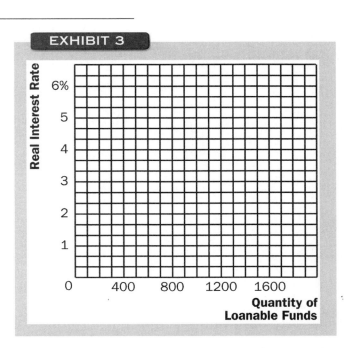

e. With regard to (c) and (d), which policy is most likely to increase growth? Why?

_____

_____

_____

Short-Answer Questions

1. Explain why a mutual fund is likely to be less risky than an individual stock.

_____

_____

_____

2. Which is likely to give you a greater rate of return: a checking deposit at a bank or the purchase of a corporate bond? Why?

_____

_____

_____

_____

3. What is the difference between debt finance and equity finance? Provide an example of each.

_____

_____

_____

4. What is meant by the words "saving" and "investment" in the national income accounts and how does it differ from the casual use of the words?

_____

_____

_____

_____

5. In a closed economy, why can't investment ever exceed saving?

_____

_____

_____

_____

6. What is private saving? What is public saving?

_____

_____

7. Utilizing the national income identities, if government purchases were to rise, and if output, taxes, and consumption were to remain unchanged, what would happen to national saving, investment, and growth?

_____

_____

_____

8. Suppose Americans become more frugal. That is, they consume a smaller percent of their income and save a larger percent. Describe the changes in the loanable-funds market. What would likely happen to growth?

_____

_____

_____

_____

9. Suppose the government runs a smaller deficit. Describe the changes in the loanable-funds market. What would likely happen to growth?

_____

_____

_____

_____

10. An increase in the government's budget deficit forces the government to borrow more. Why doesn't an increase in the deficit increase the demand for loanable funds in the loanable-funds market?

_____

_____

_____

11. What is the fundamental difference between financial markets and financial intermediaries?

_____

_____

_____

SELF-TEST

True/False Questions

_____ F 1. When a business firm sells a bond, it has engaged in ~~equity~~ *debt* finance.

_____ F 2. People who buy stock in a firm ~~have loaned~~ *are owners* money to the firm.

_____ T 3. Mutual funds reduce a shareholder's risk by purchasing a diversified portfolio.

_____ T 4. Municipal bonds pay less interest than comparable risk corporate bonds because the interest payments are tax exempt to the bond holder.

_____ T 5. In a closed economy, saving is what remains after consumption expenditures and government purchases.

_____ F 6. Public saving is always positive.

_____ T 7. In a closed economy, investment is always equal to saving regardless of where the saving came from—public or private sources.

_____ T 8. Investment is the purchase of capital equipment and structures.

_____ F 9. If you save money this week and lend it to your roommate to buy food for consumption, your act of personal saving has increased national saving.

_____ T 10. The quantity supplied of loanable funds is greater if real interest rates are higher.

F 11. If the real interest rate in the loanable-funds market is temporarily held above the equilibrium rate, desired borrowing will exceed desired lending and the real interest rate will fall.

T 12. A reduction in the budget deficit should shift the supply of loanable funds to the right, lower the real interest rate, and increase the quantity demanded of loanable funds.

T 13. Public saving and the government's budget surplus are the same thing.

F 14. If the government wanted to increase the rate of growth, it should raise taxes on interest and dividends to shift the supply of loanable funds to the right.

F 15. An increase in the budget deficit that causes the government to increase its borrowing shifts the demand for loanable funds to the right.

Multiple-Choice Questions

1. Which of the following is an example of equity finance?
   a. corporate bonds
   b. municipal bonds
   c. stock
   d. bank loan
   e. All of the above are equity finance.

2. Credit risk refers to a bond's
   a. term to maturity.
   b. probability of default.
   c. tax treatment.
   d. dividend.
   e. price-earnings ratio.

3. A financial intermediary is a middleperson between
   a. labor unions and firms.
   b. husbands and wives.
   c. buyers and sellers.
   d. borrowers and lenders.

4. National saving (or just saving) is equal to
   a. private saving + public saving.
   b. investment + consumption expenditures.
   c. GDP – government purchases.
   d. GDP + consumption expenditures + government purchases.
   e. none of the above.

5. Which of the following statements is true?
    a. A stock index is a directory used to locate information about selected stocks.
    b. Longer term bonds tend to pay less interest than shorter term bonds.
    c. Municipal bonds pay less interest than comparable corporate bonds.
    d. Mutual funds are riskier than single stock purchases because the performance of so many different firms can affect the return of a mutual fund.

6. If government spending exceeds tax collections,
    a. there is a budget surplus.
    b. there is a budget deficit.
    c. private saving is positive.
    d. public saving is positive.
    e. none of the above

7. If GDP = $1,000, consumption = $600, taxes = $100, and government purchases = $200, how much is saving and investment?
    a. saving = $200, investment = $200
    b. saving = $300, investment = $300
    c. saving = $100, investment = $200
    d. saving = $200, investment = $100
    e. saving = $0, investment = $0

8. If the public consumes $100 billion less and the government purchases $100 billion more (other things unchanging), which of the following statement is true?
    a. There is an increase in saving and the economy should grow more quickly.
    b. There is a decrease in saving and the economy should grow more slowly.
    c. Saving is unchanged.
    d. There is not enough information to determine what will happen to saving.

9. Which of the following financial market securities would likely pay the highest interest rate?
    a. a municipal bond issued by the state of Texas
    b. a mutual fund with a portfolio of blue chip bonds
    c. a bond issued by a blue chip company
    d. a bond issued by a start up company

10. Investment is
    a. the purchase of stocks and bonds.
    b. the purchase of capital equipment and structures.
    c. when we place our saving in the bank.
    d. the purchase of goods and services.

11. If Americans become more thrifty, we would expect
    a. the supply of loanable funds to shift to the right and the real interest rate to rise.
    b. the supply of loanable funds to shift to the right and the real interest rate to fall.
    c. the demand for loanable funds to shift to the right and the real interest rate to rise..
    d. the demand for loanable funds to shift to the right and the real interest rate to fall.

12. Which of the following sets of government policies is the most growth oriented?
    a. lower taxes on the returns to saving, provide investment tax credits, and lower the deficit
    b. lower taxes on the returns to saving, provide investment tax credits, and increase the deficit
    c. increase taxes on the returns to saving, provide investment tax credits, and lower the deficit
    d. increase taxes on the returns to saving, provide investment tax credits, and increase the deficit

13. An increase in the budget deficit that causes the government to increase its borrowing
    a. shifts the demand for loanable funds to the right.
    b. shifts the demand for loanable funds to the left.
    c. shifts the supply of loanable funds to the left.
    d. shifts the supply of loanable funds to the right.

14. An increase in the budget deficit will
    a. raise the real interest rate and decrease the quantity of loanable funds demanded for investment.
    b. raise the real interest rate and increase the quantity of loanable funds demanded for investment.
    c. lower the real interest rate and increase the quantity of loanable funds demanded for investment.
    d. lower the real interest rate and decrease the quantity of loanable funds demanded for investment.

15. If the supply of loanable funds is very inelastic (steep), which policy would likely increase saving and investment the most?
    a. an investment tax credit
    b. a reduction in the budget deficit
    c. an increase in the budget deficit
    d. none of the above

16. An increase in the budget deficit is
    a. a decrease in public saving.
    b. an increase in public saving.
    c. a decrease in private saving.
    d. an increase in private saving.
    e. none of the above.

17. If an increase in the budget deficit reduces national saving and investment, we have witnessed a demonstration of
    a. equity finance.
    b. the mutual fund effect.
    c. intermediation.
    d. crowding out.

18. If Americans become less concerned with the future and save less at each real interest rate,
    a. real interest rates fall and investment falls.
    b. real interest rates fall and investment rises.
    c. real interest rates rise and investment falls.
    d. real interest rates rise and investment rises.

19. If the government increases investment tax credits and reduces taxes on the return to saving at the same time,
    a. the real interest rate should rise.
    b. the real interest rate should fall.
    c. the real interest rate should not change.
    d. the impact on the real interest rate is indeterminate.

20. An increase in the budget surplus
    a. shifts the demand for loanable funds to the right and increases the real interest rate.
    b. shifts the demand for loanable funds to the left and reduces the real interest rate.
    c. shifts the supply of loanable funds to the left and increases the real interest rate.
    d. shifts the supply of loanable funds to the right and reduces the real interest rate.

ADVANCED CRITICAL THINKING

You are watching a presidential debate. When a candidate is questioned about his position on economic growth, the presidential candidate steps forward and says, "We need to get this country growing again. We need to use tax incentives to stimulate saving and investment, and we need to get that budget deficit down so that the government stops absorbing our nation's saving."

1. If government spending remains unchanged, what inconsistency is implied by the presidential candidate's statement?

_____

_____

_____

_____

2. If the presidential candidate truly wishes to decrease taxes and decrease the budget deficit, what has the candidate implied about his plans for government spending?

_____

_____

3. If policymakers want to increase growth, and if policymakers have to choose between tax incentives to stimulate saving and tax incentives to stimulate investment, what might they want to know about supply and demand in the loanable-funds market before making their decision? Explain.

_____

_____

_____

_____

_____

_____

_____

_____

SOLUTIONS

Terms and Definitions

_5_ Financial system

_12_ Financial markets

_4_ Financial intermediaries

_10_ Bank

_1_ Medium of exchange

_18_ Bond

_13_ Stock

_11_ Mutual fund

_3_ Closed economy

_15_ National saving (saving)

_7_ Private saving

_14_ Budget surplus

_2_ Budget deficit

_8_ Government debt

_17_ Investment

_6_ Demand for loanable funds

_9_ Supply of loanable funds

_16_ Crowding out

Practice Problems

1. a. Long term, because it is more likely that you may need to sell the long-term bond at a depressed price prior to maturity.
    b. Yes, the credit risk has increased and lenders would demand a higher rate of return.
    c. Fly-by-night. Unlike municipal bonds, interest receipts are taxable to the owners of corporate bonds.
    d. Owners of stock demand a higher rate of return because it is riskier.
    e. It is safer to put money in a mutual fund because it is diversified (not all of your eggs in one basket).

2. a. ($6,000 – $1,000 – $4,000) + ($1,000 – $1,200) = $800 billion
    b. $6,000 – $1,000 – $4,000 = $1,000 billion
    c. $1,000 – $1,200 = –$200 billion
    d. It is harming growth because public saving is negative so less is available for investment.

3. a. Equilibrium real interest rate = 4%, equilibrium S and I = $1000 billion. Exhibit 4.
    b. At 2 percent interest, the quantity demanded of loanable funds exceeds the quantity supplied by $900 billion. This excess demand for loans (borrowing) will drive interest rates up to 4 percent.
    c. Equilibrium real interest rate = 5%, equilibrium S and I = $800 billion. Exhibit 5

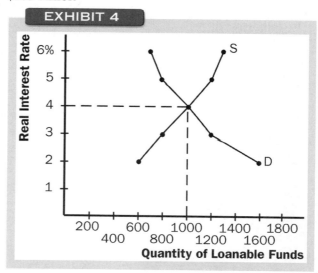

EXHIBIT 4

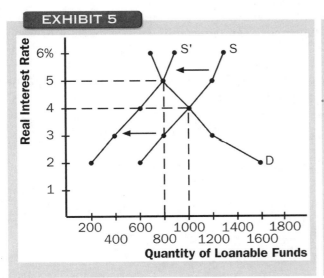

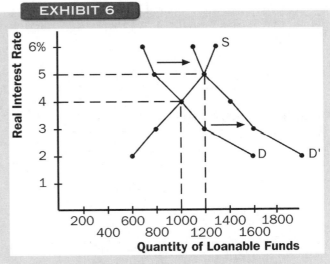

   d. Equilibrium real interest rate = 5%, equilibrium S and I = $1200 billion. (See Exhibit 6.)

   e. An investment tax credit, because it shifts the demand for loanable funds to invest in capital to the right, raising the level of investment in capital and stimulating growth.

Short-Answer Questions

1. Because a mutual fund is diversified. When one stock in the fund is performing poorly, it is likely that another stock is performing well.

2. A corporate bond, because the bond is riskier and because "direct" lending through a financial market has fewer overhead costs than "indirect" lending through an intermediary.

3. Debt finance is borrowing such as when a firm sells a bond. Equity finance is taking on additional partners such as when a firm sells stock.

4. Saving is what remains after consumption and government purchases. Investment is the purchase of equipment and structures. In casual conversation, saving is what remains out of our income (even if someone else borrows it for consumption) and investment is the purchase of stocks and bonds.

5. Because saving is the GDP left over after consumption expenditures and government purchases, and this is the limit of the output available to be used to purchase equipment and structures.

6. Private saving = $Y - T - C$, public saving = $T - G$.

7. Public saving would decrease and cause national saving and investment to decrease by the same amount, slowing growth.

8. The supply of loanable funds would shift right, the real interest rate would fall, and the quantity demanded of loanable funds to purchase capital would increase. Growth would increase.

9. The supply of loanable funds would shift right, the real interest rate would fall, and the quantity demanded of loanable funds to purchase capital would increase. Growth would increase.

10. The demand for loanable funds is defined as private demand for borrowing to purchase capital equipment and structures. An increase in the deficit absorbs saving and reduces the supply of loanable funds.

11. In a financial market, savers lend directly to borrowers. Through financial intermediaries, savers lend to an intermediary who then lends to the ultimate borrower.

True/False Questions

1. F; to sell a bond is to engage in debt finance.

2. F; stockholders are owners.

3. T

4. T

5. T

6. F; public saving is negative when there is a government budget deficit.

7. T

8. T

9. F; consumption loans do not increase national saving.

10. T

11. F; desired lending exceeds desired borrowing.

12. T

13. T

14. F; it should lower taxes on interest and dividends.

15. F; it decreases the supply of loanable funds.

Multiple-Choice Questions

1. c	5. c	9. d	13. c	17. d
2. b	6. b	10. b	14. a	18. c
3. d	7. a	11. b	15. b	19. d
4. a	8. c	12. a	16. a	20. d

Advanced Critical Thinking

1. Tax incentives to stimulate saving and investment require a reduction in taxes. This would increase the deficit, which would reduce national saving and investment.

2. The candidate plans to reduce government spending.

3. Policymakers would want to know the elasticity (similar to the steepness) of the supply and demand curves. If loanable funds demand is inelastic, changes in loanable funds supply have little effect on saving and investment, so tax incentives to increase saving at each interest rate do little for growth. If loanable funds supply is inelastic, changes in loanable funds demand have little effect on saving and investment, so tax incentives to increase investment at each interest rate do little for growth.

THE BASIC TOOLS OF FINANCE

14

GOALS

In this chapter you will

Learn the relationship between present value and future value

Consider the effects of compound growth

Learn how risk-averse people reduce the risk they face

Analyze how asset prices are determined

OUTCOMES

After accomplishing these goals, you should be able to

Choose between receiving $100 now or $120 two years from now, given an interest rate of 8 percent

Explain why two people whose incomes grow at slightly different rates may end up with significantly different incomes after a number of years

Explain the benefits of diversification

Show why randomly choosing stocks may be as good as more sophisticated stock picking methods

CHAPTER OVERVIEW

Context and Purpose

Chapter 14 is the third chapter in a four-chapter sequence on the level and growth of output in the long run. In Chapter 12, we learned that capital and labor are among the primary determinants of output and growth. In Chapter 13, we addressed how saving and investment in capital goods affect the production of output. In Chapter 14, we will learn about some of the tools people and firms use when choosing capital projects in which to invest. Since both capital and labor are among the primary determinants of output, Chapter 15 will address the market for labor.

The purpose of Chapter 14 is to introduce you to some tools that people use when they participate in financial markets. We will learn how people compare different sums of money at different points in time, how they manage risk, and how these concepts combine to help determine the value of a financial asset, such as a share of stock.

CHAPTER REVIEW

Introduction

Financial markets coordinate saving and investment. Financial decisions involve two elements—time and risk. For example, people and firms must make decisions today about saving and investment based on expectations of future earnings, but future returns are uncertain. The field of **finance** studies how people make decisions regarding the allocation of resources over time and the handling of risk. We will learn how people compare different sums of money at different points in time, how they manage risk, and how these concepts combine to help determine the value of a financial asset, such as a share of stock.

Present Value: Measuring the Time Value of Money

The **present value** of any future value is the amount today that would be needed, at current interest rates, to produce that future sum. The **future value** is the amount of money in the future that an amount of money today will yield, given prevailing interest rates. Suppose r = the interest rate expressed in decimal form, n = years to maturity, PV = present value, and FV = future value. Further, suppose that interest is paid annually and that the interest is put in the account to earn more interest—a process called **compounding**. Then:

(1) $$PV(1 + r)^n = FV, \text{ and}$$

(2) $$FV/(1 + r)^n = PV.$$

For example, suppose a person deposited $100 into a bank account for 3 years earning 7 percent interest. Using equation (1) where $r = 0.07$, $PV = \$100$, and $n = 3$, we find that in three years the account will hold about $122.50. That is, the future value is $122.50.

Alternatively, suppose you were offered a bank deposit that would provide you with $122.50 three years from now. At an interest rate of 7 percent, what would you pay for that account today? Using equation (2) where $r = 0.07$, $FV = \$122.50$, and $n = 3$, we find that the present value of $122.50 three years from today is $100.

The relationship between present value and future value demonstrates the following:

- Receiving a given sum in the present is preferred to receiving the same sum in the future. The larger the interest rate, the more pronounced is this result.

- In order to choose between two sums, a value today or a larger value at some later date, find the present value of the larger future sum and compare it to the value today.

- Firms undertake investment projects if the present value of the future returns exceeds the cost. The larger the interest rate, the less likely the project will be undertaken because the present value of the project becomes smaller. Thus, investment declines as interest rates rise.

Small differences in growth rates can make enormous differences in a country's level of income after many years. This result is also true for an individual's income or for money deposited in a bank. The concept of *compound growth* shows why. Each year's growth is based on the previous year's accumulated growth or, in the case of interest, interest is earned on previously earned interest. The effects of compound growth are demonstrated by the *rule of 70*, which states that if some variable grows at a rate of x percent per year, its value will double in approximately $70/x$ years. If your income grows at 1 percent per year, it will about double in 70 years. However, if your income grows at 4 percent, it will double in approximately 17.5 years.

Managing Risk

Most people are **risk averse,** which means that they dislike bad things more than they like comparable good things. This is because people's utility functions exhibit diminishing marginal utility of wealth. Thus, the utility lost from losing a $1,000 bet is greater than that gained from winning a $1,000 bet. People can reduce risk by buying insurance, diversifying their risk, and accepting a lower return on their assets.

- *People can reduce the risk they face by buying insurance.* Insurance allows the economy to spread the risk more efficiently because it is easier for 100 people to bear 1/100 of the group's risk of a house fire than for each to bear the entire risk of one house fire alone. There are two problems with insurance markets. *Adverse selection* occurs because a high-risk person is more likely to buy insurance than a low-risk person. *Moral hazard* occurs because after people buy insurance, they have less incentive to be careful. Some low-risk people don't buy insurance because these problems may cause the price of insurance to be too high for low-risk people.

- *People can reduce the risk they face through diversification.* **Diversification** is the reduction of risk achieved by replacing a single risk with a large number of smaller unrelated risks. This is summarized by the phrase, "Don't put all of your eggs in one basket." Risk is diversified through insurance because it is easier for 100 people to bear 1/100 of the group's risk of a house fire than for each to bear the entire risk of one house fire alone. The risk on a portfolio of stocks, as measured by the *standard deviation* (volatility) of the returns, is reduced by diversifying the portfolio—buying a small amount of a large number of stocks instead of a large amount of one stock. Diversification can eliminate **idiosyncratic risk**—the uncertainty associated with specific companies. It cannot eliminate **aggregate risk**—the uncertainty associated with the entire economy.

- *People can reduce the risk they face by accepting a lower rate of return on their investments.* People face a tradeoff between risk and return in their portfolio. In order to earn greater returns, people must accept more risk. In order to have less risk, people must accept lower returns. The optimal combination of risk and return for a person depends on the person's degree of risk aversion, which depends on the person's preferences.

Asset Valuation

The price of a share of stock is determined by supply and demand. People often try to buy stock that is *undervalued*—shares of a business whose value exceeds its price. If the price exceeds the value, the stock is considered *overvalued* and if the price and value are equal, the stock is *fairly valued.* The price of the stock is known. The value of a stock is uncertain because it is the present value of the future stream of dividends and the final sales price. The dividends and final sales price depend on the firm's future profitability. **Fundamental analysis** is a detailed analysis of a company's accounting statements and future prospects to determine its value. You can perform fundamental analysis yourself, rely on Wall Street analysts, or buy a mutual fund whose manager does fundamental analysis.

According to the **efficient markets hypothesis,** asset prices reflect all publicly available information about the value of an asset. This theory argues that professional money managers monitor news to determine a stock's value. The stock's price is set by supply and demand so at any point in time shares sold equal shares bought, implying that an equal number believe that the stock is overvalued as think it is undervalued. Thus, the average analyst thinks it is fairly valued all the time. According to this theory, the stock market is **informationally efficient**, which means that prices in the stock market reflect all available information in a rational way. If this is true, stock prices should follow a **random walk,** the path of which is impossible to predict from available information because all available information has already been incorporated into the price. As a result, no stock is a better buy than any other and the best you can do is to buy a diversified portfolio.

Index funds provide evidence in support of the efficient markets hypothesis. Index funds are mutual funds that buy all of the stocks in a particular stock index. Actively managed funds use research to try to buy only the best stocks. Actively managed funds fail to outperform index funds because they trade more frequently, incurring trading costs plus they charge fees for their alleged expertise.

Some people suggest that markets are irrational. That is, stock prices often move in ways that are hard to explain on the basis of rational analysis of news and so appear to be driven by psychological trends. However, if this were true, traders should be able to take advantage of this fact and buy better than average stocks, but beating the market is nearly impossible.

Evidence from behavioral economics studies suggests that men suffer from "self-serving attribution bias." Men think that their successes are the result of skill rather than luck. If people are overconfident in their investment choices, they can create speculative bubbles in the stock market (pushing overvalued stocks even higher) and they can fail to diversify their own portfolios. Thus, it may not be unreasonable to restrict people's choices for their retirement options through mandated saving plans such as defined-benefit pension plans and Social Security.

Conclusion

The concept of present value shows us that a dollar today is worth more than a dollar at a later date, and it allows us to compare sums at different points in time. Risk management shows us ways that risk-averse people can reduce their risk exposure. Asset valuation reflects a firm's future profitability. There is controversy regarding whether stock prices are a rational estimate of a company's true value.

HELPFUL HINTS

1. Compound growth is the same as compound interest. Compound interest is when you earn interest on your previously earned interest. Assuming annual compounding, when you deposit $100 in a bank at 10 percent, you receive $110 at the end of the year. If you leave it in for two years, you receive compound interest in that you receive $121 at the end of two years—the $100 principal, $10 interest from the first year, $10 interest from the second year, *plus $1 interest on the first year's $10 interest payment*. Next year, interest would be earned not on $100, or $110, but on $121, and so on.

In like manner, after a number of years, a faster growing economy is applying its percentage growth rate to a much larger base (size of economy) and total output accelerates away from economies that are growing more slowly. For example, applying the rule of 70, an economy that is growing at 1% should double in size after about 70 years (70/1). An economy growing at 4 percent should double in size every 17 1/2 years (70/4). After 70 years, the 4 percent growth economy is 16 times its original size (2^4) while the 1 percent growth economy is only twice its original size. If both economies started at the same size, the 4 percent growth economy is now eight times the size of the 1 percent growth economy thanks to compound growth.

2. Risk-averse people benefit from insurance because, due to their diminishing marginal utility of wealth, the reduction in utility from a single big expense exceeds the reduction in utility from a number of small payments into the insurance fund. For example, suppose there are 50 people in town. One house burns down each year so each person has a 1 in 50 chance of losing his entire home in any given year. People can pay 1/50 of the value of their home into the insurance fund each year and, thus, they will have paid premiums equal to the value of their home after 50 years. Alternatively, they can fail to buy insurance but they will replace their home once every 50 years due to fire. Although the expected value of these two expenses are the same, risk-averse people choose to buy insurance because the reduction in utility from paying once for one entire home exceeds the reduction in utility from paying 50 times for 1/50 of a home.

3. The volatility of the return of a stock portfolio decreases as the number of stocks in the portfolio increases. When a portfolio is comprised of just one stock, the volatility of the portfolio is the same as the volatility of the single stock. When a portfolio is comprised of two stocks, it could be that when one stock is paying a return that is less than its average the other may be paying more than its average and the two tend to cancel out. As a result, the portfolio has less volatility than each of the stocks in the portfolio. This effect continues as the number of stocks in the portfolio increases. However, the majority of the risk reduction occurs by the time there are 20 or 30 stocks in the portfolio. Note that in order to achieve the projected risk reduction from diversification, the risks on the stocks must be unrelated. Therefore, randomly choosing stocks should generate more risk reduction than choosing stocks of firms that are, for example, all in the same industry or all located in the same geographic area.

4. The price of a stock depends on supply and demand. The demand for a stock depends on the present value of the stream of dividend payments and the final sales price. Therefore, an increase in either the expected dividends or the final sales price, or a decrease in the prevailing interest rate, will increase the demand for a stock and increase its price. The demand for a stock also depends on risk factors associated with the stock. Because people are risk averse, an increase in aggregate risk will reduce the demand for all stocks and all stock prices should decrease. Oddly, an increase in idiosyncratic risk (the portion of the standard deviation in the returns on a particular stock that are associated with the specific company) should not affect the demand for the stock because this type of risk can be eliminated through diversification.

TERMS AND DEFINITIONS

Choose a definition for each key term.

Key terms:

____ Finance

____ Present value

____ Future value

____ Compounding

____ Diversification

____ Idiosyncratic risk

____ Aggregate risk

____ Fundamental Analysis

____ Efficient markets hypothesis

____ Informationally efficient

____ Random walk

Definitions:

1. Reflecting all available information in a rational way

2. The amount of money today that would be needed to produce, using prevailing interest rates, a given future amount of money

3. The study of a company's accounting statements and future prospects to determine its value

4. The field that studies how people make decisions regarding the allocation of resources over time and the handling of risk

5. The path of a variable whose changes are impossible to predict

6. Risk that affects only a single economic actor

7. The accumulation of a sum of money in an account where interest is earned on previously paid interest

8. The theory according to which asset prices reflect all publicly available information about the value of an asset

9. The amount of money in the future that an amount of money today will yield, given prevailing interest rates

10. The reduction of risk achieved by replacing a single risk with a large number of smaller unrelated risks

11. Risk that affects all economic actors at once

PROBLEMS AND SHORT-ANSWER QUESTIONS

Practice Problems

1. Whitewater Raft Tour Company can purchase rafts today for $100,000. They will earn a $40,000 return on the rafts at the end of each of the next three years.
   a. If the interest rate were 12 percent, what is the present value of each of the future returns that Whitewater Raft expects to receive?

   _____

   _____

b. If the interest rate were 12 percent, should Whitewater Raft invest in the rafts? Explain.

_____

_____

c. If the interest rate were 7 percent, should Whitewater Raft invest in the rafts? Explain.

_____

_____

d. Compare your answers to parts (b) and (c) above. What general principle about the relationship between investment and the interest rate is demonstrated?

_____

_____

2. Use the *rule of 70* to answer the following questions. Suppose that real GDP/person in Fastcountry grows at an annual rate of 2 percent and that real GDP/person in Slowcountry grows at an annual rate of 1 percent.
   a. How many years does it take for real GDP/person to double in Fastcountry?

   _____

   _____

   b. If real GDP/person in Fastcountry is $2000 in 1930, how much will it be in the year 2000?

   _____

   _____

   c. How many years does it take for real GDP/person to double in Slowcountry?

   _____

   _____

   d. If real GDP/person in Slowcountry is $2000 in 1930, how much will it be in the year 2000?

   _____

   _____

e. Use the numbers you calculated above to help explain the concept of compound growth.

_____

_____

_____

_____

f. If Fastcountry stopped growing in the year 2000, how many years would it take for the standard of living in Slowcountry to catch that of Fastcountry?

_____

_____

_____

3. For each of the following, determine the type of problem from which the insurance market suffers (adverse selection or moral hazard) and explain.
   a. Susan buys health insurance at the nonsmoker rate. After she obtains the insurance, she begins smoking again.

   _____

   _____

   b. Bryce discovers that he has a liver condition that will shorten his life. He seeks life insurance to help pay for his children's college expenses.

   _____

   _____

   c. Fred gets a new job and will have to commute to Chicago. Fearing that he will get into an auto accident in the heavy traffic, he increases his auto coverage.

   _____

   _____

   d. After Lisa gets fire insurance on her house, she burns fires in the fireplace without closing the fireplace doors.

   _____

   _____

   _____

4. Rachel is an extremely picky eater. When choosing a restaurant, she always chooses to eat at a buffet. At a buffet, she doesn't have to order off a menu so she doesn't have to risk ordering something she may not like. Rachel knows that buffet food is very ordinary and, because she avoids nice restaurants, she misses the chance to eat some exceptional foods that she would enjoy very much. On the other hand, she never has a meal that she is unwilling to eat.

   a. Does Rachel gain as much utility from a truly great meal as she loses from eating a meal she dislikes? Explain.

   _____

   _____

   b. What can you say about Rachel's utility function with regard to her preferences toward risk? Explain.

   _____

   _____

   _____

   c. How does the availability of a buffet help Rachel reduce her risk? Explain.

   _____

   _____

   _____

Short-Answer Questions

1. Suppose that the interest rate is 6 percent. Which would you prefer to receive: $100 today or $110 one year from today? Why?

   _____

   _____

   _____

2. Suppose you put $100 in your savings account at your bank. If your account earns 8 percent interest and it is compounded annually, how much will be in your account after one year? After two years? How much more interest did you earn in the second year? Why?

   _____

   _____

   _____

3. You just won a lottery that pays you $100,000 at the end of each of the next three years. Alternatively, the lottery is willing to pay you a lesser amount in one lump sum today. What is the least you should accept in a lump sum payment today if the interest rates is 9 percent? Explain.

    _____

    _____

    _____

4. According to the *rule of 70*, how long will it take for your income to double if you get a 5 percent raise every year? If you start work at the age of 23 earning $40,000 per year and get a 5 percent raise every year, how much will you be earning if you retire at 65?

    _____

    _____

    _____

5. What property of an individual's utility function is necessary for that individual to be risk averse? Explain.

    _____

    _____

    _____

6. Suppose that people wreck their autos once every ten years and the autos are a total loss. People can buy insurance with annual premiums of 1/10 of the value of a car. Would a risk-averse person buy collision insurance for his auto? Why?

    _____

    _____

    _____

7. What are the two types of problems from which insurance markets suffer? Explain. What problem does this cause for low-risk people?

    _____

    _____

    _____

8. What are the two types of risk someone faces when they buy stock? Which type of risk can be reduced with diversification and which type cannot? Explain.

_____

_____

_____

_____

9. Which are riskier, stocks or government bonds? Why? How can people use this information to adjust the amount of risk they face? If people reduce risk in this way, what happens to their return? Explain.

_____

_____

_____

10. What are three ways that people can reduce the risk they face in their investment portfolios?

_____

_____

11. Why might it be reasonable to restrict people's choices of retirement plans by forcing people to contribute to such things as company pension plans or Social Security?

_____

_____

_____

12. What is fundamental analysis and what are three ways to perform fundamental analysis?

_____

_____

_____

SELF-TEST

True/False Questions

_____ 1. If the prevailing interest rate is 10 percent, a rational person should be indifferent between receiving $1,000 today and $1,000 one year from today.

_____ 2. You are going to receive a $100,000 inheritance in ten years. If the prevailing interest rate is 6 percent, the present value of your inheritance is $55,839.48.

_____ 3. The rule of 70 suggests that, on average, people's incomes double every 70 years.

_____ 4. If interest is compounded annually, $100 placed in a bank account earning 10 percent interest should generate $30 interest after three years.

_____ 5. According to the rule of 70, if your income grows at 7 percent per year, it will double in ten years.

_____ 6. The present value of a future sum is the amount of money today that would be needed, at prevailing interest rates, to produce that future sum.

_____ 7. If people are risk averse, the utility gained from winning $1,000 is equal to the utility lost from losing a $1,000 bet.

_____ 8. If someone's utility function exhibits diminishing marginal utility of wealth, this person is risk averse.

_____ 9. The insurance market demonstrates the problem of adverse selection when those that are sicker than average seek health insurance.

_____10. People can reduce what is known as _aggregate risk_ by diversifying their portfolios.

_____11. Increasing the diversification of a portfolio from 1 stock to 10 stocks reduces the portfolio's risk by the same amount as increasing the diversification from 10 to 20 stocks.

_____12. As a person allocates more of his savings to stocks and less to government bonds, he will earn a higher rate of return but he must accept additional risk.

_____13. The efficient markets hypothesis suggests that since markets are efficient, it is easy to engage in fundamental analysis to purchase undervalued stock and then earn greater than average market returns.

_____14. If the efficient markets hypothesis is true, stock prices follow a random walk. Therefore, buying a diversified portfolio, by purchasing an index fund or by throwing darts at the stock page, is probably the best that you can do.

_____15. The value of a stock is based on the present value of the future stream of dividend payments and the final sales price.

Multiple-Choice Questions

1. The amount today that would be needed, at prevailing interest rates, to produce a particular sum in the future is know as
   a. compound value.
   b. future value.
   c. present value.
   d. fair value.
   e. beginning value.

2. If a depositor puts $100 in a bank account that earns 4 percent interest compounded annually, how much will be in the account after five years?
   a. $104.00
   b. $120.00
   c. $121.67
   d. $123.98
   e. $400.00

3. General Electric has the opportunity to purchase a new factory today that will provide them with a $50 million return four years from now. If prevailing interest rates are 6 percent, what is the maximum that the project can cost for General Electric to be willing to undertake the project?
   a. $34,583,902
   b. $39,604,682
   c. $43,456,838
   d. $50,000,000
   e. $53,406,002

4. An increase in the prevailing interest rate
   a. decreases the present value of future returns from investment, and decreases investment.
   b. decreases the present value of future returns from investment, and increases investment.
   c. increases the present value of future returns from investment, and decreases investment.
   d. increases the present value of future returns from investment, and increases investment.

5. If two countries start with the same real GDP/person, and one country grows at 2 percent while the other grows at 4 percent,
   a. one country will always have 2 percent more real GDP/person than the other.
   b. the standard of living in the country growing at 4 percent will start to accelerate away from the slower growing country due to compound growth.
   c. the standard of living in the two countries will converge.
   d. next year the country growing at 4 percent will have twice the GDP/person as the country growing at 2 percent.

6. Using the *rule of 70*, if your income grows at 10 percent per year, your income will double in approximately
   a. 700 years.
   b. 70 years.
   c. 10 years.
   d. 7 years.
   e. There is not enough information to answer this question.

7. Using the *rule of 70*, if your parents place $10,000 in a deposit for you on the day you are born, approximately how much will be in the account when you retire at 70 years old if the deposit earns 3 percent per year?
   a. $300
   b. $3,000
   c. $20,000
   d. $70,000
   e. $80,000

8. If people are risk averse, then
   a. they dislike bad things more than the like comparable good things.
   b. their utility functions exhibit the property of diminishing marginal utility of wealth.
   c. the utility they would lose from losing a $50 bet would exceed the utility they would gain from winning a $50 bet.
   d. all of the above are true.
   e. none of the above are true.

9. Which of the following does *not* help reduce the risk that people face?
   a. buying insurance
   b. diversifying their portfolio
   c. increasing the rate of return within their portfolio
   d. All of the above help reduce risk.

10. Which of the following is an example of moral hazard?
    a. After Joe buys fire insurance, he begins to smoke cigarettes in bed.
    b. Doug has been feeling poorly lately so he seeks health insurance.
    c. Both of Susan's parents lost their teeth due to gum disease, so Susan buys dental insurance.
    d. All of the above demonstrate moral hazard.
    e. None of the above demonstrate moral hazard.

11. Idiosyncratic risk is the
    a. uncertainty associated with the entire economy.
    b. uncertainty associated with specific companies.
    c. risk associated with moral hazard.
    d. risk associated with adverse selection.

12. Diversification of a portfolio can
    a. reduce aggregate risk.
    b. reduce idiosyncratic risk.
    c. eliminate all risk.
    d. increase the standard deviation of the portfolio's return.

13. Compared to a portfolio composed entirely of stock, a portfolio that is 50 percent government bonds and 50 percent stock will have a
    a. higher return and a higher level of risk.
    b. higher return and a lower level of risk.
    c. lower return and a lower level of risk.
    d. lower return and a higher level of risk.

14. The study of a company's accounting statements and future prospects to determine its value is known as
    a. diversification.
    b. risk management.
    c. information analysis.
    d. fundamental analysis.

15. If the efficient markets hypothesis is true, then
    a. stocks tend to be overvalued.
    b. the stock market is informationally efficient so stock prices should follow a random walk.
    c. fundamental analysis is a valuable tool for increasing one's stock returns.
    d. an index fund is a poor investment.
    e. all of the above

16. Which of the following reduces risk in a portfolio the greatest?
    a. increasing the number of stocks in the portfolio from 1 to 10
    b. increasing the number of stocks from 10 to 20
    c. increasing the number of stocks from 20 to 30
    d. All of the above provide the same amount of risk reduction.

17. Which of the following should cause the price of a share of stock to rise?
    a. a reduction in aggregate risk
    b. an increase in expected dividends
    c. a reduction in the interest rate
    d. all of the above
    e. none of the above

18. Speculative bubbles may occur in the stock market
    a. when stocks are fairly valued.
    b. only when people are irrational.
    c. because rational people may buy an overvalued stock if they think they can sell it to someone for even more at a later date.
    d. during periods of extreme pessimism because so many stocks become undervalued.

19. Stock prices will follow a random walk if
    a. people behave irrationally when choosing stock.
    b. markets reflect all available information in a rational way.
    c. stocks are undervalued.
    d. stocks are overvalued.

20. It is difficult for an actively managed mutual fund to out perform an index fund because
    a. index funds generally do better fundamental analysis.
    b. stock markets tend to be inefficient.
    c. actively managed funds trade more often and charge fees for their alleged expertise.
    d. index funds are able to buy undervalued stocks.
    e. all of the above

ADVANCED CRITICAL THINKING

You are a student in the business college at an exclusive private university. The tuition is extremely expensive. Near the end of your senior year, your parents come to visit you in your dorm room. As they enter the room, they see you throwing darts at the stock pages on your bulletin board. You inform them that you received an enormous signing bonus from the company for which you agreed to work after graduation. You are now in the process of picking the stocks in which you plan to invest. Your parents are horrified and they want their money back for your expensive education. Your father says, "There's got to be a better way to choose stocks. I can give you the phone number of my stock analyst or you could at least buy a well-known, well-managed mutual fund."

1. What is the stock valuation method to which your father is referring, and what is its goal?

_____

_____

_____

_____

_____

2. Explain the efficient markets hypothesis to your parents. If the efficient markets hypothesis is true, can your father's method for picking stocks achieve its goal?

_____

_____

_____

_____

_____

3. If the efficient markets hypothesis is true, what is the only goal of your dart throwing exercise? Explain.

_____

_____

4. If the efficient markets hypothesis is true, which will likely provide the greater return in the long run: your dart throwing exercise or an actively managed mutual fund? Why?

_____

_____

_____

_____

SOLUTIONS

Terms and Definitions

_4_   Finance

_2_   Present value

_9_   Future value

_7_   Compounding

_10_   Diversification

_6_   Idiosyncratic risk

_11_   Aggregate risk

_3_   Fundamental analysis

_8_   Efficient markets hypothesis

_1_   Informationally efficient

_5_   Random walk

Practice Problems

1. a. $\$40,000/1.12 = \$35,714.29$; $\$40,000/(1.12)^2 = \$31,887.76$; $\$40,000/(1.12)^3 = \$28,471.21$
    b. No, the cost is $\$100,000$ but the present value of the return is only $\$96,073.26$.
    c. Yes. Although the cost is still $\$100,000$, the present value of the returns is now the sum of $\$40,000/1.07$; $\$40,000/(1.07)^2$; $\$40,000/(1.07)^3$ which is $\$104,972.65$.
    d. Investment is inversely related to the interest rate—lower interest rates stimulate investment.

2. a. $70/2 = 35$ years.
    b. $\$8,000$
    c. $70/1 = 70$ years.
    d. $\$4,000$
    e. Fastcountry adds $\$2,000$ to its GDP/person in the first 35 years. Growing at the same percent, it adds $\$4,000$ to its GDP over the next 35 years because the same growth rate is now applied to a larger base.
    f. Another 70 years.

3. a. Moral hazard, because after she obtained the insurance, she is less careful with her health.
    b. Adverse selection, because after he knows that his probability of death is higher than average, he seeks life insurance.
    c. Adverse selection, because after he knows that his probability of an accident is higher than average, he seeks more auto insurance.
    d. Moral hazard, because after she obtains the insurance, she becomes less careful with fire.

4. a. No. She dislikes bad food more than she likes good food.
    b. Rachel is risk averse because she exhibits diminishing marginal utility of wealth (she dislikes spending, say, $\$30$ on a meal she dislikes more than she enjoys spending $\$30$ on a meal she loves.)

c. She can diversify her risk at a buffet—she does not "put all of her eggs in one basket" at a buffet. This reduces her standard deviation of meals because her meals are always adequate but never terrible or great. A buffet is like a mutual fund of food.

Short-Answer Questions

1. You should prefer $110 one year from today because the PV of $110 one year from today is $110/1.06 = $103.77 and this is greater than $100.

2. After one year: $100(1.08) = $108. After two years: $100(1.08)^2 = $100(1.1664) = $116.64. The account earned $0.64 more interest in the second year because the account earned interest on the first year's interest payment: 0.08($8) = $0.64

3. The least you should accept is the present value of the future stream of payments which is: $100,000/1.09 + $100,000/(1.09)^2 + $100,000/(1.09)^3 = $91,743.12 + $84,168.00 + $77,218.35 = $253,129.47.

4. 70/5 = 14 years. Your income would double three time in the 42 year period or $40,000(2)^3 = $320,000 per year.

5. Diminishing marginal utility of wealth. Therefore, the increase in utility from a $1 gain is less than the decrease in utility from a $1 loss.

6. Yes. Due to diminishing marginal utility of wealth, the reduction in utility from a lump sum payment to replace a car exceeds the reduction in utility from the payment of 10 premiums of 1/10 of the value of a car.

7. Adverse selection: A high risk person is more likely to apply for insurance than a low risk person. Moral hazard: After people buy insurance, they have less incentive to be careful. As a result, the price of insurance is often too high for low risk people so they don't buy it.

8. Idiosyncratic risk—the uncertainty associated with specific companies, and aggregate risk—the uncertainty associated with the entire economy. Idiosyncratic risk can be eliminated with diversification because when one firm does poorly another unrelated firm may do well reducing the volatility in returns. Aggregate risk cannot be reduced because when the entire economy does poorly, the market portfolio does poorly.

9. Stocks, because the standard deviation in the returns to government bonds is zero while the standard deviation in stock returns is significantly higher. People can vary the proportion they invest in stocks versus risk free government bonds. Low risk assets generate low returns, so putting a larger portion of the portfolio in government bonds lowers the return of the portfolio.

10. Buy insurance, diversify a portfolio, and accept a lower return on the portfolio.

11. Some people exhibit little self-control, poor decision making, and overconfidence. This can cause them to fail to diversify their portfolios and accept too much risk.

12. Determining a company's value by analyzing its accounting statements and future prospects. You can do it yourself, rely on Wall Street analysts, or buy a mutual fund that is actively managed.

True/False Questions

1. F; the present value of $1,000 one year from today is $1,000/1.10 = $909.09.

2. T

3. F; if people's incomes grow at x percent, they double in $70/x$ years.

4. F; $10 the first year, $11 the second year, $12.10 the third year for a total of $33.10.

5. T

6. T

7. F; the utility lost from losing $1,000 is greater.

8. T

9. T

10. F; diversification reduces idiosyncratic risk.

11. F; diversification of a portfolio from 1 stock to 10 stocks reduces the portfolio's risk to a greater degree.

12. T

13. F; if markets are efficient, stocks are always fairly valued.

14. T

15. T

Multiple-Choice Questions

1. c	5. b	9. c	13. c	17. d
2. c	6. d	10. a	14. d	18. c
3. b	7. e	11. b	15. b	19. b
4. a	8. d	12. b	16. a	20. c

Advanced Critical Thinking

1. Fundamental analysis is the detailed analysis of a firm's accounting statements and future prospects to determine its value. The goal is to choose stocks that are undervalued—those whose stock prices are less than their values.

2. The efficient markets hypothesis argues that the stock market is informationally efficient in that it reflects all available information about the value of the traded stocks. That is, market participants monitor news that affects the value of a stock. Since at any given time the number of buyers of a stock equals the number of sellers, an equal number of people think a stock is undervalued as overvalued. Thus, stock is fairly valued all the time and its price should follow a random walk. If true, it is not possible to consistently buy undervalued stock.

3. The only thing a person can do is diversify their portfolio to reduce idiosyncratic risk.

4. If you throw enough darts to remove most of the idiosyncratic risk (your portfolio starts to resemble the entire market like an index fund) and if you bought and held the stock (you didn't trade often), then it is likely that throwing darts would give you the greater return. This is because active managers of mutual funds tend to trade frequently incurring trading costs and they charge fees as compensation for their alleged expertise, yet they cannot reduce aggregate risk.

UNEMPLOYMENT AND
ITS NATURAL RATE

CHAPTER OVERVIEW

Context and Purpose

Chapter 15 is the fourth chapter in a four-chapter sequence on the level and growth of output in the long run. In Chapter 12, we learned that capital and labor are among the primary determinants of output and growth. In Chapter 13, we addressed how saving and investment in capital goods affect the production of output. In Chapter 14, we learned about some of the tools people and firms use when choosing capital projects in which to invest. In Chapter 15, we see how full utilization of our labor resources improves the level of production and our standard of living.

The purpose of Chapter 15 is to introduce you to the labor market. We will see how economists measure the performance of the labor market using unemployment statistics. We will also address a number of sources of unemployment and some policies that the government might use to lower certain types of unemployment.

15

GOALS

In this chapter you will

Learn about the data used to measure the amount of unemployment

Consider how unemployment arises from the process of job search

Consider how unemployment can result from minimum-wage laws

See how unemployment can arise from bargaining between firms and unions

Examine how unemployment results when firms choose to pay efficiency wages

OUTCOMES

After accomplishing these goals, you should be able to

Use data on the number of employed, unemployed, and not in the labor force to calculate the unemployment rate and the labor-force participation rate

Explain why some job search unemployment is inevitable

Diagram the impact of the minimum wage on high wage and low wage sectors

List the reasons why unions cause unemployment and, alternatively, why unions might increase efficiency in some cases

Describe the four reasons why firms may choose to pay wages in excess of the competitive wage

CHAPTER REVIEW

Introduction

If a country keeps its workers fully employed, it achieves a higher level of GDP than if it leaves many workers idle. In this chapter, we are concerned largely with the **natural rate of unemployment,** which is the amount of unemployment that the economy normally experiences. "Natural" does not mean constant or impervious to economic policy. It means that it is the unemployment that doesn't go away on its own. This chapter addresses the measurement and interpretation of unemployment statistics, and some causes and cures for unemployment.

Identifying Unemployment

The Bureau of Labor Statistics (BLS) uses the Current Population Survey to categorize all surveyed adults (16 and older) as employed, unemployed, or not in the labor force.

- employed: worked most of the previous week at a paid job

- unemployed: on temporary layoff, or looked for a job, or waiting to start a new job

- not in the labor force: not in previous two categories (student, homemaker, retired)

BLS then computes:

- labor force = number of employed + number of unemployed

- unemployment rate = (number of unemployed / labor force) × 100

- labor-force participation rate = (labor force / adult pop.) × 100

The **labor force** includes all people who have made themselves available for work. The **unemployment rate** is the percent of the labor force that is unemployed. The **labor-force participation rate** is the percent of the total adult population who are in the labor force. The unemployment rate and the labor-force participation rate varies widely across demographic groups-men, women, black, white, young, old. Women have lower labor-force participation rates than men, but once in the labor force they have similar unemployment rates. Blacks and teenagers have higher unemployment rates than whites and older workers.

The normal rate of unemployment around which the unemployment rate fluctuates is the *natural rate of unemployment*. The deviation in unemployment from the natural rate is known as **cyclical unemployment.** In recent history, the natural rate of unemployment in the United States has been about 5.5 percent. This chapter is concerned with explaining the characteristics and causes of the natural rate.

Because people move into and out of the labor force so often, unemployment is difficult to measure and interpret. For example, over one-third of the unemployed are recent entrants to the labor force and half of all spells of unemployment end when the unemployed person leaves the labor force. In addition, unemployment may be inaccurately measured because:

- Some people are counted in the labor force but unemployed even though they are only pretending to look for work so that they can collect government assistance or because they are being paid "under the table." This behavior biases the unemployment statistics upward.

- Some people have had an unsuccessful search for a job and have given up looking for work so they are not counted in the labor force. These individuals are called **discouraged workers.** This behavior biases the unemployment statistics downward.

Because of these and other problems, the BLS calculates alternative measures of labor underutilization, known as U1 through U6. These statistics attempt to measure the impact on the labor market of long-term unemployment, temporary jobs, discouraged workers, part-time workers, and marginally attached workers.

Knowledge about the duration of unemployment spells may help us design corrective policies for unemployment. Evidence suggests that *most spells are short-term, but most unemployment at any given time is long-term.* This means that many people are unemployed for short periods, but a few people are unemployed for very long periods. Economists think short-term unemployment is much less of a social problem than long-term unemployment.

In most markets, prices adjust to balance supply and demand. In the ideal labor market, wages would adjust so that there would be no unemployment. However, even when the economy is doing well, the unemployment rate never falls to zero. The following sections address four reasons why the labor market falls short of the ideal market. The first source of unemployment we discuss is due to job search. **Frictional unemployment** is the unemployment that results from the time it takes for workers to search for the jobs that best suit their tastes and skills. The next three sources of unemployment fall within the category of structural unemployment. **Structural unemployment** is the unemployment that results because the number of jobs available in some labor markets is insufficient for everyone who wants a job to get one. Structural unemployment occurs because the wage is held above the equilibrium wage. Three possible sources to an excessive wage are minimum-wage laws, unions, and efficiency wages. Frictional unemployment tends to explain shorter spells of unemployment while structural unemployment tends to explain longer spells of unemployment.

Job Search

Job search is the process of matching workers and jobs. Just as workers differ in their skills and tastes, jobs differ in their attributes. Moreover, information about jobs disseminates slowly. Therefore, it takes time for job candidates and job vacancies to match. *Frictional unemployment* is due to this search time.

Frictional unemployment is inevitable in a dynamic economy. As the demand for products changes, some industries and regions will experience growth while others will contract. These changes in the composition of demand among industries or regions are called *sectoral shifts*. Sectoral shifts cause temporary frictional unemployment as workers in contracting sectors lose their jobs and search for work in the growing sectors.

Frictional unemployment may be reduced by improved information about job openings provided by the Internet. Government may be able to lower frictional unemployment by engaging in activities that shorten the job search time. Two such programs are (1) government-run employment agencies to help match workers and jobs, and (2) worker-training programs to retrain workers laid off from contracting sectors. Critics argue that government is ill-suited to do these things and that the market does a more efficient job at matching and retraining.

Unemployment insurance pays laid off workers a portion of their original salaries for a period of time. Unemployment insurance increases frictional unemployment because unemployed workers are more likely to (1) devote less effort to their job search, (2) turn down unattractive job offers, and (3) be less concerned with job security. This does not mean unemployment insurance is bad. Unemployment insurance does provide the worker partial protection against job loss and it may improve the efficiency of the job market by allowing workers to search longer for the best job match.

German unemployment benefits may be so generous that many unemployed workers have little incentive to find work.

Minimum-Wage Laws

Structural unemployment results when the number of jobs is insufficient for the number of workers. Minimum-wage laws are one source of structural unemployment. Recall that minimum-wage laws force the wage to remain above the equilibrium wage. This causes the quantity of labor supplied to exceed the quantity of labor demanded. There is a surplus of labor or unemployment. Since the equilibrium wage for most workers exceeds the minimum wage, the minimum wage tends to cause unemployment only for the least skilled and least experienced, such as teenagers.

Although only a small portion of total unemployment is due to the minimum wage, an analysis of the minimum wage points out a general rule: *If a wage is held above the equilibrium level, the result is unemployment.* The next two sections develop two additional reasons why the wage may be held above the equilibrium level. That is, the next two sections provide two additional sources for structural unemployment.

Note that with frictional unemployment, workers are *searching* for the right job even if the wage is at the competitive equilibrium. In contrast, structural unemployment exists because the wage exceeds the competitive equilibrium wage and workers are *waiting* for jobs to open up.

Unions and Collective Bargaining

A **union** is a worker association that engages in **collective bargaining** with employers over wages and working conditions. A union is a cartel because it is a group of sellers organized to exert market power. If the union and firm fail to reach an agreement, the union can **strike**—that is, withdraw its labor services from the firm. Because of the threat of a strike, workers in unions earn about 10 to 20 percent more than nonunion workers. Less-educated workers gain a greater financial advantage from union membership than do better educated workers.

Unions benefit *insiders* (members) at the expense of *outsiders* (nonmembers). When the union raises the wage above the equilibrium wage, unemployment results. Insiders earn higher wages and outsiders are either unemployed or must take jobs with nonunion firms. This increases the supply of labor in the nonunion sector and lowers the wage further for nonunion workers.

Most cartels are illegal, but unions are exempt from antitrust legislation. Indeed legislation, such as the Wagner Act of 1935, promotes the establishment of labor unions. Alternatively, state *right-to-work laws* discourage union membership by making it illegal to require union membership for employment.

There is little agreement about whether unions are good or bad for the economy. Critics argue that unions are cartels that raise the price of labor above the competitive equilibrium. This is inefficient (causes unemployment) and inequitable (insiders gain at the expense of outsiders). Supporters of unions argue that firms have market power and are able to depress the wage, so unions are just a counterbalance to the firm's power. This is most likely to be true in a *company town* where one firm hires most of the workers in the region. Supporters also argue that unions are efficient because firms don't have to bargain with individual workers about salary and benefits. That is, unions may reduce transactions costs.

The Theory of Efficiency Wages

The theory of **efficiency wages** suggests that firms may intentionally hold wages above the competitive equilibrium because it is efficient for them to do so. Efficiency wages are similar to minimum-wage laws and unions because, in all three cases, unemployment results from wages being held above the equilibrium wage. However, an efficiency wage is unusual in that it is paid voluntarily by the firm. Below, we address four reasons why firms may find it efficient (or profitable) to pay a wage in excess of the competitive equilibrium:

- *Worker health* may be improved by paying a higher wage. Better-paid workers eat a better diet and are more productive. This is more applicable to firms in developing nations and is probably not relevant for firms in the United States.

- *Worker turnover* may be reduced by paying a higher wage because workers will find it difficult to find alternative jobs at the higher wage. Firms may find it profitable to reduce worker turnover because there is a cost associated with hiring and training new workers and because new workers are not as experienced.

- *Worker effort* may be increased by paying a higher wage. When a worker's effort cannot be easily monitored, workers may shirk their responsibilities. If caught and fired, a worker earning the competitive equilibrium wage can easily find another job at the same wage. Higher wages make workers eager to keep their jobs and work hard.

- *Worker quality* can be improved by paying a higher wage. Firms cannot perfectly gauge the quality of their job applicants. Higher quality workers have a higher *reservation wage*—the minimum wage they are willing to accept. By paying a wage above the competitive equilibrium, firms have a higher probability of attracting high quality applicants for a job opening.

HELPFUL HINTS

1. Job search takes time even at the competitive equilibrium wage. Minimum-wage laws, unions, and efficiency wages all create an excess supply of labor (unemployment) by holding the wage above the competitive equilibrium wage. Frictional unemployment, however, exists even at the competitive equilibrium wage because it is inevitable that it takes time for workers and firms to match regardless of the wage. For this reason, structural unemployment resulting from the wage being held above the equilibrium wage can often be thought of as additional unemployment beyond the inherent frictional unemployment.

2. The natural rate of unemployment is persistent, not constant. Changes in minimum-wage laws, unions, efficiency wages, and changes in the job search process due to the information revolution all have an impact on the natural rate of unemployment. Therefore, the natural rate will change as government policies, institutions, and behaviors change. But since policies,

institutions, and behaviors change slowly, so does the natural rate of unemployment. Note then, that although we have suggested that the natural rate has been about 5.5 percent for the last 40 years, it may be better to think of the natural rate as having been consistently in the range of about 5 percent to 6 percent.

TERMS AND DEFINITIONS

Choose a definition for each key term.

Key terms:

_7_ Natural rate of unemployment

_2_ Cyclical unemployment

_14_ Labor force

_16_ Unemployment rate

_8_ Labor-force participation rate

_1_ Discouraged workers

_15_ Structural unemployment

_11_ Union

_17_ Collective bargaining

_10_ Strike

_12_ Insiders

_18_ Outsiders

_9_ Right-to-work laws

_3_ Efficiency wages

_5_ Reservation wage

_6_ Frictional unemployment

_4_ Sectoral shifts

_13_ Unemployment insurance

Definitions:

1. Workers who stop looking for work due to an unsuccessful search

2. The deviation of the unemployment rate from its natural rate

3. Wages voluntarily paid in excess of the competitive equilibrium wage to increase worker productivity

4. Changes in the composition of demand across industries or regions

5. The lowest wage a worker will accept

6. Unemployment due to the time it takes for workers to search for the jobs that best suit their tastes and skills

7. Normal rate of unemployment about which the unemployment rate fluctuates

8. Percentage of the adult population in the labor force

9. Legislation that makes it illegal to require union membership for employment

10. An organized withdrawal of labor from the firm

11. Worker association that bargains with employers over wages and working conditions

12. Those employed in union jobs

13. A government program that pays laid off workers a portion of their original salaries

14. The total number of workers, which is the sum of the unemployed and the employed

15. Unemployment that results because the number of jobs available in some labor market is insufficient for everyone who wants a job to get one.

16. Percentage of the labor force that is unemployed

17. The process by which unions and firms agree on labor contracts

18. Those not employed in union jobs

PROBLEMS AND SHORT-ANSWER QUESTIONS

Practice Problems

1. Use the following information about Employment Country to answer question 1. Numbers are in millions.

	2001	**2002**
population	223.6	226.5
adult population	168.2	169.5
number of unemployed	7.4	8.1
number of employed	105.2	104.2

a. What is the labor force in 2001 and 2002?

_____

_____

b. What is the labor force participation rate in 2001 and 2002?

_____

_____

c. What is the unemployment rate in 2001 and 2002?

_____

_____

d. From 2001 to 2002, the adult population went up while the labor force went down. Provide a number of explanations why this might have occurred.

_____

_____

_____

_____

e. If the natural rate of unemployment in Employment Country is 6.6 percent, how much is cyclical unemployment in 2001 and 2002? Is Employment Country likely to be experiencing a recession in either of these years?

_____

_____

_____

_____

2. Suppose the labor market is segmented into two distinct markets: the market for low-skill workers and the market for high-skill workers. Further, suppose the competitive equilibrium wage in the low-skill market is $3.00/hour while the competitive equilibrium wage in the high-skill market is $15.00/hour.

   a. If the minimum wage is set at $5.00/hour, which market will exhibit the greatest amount of unemployment? Demonstrate it graphically.

   _____

   _____

EXHIBIT 1

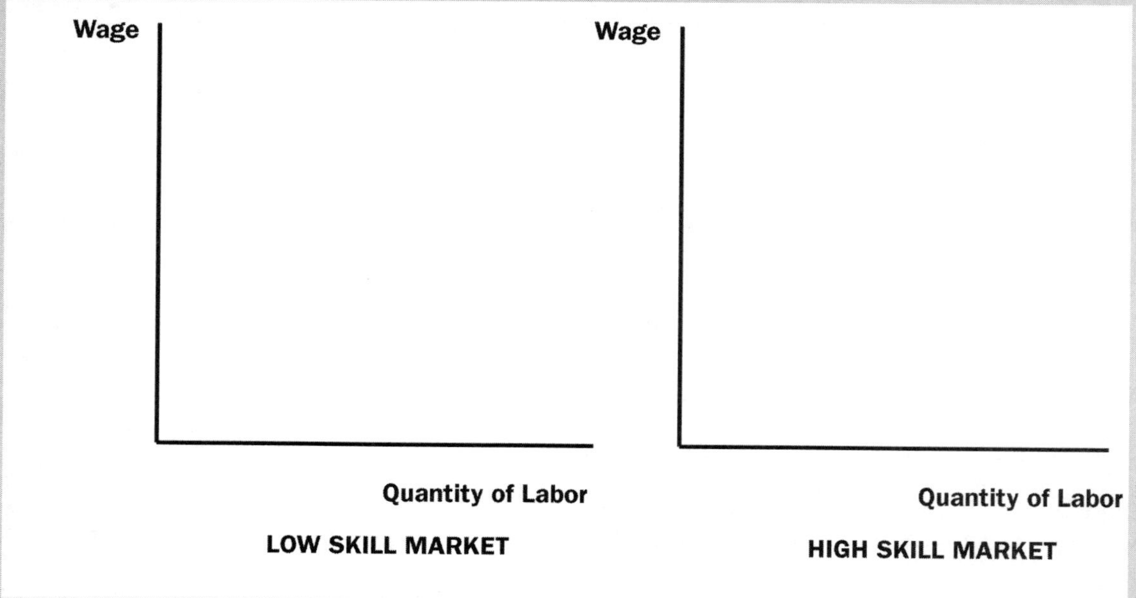

Wage   Wage

Quantity of Labor   Quantity of Labor

LOW SKILL MARKET   **HIGH SKILL MARKET**

   b. Does the minimum wage have any impact on the high skill market? Why?

   _____

   _____

   c. Do your results seem consistent with labor market statistics? Explain.

   _____

   _____

d. Suppose the high-skill market becomes unionized and the new negotiat-ed wage is $18.00/hour. Will this have any affect on the low skill market? Explain.

_____

_____

_____

_____

_____

3. Answer the following questions about the composition of unemployment.
   a. What are some of the sources of unemployment?

   _____

   _____

   b. Which type of unemployment is initiated by the firm?

   _____

   _____

   c. Why might a firm pay wages in excess of the competitive equilibrium?

   _____

   _____

   d. Which type of efficiency wage is unlikely to be relevant in the United States? Why?

   _____

   _____

   e. How does frictional unemployment differ from the other sources of unemployment?

   _____

   _____

Short-Answer Questions

1. Name two reasons why the unemployment rate is an imperfect measure of joblessness.

   _____

   _____

   _____

2. Explain the statement, "Most spells of unemployment are short, and most unemployment observed at any given time is long term."

   _____

   _____

   _____

3. Where would a labor union be more likely to increase efficiency rather than reduce it: a small remote town with one large employer or a major city with many employers? Why?

   _____

   _____

   _____

4. Name two ways that a union increases the disparity in wages between members and nonmembers.

   _____

   _____

   _____

5. Which alternative measure of unemployment attempts to include the impact of discouraged workers in the unemployment statistics? Explain. Is it higher or lower than the official unemployment rate? Explain.

   _____

   _____

   _____

6. Does the minimum wage cause much unemployment in the market for accountants? Why?

_____

_____

_____

7. Which type of unemployment will occur even if the wage is at the competitive equilibrium? Why?

_____

_____

_____

8. How does unemployment insurance increase frictional unemployment?

_____

_____

_____

9. How might the government help reduce frictional unemployment?

_____

_____

_____

10. Which of the following individuals is most likely to be unemployed for the long term: a buggy whip maker who loses his job when automobiles become popular, or a waitress who is laid off when a new cafe opens in town? Why?

_____

_____

_____

SELF-TEST

True/False Questions

_____ 1. The natural rate of unemployment is the amount of unemployment that won't go away on its own, even in the long run.

_F_ 2. If the unemployment rate falls, we can be certain that more workers have jobs.

_T_ 3. In post–World War II United States, the labor-force participation rate has been rising for women and has been falling for men.

_F_ 4. The unemployment rate is about the same for the various demographic groups: men, women, black, white, young, old.

_F_ 5. A minimum wage is likely to have a greater impact on the market for skilled workers than on the market for unskilled workers.

_T_ 6. The presence of a union tends to raise the wage for insiders and lower the wage for outsiders.

_T_ 7. A union is a labor cartel.

_T_ 8. Unions may increase efficiency in some circumstances because they decrease the cost of bargaining between labor and management.

_F_ 9. An efficiency wage is like a minimum wage in that firms are required by legislation to pay it.

_F_ 10. Paying efficiency wages tends to increase worker turnover because workers can get continually higher wages if they "job hop."

_T_ 11. Firms may voluntarily pay wages above the level that balances the supply and demand for workers because the higher wage improves the average quality of workers that apply for employment.

_F_ 12. If wages were always at the competitive equilibrium, there would be absolutely no unemployment.

_F_ 13. Due to the existence of "discouraged workers," the official unemployment rate may overstate true unemployment.

_F_ 14. The presence of unemployment insurance tends to decrease the unemployment rate because recipients of unemployment benefits are not counted in the labor force.

_T_ 15. Whenever the wage rises above the competitive equilibrium, regardless of the source, the result is additional unemployment.

Multiple-Choice Questions

1. The amount of unemployment that the economy normally experiences is known as
   a. efficiency wage unemployment.
   b. frictional unemployment.
   c. cyclical unemployment.
   d. the natural rate of unemployment.

2. According to the Bureau of Labor Statistics, a husband who chooses to stay
    home and take care of the household is
    a. unemployed.
    b. employed.
    c. not in the labor force.
    d. a discouraged worker.

Use the following table for questions 3 through 5. Numbers are in millions.

total population	195.4
adult population	139.7
number of unemployed	5.7
number of employed	92.3

3. The labor force is
    a. 92.3 million.
    b. 98.0 million.
    c. 134.0 million.
    d. 139.7 million.
    e. none of the above.

4. The unemployment rate is
    a. 3.2 percent.
    b. 5.7 percent.
    c. 5.8 percent.
    d. 6.2 percent.
    e. Not enough information is available to to answer.

5. The labor-force participation rate is
    a. 47.1 percent.
    b. 50.2 percent.
    c. 65.9 percent.
    d. 70.2 percent.
    e. none of the above.

6. An accountant with a CPA designation that has been unable to find work for
    so long that she has stopped looking for work is considered to be
    a. employed.
    b. unemployed.
    c. not in the labor force.
    d. not in the adult population.

7. Which of the following statements is true?
    a. Women tend to have similar unemployment rates as men.
    b. The labor-force participation rate of men is rising.
    c. Blacks have a lower unemployment rate than whites.
    d. Most spells of unemployment are long term but most unemployment
        observed at any given time is short term.
    e. All of the above are true.

8. A minimum-wage law tends to
   a. create more unemployment in high-skill job markets than in low-skill job markets.
   b. create more unemployment in low-skill job markets than in high-skill job markets.
   c. have no impact on unemployment as long as it is set above the competitive equilibrium wage.
   d. help all teenagers because they receive a higher wage than they would otherwise.

9. Which one of the following types of unemployment results from the wage being held above the competitive equilibrium wage?
   a. structural unemployment
   b. cyclical unemployment
   c. frictional unemployment
   d. sectoral unemployment
   e. none of the above

10. If, for any reason, the wage is held above the competitive equilibrium wage,
    a. unions will likely strike and the wage will fall to equilibrium.
    b. the quality of workers in the applicant pool will tend to fall.
    c. the quantity of labor supplied will exceed the quantity of labor demanded and there will be unemployment.
    d. the quantity of labor demanded will exceed the quantity of labor supplied and there will be a labor shortage.

11. A "reservation wage" is the
    a. maximum wage the firm is willing to pay.
    b. minimum wage the worker is willing to accept.
    c. tip necessary to get a waiter to reserve a table.
    d. competitive equilibrium wage.

12. Which of the following government policies would fail to lower the unemployment rate?
    a. reduce unemployment benefits
    b. establish employment agencies
    c. establish worker training programs
    d. raise the minimum wage
    e. establish right-to-work laws

13. Sectoral shifts tend to raise which type of unemployment?
    a. frictional unemployment
    b. structural unemployment
    c. unemployment due to unions
    d. unemployment due to efficiency wages

14. Which of the following is an example of a reason why firms might pay effi-
    ciency wages?
    a. At equilibrium wages, workers often quit to find better jobs.
    b. At equilibrium wages, workers sleep when the boss is not looking
       because workers are not deeply concerned about being fired.
    c. At equilibrium wages, only minimally qualified workers apply for the
       job.
    d. At equilibrium wages, workers cannot afford a healthy diet so they fall
       asleep at work due to a lack of energy.
    e. all of the above

15. Some frictional unemployment is inevitable because
    a. efficiency wages may hold the wage above the equilibrium wage.
    b. of minimum wage laws.
    c. there are changes in the demand for labor among different firms.
    d. of unions.
    e. all of the above

16. Unions might increase efficiency in the case where they
    a. raise the wage for insiders above the competitive equilibrium.
    b. offset the market power of a large firm in a "company town."
    c. lower the wage of local outsiders.
    d. threaten a strike but don't actually follow through so there are no lost
       hours of work.

17. Which of the following statements about efficiency wage theory is true?
    a. Firms do not have a choice about whether they pay efficiency wages or
       not because these wages are determined by law.
    b. Paying the lowest possible wage is always the most efficient (profitable).
    c. Paying above the competitive equilibrium wage tends to cause workers
       to shirk their responsibilities.
    d. Paying above the competitive equilibrium wage may improve worker
       health, lower worker turnover, improve worker quality, and increase
       worker effort.

18. Unions tend to increase the disparity in pay between insiders and outsiders by
    a. increasing the wage in the unionized sector, which may create an increase
       in the supply of workers in the nonunionized sector.
    b. increasing the wage in the unionized sector, which may create a decrease
       in the supply of workers in the nonunionized sector.
    c. decreasing the demand for workers in the unionized sector.
    d. increasing the demand for workers in the unionized sector.

19. Which of the following types of unemployment will exist even if the wage
    is at the competitive equilibrium?
    a. unemployment due to minimum-wage laws
    b. unemployment due to unions
    c. unemployment due to efficiency wages
    d. frictional unemployment

20. If unemployment insurance were so generous that it paid laid off workers 95 percent of their regular salary,
    a. the official unemployment rate would probably understate true unemployment.
    b. the official unemployment rate would probably overstate true unemployment.
    c. there would be no impact on the official unemployment rate.
    d. frictional unemployment would fall.
    e. none of the above

ADVANCED CRITICAL THINKING

You are watching the national news with your roommate. The news anchor says, "Unemployment statistics released by the Department of Labor today show an increase in unemployment from 6.1 percent to 6.2 percent. This is the third month in a row where the unemployment rate has increased." Your roommate says, "Every month there are fewer and fewer people with jobs. I don't know how much longer the country can continue like this."

1. Can your roommate's statement be deduced from the unemployment rate statistic? Why?

   _____

   _____

   _____

   _____

2. What information would you need to determine whether there are really fewer people with jobs?

   _____

   _____

   _____

SOLUTIONS

Terms and Definitions

 7 Natural rate of unemployment

 2 Cyclical unemployment

 14 Labor force

 16 Unemployment rate

 8 Labor-force participation rate

 1 Discouraged workers

 15 Structural unemployment

 11 Union

 17 Collective bargaining

 10 Strike

 12 Insiders

 18 Outsiders

 9 Right-to-work laws

 5 Reservation wage

 6 Frictional unemployment

 4 Sectoral shifts

 13 Unemployment insurance

 3 Efficiency wages

Practice Problems

1. a. 2001: 7.4 + 105.2 = 112.6 million
       2002: 8.1 + 104.2 = 112.3 million
    b. 2001: (112.6 / 168.2) × 100 = 66.9%
       2002: (112.3/169.5) × 100 = 66.3%
    c. 2001: (7.4 / 112.6) × 100 = 6.6%
       2002: (8.1/112.3) × 100 = 7.2%
    d. Earlier retirements, students staying in college longer, more parents staying at home with children, discouraged workers discontinuing their job search.
    e. 2001: 6.6% − 6.6% = 0%
       2002: 7.2% − 6.6% = 0.6%
       In 2001, unemployment is "normal" for Employment Country; therefore, there is no recession. However, in 2002, unemployment is above normal (positive cyclical unemployment), so Employment Country may be in a recession.

EXHIBIT 2

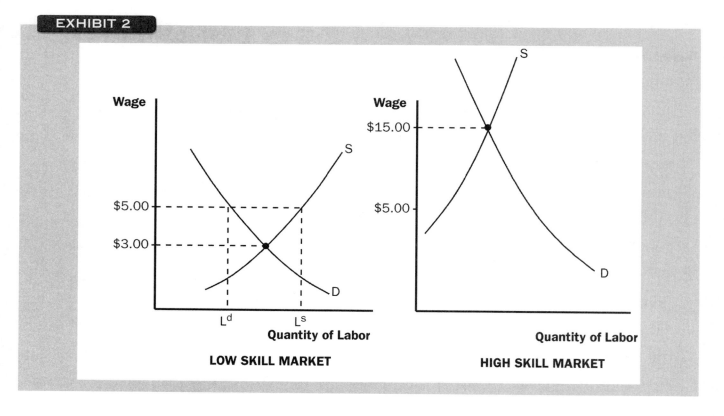

LOW SKILL MARKET

HIGH SKILL MARKET

2. a. The low-skill market will experience unemployment because there will be an excess supply of labor. (See Exhibit 2.)
   b. No, because the competitive equilibrium wage is above the wage floor.
   c. Yes. We observe a greater amount of unemployment among low-skill workers who are often young and inexperienced.
   d. Yes. The excess supply of skilled workers may cause some skilled workers to move to the unskilled market increasing the supply of labor in the unskilled market, further reducing the competitive equilibrium wage and causing even more unemployment there.

3. a. Job search, minimum wage, unions, efficiency wages.
   b. Efficiency wages.
   c. To improve worker health, lower worker turnover, increase worker effort, improve worker quality.
   d. Worker health, because in the U.S. workers' wages are significantly above subsistence.
   e. Frictional unemployment exists even when the wage is at a competitive equilibrium.

Short-Answer Questions

1. Some people claim to be looking for work just to collect unemployment benefits or they are being paid "under the table." Others are discouraged workers and have stopped looking for work due to an unsuccessful search.

2. Many people are unemployed for short periods. A few people are unemployed for very long periods.

3. In a small "company" town where a single company has market power that may depress the wage below the competitive equilibrium. This may need to be offset by organized labor.

4. It raises the wage above the competitive equilibrium in the unionized sector. Some of those unemployed in the unionized sector move to the nonunionized sector increasing the supply of labor and lowering the wage in the nonunion sector.

5. U4. It is total unemployed plus discouraged workers as a percent of the civilian labor force plus discouraged workers. It is a little higher than the official unemployment rate because it includes some non-working people that have given up looking for work and have fallen out of the labor force.

6. No, because the competitive equilibrium wage for accountants exceeds the minimum wage and, hence, the minimum wage is not a binding constraint for accountants.

7. Frictional unemployment, because job matching takes time even when the wage is at the competitive equilibrium. Also, continuous sectoral shifts and new entrants into the job market make some frictional unemployment inevitable.

8. Unemployed workers devote less effort to their job search, turn down unattractive job offers, and are less concerned with job security.

9. By establishing employment agencies and worker training programs to retrain workers laid off in the contracting sectors.

10. The buggy whip maker. He will have to retrain because the contraction of the buggy whip business is permanent, while the waitress may just have to relocate, possibly just down the street.

True/False Questions

1. T

2. F; the unemployment rate falls when unemployed workers leave the labor force.

3. T

4. F; unemployment differs across demographic groups.

5. F; a minimum wage has a greater impact on low wage workers.

6. T

7. T

8. T

9. F; efficiency wages are paid voluntarily by firms.

10. F; efficiency wages reduce turnover.

11. T

12. F; there would still be frictional unemployment.

13. F; the official unemployment rate may understate true unemployment.

14. F; unemployment insurance increases the unemployment rate because it increases frictional unemployment.

15. T

Multiple-Choice Questions

1. d	5. d	9. a	13. a	17. d
2. c	6. c	10. c	14. e	18. a
3. b	7. a	11. b	15. c	19. d
4. c	8. b	12. d	16. b	20. b

Advanced Critical Thinking

1. No. The unemployment rate is the ratio of the number of unemployed to the labor force. If the labor force grows (new graduates, house wives and house husbands entering the labor force) and if few of the new members of the labor force find work, then the unemployment rate will rise but the number of employed could stay the same or rise.

2. The number of employed is a component of the labor force and you can get information on that number directly.

16

GOALS

⌈In this chapter you will

Consider what money is and what functions money has in the economy

Learn what the Federal Reserve System is

Examine how the banking system helps determine the supply of money

See what tools the Federal Reserve uses to alter the supply of money

OUTCOMES

⌈After accomplishing these goals, you should be able to

Define money and list the three functions of money

Explain the role of the Fed in money creation

Explain the money multiplier in a fractional reserve banking system

List and explain the three tools the Fed uses to change the money supply

THE MONETARY SYSTEM

CHAPTER OVERVIEW

Context and Purpose

Chapter 16 is the first chapter in a two-chapter sequence dealing with money and prices in the long run. Chapter 16 describes what money is and develops how the Federal Reserve controls the quantity of money. Since the quantity of money influences the rate of inflation in the long run, the following chapter concentrates on the causes and costs of inflation.

The purpose of Chapter 16 is to help you develop an understanding of what money is, what forms money takes, how the banking system helps create money, and how the Federal Reserve controls the quantity of money. An understanding of money is important because the quantity of money affects inflation and interest rates in the long run, and production and employment in the short run.

CHAPTER REVIEW

Introduction

If there were no such thing as money, people would have to rely on barter. Barter is when people trade goods and services directly for other goods and services. Barter requires that there be a double coincidence of wants. For a trade to take place, each trader has to have what the other one wants—an unlikely event. The existence of money facilitates production and trade, which allow people to specialize in what they do best and raise the standard of living.

The Meaning of Money

Money is the set of assets commonly used to buy goods and services. That is, money is the portion of someone's wealth that is directly spendable or exchangeable for goods and services.

There are three functions of money:

- Money serves as a **medium of exchange** because money is the most commonly accepted asset when a buyer purchases goods and services from a seller.

- Money serves as a **unit of account** because money is the yardstick with which people post prices and record debts.

- Money serves as a **store of value** because people can use money to transfer purchasing power from the present to the future. Other types of wealth—stocks, bonds, rare art—may be a better store of value, but they are not as good at providing liquidity. **Liquidity** is the ease with which an asset can be converted into a medium of exchange. Money is liquid, but loses value when prices rise. The value of rare art tends to rise with inflation but it is much less liquid.

Money can be divided into two fundamental types—commodity money and fiat money.

- **Commodity money** is money that has "intrinsic value." That is, it has value independent of its use as money. Gold, silver, and cigarettes in a prisoner-of-war camp are all examples of commodity money. When a country uses gold as money, it is operating under a gold standard.

- **Fiat money** is money without intrinsic value. It is money by government fiat or declaration. Paper dollars are an example of fiat money.

When we measure the quantity of money, sometimes called the money stock, we should clearly include **currency** (paper bills and coins in the hands of the public) and **demand deposits** (balances in bank accounts that can be accessed on demand by check) because these assets are a medium of exchange. Savings balances, however, can easily be transferred into checking; other more restrictive checking accounts, such as money market mutual funds, offer some degree of spendability. In an economy with a complex financial system, it is difficult to draw the line between assets that are money and assets that are not. For this reason, in the United States we calculate multiple measures of the money stock, two of which are shown below:

- M1: Currency, demand deposits, traveler's checks, other checkable deposits

- M2: M1, savings deposits, small time deposits, money market mutual funds, a few minor categories

For our purposes, consider money in the United States to be currency and spendable deposits.

Credit cards are not counted in the stock of money because they are not a method of payment but are instead a method of deferring payment. Debit cards are like an electronic check in that money from the buyer's account is directly transferred to the seller's account. Thus, the value is already captured by the account balance.

In comparison to the size of the U.S. population, there is an unusually large amount of currency in circulation. It is likely that a large prtion of this currency is circulating overseas or used by criminal enterprises.

The Federal Reserve System

The **Federal Reserve (Fed)** is the **central bank** of the United States. It is designed to oversee the banking system and regulate the quantity of money in the economy.

The Fed was created in 1914 in response to a series of bank failures in 1907. The Fed is run by the Board of Governors, which has seven members appointed by the president and approved by the Senate. The members of the Board of Governors have 14-year terms to insulate them from political pressures. One of the seven members of the Board of Governors is appointed by the president to serve as Chairman for a four-year term. The Federal Reserve System is composed of the Federal Reserve Board in Washington, D.C. and 12 regional Federal Reserve Banks.

The Fed has two main jobs:

- to regulate the banks and ensure the health of the banking system. The Fed monitors each bank's financial condition and helps clear checks. In a crisis, when banks find themselves short of cash, the Fed may act as the *lender of last resort* to the banks.

- to control the quantity of money in the economy, called the **money supply**. The Fed's decisions about the money supply are called **monetary policy**.

The monetary policy branch of the Fed is the Federal Open Market Committee (FOMC). There are twelve voting members on the FOMC—the seven members of the Board of Governors plus five of the twelve regional bank presidents. The voting among the regional bank presidents is rotated. The FOMC meets about every six weeks to discuss the condition of the economy and to vote on changes in monetary policy.

The Fed primarily changes the money supply with **open-market operations,** which are the purchase and sale of U.S. government bonds by the Fed in the open market for debt (thus, the name Federal Open Market Committee).

- To increase the money supply, the Fed creates dollars and uses them to purchase government bonds. After the transaction, additional dollars are in the hands of the public, so the money supply is larger.

- To decrease the money supply, the Fed sells government bonds to the public. After the transaction, fewer dollars are in the hands of the public, so the money supply is smaller.

Changing the money supply changes inflation in the long run and may change employment and output in the short run.

Banks and the Money Supply

Recall that the public can hold its money as currency or demand deposits. Since these deposits are in banks, the behavior of banks affects the money supply. This complicates the Fed's task of controlling the money supply.

The impact that banks have on the money supply can be seen by going through the following three cases:

- Suppose there are *no banks*. Then currency is the only money. If there is $1,000 of currency, there is $1,000 of money.

- Suppose there is *100-percent-reserve banking*. Deposits that are received by a bank but are not loaned out are called **reserves.** With 100-percent-reserve banking, banks are safe places to store money, but they are not lenders. If the public deposits all $1,000 of its currency in Bank 1, Bank 1's T-account, which records changes in the bank's assets and liabilities, would be the following:

Bank 1

assets		liabilities	
reserves	$1000	deposits	$1000

Bank 1 has liabilities of $1,000 because it owes the $1,000 deposit back to the depositor. It has assets of $1,000 because it has cash reserves of $1,000 in its vault. Since currency held by the public has gone down by $1,000 and deposits held by the public have increased by $1,000, the money supply is unaffected. *If banks hold all deposits on reserve, banks do not influence the money supply.*

- Suppose there is **fractional-reserve banking.** Since few people request the return of their deposit on any given day, Bank 1 need not hold all $1,000 of the deposit as cash reserves. It could lend some of the $1,000 and keep only the remainder on reserve. This is called fractional reserve banking. The fraction of deposits held as reserves is the **reserve ratio.** The Fed sets the minimum reserve ratio with a reserve requirement. Suppose Bank 1 has a *reserve ratio* of 10 percent which means that it keeps 10 percent of its deposits on reserve and lends out the rest. Its T-account becomes:

Bank 1

assets		liabilities	
reserves	$100	deposits	$1000
loans	$900		

Bank 1 has created money because it still holds a $1,000 deposit but now a borrower has $900 in currency. *When banks hold only a fraction of deposits as reserves, banks create money.*

This story is not complete. Suppose the borrower of the $900 spends it and the receiver of the $900 deposits it in Bank 2. If Bank 2 also has a reserve ratio of 10 percent, its T-account becomes:

Bank 2

assets		liabilities	
reserves	$90	deposits	$900
loans	$810		

Bank 2 has created another $810 by its lending activity. Each time money is deposited and a portion of it loaned, more money is created.

If this process continues forever, the total amount of money created by the banking system from the original deposit of $1,000 is $1,000 + $900 + $810 + $729 + . . . = $10,000 (in this case, each loan is 90 percent of the previous loan).

The amount of money the banking system creates from each dollar of reserves is called the **money multiplier.** The money multiplier is the reciprocal of the reserve ratio. If R is the reserve ratio, then the money multiplier is $1/R$. In the case described above, the money multiplier is $1/.10$ or 10. Thus, $1,000 of new reserves created from the original $1,000 deposit can create a total of $10,000 in deposits.

The smaller the reserve ratio, the greater the amount of lending from the same amount of reserves and, hence, the larger the money multiplier. The larger the reserve ratio, the smaller the multiplier.

Fractional-reserve banking does not create net wealth because when a bank loans reserves, which creates money (someone's asset), it also creates an equal value debt contract (someone's liability).

The Fed has three main tools it uses to alter the money supply:

- *Open-market operations:* Recall, when the Fed buys government bonds from the public, the dollars it uses to pay for them increase the dollars in circulation. Each new dollar held as currency increases the money supply one dollar. Each dollar deposited with banks increases bank reserves and, thus, increases the money supply by some multiple. When the Fed sells government securities, dollars are removed from circulation and reserves are reduced at banks. This reduces lending, and further reduces the money supply. Open market operations can easily be used for small or large changes in the money supply. Hence, it is the day-to-day tool of the Fed.

- *Reserve requirements:* **Reserve requirements** set the minimum reserve ratio for a bank. An increase in the reserve requirement reduces the money multiplier and decreases the money supply. A decrease in the reserve requirement increases the money multiplier and increases the money supply. The Fed rarely changes reserve requirements because changes in reserve requirements disrupt the business of banking. For example, an increase in reserve requirements immediately restricts bank loans.

- *Discount rate:* The **discount rate** is the interest rate the Fed charges on loans to banks. When the Fed raises the discount rate, banks tend to borrow fewer reserves from the Fed and the money supply decreases. When the Fed decreases the discount rate, banks tend to borrow more reserves from the Fed and the money supply increases. The Fed also acts as a lender of last resort to banks during a crisis when depositors withdraw unusually large amounts of their deposits from banks.

The Fed's control of the money supply is not precise because:

- The Fed does not control the amount of money people choose to hold as deposits versus currency. When the public deposits a greater amount of their currency, bank reserves increase and the money supply increases.

- The Fed does not control the amount of reserves that the banks lend. The reserve requirement sets the minimum reserve ratio, but banks can hold *excess reserves*—reserves in excess of those required. If banks increase their excess reserves, lending decreases and the money supply decreases.

In times prior to the existence of deposit insurance, if depositors feared that a bank had made unsound loans with their deposits and that the bank might become bankrupt, they would "run" to the bank to remove their deposit. This is known as a "bank run." With fractional reserves, only a few depositors can immediately get their money back. This behavior causes a decrease in the money supply for two reasons. First, people increase their holdings of currency by withdrawing deposits from banks. This reduces reserves, bank lending, and the money supply. Second, banks, fearing deposit withdrawal, hold excess reserves and further decrease lending and the money supply. This is no longer a problem due to the Federal Deposit Insurance Corporation (FDIC). Also, the Fed collects weekly data on reserves and deposits so it can detect changes in depositor and bank behavior.

HELPFUL HINTS

1. Fiat money maintains value due to artificial scarcity. Gold has value because people desire it for its intrinsic value and because it is naturally scarce (alchemists have never been able to create gold). However, fiat money is cheap and easy to produce. Therefore, fiat money maintains its value only because of self-restraint on the part of the producer. If U.S. dollars are a quality store of value, it is because the dollar is difficult to counterfeit and the Fed shows self-restraint in the production of dollars.

2. Paper dollars are considered "currency" only when in the hands of the non-bank public. When economists use the word currency, we mean "currency in the hands of the non-bank public." When you deposit currency in the bank, you now own a deposit and your paper dollars are now the "reserves" of the bank. Currency in the hands of the non-bank public has decreased while deposits have increased by an equal amount. At this point, the money supply is unaltered because money is the sum of currency (in the hands of the non-bank public) and deposits.

3. The money multiplier is most easily understood in words. If we state the relationship between reserves, deposits, and the multiplier in words, it clarifies the relationship. Since a fractional reserve system implies that "reserves are some percent of deposits," it follows that "deposits are some multiple of reserves." For example, if reserves are 1/5 (or 20 percent) of deposits, then deposits are five times (or 1/.20) reserves. Since deposit expansion actually takes place due to banks' lending some of their reserves, it is most useful to us to think in terms of "deposits are some multiple of reserves."

4. It is easy to remember the impact of open-market operations by asking yourself, "Who pays?" When the Fed buys a government bond from the public, the Fed pays with "new dollars" and the money supply expands. When the Fed sells government bonds, the public pays with dollars and the Fed "retires" the dollars. That is, the dollars cease to exist when the Fed receives payment. Note that when the Fed sells bonds, it is not "issuing" bonds. It is selling existing bonds that were previously issued by the U.S. Government.

TERMS AND DEFINITIONS

Choose a definition for each key term.

Key terms:

____ Barter

____ Double coincidence of wants

____ Money

____ Medium of exchange

____ Unit of account

____ Store of value

____ Liquidity

____ Commodity money

____ Fiat money

____ Currency

____ Demand deposits

____ Federal Reserve (Fed)

____ Central bank

____ Money supply

____ Monetary policy

____ Federal Open Market Committee

____ Open-market operations

____ Reserves

____ Fractional-reserve banking

____ Reserve ratio

____ Money multiplier

____ Reserve requirements

____ Discount rate

____ Excess reserves

Definitions:

1. A banking system in which banks hold only a fraction of deposits as reserves

2. Paper bills and coins in the hands of the public

3. The function of money when used to transfer purchasing power to the future

4. The interest rate the Fed charges on loans to banks

5. Trading goods and services directly for goods and services

6. The function of money when used as a yardstick to post prices and record debts

7. Money in the form of a commodity with intrinsic value

8. The central bank of the United States

9. The set of assets generally accepted in trade for goods and services

10. The fraction of deposits held as reserves

11. Reserves held beyond the minimum reserve requirement

12. The quantity of money in the economy

13. Money without intrinsic value

14. The function of money when used to purchase goods and services

15. The purchase and sale of U.S. government bonds by the Fed

16. The accident that two people bartering have what the other wants

17. The minimum legal percent of deposits that banks must hold as reserves

18. Decisions by the central bank concerning the money supply

19. Balances in bank accounts that can be accessed on demand by check

20. The amount of money the banking system generates from each dollar of reserves

21. The monetary policy committee within the Federal Reserve

22. An institution designed to regulate the banking system and money supply

23. The ease with which an asset can be converted into the economy's medium of exchange

24. Deposits that banks have received but have not lent out

PROBLEMS AND SHORT-ANSWER QUESTIONS

Practice Problems

1. Suppose the Federal Reserve purchases a U.S. Government Bond from you for $10,000.
   a. What is the name of the Fed's action?

   _____

   b. Suppose you deposit the $10,000 in First Student Bank. Show this transaction on First Student Bank's T-account.

   First Student Bank

assets	liabilities

   c. Suppose the reserve requirement is 20 percent. Show First Student Bank's T-account if they loan out as much as they can.

   First Student Bank

assets	liabilities

   d. At this point, how much money has been created from the Fed's policy action?

   _____

   e. What is the value of the money multiplier?

   _____

   f. After infinite rounds of depositing and lending, how much money could be created from the Fed's policy action?

   _____

   g. If during the rounds of depositing and lending some people keep extra currency and fail to deposit all of their receipts, will there be more or less money created from the Fed's policy action than you found in part (f)? Why?

   _____

   _____

h. If during the rounds of depositing and lending, some banks fail to loan the maximum amount of reserves allowed but instead keep excess reserves, will there be more or less money created from the Fed's policy action than you found in part (f)? Why?

_____

_____

_____

2. Suppose the entire economy contains $1,000 worth of one dollar bills.
   a. If people fail to deposit any of the dollars but instead hold all $1,000 as currency, how large is the money supply? Explain.

_____

_____

   b. If people deposit the entire $1,000 worth of bills in banks that are required to observe a 100 percent reserve requirement, how large is the money supply? Explain.

_____

_____

   c. If people deposit the entire $1,000 worth of bills in banks that are required to observe a 20 percent reserve requirement, how large could the money supply become? Explain.

_____

_____

   d. In part (c), what portion of the money supply was created due to the banks? (Hint: $1,000 of bills already existed).

_____

_____

_____

   e. If people deposit the entire $1,000 worth of bills in banks that are required to observe a 10 percent reserve requirement, how large could the money supply become?

_____

_____

f. Compare your answer in part (e) to part (c). Explain why they are different.

_____

_____

_____

g. If people deposit the entire $1,000 worth of bills in banks that are required to observe a 10 percent reserve requirement, but they choose to hold another 10 percent as excess reserves, how large could the money supply become?

_____

_____

h. Compare your answer in part (c) to part (g). Are these answers the same? Why?

_____

_____

_____

Short-Answer Questions

1. What is barter and why does it limit trade?

_____

_____

_____

2. What are the three functions of money?

_____

_____

3. What are the two basic kinds of money?

_____

_____

4. What two main assets are clearly money in the United States and how do they differ from all other assets? (i.e. define money)

_____

_____

_____

5. What are the two main jobs of the Federal Reserve?

_____

_____

_____

6. What are the three monetary policy tools of the Fed?

_____

_____

7. If the Fed wished to expand the money supply, how should they adjust each of the three policy instruments described in question 6 above?

_____

_____

_____

8. If the Fed buys $1,000 of government bonds from you and you hold all of the payment as currency at home, by how much does the money supply rise?

_____

9. If the Fed buys $1,000 of government bonds from you, you deposit the entire $1,000 in a demand deposit at your bank, and banks observe a 10 percent reserve requirement, by how much could the money supply increase?

_____

_____

10. Suppose the reserve requirement is 20 percent. If you write a check on your account at Bank 1 to buy a $1,000 government bond from your roommate, and your roommate deposits the $1,000 in her account at Bank 2, by how much will the money supply change?

_____

_____

11. Suppose there is no deposit insurance. Suppose rumors circulate that banks have made many bad loans and may be unable to repay their depositors. What would you expect depositors and banks to do, and what would their behavior do to the money supply?

_____

_____

_____

SELF-TEST

True/False Questions

___F___ 1. Money and wealth are the same thing.

___F___ 2. Fiat money is money that is used in Italy.

___T___ 3. Commodity money has value independent of its use as money.

___T___ 4. The M1 money supply is composed of currency, demand deposits, traveler's checks, and other checkable deposits.

___F___ 5. When you are willing to go to sleep tonight with $100 in your wallet and you have complete confidence that you can spend it tomorrow and receive the same amount of goods as you would have received had you spent it today, money has demonstrated its function as a medium of exchange.

___F___ 6. Money has three functions: It acts as a medium of exchange, a unit of account, and a hedge against inflation.

___F___ 7. Credit cards are part of the M2 money supply and are valued at the maximum credit limit of the card holder.

___T___ 8. The Federal Reserve is the central bank of the United States and is run by the seven members of the Board of Governors.

___T___ 9. The Federal Open-Market Committee (FOMC) meets about every six weeks and discusses the condition of the economy and votes on changes in monetary policy.

___T___ 10. If there is 100 percent reserve banking, the money supply is unaffected by the proportion of the dollars that the public chooses to hold as currency versus deposits.

___F___ 11. If the Fed purchases $100,000 of government bonds, and the reserve requirement is 10 percent, the maximum increase in the money supply is $10,000.

___T___ 12. If the Fed desires to contract the money supply, it could do any of the following: sell government bonds, raise the reserve requirement, and raise the discount rate.

___T___ 13. If the Fed sells $1,000 of government bonds, and the reserve requirement is 10 percent, deposits could fall by as much as $10,000.

___F___ 14. An increase in the reserve requirement increases the money multiplier and increases the money supply.

___T___ 15. If banks choose to hold excess reserves, lending decreases and the money supply decreases.

Multiple-Choice Questions

1. Which of the following is not a function of money?
   a. unit of account
   b. store of value
   c. hedge against inflation
   d. medium of exchange

2. The M1 money supply is composed of
   a. currency, demand deposits, traveler's checks, and other checkable accounts.
   b. currency, demand deposits, savings deposits, money market mutual funds, and small time deposits.
   c. currency, government bonds, gold certificates, and coins.
   d. currency, NOW accounts, savings accounts, and government bonds.
   e. none of the above.

3. An example of fiat money is
   a. gold.
   b. paper dollars.
   c. coins.
   d. cigarettes in a prisoner-of-war camp.

4. The Board of Governors of the Federal Reserve System consists of
   a. 7 members appointed by Congress and 7 appointed by the president.
   b. 7 members elected by the Federal Reserve Banks.
   c. 12 members appointed by Congress.
   d. 7 members appointed by the president.
   e. 5 members appointed by the president and 7 rotating presidents of the Federal Reserve Banks.

5. Commodity money
   a. has no intrinsic value.
   b. has intrinsic value.
   c. is used exclusively in the United States.
   d. is used as reserves to back fiat money.

6. To insulate the Federal Reserve from political pressure,
   a. the Board of Governors are elected by the public.
   b. the Board of Governors have life-time tenure.
   c. the Board of Governors are supervised by the House Banking Committee.
   d. the Board of Governors are appointed to 14-year terms.

7. Which of the following statements is true?
   a. The FOMC meets once per year to discuss monetary policy.
   b. The Federal Reserve was created in 1871 in response to the Civil War.
   c. When the Fed sells government bonds, the money supply decreases.
   d. The primary tool of monetary policy is the reserve requirement.

8. Required reserves of banks are a fixed percentage of their
   a. loans.
   b. assets.
   c. deposits.
   d. government bonds.

9. If the reserve requirement is 25 percent, the value of the money multiplier is
   a. 0.25.
   b. 4.
   c. 5.
   d. 25.
   e. none of the above.

10. Which of the following policy actions by the Fed is likely to increase the money supply?
    a. reducing reserve requirements
    b. selling government bonds
    c. increasing the discount rate
    d. All of these will increase the money supply.

11. Suppose Joe changes his $1,000 demand deposit from Bank A to Bank B. If the reserve requirement is 10 percent, what is the potential change in demand deposits as a result of Joe's action?
    a. $1,000
    b. $9,000
    c. $10,000
    d. $0

12. A decrease in the reserve requirement causes
    a. reserves to rise.
    b. reserves to fall.
    c. the money multiplier to rise.
    d. the money multiplier to fall.
    e. none of the above.

13. The discount rate is
    a. the interest rate the Fed pays on reserves.
    b. the interest rate the Fed charges on loans to banks.
    c. the interest rate banks pay on the public's deposits.
    d. the interest rate the public pays when borrowing from banks.

14. Which of the following policy combinations would consistently work to increase the money supply?
    a. sell government bonds, decrease reserve requirements, decrease the discount rate
    b. sell government bonds, increase reserve requirements, increase the discount rate
    c. buy government bonds, increase reserve requirements, decrease the discount rate
    d. buy government bonds, decrease reserve requirements, decrease the discount rate
    e. none of the above

15. Suppose the Fed purchases a $1,000 government bond from you. If you deposit the entire $1,000 in your bank, what is the total potential change in the money supply as a result of the Fed's action if reserve requirements are 20 percent?
    a. $1,000
    b. $4,000
    c. $5,000
    d. $0

16. Suppose all banks maintain a 100 percent reserve ratio. If an individual deposits $1,000 of currency in a bank,
    a. the money supply is unaffected.
    b. the money supply increases by more than $1,000.
    c. the money supply increases by less than $1,000.
    d. the money supply decreases by more than $1,000.
    e. the money supply decreases by less than $1,000.

17. If the Fed engages in an open-market purchase and, at the same time, it raises reserve requirements,
    a. the money supply should rise.
    b. the money supply should fall.
    c. the money supply should remain unchanged.
    d. we cannot be certain what will happen to the money supply.

18. Given the following T-account, what is the largest new loan this bank can prudently make if the reserve requirement is 10 percent?

Test Bank

assets		liabilities	
reserves	$150	deposits	$1000
loans	$850		

    a. $0
    b. $50
    c. $150
    d. $1,000
    e. none of the above

19. The three main tools of monetary policy are
    a. government expenditures, taxation, and reserve requirements.
    b. the money supply, government purchases, and taxation.
    c. coin, currency, and demand deposits.
    d. open-market operations, reserve requirements, and the discount rate.
    e. fiat, commodity, and deposit money.

20. Suppose the Fed purchases a government bond from a person who deposits the entire amount from the sale in her bank. If the bank holds some of the deposit as excess reserves, the money supply will
    a. rise less than the money multiplier would suggest.
    b. rise more than the money multiplier would suggest.
    c. fall less than the money multiplier would suggest.
    d. fall more than the money multiplier would suggest.

ADVANCED CRITICAL THINKING

Suppose you are a personal friend of Alan Greenspan (the chairman of the Board of Governors on the date of publication of this *Study Guide*). He comes over to your house for lunch and notices your couch. Mr. Greenspan is so struck by the beauty of your couch that he simply must have it for his office. Mr. Greenspan buys it from you for $1,000 and, since it is for his office, pays you with a check drawn on the Federal Reserve Bank of New York.

1. Are there more dollars in the economy than before? Why?

    _____

    _____

2. Why do you suppose that the Fed doesn't buy and sell couches, real estate, and so on, instead of government bonds when they desire to change the money supply?

    _____

    _____

    _____

3. If the Fed doesn't want the money supply to rise when it purchases new furniture, what might it do to offset the purchase?

    _____

    _____

    _____

SOLUTIONS

Terms and Definitions

_5_ Barter

_16_ Double coincidence of wants

_9_ Money

_14_ Medium of exchange

_6_ Unit of account

_3_ Store of value

_23_ Liquidity

_7_ Commodity money

_13_ Fiat money

_2_ Currency

_19_ Demand deposits

_8_ Federal Reserve (Fed)

_22_ Central bank

_12_ Money supply

_18_ Monetary policy

_21_ Federal Open Market Committee

_15_ Open-market operations

_24_ Reserves

_1_ Fractional-reserve banking

_10_ Reserve ratio

_20_ Money multiplier

_17_ Reserve requirements

_4_ Discount rate

_11_ Excess reserves

Practice Problems

1. a. Open market operations
    b.

    First Student Bank

assets		liabilities	
Reserves	$10,000	Deposits	$10,000

    c.

    First Student Bank

assets		liabilities	
Reserves	$2,000	Deposits	$10,000
Loans	$8,000		

    d. $10,000 + $8,000 = $18,000
    e. $1/.20 = 5$
    f. $\$10,000 \times 5 = \$50,000$
    g. Less, because a smaller amount of each loan gets redeposited to be available to be loaned again.
    h. Less, because a smaller amount of each deposit gets loaned out to be available to be deposited again.

2. a. $1,000, because there is $1,000 of currency and $0 of deposits.
    b. $1,000, because there is now $0 of currency and $1,000 of deposits.
    c. $\$1,000 \times (1/.20) = \$5,000$, because $1,000 of new reserves can support $5,000 worth of deposits.

d. The total potential increase is $5,000, but $1,000 was currency already in the system. Thus, an additional $4,000 was created by the banks.

e. $1,000 × (1/.10) = $10,000.

f. Banks can create more money from the same amount of new reserves when reserve requirements are lower because they can lend a larger portion of each new deposit.

g. $1,000 × 1/(.10+.10) = $5,000.

h. Yes, they are the same. With regard to deposit creation, it doesn't matter why banks hold reserves. It only matters how much they hold.

Short-Answer Questions

1. Barter is trading goods and services directly for other goods and services. It requires a double coincidence of wants.

2. Medium of exchange, unit of account, store of value.

3. Commodity money, fiat money.

4. Currency and demand deposits. They are the assets that are directly spendable or are commonly accepted in trade for goods and services.

5. To regulate banks and insure the health of the banking system, and to control the quantity of money in the economy.

6. Open-market operations, reserve requirements, and the discount rate.

7. Buy U.S. government bonds, lower the reserve requirement, and lower the discount rate.

8. $1,000

9. $1,000 × (1/.10) = $10,000

10. The money supply will not change at all. In this case, reserves are only moved from one bank to another.

11. Depositors will withdraw their deposits reducing bank reserves. Banks will try to hold excess reserves to prepare for the deposit withdrawal. Both will reduce bank lending and the money supply.

True/False Questions

1. F; money is the spendable portion of one's wealth.

2. F; fiat money is money without intrinsic value.

3. T

4. T

5. F; money demonstrated its function as a store of value.

6. F; store of value, not a hedge against inflation.

7. F; credit cards are not included in the money supply.

8. T

9. T

10. T

11. F; the maximum increase in the money supply is $100,000 \times (1/0.10) = \$1,000,000$.

12. T

13. T

14. F; an increase in the reserve requirement decreases the money multiplier, which decreases the money supply.

15. T

Multiple-Choice Questions

1. c	5. b	9. b	13. b	17. d
2. a	6. d	10. a	14. d	18. b
3. b	7. c	11. d	15. c	19. d
4. d	8. c	12. c	16. a	20. a

Advanced Critical Thinking

1. Yes. When the Fed purchases anything, it pays with newly created dollars, and there are more dollars in the economy.

2. The transactions costs and storage costs would be staggering. Also, the value of the inventory of "items" would never be certain. The open market for government bonds is much more efficient.

3. The Fed could sell government bonds of equal value to offset other purchases.

17

MONEY GROWTH
AND INFLATION

GOALS

In this chapter you will

See why inflation results from rapid growth in the money supply

Learn the meaning of the classical dichotomy and monetary neutrality

See why some countries print so much money that they experience hyperinflation

Examine how the nominal interest rate responds to the inflation rate

Consider the various costs that inflation imposes on society

OUTCOMES

After accomplishing these goals, you should be able to

Demonstrate the link between money and prices with the quantity equation

Explain why money has no impact on real variables in the long run

Explain the concept of an inflation tax

Show the relationship between the nominal interest rate, the real interest rate, and the inflation rate

Explain who gains and who loses on a loan contract when inflation rises unexpectedly

CHAPTER OVERVIEW

Context and Purpose

Chapter 17 is the second chapter in a two-chapter sequence dealing with money and prices in the long run. Chapter 16 explained what money is and how the Federal Reserve controls the quantity of money. Chapter 17 establishes the relationship between the rate of growth of money and the inflation rate.

The purpose of this chapter is to acquaint you with the causes and costs of inflation. You will find that, in the long run, there is a strong relationship between the growth rate of money and inflation. You will also find that there are numerous costs to the economy from high inflation, but that there is not a consensus on the importance of these costs when inflation is moderate.

CHAPTER REVIEW

Introduction

Inflation is an increase in the overall level of prices. Deflation is a decrease in the overall level of prices. Hyperinflation is extraordinarily high inflation. There is great variation in inflation over time and across countries. In this chapter, we address two questions: what causes inflation and why is inflation a problem? The answer to the first question is that inflation is caused when the government prints

EXHIBIT 1

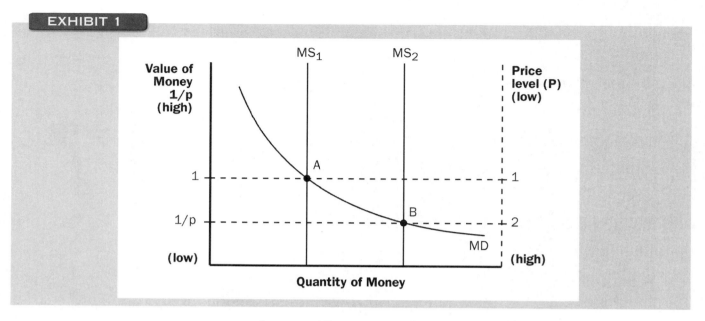

too much money. The answer to the second question requires more thought and will be the focus of the second half of this chapter.

The Classical Theory of Inflation

This section develops and employs the **quantity theory of money** as an explanation of the price level and inflation.

When prices rise, it is rarely because products are more valuable, but rather because the money used to buy them is less valuable. Thus, *inflation is more about the value of money than about the value of goods.* An increase in the overall price level is equivalent to a proportionate fall in the value of money. If P is the price level (the value of goods and services measured in money) then $1/P$ is the value of money measured in terms of goods and services. If prices double, the value of money has fallen to $1/2$ its prior value.

The value of money is determined by the supply and demand for money. If we ignore the banking system, the Fed controls the money supply. Money demand reflects how much wealth people want to hold in liquid form. While money demand has many determinants, in the long run one is dominant—the price level. People hold money because it is a medium of exchange. If prices are higher, more money is needed for the same transaction, and the quantity of money demanded is higher.

Money supply and money demand need to balance for there to be monetary equilibrium. Monetary equilibrium is shown in Exhibit 1 for money supply MS_1 at point A. Recall that the value of money measured in goods and services is $1/P$. When the value of money is high, the price level is low and the quantity of money demanded is low. Therefore, the money demand curve slopes negatively in the graph. Since the Fed fixes the quantity of money, the money supply curve is vertical. In the long run, the overall level of prices adjusts to equate the quantity of money demanded to the quantity of money supplied.

Suppose the Fed doubles the quantity of money in the economy from MS_1 to MS_2. There is now an excess supply of money at the original price level. Since people now are holding more money than they desire, they will rid themselves of the excess supply of money by buying things—goods and services or bonds. Even if people buy bonds (lend money), the bond issuer (borrower) will take the money and buy goods and services. Either way, an injection of money increases the demand for goods and services. Since the ability of the economy to produce goods and services has not changed, an increase in the demand for goods and services raises the price level. The price level will continue to rise (and the value of money will fall) until the quantity of money demanded is raised to the level of the quantity of money supplied (point B). That is, the price level adjusts to equate money supply and money demand. Thus, the conclusions of the *quantity theory of money* are: (1) the quantity of money in the economy determines the price level (and the value of money) and (2) an increase in the money supply increases the price level which means that growth in the money supply causes inflation.

The **classical dichotomy** suggests that economic variables can be divided into two groups—**nominal variables** (those measured in monetary units) and **real variables** (those measured in physical units). Although prices are nominal variables, relative prices are real variables. For example, the ratio of your earnings per hour to the price of candy bars is a real variable measured in candy bars per hour. Changes in the money supply affect nominal variables but not real variables. Real output is determined by productivity and factor supplies, and not by the quantity of money. However, the value of nominal variables is determined by and is *proportional* to the quantity of money. For example, if the money supply doubles, prices double, wages double, and all dollar values double but real output, employment, real interest rates, and real wages remain unchanged. This result is known as **monetary neutrality.** Money is unlikely to be neutral in the short run, but it is likely to be neutral in the long run.

The classical dichotomy and monetary neutrality can be demonstrated with the **quantity equation**. To begin, we define velocity as the speed of circulation of money. Then $V = (P \times Y)/M$ where V is the **velocity of money,** P is the price of output, and Y is the amount of real output (and $P \times Y$ = nominal GDP), and M is the quantity of money. If nominal output is $500 (500 items at $1 each) and M is $100, then $V = 5$. That is, in order for $100 to accommodate $500 of purchases and sales, each dollar must be spent, on average, 5 times.

Rearranged, we get the **quantity equation:** $M \times V = P \times Y$. If the quantity of money increases, P or Y must rise, or V must fall. Our theory of inflation takes five steps:

- V is relatively stable in the long run.

- Therefore, changes in M cause proportional changes in nominal output ($P \times Y$).

- Real output (Y) is determined by productivity and factor supplies in the long run and is not affected by changes in M.

- Because Y is fixed, an increase in M causes *proportional* changes in P.

- Thus, inflation results from rapid growth in the money supply.

Hyperinflation is sometimes defined as inflation that exceeds 50 percent per month. In those cases, the data show that there is a close link between money growth and inflation. This supports the conclusions of the quantity theory.

Why do countries print too much money if they know it causes inflation? Governments do it to pay for expenditures. When governments spend, they get the money by taxing, borrowing, or printing more money. Countries that have high spending, inadequate tax revenue, and limited ability to borrow, may turn to printing money. When a government raises revenue by printing money, it has engaged in an **inflation tax.** When the government prints money and prices rise, the value of the existing money held by people falls. An inflation tax is a tax on people who hold money. Russia employed an inflation tax during the 1990s.

If money is neutral, changes in money will have no effect on the real interest rate. Recall the relationship between the real interest rate, nominal interest rate, and inflation:

$$\text{real interest rate} = \text{nominal interest rate} - \text{inflation rate}$$

Solving for the nominal interest rate:

$$\text{nominal interest rate} = \text{real interest rate} + \text{inflation rate}$$

The real interest rate depends on the supply and demand for loanable funds. In the long run, money is neutral and only affects nominal variables, not real variables. Thus, when the Fed increases the growth rate of money, there is an increase in the inflation rate and a one-for-one increase in the nominal interest rate while the real interest rate remains unchanged. The one-for-one adjustment of the nominal interest rate to inflation is called the **Fisher effect.** Note that the nominal interest rate is set when the loan is first made and, thus, the Fisher effect actually says that the nominal interest rate adjusts one-for-one with *expected inflation*.

The Costs of Inflation

People often argue that inflation is a serious economic problem because when prices rise, their incomes can't buy as many goods and services. Thus, they believe that inflation directly lowers their standard of living. This argument, however, has a fallacy. Since people earn incomes by selling services, such as labor, inflation in nominal incomes goes hand in hand with inflation in prices. Therefore, inflation generally does not directly affect people's real purchasing power.

There are, however, a number of more subtle costs of inflation:

- *Shoeleather costs:* Recall, inflation is a tax on people who hold money. To avoid the tax, people hold less money and keep more invested in interest bearing assets when inflation is high than they do when inflation is low. As a result, people have to go to the bank and withdraw money more often than they would if there were no inflation. These costs are sometimes metaphorically called **shoeleather costs** (since your shoes are worn out from all those trips to the bank). The actual cost of holding less cash is wasted time and inconvenience. At high rates of inflation, this cost is more than trivial.

- *Menu costs:* There are numerous costs associated with changing prices—the cost of printing new menus, price lists, and catalogs, mailing costs to distribute them, the cost of advertising new prices, and the cost of deciding the new prices themselves.

- *Relative-price variability and the misallocation of resources:* Since it is costly to change prices, firms change prices as rarely as possible. When there is inflation, the relative price of goods whose price is held constant for a period of time is falling with respect to the average price level. This misallocates resources because economic decisions are based on relative prices. A good whose price is changed only once per year is artificially expensive at the beginning of the year and artificially inexpensive by the end of the year.

- *Inflation-induced tax distortions:* Inflation raises the tax burden on income earned from saving, and thus, discourages saving and growth. Inflation affects two types of taxes on saving:

(1) *Capital gains* are the profits made from selling an asset for more than its purchase price. Nominal capital gains are subject to taxation. Suppose you buy a stock for $20 and sell it for $50. Also suppose the price level doubles while you owned the stock. You only have a $10 real gain (because you would need to sell the stock for $40 just to break even) yet you must pay taxes on the $30 nominal capital gain because the tax code does not account for inflation.

(2) *Nominal interest* is taxed even though part of the nominal interest rate is to compensate for inflation. When government takes a fixed percent of the nominal interest rate as taxes, the after-tax real return grows smaller as inflation increases. This is because the nominal interest rate rises one for one with inflation and taxes increase with the nominal interest rate, yet the pretax real return is unaffected by inflation. Therefore, the after-tax real return falls.

Because there are taxes on nominal capital gains and nominal interest, inflation lowers the after-tax real return on saving, and thus, inflation discourages saving and growth. This problem can be solved by eliminating inflation or by indexing the tax system so that taxes are assessed only on real gains.

- *Confusion and inconvenience:* Money serves as the unit of account, which means that the dollar is the yardstick by which we measure economic values. When the Fed increases the money supply and causes inflation, it decreases the value of money and shrinks the size of the economic measuring stick. This makes accounting for firms' profits more difficult and, thus, makes choosing investments more complicated. It also makes daily transactions more confusing.

- *A special cost of unexpected inflation—arbitrary redistribution of wealth:* The costs of inflation described above exist even if inflation is stable and predictable. Inflation has an additional cost to the economy, however, if it is unexpected because it arbitrarily redistributes wealth. For example, the terms of a loan are generally expressed in nominal values based on a certain amount of expected inflation (see the Fisher effect equation). However, if inflation becomes higher than expected, borrowers are allowed to repay the loan with dollars that purchase less than expected. Borrowers gain at the expense of lenders. The opposite is true when inflation is less than expected. If inflation were perfectly predictable, regardless of its size, this redistribution would not take place. However, high inflation is never stable. Therefore, low inflation is preferred because it is more stable and predictable.

The U.S. Treasury has just begun to issue bonds that automatically adjust the interest payment based on inflation thereby maintaining a stable real return. These bonds cannot accidentally redistribute wealth. "Inflation-indexed bonds" have been sold in other countries for a number of years.

HELPFUL HINTS

1. The price of money is $1/P$. Since we measure the price of goods and services in terms of money, we measure the price of money in terms of the quantity of goods and services for which money can be exchanged. For example, if a basket of goods and services costs $5, then $P = \$5$. The price of a dollar is then $1/P$ or 1/5 of the basket of goods. That is, one dollar exchanges for 1/5 of the basket of goods. If the price of the basket of goods doubles so that it now sells for $10, the price of money has fallen to one half its original

value. Numerically, since the price of the basket is now $10, or $P = \$10$, the price of money has fallen to $1/P$ or $1/10$ of the basket of goods. To summarize, when the price of a basket of goods and services double from $5 to $10, the price of money falls by half from $1/5$ to $1/10$ of the basket of goods.

2. When dealing with the quantity theory, imagine you are at an auction. At the end of the auction, we can calculate the number of items sold and the average price of each item sold. Suppose we repeat the auction, only now the doorman doubles the money each buyer takes into the auction—if you had $20, you now have $40, and so on. If all participants spend the same percent of their money as at the prior auction (equivalent to a constant velocity) and if the items available to buy are unchanged (equivalent to a constant real output), what must happen to the average price of goods sold at the auction? Prices at the auction will precisely double, showing that prices are proportional to the quantity of money.

3. Unexpected inflation works like a tax on future receipts. We know that unexpected inflation redistributes wealth. Although it can be difficult to remember who wins and who loses on nominal contracts through time, you can always keep things straight if you remember that *unexpected inflation works like a tax on future receipts and a subsidy to future payments*. Therefore, when inflation turns out to be higher than we thought it would be when a loan contract was written, the recipient of the future payments is worse off because they receive dollars with less purchasing power than they had bargained for. The person who borrowed is better off because they were able to use the money when it had greater value, yet they were allowed to repay the loan with money of lower value. Therefore, when inflation is higher than expected, wealth is redistributed from lenders to borrowers. Alternatively, when inflation is less than expected, winners and losers are reversed.

This concept can be applied to any contract that extends through time. Consider a labor contract. Recall, when inflation is greater than we expected, those who receive money in the future are harmed and those who pay are helped. Therefore, firms gain at the expense of workers when inflation is greater than anticipated. When inflation is less than expected, winners and losers are reversed.

TERMS AND DEFINITIONS

Choose a definition for each key term.

Key terms:

_2___ Inflation

_16__ Deflation

_10__ Hyperinflation

_3___ Quantity theory of money

_____ Nominal variables

_____ Real variables

_____ Classical dichotomy

_____ Monetary neutrality

_15__ Velocity of money

_11__ Quantity equation

_____ Inflation tax

_6___ Nominal interest rate

_13__ Real interest rate

_____ Fisher effect

_____ Shoeleather cost

_____ Menu cost

_____ Capital gains

Definitions:

1. Resources wasted when inflation causes people to economize on money holdings

2. The practice of a government raising revenue by printing money

3. The theory that the quantity of money determines prices and the growth rate of money determines inflation

4. Variables measured in physical units

5. The costs associated with changing prices

6. Interest rate uncorrected for inflation

7. Profits made from selling an asset for greater than the purchase price

8. The one-to-one adjustment of the nominal interest rate to inflation

9. An increase in the overall level of prices

10. Extraordinarily high inflation

11. $M \times V = P \times Y$

12. The theoretical separation of nominal and real variables

13. Interest rate corrected for inflation

14. Variables measured in monetary units

15. Rate at which money circulates

16. A decrease in the overall level of prices

17. The property that changes in the money supply affect nominal variables but not real variables

PROBLEMS AND SHORT-ANSWER QUESTIONS

Practice Problems

1. Use the quantity equation for this problem. Suppose the money supply is $200, real output is 1,000 units, and the price per unit of output is $1.
   a. What is the value of velocity?

   _____

   b. If velocity is fixed at the value you solved for in part (a), what does the quantity theory of money suggest will happen if the money supply is increased to $400?

   _____

   _____

   c. Is your answer in part (b) consistent with the classical dichotomy? Explain.

   _____

   _____

   _____

   d. Suppose that when the money supply is doubled from $200 to $400, real output grows a small amount (say 2 percent). Now what will happen to prices? Do prices more than double, less than double, or exactly double? Why?

   _____

   _____

   _____

   e. When inflation gets very high, people do not like to hold money because it is losing value quickly. Therefore, they spend it faster. If when the money supply is doubled, people spend money more quickly, what happens to prices? Do prices more than double, less than double, or exactly double? Why?

   _____

   _____

   _____

   f. Suppose the money supply at the beginning of this problem refers to M1. That is, the M1 money supply is $200. What would the M2 quantity equation look like if the M2 money supply were $500 (and all other values were as stated at the beginning of the problem)?

_____

_____

2. The following questions are related to the Fisher effect.
   a. To demonstrate your understanding of the Fisher effect, complete the following table.

Real interest rate	Nominal interest rate	Inflation rate
3%	10%	
	6	2%
5		3

   The following questions about the Fisher effect are unrelated to the table above.
   b. Suppose people expect inflation to be 3 percent and suppose the desired real interest rate is 4 percent. What is the nominal rate?

_____

_____

   c. Suppose inflation turns out to be 6 percent. What is the actual real interest rate on loans that were signed based on the expectations in part (b)?

_____

_____

   d. Was wealth redistributed to the lender from the borrower or to the borrower from the lender when inflation was expected to be 3 percent, but in fact, turned out to be 6 percent?

_____

_____

   e. What would have happened had inflation turned out to be only 1 percent?

_____

_____

_____

3. Income taxes treat nominal interest earned on savings as income even though much of the nominal interest is simply to compensate for inflation.
   a. To see what this does to the incentive to save, complete the following table for both the low inflation and high inflation country.

	Low inflation country	High inflation country
Real interest rate	5%	5%
Inflation rate	3	11
Nominal interest rate		
Reduced interest rate due to a 25% tax		
After-tax nominal interest rate		
After-tax real interest rate		

   b. In which country is there a greater incentive to save? Why?

   _____

   _____

   _____

   c. What could the government do to eliminate this problem?

   _____

   _____

Short-Answer Questions

1. If the money supply doubles, what must happen in the long run to the quantity of money demanded and the price level?

   _____

   _____

   _____

2. Explain the classical dichotomy.

   _____

   _____

   _____

3. Within the framework of the classical dichotomy, which type of variables are affected by changes in money and which type are not? What phrase do we use to capture this effect?

_____

_____

4. Is money more likely to be neutral in the long run or the short run? Why?

_____

_____

_____

5. Suppose the money supply were to increase by 10 percent. Explain what would happen to each variable in the quantity equation.

_____

_____

6. What are the three sources of revenue a government can use to support its expenditures? Which method causes inflation and who bears the burden of this method of raising revenue?

_____

_____

7. In the long run, what does an increase in the growth rate of the money supply do to real and nominal interest rates?

_____

_____

_____

8. Does inflation erode the value of our income and thereby lower our standard of living? Explain.

_____

_____

9. What are the costs of inflation when inflation is perfectly anticipated?

_____

_____

_____

10. Suppose inflation turns out to be lower than we had expected. Who is likely to gain: borrowers or lenders? union workers or firms? Why?

_____

_____

_____

11. What is the inconsistency in the following statement? "When inflation is high but stable and predictable, inflation does not redistribute wealth."

_____

_____

12. Does inflation (if correctly anticipated) make borrowers worse off and lenders better off when it raises nominal interest rates? Why?

_____

_____

_____

SELF-TEST

True/False Questions

_____ 1. An increase in the price level is the same as a decrease in the value of money.

_____ 2. The quantity theory of money suggests that an increase in the money supply increases real output proportionately.

_____ 3. If the price level were to double, the quantity of money demanded would double because people would need twice as much money to cover the same transactions.

_____ 4. In the long run, an increase in the money supply tends to have an effect on real variables but no effect on nominal variables.

_____ 5. If the money supply is $500, real output is 2,500 units, and the average price of a unit of real output is $2, the velocity of money is 10.

_____ 6. The Fisher effect suggests that, in the long run, if the rate of inflation rises from 3 percent to 7 percent, the nominal interest rate should increase 4 percent and the real interest rate should remain unchanged.

_____ 7. An inflation tax is "paid" by those that hold money because inflation reduces the value of their money holdings.

___F___ 8. Monetary neutrality means that a change in the money supply doesn't cause a change in anything at all.

___F___ 9. Inflation erodes the value of people's wages and reduces their standard of living.

___T___ 10. Inflation reduces the relative price of goods whose prices have been temporarily held constant to avoid the costs associated with changing prices.

___F___ 11. The shoeleather costs of inflation should be approximately the same for a medical doctor and for an unemployed worker.

___F___ 12. Inflation tends to stimulate saving because it raises the after tax real return to saving.

___T___ 13. Countries that spend more money than they can collect from taxing or borrowing tend to print too much money which causes inflation.

___F___ 14. If inflation turns out to be higher than people expected, wealth is redistributed to lenders from borrowers.

___F___ 15. If the nominal interest rate is 7 percent and the inflation rate is 5 percent, the real interest rate is 12 percent.

Multiple-Choice Questions

1. In the long run, inflation is caused by
   a. banks that have market power and refuse to lend money.
   b. governments that raise taxes so high that it increases the cost of doing business and, hence, raises prices.
   c. governments that print too much money.
   d. increases in the price of inputs, such as labor and oil.
   e. none of the above.

2. When prices rise at an extraordinarily high rate, it is called
   a. inflation.
   b. hyperinflation.
   c. deflation.
   d. hypoinflation.
   e. disinflation.

3. If the price level doubles,
   a. the quantity demanded of money falls by half.
   b. the money supply has been cut by half.
   c. nominal income is unaffected.
   d. the value of money has been cut by half.
   e. none of the above.

4. In the long run, the demand for money is most dependent upon
   a. the level of prices.
   b. the availability of credit cards.
   c. the availability of banking outlets.
   d. the interest rate.

5. The quantity theory of money concludes that an increase in the money supply causes
   a. a proportional increase in velocity.
   b. a proportional increase in prices.
   c. a proportional increase in real output.
   d. a proportional decrease in velocity.
   e. a proportional decrease in prices.

6. An example of a real variable is
   a. the nominal interest rate.
   b. the ratio of the value of wages to the price of soda.
   c. the price of corn.
   d. the dollar wage.
   e. None of the above are real variables.

7. The quantity equation states that
   a. money × price level = velocity × real output.
   b. money × real output = velocity × price level.
   c. money × velocity = price level × real output.
   d. none of the above.

8. If money is neutral,
   a. an increase in the money supply does nothing.
   b. the money supply cannot be changed because it is tied to a commodity such as gold.
   c. a change in the money supply only affects real variables such as real output.
   d. a change in the money supply only affects nominal variables such as prices and dollar wages.
   e. a change in the money supply reduces velocity proportionately; therefore there is no effect on either prices or real output.

9. If the money supply grows 5 percent, and real output grows 2 percent, prices should rise by
   a. 5 percent.
   b. less than 5 percent.
   c. more than 5 percent.
   d. none of the above.

10. Velocity is
    a. the annual rate of turnover of the money supply.
    b. the annual rate of turnover of output.
    c. the annual rate of turnover of business inventories.
    d. highly unstable.
    e. impossible to measure.

11. Countries that employ an inflation tax do so because
    a. the government doesn't understand the causes and consequences of inflation.
    b. the government has a balanced budget.
    c. government expenditures are high and the government has inadequate tax collections and difficulty borrowing.
    d. an inflation tax is the most equitable of all taxes.
    e. an inflation tax is the most progressive (paid by the rich) of all taxes.

12. An inflation tax
    a. is an explicit tax paid quarterly by businesses based on the amount of increase in the prices of their products.
    b. is a tax on people who hold money.
    c. is a tax on people who hold interest bearing savings accounts.
    d. is usually employed by governments with balanced budgets.
    e. none of the above.

13. Suppose the nominal interest rate is 7 percent while the money supply is growing at a rate of 5 percent per year. If the government increases the growth rate of the money supply from 5 percent to 9 percent, the Fisher effect suggests that, in the long run, the nominal interest rate should become
    a. 4 percent.
    b. 9 percent.
    c. 11 percent.
    d. 12 percent.
    e. 16 percent.

14. If the nominal interest rate is 6 percent and the inflation rate is 3 percent, the real interest rate is
    a. 3 percent.
    b. 6 percent.
    c. 9 percent.
    d. 18 percent.
    e. none of the above.

15. If actual inflation turns out to be greater than people had expected, then
    a. wealth was redistributed to lenders from borrowers.
    b. wealth was redistributed to borrowers from lenders.
    c. no redistribution occurred.
    d. the real interest rate is unaffected.

16. Which of the following costs of inflation does not occur when inflation is constant and predictable?
    a. shoeleather costs
    b. menu costs
    c. costs due to inflation induced tax distortions
    d. arbitrary redistributions of wealth
    e. costs due to confusion and inconvenience

17. Suppose that, because of inflation, a business in Russia must calculate, print, and mail a new price list to its customers each month. This is an example of
    a. shoeleather costs.
    b. menu costs.
    c. costs due to inflation induced tax distortions.
    d. arbitrary redistributions of wealth.
    e. costs due to confusion and inconvenience.

18. Suppose that, because of inflation, people in Brazil economize on currency and go to the bank each day to withdraw their daily currency needs. This is an example of
    a. shoeleather costs.
    b. menu costs.
    c. costs due to inflation induced tax distortions.
    d. costs due to inflation induced relative price variability which misallocates resources.
    e. costs due to confusion and inconvenience.

19. If the real interest rate is 4 percent, the inflation rate is 6 percent, and the tax rate is 20 percent, what is the after tax real interest rate?
    a. 1 percent
    b. 2 percent
    c. 3 percent
    d. 4 percent
    e. 5 percent

20. Which of the following statements is true about a situation where real incomes are rising at 3 percent per year.
    a. If inflation were 5 percent, people should receive raises of about 8 percent per year.
    b. If inflation were 0 percent, people should receive raises of about 3 percent.
    c. If money is neutral, an increase in the money supply will not alter the rate of growth of real income.
    d. All of the above are true.
    e. None of the above is true.

ADVANCED CRITICAL THINKING

Suppose you explain the concept of an "inflation tax" to a friend. You correctly tell them, "When a government prints money to cover its expenditures instead of taxing or borrowing, it causes inflation. An inflation tax is simply the erosion of the value of money from this inflation. Therefore, the burden of the tax lands on those who hold money." Your friend responds, "What's so bad about that? Rich people have all the money so an inflation tax seems fair to me. Maybe the government should finance all of its expenditures by printing money."

1. Is it true that rich people hold more money than poor people?

   _____

   _____

2. Do rich people hold a higher percent of their income as money than poor people?

   _____

   _____

   _____

3. Compared to an income tax, does an inflation tax place a greater or lesser burden on the poor?

_____

_____

_____

_____

4. Are there any other reasons why engaging in an inflation tax is not good policy?

_____

_____

_____

SOLUTIONS

Terms and Definitions

_9_   Inflation

_16_   Deflation

_10_   Hyperinflation

_3_   Quantity theory of money

_14_   Nominal variables

_4_   Real variables

_12_   Classical dichotomy

_17_   Monetary neutrality

_15_   Velocity of money

_11_   Quantity equation

_2_   Inflation tax

_6_   Nominal interest rate

_13_   Real interest rate

_8_   Fisher effect

_1_   Shoeleather cost

_5_   Menu cost

_7_   Capital gains

Practice Problems

1. a. $(1,000 \times \$1)/\$200 = 5$
    b. $\$400 \times 5 = \$2 \times 1,000$, prices will double from $1 to $2
    c. Yes. The classical dichotomy divides economic variables into real and nominal. Money affects nominal variables proportionately and has no impact on real variables. In part (b), prices double, but real output remains constant.
    d. The quantity equation says that nominal output must change in proportion to money. Prices will still rise, but since real output is larger, prices will less than double.
    e. Money has a proportional impact on nominal output if V is constant. If V grows, a doubling of M will cause P to more than double.
    f. $\$500 \times 2 = \$1 \times 1,000$, M2 velocity is 2.

2. a.

Real interest rate	Nominal interest rate	Inflation rate
3%	10%	7%
4	6	2
5	8	3

b. 3% + 4% = 7%

c. People would have signed loan contracts for 7 percent nominal interest. Therefore, 7% − 6% = 1%.

d. People expected a real interest rate of 4 percent, but the actual real interest rate turned out to be 1 percent. Wealth was redistributed to the borrower from the lender.

e. The original loan contract would be the same. Thus 7% − 1% = 6%. The actual real rate is 6 percent instead of 4 percent so wealth is redistributed to lenders from borrowers.

3. a.

	Low-Inflation Country	High-Inflation Country
Real interest rate	5%	5%
Inflation rate	3	11
Nominal interest rate	8	16
Reduced interest rate due to a 25% tax	2	4
After-tax nominal interest rate	6	12
After-tax real interest rate	3	1

b. In the low inflation country because the after tax real interest rate is larger.

c. They could eliminate inflation or tax only real interest income.

Short-Answer Questions

1. The quantity of money demanded must double to maintain monetary equilibrium because spending will double on the same amount of goods causing prices to double and the value of money to fall by half.

2. The view that macroeconomic variables can be divided into two groups: real (measured in physical units) and nominal (measured in monetary units).

3. Nominal are affected. Real are not. Monetary neutrality.

4. In the long run, because it takes time for people and markets to adjust prices in response to a change in the money supply. In the short run, mistakes are likely to be made.

5. V remains constant. Y remains constant. M rises by 10 percent and P rises by 10 percent.

6. Taxes, borrowing, and printing money. Printing money. Those that hold money because its value decreases.

7. No impact on the real interest rate. Raises the nominal interest rate one-to-one with the increase in the growth rate of money and prices.

8. No. Income is a result of selling labor services, the value of which rises along with other prices during an inflation.

9. Shoeleather costs, menu costs, costs due to relative-price variability which misallocates resources, tax distortions, confusion and inconvenience.

10. Lenders and workers. Those that receive dollars in the future on contract receive dollars of greater value that they bargained for.

11. When inflation is high, it is always unstable and difficult to predict.

12. No. The nominal interest rate adjusts one-to-one with the rise in inflation so that the real rate is unaffected. Neither the borrower nor lender gain.

True/False Questions

1. T

2. F; it increases price proportionately.

3. T

4. F; the money supply tends to have an effect on nominal variables but not real variables.

5. T

6. T

7. T

8. F; it doesn't cause a change in real variables.

9. F; inflation in incomes goes hand in hand with inflation in prices.

10. T

11. F; the opportunity costs of trips to the bank are greater for a medical doctor.

12. F; inflation tends to reduce the after-tax return to saving.

13. T

14. F; wealth is redistributed to borrowers from lenders.

15. F; the real interest rate is 2 percent because $7\% - 5\% = 2\%$.

Multiple-Choice Questions

1. c	5. b	9. b	13. c	17. b
2. b	6. b	10. a	14. a	18. a
3. d	7. c	11. c	15. b	19. b
4. a	8. d	12. b	16. d	20. d

Advanced Critical Thinking

1. Yes, rich people probably hold more dollars than poor people.

2. No, by a wide margin, poor hold a larger percent of their income as money. In fact, the poor may have no other financial asset at all.

3. An inflation tax places a far greater burden on the poor than on the rich. The rich are able to keep most of their assets in inflation-adjusted, interest-bearing assets. We observed this in Brazil and Argentina during periods of high inflation.

4. Inflation imposes many other costs on the economy besides the inflation tax: shoeleather costs, menu costs, tax distortions, confusion, etc.

OPEN-ECONOMY MACROECONOMICS: BASIC CONCEPTS

CHAPTER OVERVIEW

Context and Purpose

Chapter 18 is the first chapter in a two-chapter sequence dealing with open-economy macroeconomics. Chapter 18 develops the basic concepts and vocabulary associated with macroeconomics in an international setting: net exports, net capital outflow, real and nominal exchange rates, and purchasing-power parity. The next chapter, Chapter 19, builds an open-economy macroeconomic model that shows how these variables are determined simultaneously.

The purpose of Chapter 18 is to develop the basic concepts macroeconomists use to study open economies. We address why a nation's net exports must equal its net capital outflow. We also address the concepts of the real and nominal exchange rate and develop a theory of exchange rate determination known as purchasing-power parity.

CHAPTER REVIEW

Introduction

Earlier in the text, we learned that people gain from trade because they can specialize in the production of goods for which they have a comparative advantage and trade for other people's production. However, until now, most of our study of macroeconomics has been based on a **closed economy:** one which does not interact with other countries. We now begin the study of macroeconomics in an **open economy:** an economy that interacts with other economies.

The International Flows of Goods and Capital

An open economy interacts with other economies in two ways: It buys and sells goods and services in world product markets, and it buys and sells capital assets in world financial markets.

The Flow of Goods and Services: Exports, Imports, and Net Exports **Exports** are domestically produced goods and services sold abroad while **imports** are foreign produced goods and services sold domestically. **Net exports** are the value of a country's exports minus the value of its imports. Net exports are also called the **trade balance.** If exports exceed imports, net exports are positive and the country is said to have a **trade surplus.** If imports exceed exports, net exports are negative and the country is said to have a **trade deficit.** If imports equal exports, net exports are zero and there is **balanced trade.**

Net exports are influenced by the tastes of consumers for domestic versus foreign goods, the relative prices of foreign and domestic goods, exchange rates, foreign and domestic incomes, international transportation costs, and government policies toward trade. These factors will be addressed in the following chapter.

The U.S. economy has engaged in an increasing amount of international trade during the last four decades for the following reasons: (1) improved transportation such as larger cargo ships, (2) advances in telecommunications which allow for better overseas communication, (3) technologically advanced goods are more valuable per pound and easier to transport, and (4) governments look more favorably on trade as evidenced by their support of the North American Free Trade Agreement (NAFTA) and the General Agreement on Tariffs and Trade (GATT).

The Flow of Financial Resources: Net Capital Outflow   **Net capital outflow** is the purchase of foreign assets by domestic residents minus the purchase of domestic assets by foreigners. When a domestic resident buys and controls capital in a foreign country, it is known as *foreign direct investment*. When a domestic resident buys stock in a foreign corporation but has no direct control of the company, it is known as *foreign portfolio investment*.

Net capital outflow is influenced by the relative real interest rates paid on foreign versus domestic assets, the relative economic and political risks, and government policies that affect ownership of foreign assets. These factors will be addressed in the following chapter.

The Equality of Net Exports and Net Capital Outflow   Net exports measure the imbalance of a country's imports and exports. Net capital outflow is the imbalance of a country's purchase and sale of assets. These two imbalances offset each other. That is, net capital outflow (NCO) equals net exports (NX):

$$NCO = NX$$

This is an identity because every international transaction is an exchange. When Ford sells a car to a Mexican resident, Ford receives pesos. NX has increased and NCO has increased because Ford is now holding additional foreign assets (pesos). If Ford chooses not to hold the pesos, any subsequent transaction undertaken by Ford preserves the equality of NX and NCO. For example, Ford could use the pesos to purchase Mexican goods of equal value, reversing the transaction so that NX and NCO return to their original values. Alternatively, Ford could use the pesos to buy other Mexican assets (stocks, etc.), maintaining the increase in *NX* and *NCO*. Finally, Ford could exchange the pesos for dollars. The new owners of the pesos could buy Mexican assets, maintaining the increase in *NX* and *NCO*, or they could buy Mexican goods, reducing *NX* and *NCO* to their original levels. Simply put, when someone exports goods and receives foreign currency, the foreign currency will either be held, used to buy goods from the importing country, or used to buy assets from the importing country. In each case, *NX* = *NCO* is maintained.

Saving and Investment in an Open Economy Saving and investment are important for growth. Saving is the income of a nation that is left over after paying for consumption and government purchases. Recall, gross domestic product (*Y*) is the sum of consumption (*C*), investment (*I*), government purchases (*G*), and net exports (*NX*). Therefore,

$$Y = C + I + G + NX$$

and saving is,

$$Y - C - G = I + NX$$

or,

$$S = I + NX.$$

Since *NX* = *NCO* we can write,

$$S = I + NCO.$$

Thus, in an open economy, when the U.S. economy saves a dollar, it can invest in domestic capital (*I*) or foreign capital (*NCO*). It does not have to invest only in domestic capital (*I*).

In summary, if a country runs a trade surplus, net exports (*NX*) are positive, domestic saving is greater than domestic investment, and net capital outflow (*NCO*) is positive. If a country runs a trade deficit, net exports (*NX*) are negative, domestic saving is less than domestic investment, and net capital outflow (*NCO*) is negative. If a country has balanced trade, net exports (*NX*) are zero, domestic saving is equal to domestic investment, and net capital outflow (*NCO*) is zero.

When the U.S. trade deficit increased from 1980 to 1987, the accompanying decrease in net capital outflow (foreigners invested more in the United States) was largely due to a decrease in U.S. saving. While this is not the preferred method to finance investment, it is better to have foreigners than no one invest in the United States. When the U.S. trade deficit increased from 1991 to 2000, the accompanying decrease in net capital outflow (foreigners invested more in the United States) was largely due to an increase in U.S. investment. This type of trade deficit induced capital inflow in a country is not necessarily bad as long as the investment projects yield the desired returns.

The Prices for International Transactions: Real and Nominal Exchange Rates

The **nominal exchange rate** is the rate at which people can trade one currency for another currency. An exchange rate between dollars and any foreign currency can be expressed in two ways: foreign currency per dollar or dollars per unit of foreign currency. For example, if 80 yen are equal to 1 dollar, the nominal exchange rate is 80 yen per dollar or .0125 (which is 1/80) dollars per yen. We will always express exchange rates as foreign currency per dollar. When the dollar buys more foreign currency, there has been an **appreciation** of the dollar. When the dollar buys less foreign currency, there has been a **depreciation** of the dollar. Because there are so many currencies in the world, the dollar exchange rate is often expressed by an exchange rate index that compares a group of currencies to the dollar.

The **real exchange rate** is the rate at which people can trade the goods and services of one country for the goods and services of another. Two things are considered when we directly compare the value of goods in one country to those in another: the relative values of the currencies (nominal exchange rate) and the relative prices of the goods to be traded. The real exchange rate is defined as:

$$\text{real exchange rate} = \frac{\text{nominal exchange rate} \times \text{domestic price}}{\text{foreign price}}$$

Just as the nominal exchange rate is expressed as units of foreign currency per unit of domestic currency, the real exchange rate is expressed as units of foreign goods per unit of domestic goods. For example: Suppose that a case of Mexican beer is 20 pesos while a case of U.S. beer is $10 and that the nominal exchange rate is 4 pesos per dollar. The real exchange rate of Mexican beer to U.S. beer is

$$\text{real exchange rate} = \frac{(4 \text{ pesos}/1 \text{ dollar}) \times (\$10/\text{case U.S. beer})}{(20 \text{ pesos}/\text{case Mexican beer})}$$

$$= \frac{40 \text{ pesos}/\text{case U.S. beer}}{20 \text{ pesos}/\text{case Mexican beer}}$$

$$= \frac{40 \text{ pesos}}{\text{case U.S. beer}} \times \frac{\text{case Mexican beer}}{20 \text{ pesos}}$$

$$= \frac{2 \text{ cases Mexican beer}}{1 \text{ case U.S. beer}}$$

The real exchange rate is the true relative cost of goods across borders.

Since macroeconomists are concerned with the economy as a whole, they are concerned with overall prices rather than individual prices. Therefore, instead of using the price of beer to compute the real exchange rate, macroeconomists use each country's price index:

$$\text{real exchange rate} = (e \times P)/P^*$$

where e is the nominal exchange rate, P is a domestic price index, and P^* is a foreign price index.

When this measure of the real exchange rate rises, U.S. goods are more expensive relative to foreign goods and net exports fall. When this measure of the real exchange rate falls, U.S. goods are cheaper relative to foreign goods and net exports rise.

Many European countries now share a common currency called the *euro*. It has replaced the French franc, German mark, Italian lira, and so on. The euro is controlled by the European Central Bank (ECB). A single currency makes trade easier, is more convenient, and helps reduce nationalistic feelings in Europe.

A First Theory of Exchange-Rate Determination: Purchasing-Power Parity

The simplest explanation of why an exchange rate takes on a particular value is called **purchasing-power parity.** This theory says that a unit of any given currency should buy the same quantity of goods in all countries. The logic of this theory is based on the *law of one price*. The law of one price says that a good must sell for the same price in all locations because, if there were different prices for the same good, people would buy the good where it is cheap and sell it where it is expensive. This behavior will continue to drive up the price where it was low and drive down the price where it was high until the prices are equalized. This process is called *arbitrage*. Thus, a dollar should buy the same amount of beer in Mexico as it buys in the United States. If it did not, there would be opportunities for profit and traders would buy where it is cheap and sell where it is expensive.

If purchasing-power parity is true, the nominal exchange rate between two country's currencies depends on the price levels in those two countries. For example, if beer in Mexico is 20 pesos per case while beer in the U.S. is $10 per case, then the exchange rate should be 20 pesos per $10, or 2 pesos/dollar so that one dollar buys the same amount of beer in both countries. Notice, *the nominal exchange rate of 2 pesos/dollar is simply the ratio of the prices in the two countries.*

To put this concept into a formula, suppose P is the U.S. price level, P^* is the foreign price level, and e is the exchange rate in terms of foreign currency per dollar. A dollar can buy $1/P$ units in the United States and e/P^* units in the foreign country. Purchasing-power parity suggests that a dollar should buy the same amount in each country.

$$1/P = e^*/P$$

Solving for e,

$$e = P^*/P.$$

Thus, if purchasing-power parity holds, the nominal exchange rate is the ratio of the foreign price level to the domestic price level.

Recall, a country's price level depends on how much money its central bank creates. If a central bank creates more money, its currency will buy fewer goods and services and fewer units of other currencies. That is, its currency will depreciate.

Purchasing-power parity is most likely to hold in the long run. However, even in the long run, the theory of purchasing-power parity is not completely accurate because (1) some goods are not easily traded (such as services) and (2) even tradable goods are not always perfect substitutes.

HELPFUL HINTS

1. Negative net capital outflow augments domestic investment. National saving is used to support domestic investment and net capital outflow:

    $$S = I + NCO.$$

    If *NCO* is negative, as it is for the United States, it means that foreigners invest more in the United States than Americans invests abroad. This allows domestic investment to remain adequate in spite of very small saving on the part of Americans. For example, suppose saving is $700 billion and net capital outflow is – $200 billion. Domestic investment is $I = \$700 + \$200$ or $900 billion.

2. Always express nominal and real exchange rates in terms of foreign units to domestic units. Expressing exchange rates in terms of foreign units relative to domestic units helps avoid confusion because a rise in this exchange rate is associated with a rise in the value of the domestic unit. For example, suppose the nominal exchange rate between the yen and the dollar is expressed as 200 yen/dollar. If the exchange rate rises to 210 yen/dollar, the value of the dollar has risen.

3. When generating nominal or real exchange rates, always identify the units of measurement. A common mistake committed by students when calculating exchange rates (particularly real exchange rates) is to fail to identify the units of measurement throughout the problem and to try to attach the units of measurement at the end of the problem after a numerical solution has been found. This leaves much room for error and confusion. Notice in the real exchange rate example about Mexican and American beer that the units are attached to the numbers throughout. This is not just for your convenience. It is necessary to avoid making mistakes even if you have done it numerous times.

4. Purchasing-power parity should hold for goods of high value and low transportation costs. The law of one price applies to goods for which arbitrage is most likely. Hence, we might expect the dollar price of diamonds to be the same in all countries because small deviations in the price of diamonds create substantial profit opportunities. However, large deviations in prices of shoe shines between London and New York are unlikely to create profit opportunities and a movement of goods or services. While many goods and services are not currently traded across borders, growth in the production and trade of light, high technology, high value commodities should increase the applicability of the purchasing-power parity theory.

TERMS AND DEFINITIONS

Choose a definition for each key term.

Key terms:

7 Closed economy

11 Open economy

2 Exports

13 Imports

8 Net exports

1 Trade surplus

12 Trade deficit

14 Net capital outflow

5 Nominal exchange rate

10 Appreciation

6 Depreciation

3 Real exchange rate

9 Purchasing-power parity

4 Arbitrage

Definitions:

1. The amount by which exports exceed imports

2. Goods and services produced domestically and sold abroad

3. The rate at which people can trade the goods and services of one country for those of another country

4. Taking advantage of two prices for the same commodity by buying where it is cheap and selling where it is expensive

5. The rate at which people can trade one currency for another currency

6. A decrease in the value of a currency measured in terms of other currencies

7. An economy that does not interact with other economies

8. The value of exports minus the value of imports or the trade balance

9. The theory that a unit of a country's currency should buy the same quantity of goods in all countries.

10. An increase in the value of a currency measured in terms of other currencies

11. An economy that interacts with other economies

12. The amount by which imports exceed exports

13. Goods and services produced in foreign countries and sold domestically

14. The purchase of foreign assets by domestic residents minus the purchase of domestic assets by foreigners

PROBLEMS AND SHORT-ANSWER QUESTIONS

Practice Problems

1. How would each of the following transactions affect U.S. *NCO*? Does the transaction affect direct investment or portfolio investment?
   a. Ford buys stock in Mazda.

_____

_____

b. Ford buys steel from a Japanese manufacturer to use in the production of its cars.

_____

_____

_____

c. Mazda expands its plant in Tennessee.

_____

_____

d. A Japanese mutual fund buys shares of stock in Ford.

_____

_____

e. Dow Chemical builds a plant in Germany.

_____

_____

2. Suppose a resident of Great Britain buys a computer from a U.S. manufacturer using British pounds.
   a. If the U.S. manufacturer holds on to the British pounds, does $NX = NCO$ in this case? Explain.

   _____

   _____

   b. Suppose the U.S. manufacturer uses the pounds to help build a factory in Great Britain. Does $NX = NCO$ in this case? Explain. What kind of foreign investment is this?

   _____

   _____

   c. Suppose the U.S. manufacturer uses the pounds to buy stock in a British corporation. Does $NX = NCO$ in this case? Explain. What kind of foreign investment is this?

   _____

   _____

d. Suppose the U.S. manufacturer uses the pounds to buy computer chips manufactured in Great Britain. Does $NX = NCO$ in this case? Explain.

_____

_____

_____

3. Suppose the nominal exchange rate is 100 yen per dollar. Further, suppose the price of a bushel of American corn is $5 per bushel and the price of a bushel of Japanese corn is 750 yen.

a. What is the real exchange rate between Japan and the United States in terms of corn?

_____

_____

b. Does a dollar have purchasing-power parity in the United States and Japan? Explain.

_____

_____

_____

c. Is there a profit opportunity that you could exploit with arbitrage? Where would you buy and where would you sell?

_____

_____

d. If the nominal exchange rate stayed the same, what should happen to the price of corn in the United States and Japan? Explain.

_____

_____

e. Suppose prices move as you have suggested in part (d). What has happened to the real exchange rate?

_____

_____

_____

4. Suppose the price of a pair of Lee jeans is $40 in the United States and 400 pesos in Mexico.

   a. What is the nominal peso/dollar exchange rate if purchasing-power parity holds?

   _____

   _____

   b. Suppose Mexico's central bank is politically pressured to double its money supply, which doubles its price level. If purchasing-power parity holds, what is the new peso/dollar exchange rate? Did the peso appreciate or depreciate?

   _____

   _____

   c. Suppose the Fed now doubles the U.S. money supply, which doubles the U.S. price level. If purchasing-power parity holds, what is the value of the peso/dollar exchange rate? Did the dollar appreciate or depreciate?

   _____

   _____

   _____

   d. Compare your answer to part (a) and part (c). What has happened to the exchange rate? Why?

   _____

   _____

   _____

Short-Answer Questions

1. Identify four reasons why the U.S. economy has engaged in an increasing amount of trade over the last 40 years.

   _____

   _____

   _____

2. Define net capital outflow. When foreigners invest in the United States, what happens to the value of U.S. *NCO*?

_____

_____

_____

3. What are the two mutually exclusive locations where national saving can be invested?

_____

_____

4. If national saving is held constant, what happens to domestic investment if *NCO* decreases? Why?

_____

_____

5. Suppose the U.S. dollar appreciates relative to world currencies. Would Pier One Imports (a domestic chain selling "exotic" foreign goods) be pleased or upset?

_____

_____

_____

6. In terms of the real exchange rate, what three variables could change to make the United States more competitive internationally?

_____

_____

_____

7. Suppose a Ford Escort sells for 10,000 U.S. dollars in the United States and 12,000 Canadian dollars in Canada. If purchasing-power parity holds, what is the Canadian dollar/American dollar exchange rate? How many U.S. dollars will a Canadian dollar buy?

_____

_____

8. Suppose trade increases between countries. Would this increase or decrease the predictive accuracy of the purchasing-power parity theory of exchange rate determination?

_____

_____

9. If the money supply grows at an average annual rate of five percent in the United States and at an average annual rate of 35 percent in Mexico, what should happen over time to the peso/dollar exchange rate if purchasing-power parity holds? Why?

_____

_____

_____

10. Why might purchasing-power parity fail to be completely accurate?

_____

_____

SELF-TEST

True/False Questions

_F_ 1. Net exports are defined as imports minus exports.

_T_ 2. U.S. net capital outflow falls when Toyota buys stock in Hilton Hotels, an American corporation.

_T_ 3. For any country, net exports are always equal to net capital outflow because every international transaction involves an exchange of an equal value of some combination of goods and assets.

_T_ 4. For a given amount of U.S. national saving, an increase in U.S. net capital outflow decreases U.S. domestic investment.

_F_ 5. Valuable technologically advanced goods are less likely to be traded internationally because shipping costs absorb too much of the potential profit.

_F_ 6. A country that exports more than it imports is said to have a trade deficit.

_T_ 7. If the yen/dollar exchange rate rises, the dollar has appreciated.

_F_ 8. If a case of Pepsi costs $8 in the U.S. and 720 yen in Japan, then according to the purchasing-power parity theory of exchange rates, the yen/dollar exchange rate should be 5,760 yen/dollar.

_T_ 9. If purchasing-power parity holds, the real exchange rate is always equal to 1.

_F_ 10. If Great Britain's money supply grows faster than Mexico's, the value of the British pound should rise relative to the value of the peso.

_T_ 11. If the nominal exchange rate is 2 British pounds to the dollar, and if the price of a Big Mac is $2 in the U.S. and 6 pounds in Great Britain, then the real exchange rate is 2/3 British Big Mac per American Big Mac.

_T_ 12. In order to increase domestic investment, a country must either increase its saving or decrease its net foreign investment.

_T_ 13. Arbitrage is the process of taking advantage of differences in prices of the same good by buying where the good is cheap and selling where it is expensive.

_F_ 14. Arbitrage tends to cause prices for the same good to ~~diverge~~ *converge* from one another.

_F_ 15. If a company based in the United States prefers a strong dollar (a dollar with a high exchange value), then the company likely exports more than it imports.

Multiple-Choice Questions

1. An economy that interacts with other economies is known as
   a. a balanced trade economy.
   b. an export economy.
   c. an import economy.
   d. a closed economy.
   e. an open economy.

2. Each of the following is a reason why the U.S. economy continues to engage in greater amounts of international trade *except* which one?
   a. There are larger cargo ships and airplanes.
   b. High technology goods are more valuable per pound and, thus, more likely to be traded.
   c. NAFTA imposes requirements for increased trade between countries in North America.
   d. There have been improvements in technology that have improved telecommunications between countries.
   e. All of the above are reasons for increased trade by the United States.

3. Which of the following statements is true about a country with a trade deficit?
   a. Net capital outflow must be positive.
   b. Net exports are negative.
   c. Net exports are positive.
   d. Exports exceed imports.
   e. none of the above

4. Which of the following would directly increase U.S. net capital outflow?
   a. General Electric sells an aircraft engine to Airbus in Great Britain.
   b. Microsoft builds a new distribution facility in Sweden.
   c. Honda builds a new plant in Ohio.
   d. Toyota buys stock in AT&T.

5. Which of the following is an example of foreign direct investment?
   a. McDonald's builds a restaurant in Moscow.
   b. Columbia Pictures sells the rights to a movie to a Russian movie studio.
   c. General Motors buys stock in Volvo.
   d. General Motors buys steel from Japan.

6. If Japan exports more than it imports,
   a. Japan's net exports are negative.
   b. Japan's net capital outflow must be negative.
   c. Japan's net capital outflow must be positive.
   d. Japan is running a trade deficit.

7. If the U.S. saves $1,000 billion and U.S. net capital outflow is – $200 billion, U.S. domestic investment is
   a. –$200 billion.
   b. $200 billion.
   c. $800 billion.
   d. $1,000 billion.
   e. $1,200 billion.

8. If the exchange rate changes from 3 Brazilian reals per dollar to 4 reals per dollar,
   a. the dollar has depreciated.
   b. the dollar has appreciated.
   c. the dollar could have appreciated or depreciated depending what happened to relative prices in Brazil and the United States.
   d. none of the above

9. Suppose the real exchange rate between Russia and the United States is defined in terms of bottles of Russian vodka per bottle of U.S. vodka. Which of the following will increase the *real* exchange rate (that is, increase the number of bottles of Russian vodka per bottle of U.S. vodka)?
   a. a decrease in the ruble price of Russian vodka
   b. an increase in the dollar price of U.S. vodka
   c. an increase in the number of rubles for which the dollar can be exchanged
   d. All of the above will increase the real exchange rate.
   e. None of the above will increase the real exchange rate.

10. The most accurate measure of the international value of the dollar is
   a. the yen/dollar exchange rate.
   b. the Brazilian real/dollar exchange rate.
   c. the peso/dollar exchange rate.
   d. the British pound/dollar exchange rate.
   e. an exchange rate index that accounts for many exchange rates.

11. If the nominal exchange rate between British pounds and dollars is 0.5 pound per dollar, how many dollars can you get for a British pound?
    a. 2 dollars
    b. 1.5 dollars
    c. 1 dollar
    d. 0.5 of a dollar
    e. none of the above

12. Suppose the nominal exchange rate between the Japanese yen and the U.S. dollar is 100 yen per dollar. Further, suppose that a pound of hamburger costs $2 in the United States and 250 yen in Japan. What is the real exchange rate between Japan and the United States?
    a. 0.5 lb. of Japanese hamburger/lb. of American hamburger
    b. 0.8 lb. of Japanese hamburger/lb. of American hamburger
    c. 1.25 lb. of Japanese hamburger/lb. of American hamburger
    d. 2.5 lb. of Japanese hamburger/lb. of American hamburger
    e. none of the above

13. Which of the following people or firms would be pleased by a depreciation of the dollar?
    a. a U.S. tourist traveling in Europe
    b. a U.S. importer of Russian vodka
    c. a French exporter of wine to the United States
    d. an Italian importer of U.S. steel
    e. a Saudi Arabian prince exporting oil to the United States

14. Suppose a cup of coffee is 1.5 euros in Germany and $.50 in the United States. If purchasing-power parity holds, what is the nominal exchange rate between euros and dollars?
    a. 1/3 euro per dollar
    b. 3 euros per dollar
    c. 1.5 euros per dollar
    d. 0.75 euro per dollar

15. Which of the following products would likely be the least accurate if used to calculate purchasing-power parity?
    a. gold
    b. automobiles
    c. diamonds
    d. dental services

16. Suppose the money supply in Mexico grows more quickly than the money supply in the United States. We would expect that
    a. the peso should depreciate relative to the dollar.
    b. the peso should appreciate relative to the dollar.
    c. the peso should maintain a constant exchange rate with the dollar because of purchasing-power parity.
    d. none of the above

17. When people take advantage of differences in prices for the same good by buying it where it is cheap and selling it where it is expensive, it is known as
    a. purchasing-power parity.
    b. net capital outflow.
    c. arbitrage.
    d. net exports.
    e. currency appreciation.

18. Suppose a U.S. resident buys a Jaguar automobile from Great Britain and the British exporter uses the receipts to buy stock in General Electric. Which of the following statements is true from the perspective of the United States?
    a. Net exports fall, and net capital outflow falls.
    b. Net exports rise, and net capital outflow rises.
    c. Net exports fall, and net capital outflow rises.
    d. Net exports rise, and net capital outflow falls.
    e. none of the above

19. Which of the following statements is *not* true about the relationship between national saving, investment, and net capital outflow?
    a. Saving is the sum of investment and net capital outflow.
    b. For a given amount of saving, an increase in net capital outflow must decrease domestic investment.
    c. For a given amount of saving, a decrease in net capital outflow must decrease domestic investment.
    d. An increase in saving associated with an equal increase in net capital outflow leaves domestic investment unchanged.

20. Suppose the inflation rate over the last 20 years has been 10 percent in Great Britain, 7 percent in Japan, and 3 percent in the United States. If purchasing-power parity holds, which of the following statements is true? Over this period,
    a. the value of the dollar should have fallen compared to the value of the pound and the yen.
    b. the yen should have risen in value compared to the pound and fallen compared to the dollar.
    c. the yen should have fallen in value compared to the pound and risen compared to the dollar.
    d. the value of the pound should have risen compared to the value of the yen and the dollar.
    e. none of the above

ADVANCED CRITICAL THINKING

You are watching a national news broadcast with your parents. The news anchor explains that the exchange rate for the dollar just hit its lowest value in a decade. The on-the-spot report shifts to a spokesman for Caterpillar, a heavy equipment manufacturer. The spokesman reports that sales of their earth moving equipment has hit an all time high and so has the value of their stock. Your parents are shocked by the report's positive view of the low value of the dollar. They just cancelled their European vacation because of the dollar's low value.

1. Why do Caterpillar and your parents have different opinions about the value of the dollar?

_____

_____

_____

_____

2. Caterpillar imports many parts and raw materials for their manufacturing processes and they sell many finished products abroad. Since they are happy about a low dollar, what must be true about the proportions of Caterpillar's imports and exports?

_____

_____

3. If someone argues that a strong dollar is "good for America" because Americans are able to exchange some of their GDP for a greater amount of foreign GDP, is it true that a strong dollar is good for *every* American? Why?

_____

_____

_____

SOLUTIONS

Terms and Definitions

  7   Closed economy

 11   Open economy

  2   Exports

 13   Imports

  8   Net exports

  1   Trade surplus

 12   Trade deficit

 14   Net capital outflow

  5   Nominal exchange rate

 10   Appreciation

  6   Depreciation

  3   Real exchange rate

  9   Purchasing-power parity

  4   Arbitrage

Practice Problems

1. a. *NCO* rises. Foreign portfolio investment.
   b. U.S. *NX* falls and a Japanese manufacturer is holding U.S. dollars, therefore, *NCO* falls. Foreign portfolio investment.
   c. *NCO* falls. Foreign direct investment.
   d. *NCO* falls. Foreign portfolio investment.
   e. *NCO* rises. Foreign direct investment.

2. a. es, *NX* has risen by the size of the sale and *NCO* has risen an equal amount and is the size of the company's holdings of foreign currency.
   b. Yes, *NX* has risen by the size of the sale and *NCO* has risen an equal amount and is the size of the company's purchase of foreign capital. Foreign direct investment.
   c. Yes, *NX* has risen by the size of the sale and *NCO* has risen an equal amount and is the size of the company's purchase of foreign capital. Foreign portfolio investment.
   d. Yes, *NX* and *NCO* are both unchanged because exports rise by the same amount as imports, leaving *NX* unchanged. *NCO* was not involved.

3. a. $$\frac{(100 \text{ yen}/\$3) \times (\$5/\text{American bushel})}{750 \text{ yen}/\text{Japanese bushel}}$$

    = 0.67 Japanese bushel per American bushel
    b. No, $1 buys $1/$5 bushel or 0.20 of a bushel of American corn. $1 buys 100 yen and 100 yen buys 100/750 or 0.13 of a bushel of Japanese corn. (Or 1 bushel costs $5 in the United States and $7.50 in Japan.)
    c. Yes. Buy corn in the United States and sell it in Japan.
    d. The price should rise in the United States due to an increase in demand and fall in Japan due to an increase in supply.
    e. The real exchange rate will rise until it is equal to one (1 Japanese bushel to 1 American bushel).

4. a. 400 pesos/40 dollars = 10 pesos/dollar
    b. 800 pesos/40 dollars = 20 pesos/dollar, depreciate
    c. 800 pesos/80 dollars = 10 pesos/dollar, depreciate
    d. It is unchanged. When prices rise symmetrically, it has no effect on the nominal exchange rate if purchasing-power parity holds.

Short-Answer Questions

1. improved transportation, advances in telecommunications, more valuable technologically advanced products, favorable government policies.

2. Purchase of foreign assets by domestic residents minus purchase of domestic assets by foreigners. *NCO* decreases or becomes negative.

3. Domestically (*I*) or foreign countries (*NCO*) because $S = I + NCO$.

4. Domestic investment grows because less national saving is allocated abroad, and/or more foreign saving is allocated here.

5. Pleased, because a strong dollar means they can buy imports cheaply and offer lower prices to their customers.

6. If U.S. prices fall, the foreign currency/dollar exchange rate falls, or the foreign price level rises, U.S. goods are less expensive to foreigners.

7. 1.2 Canadian dollars/U.S. dollar. 1 U.S. dollar/1.2 Canadian dollars = 0.83 or 83 cents U.S.

8. Increase the accuracy because the greater the number of traded goods, the more accurate is purchasing-power parity.

9. It should rise because, in the long run, a higher rate of growth of money causes a higher rate of growth in prices. Lower inflation in the United States increases the relative value of its currency.

10. Some goods are not easily traded, and traded goods are not always perfect substitutes.

True/False Questions

1. F; net exports are exports minus imports.

2. T

3. T

4. T

5. F; they are more likely to be traded because shipping costs are a small portion of the total cost of the good.

6. F; if exports exceed imports, the country has a trade surplus.

7. T

8. F; the exchange rate should be 90 yen/dollar.

9. T

10. F; the value of the British pound should fall relative to the peso.

11. T

12. T

13. T

14. F; arbitrage causes prices to converge.

15. F; companies preferring a strong dollar import more than they export.

Multiple-Choice Questions

1. e	5. a	9. d	13. d	17. c
2. c	6. c	10. e	14. b	18. a
3. b	7. e	11. a	15. d	19. c
4. b	8. b	12. b	16. a	20. b

Advanced Critical Thinking

1. Caterpillar sells much of its equipment to foreigners and the low value of the dollar makes Caterpillar's products inexpensive to foreigners. Your parents were going to buy foreign goods and services and the dollar cost became higher.

2. Caterpillar must sell a greater amount of products abroad than they purchase. That is, they are a net exporter.

3. No. A strong dollar benefits Americans who are net importers and harms Americans who are net exporters.

A MACROECONOMIC THEORY OF THE OPEN ECONOMY

In this chapter you will

Build a model to explain an open economy's trade balance and exchange rate

Use the model to analyze the effects of government budget deficits

Use the model to analyze the macroeconomic effects of trade policies

Use the model to analyze political instability and capital flight

OUTCOMES

After accomplishing these goals, you should be able to

Explain the slope of supply and demand in the market for foreign-currency exchange

Show why a budget deficit tends to cause a trade deficit

Demonstrate that a quota on imports fails to have an effect on net exports

Show why capital flight causes a currency to depreciate

CHAPTER OVERVIEW

Context and Purpose

Chapter 19 is the second chapter in a two-chapter sequence on open economy macroeconomics. Chapter 18 explained the basic concepts and vocabulary associated with an open economy. Chapter 19 ties these concepts together into a theory of the open economy.

The purpose of Chapter 19 is to establish the interdependence of a number of economic variables in an open economy. In particular, Chapter 19 demonstrates the relationships between the prices and quantities in the market for loanable funds and the prices and quantities in the market for foreign-currency exchange. Using these markets, we can analyze the impact of a variety of government policies on an economy's exchange rate and trade balance.

CHAPTER REVIEW

Introduction

This chapter constructs a model of the open economy that allows us to analyze the impact of government policies on net exports, net capital outflow, and exchange rates. This model is based on our previous long-run analysis in two ways: (1) we assume that output is determined by technology and factor supplies so output is fixed or given, and (2) prices are determined by the quantity of money so prices are fixed or given. The model constructed in this chapter is composed of two markets—the market for loanable funds and the market for foreign-currency exchange. These markets simultaneously determine the interest rate and the exchange rate (and also the level of overall investment and the trade balance).

Supply and Demand for Loanable Funds and for Foreign-Currency Exchange

In this section, we address two markets—the market for loanable funds and the market for foreign-currency exchange.

The market for loanable funds in an open economy is just an extension of the domestic loanable-funds market. We assume that there is one financial market where savers lend and investors borrow. However, in an open economy, $S = I + NCO$. Therefore, as before, the supply of loanable funds comes from national saving (S). The supply of loanable funds (desire to lend) is positively related to the real interest rate. The demand for loanable funds, however, now comes from two sources—domestic investment (I) and net capital outflow (NCO). The demand for capital assets, both domestic and foreign, is negatively related to the real interest rate. That is, a higher real interest rate reduces the desire of domestic residents to borrow to buy U.S. capital assets, and a higher domestic real interest rate reduces the desire of U.S. residents to buy foreign assets (and increases foreigners desire to buy U.S. assets) thus reducing NCO. If NCO is positive, it adds to the demand for funds. If NCO is negative, it subtracts from it. Both the supply and demand for loanable funds are shown in panel (a) of Exhibit 1. At equilibrium, the amount people save is balanced by the amount people want to invest in domestic and foreign assets.

The second market in our model is the market for foreign-currency exchange. Recall, net capital outflow = net exports or $NCO = NX$ because if NX are positive, Americans must be using the dollars earned from net exports to increase their holdings of foreign assets which makes NCO positive by the same amount. In the market for foreign-currency exchange, NCO represents the quantity of dollars supplied to buy net foreign assets. NX represents the quantity of dollars demanded for the purpose of buying U.S. net exports. The demand for dollars is negatively related to the real exchange rate because a rise in the real exchange rate means that U.S. goods are relatively more expensive and less attractive to foreign and domestic buyers causing NX to fall. The supply of dollars on the foreign-exchange market is vertical because NCO (the source of the supply of dollars) does not depend on the real exchange rate but instead depends on the real interest rate. We assume that the real interest rate is given while addressing the foreign-exchange market. The supply and demand for dollars in the foreign-exchange market is shown in panel (c) of Exhibit 1. The supply and demand for dollars in this market determine the exchange rate. At equilibrium, the quantity of dollars demanded to buy net exports is balanced by the quantity of dollars supplied to buy net foreign assets.

Equilibrium in the Open Economy

The market for loanable funds is linked to the market for foreign-currency exchange by net capital outflow (NCO). In the market for loanable funds, NCO is a portion of demand along with private investment. In the market for foreign-currency exchange, NCO is the source of supply. The quantity of net capital outflow is negatively related to the real interest rate because when the U.S. real interest rate is high, U.S. assets are more attractive and U.S. NCO is low. This is shown in panel (b) of the previous graph.

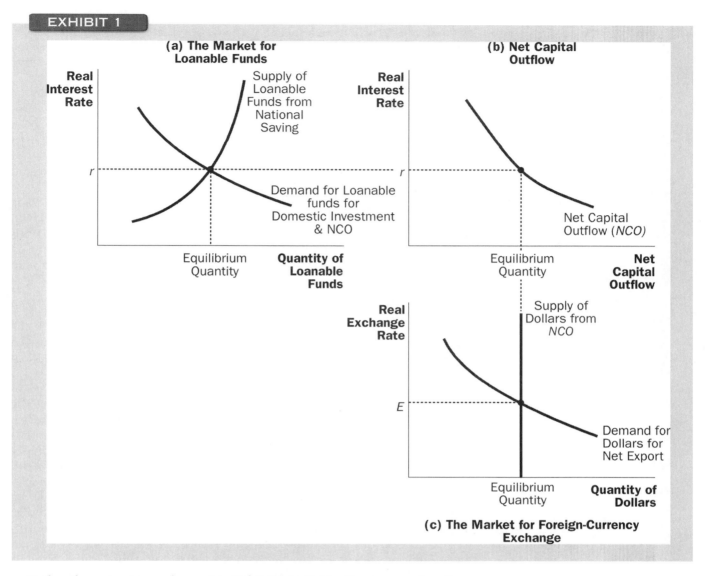

EXHIBIT 1

(a) The Market for Loanable Funds

Real Interest Rate

Supply of Loanable Funds from National Saving

r

Demand for Loanable funds for Domestic Investment & NCO

Equilibrium Quantity

Quantity of Loanable Funds

(b) Net Capital Outflow

Real Interest Rate

r

Net Capital Outflow (*NCO*)

Equilibrium Quantity

Net Capital Outflow

Real Exchange Rate

Supply of Dollars from *NCO*

E

Demand for Dollars for Net Export

Equilibrium Quantity

Quantity of Dollars

(c) The Market for Foreign-Currency Exchange

Rather than viewing each panel in Exhibit 1 individually, we can view them as a group and see how these two markets determine simultaneously the equilibrium values of the real interest rate, the real exchange rate, *NCO, NX* (the trade balance), saving, and domestic investment.

The supply and demand for loanable funds in panel (a) determine the real interest rate. The real interest rate from panel (a) determines the quantity of *NCO* in panel (b). The quantity of *NCO* is the supply of dollars in the foreign-currency exchange market in panel (c). This supply curve in conjunction with the demand for dollars (determined by *NX*) in the foreign-currency exchange market determines the real exchange rate in panel (c).

How Policies and Events Affect an Open Economy

We can use this model to see how various government policies and other events affect the equilibrium values of the variables in the model.

- *Government Budget Deficits:* An increase in the government's budget deficit reduces national saving and, thus, shifts the supply of loanable funds to the left in panel (a) of Exhibit 1. The decrease in the supply of loanable funds increases the domestic real interest rate and crowds out domestic investment. This is no different from the closed economy case. However, in an open economy, the rise in the domestic real interest rate makes foreign investments less attractive (and domestic investments more attractive to foreigners) so the quantity of net capital outflow decreases in panel (b). This reduces the supply of dollars in the foreign-currency exchange market in panel (c) because fewer people are supplying dollars to buy foreign assets. This raises the real exchange rate of the dollar and reduces net exports (to equal the reduction in NCO). Hence, an increase in the budget deficit reduces national saving, raises the real interest rate, crowds out investment, reduces NCO, raises the real exchange rate, and moves the trade balance toward deficit.

Note that our model suggests that government budget deficits cause trade deficits. Thus, budget and trade deficits are often referred to as the "twin deficits" because they are closely related. The U.S. budget deficit in the 1980s failed to crowd out domestic investment to the degree predicted by closed economy models because the increase in the trade deficit and the reduction in U.S. NCO (increased foreign investment in the United States) helped fund U.S. investment needs.

- *Trade policy:* A **trade policy** is a government policy that directly affects the quantity of country's imports or exports. A *tariff* is a tax on imported goods. An *import quota* is a limit on the quantity of a good which is produced abroad that can be sold domestically.

  Suppose the government places an import quota on autos produced in Japan for the purpose of moving the U.S. trade balance toward surplus. The import restriction reduces imports at each exchange rate and, thus, increases net exports at each exchange rate. It follows that foreigners need more dollars at each exchange rate so the demand for dollars in the foreign-currency exchange market shifts to the right in panel (c) of Exhibit 1 and raises the real exchange rate for the dollar. Since there has been no change in the loanable-funds market in panel (a) and no change in NCO in panel (b), the final net exports must remain unchanged because $S - I = NCO = NX$. Thus, the import quota reduces imports but the rise in the exchange value of the dollar offsets this effect by reducing exports, *leaving the trade balance unchanged*. As a result, the U.S. imports fewer autos (which benefits U.S. auto manufacturers) but sells fewer airplanes abroad (which harms U.S. aircraft producers), but there are no significant macroeconomic effects beyond the increase in the exchange rate. The impact of trade policy is more microeconomic than macroeconomic.

- *Political instability and capital flight:* **Capital flight** is a sudden reduction in the demand for domestic assets coupled with a sudden increase in the demand for foreign assets. It may occur due to domestic political instability.

  Suppose the U.S. becomes politically unstable. Investors might decide to sell U.S. assets and buy foreign assets. This act increases net capital outflow and shifts the demand for loanable funds to be used for foreign investment at each real interest rate to the right in panel (a) of Exhibit 1. It simultaneously shifts the NCO curve to the right in panel (b). The increase in net capital outflow increases the supply of dollars in the foreign-currency exchange market in panel (c), reducing the real exchange rate. Thus, capital flight increases the domestic real interest rate, increases net capital outflow and net exports, and reduces the value of the dollar in the foreign-currency exchange market. Note that the increase in the interest rate reduces domestic investment, which slows capital accumulation and growth. It has the opposite effect on the country to which the capital is flowing.

The U.S. trade deficit is large and has been growing for two decades. This trade deficit is associated with an equal and negative capital outflow (foreigners are buying U.S. assets). This situation could be risky because foreigners could choose to stop buying U.S. financial assets in the future. Economists suggest that the solution is to encourage higher U.S. household saving.

HELPFUL HINTS

1. A change in national saving generates the same result regardless of whether the change was from private saving or public saving. In your text there is a demonstration of the impact of an increase in a government budget deficit on an open economy. It is shown that a budget deficit causes a reduction in the public saving component of national saving and shifts the supply of loanable funds to the left. Note that a reduction in the private saving component of national savings also shifts the supply of loanable funds to the left. Thus, the example given in your text can be utilized for cases when there is a change in private saving. (The source of the change in saving will generate differences in the amount of output purchased by consumers versus government, but it will not alter any of the international analysis.)

2. To find the change in NX (net exports), remember that $NX = NCO$ (net capital outflow). When we use our model to discover the impact of a government policy or an economic event on the economic variables in an open economy, there is no way to directly read net exports (the trade balance) from any of the graphs. However, the quantity of NCO is always directly measurable from panel (b) of Exhibit 1. Since $NCO = NX$, whenever there is an increase in NCO, there is an equivalent increase in NX (which is an improvement in the trade balance). Whenever NCO declines, there is an equivalent decline in NX.

3. Capital flight reduces domestic investment. The discussion of capital flight in the text and in the chapter review above notes that capital flight increases net capital outflow and the supply of the domestic currency on the foreign-currency exchange market, which lowers the exchange value of the domestic currency. Since these activities raise net exports (improve the trade balance), why is capital flight considered bad for the economy rather than good? Look at panel (a) of Figure 7 of your text. The increase in net capital outflow within the demand for loanable funds absorbs a greater amount of national saving than the tiny increase in national saving induced by the rise in the real interest rate. Thus, domestic investment is reduced an amount similar to the increase in net exports. As a result, the prospect for long-term growth in a country exhibiting capital flight is reduced due to the reduction in domestic investment.

4. Work the examples in the text backward. The three policy problems demonstrated in your text require a significant degree of concentration to understand. Once you have mastered them, you should feel comfortable that you can follow someone else's demonstration. The next step is to work those same problems backward, alone. That is, address the effect of a reduction in the budget deficit, the lowering of a trade restriction, and the effect of

capital inflow. So that you may check your work, the first practice problem below is composed of the chapter examples where the source of the change has been reversed.

TERMS AND DEFINITIONS

Choose a definition for each key term.

Key terms:

_____ Twin deficits

_____ Trade policy

_____ Tariff

_____ Import quota

_____ Capital flight

Definitions:

1. A limit on the quantity of a good which is produced abroad that can be sold domestically

2. A government policy that directly affects the quantity of country's imports or exports

3. A sudden reduction in the demand for domestic assets coupled with a sudden increase in the demand for foreign assets

4. The government budget deficit and the trade deficit

5. A tax on imported goods

PROBLEMS AND SHORT-ANSWER QUESTIONS

Practice Problems

1. This problem is composed of the examples in the chapter except the source of the change has been reversed. Use the model described by Exhibit 1 to answer the following questions.
   a. Suppose the government reduces its budget deficit. Describe the sequence of events in the model by describing the shifts in the curves in Exhibit 1 and discuss the movements in the relevant macroeconomic variables.

   _____

   _____

   _____

   _____

b. Suppose the government reduces a quota on the importing of Japanese automobiles. Describe the sequence of events in the model by describing the shifts in the curves in Exhibit 1 and discuss the movements in the relevant macroeconomic variables.

_____

_____

_____

_____

c. Suppose there is a sudden inflow of capital into the United States because we are believed to be more politically stable than the rest of the world. Describe the sequence of events in the model by describing the shifts in the curves in Exhibit 1 and discuss the movements in the relevant macroeconomic variables.

_____

_____

_____

_____

_____

2. a. Suppose private saving increased at each real interest rate. What would happen to the important macroeconomic variables in our model of an open economy?

_____

_____

_____

_____

_____

b. Is there any difference between your answer above and the answer you would write if the government had reduced its deficit? Why?

_____

_____

_____

c. Suppose the government passes an investment tax credit that increases domestic investment at each real interest rate. How would this change the important economic variables in the model?

_____

_____

_____

_____

_____

d. Compare your answer in part (a) (an increase in saving at each real interest rate) to your answer in part (c) (an increase in domestic investment at each real interest rate). Are there any differences?

_____

_____

_____

3. Suppose the American taste for Japanese automobiles increases. (Answer this question using the open economy model from the Japanese perspective.)

a. What happens to the demand for yen in the foreign-currency exchange market?

_____

_____

b. What happens to the value of yen in the foreign-currency exchange market?

_____

_____

c. What happens to Japanese net exports? Why?

_____

_____

    d. If the Japanese are selling more cars, what must be true about Japanese imports and exports of other items?

    _____

    _____

    _____

    e. Keeping in mind your answers to (a) through (c), do you think Japan runs an overall trade surplus with the rest of the world because its autos are better built or because of its domestic saving and *NCO?* Explain.

    _____

    _____

    _____

4. Suppose Canada is perceived to be politically unstable, which induces capital flight to the United States.

    a. Describe what happens in the foreign-currency exchange market from the perspective of Canada.

    _____

    _____

    _____

    b. Describe what happens in the foreign-currency exchange market from the perspective of the United States.

    _____

    _____

    _____

    c. Are your answers to part (a) and (b) above consistent with one another? Why?

    _____

    _____

    _____

d. If the economy of Canada is small when compared to the economy of the United States, what should this event do to each country's balance of trade?

_____

_____

_____

e. Which country will tend to grow faster in the future? Why?

_____

_____

_____

Short-Answer Questions

1. Explain the slope of the demand for loanable funds in an open economy.

_____

_____

_____

2. Does net capital outflow add to, or subtract from, domestic investment when we create the demand for loanable funds? Explain.

_____

_____

_____

3. Explain the source of the supply of dollars in the market for foreign-currency exchange.

_____

_____

4. Explain the source of the demand for dollars in the market for foreign-currency exchange.

_____

_____

5. Why might certain companies and unions support tariffs and import quotas even if they know that these restrictions cannot alter the trade balance?

_____

_____

_____

6. Suppose the quality of U.S. goods and services falls and, as a result, foreigners choose to buy fewer U.S. goods. Does this affect the U.S. balance of trade? Why?

_____

_____

7. What happens to the value of a country's currency if there is capital flight from that country? Explain.

_____

_____

_____

8. What would an increase in the saving of U.S. residents do to the U.S. trade balance and the dollar exchange rate? Explain.

_____

_____

_____

_____

9. Why are the budget and trade deficits referred to as the "twin deficits?"

_____

_____

_____

_____

10. Do trade restrictions (such as tariffs and import quotas) alter *NX*?

_____

_____

_____

_____

SELF-TEST

True/False Questions

_____ 1. Net capital outflow is the purchase of domestic assets by foreigners minus the purchase of foreign assets by domestic residents.

_____ 2. A country's net capital outflow (NCO) is always equal to its net exports (NX).

_____ 3. Other things being the same, an increase in a country's real interest rate reduces net capital outflow.

_____ 4. An increase in U.S. net capital outflow increases the supply of dollars in the market for foreign-currency exchange and decreases the real exchange rate of the dollar.

_____ 5. If labor unions convince Americans to "buy American," it will improve (move toward surplus) the U.S. trade balance.

_____ 6. If a country's net capital outflow (NCO) is positive, it is an addition to its demand for loanable funds.

_____ 7. An increase in the government's budget deficit shifts the supply of loanable funds to the right.

_____ 8. An increase in the government's budget deficit tends to cause the real exchange rate of the dollar to depreciate.

_____ 9. The term "twin deficits" refers to a country's trade deficit and its government budget deficit.

_____10. If the United States raises its tariff on imported sugar, it will reduce imports and improve the trade balance.

_____11. If the United States raises its tariff on imported sugar, domestic sugar growers will benefit, but the dollar will appreciate and domestic producers of export goods will be harmed.

_____12. An increase in the government budget deficit reduces net exports.

_____13. A country experiencing capital flight will experience a reduction in its net capital outflow and its net exports.

_____14. If Americans increase their saving, the dollar will appreciate in the market for foreign-currency exchange.

_____15. A rise in Mexico's net exports (NX) will increase the demand for pesos in the market for foreign-currency exchange and the peso will appreciate in value.

Multiple-Choice Questions

1. Which of the following statements regarding the loanable-funds market is *not* true?
   a. An increase in a country's net capital outflow raises its real interest rate.
   b. An increase in a country's net capital outflow shifts the supply of loanable funds to the left.
   c. An increase in domestic investment shifts the demand for loanable funds to the right.
   d. A decrease in a country's net capital outflow shifts the demand for loanable funds to the left.

2. An increase in the government budget deficit
   a. increases the real interest rate and crowds out investment.
   b. decreases the real interest rate and crowds out investment.
   c. has no impact on the real interest rate and fails to crowd out investment because foreigners buy assets in the deficit country.
   d. none of the above

3. Which of the following statement regarding the loanable-funds market is true?
   a. An increase in private saving shifts the supply of loanable funds to the left.
   b. A decrease in the government budget deficit increases the real interest rate.
   c. An increase in the government budget deficit shifts the supply of loanable funds to the right.
   d. An increase in the government budget deficit shifts the supply of loanable funds to the left.

4. Other things unchanging, a higher U.S. real interest rate
   a. increases U.S. net capital outflow because U.S. residents and foreigners prefer to invest in the U.S.
   b. decreases U.S. net capital outflow because U.S. residents and foreigners prefer to invest in the U.S.
   c. decreases U.S. net capital outflow because U.S. residents and foreigners prefer to invest abroad.
   d. none of the above

5. An increase in Europe's taste for U.S. produced Fords would cause the dollar to
   a. depreciate and would increase U.S. net exports.
   b. depreciate and would decrease U.S. net exports.
   c. appreciate and would increase U.S. net exports.
   d. appreciate and would decrease U.S. net exports.
   e. appreciate, but the total value of U.S. net export stays the same.

6. An increase in the U.S. government budget deficit
   a. increases U.S. net exports and decreases U.S. net capital outflow.
   b. decreases U.S. net exports and increases U.S. net capital outflow.
   c. decreases U.S. net exports and U.S. net capital outflow the same amount.
   d. increases U.S. net exports and U.S. net capital outflow the same amount.

7. The phrase "twin deficits" refers to
   a. a country's trade deficit and its government budget deficit.
   b. a country's trade deficit and its net capital outflow deficit.
   c. the equality of a country's saving deficit and its investment deficit.
   d. the fact that if a country has a trade deficit, its trading partners must also have trade deficits.

8. Which of the following statements regarding the market for foreign-currency exchange is true?
   a. An increase in U.S. net exports increases the supply of dollars and the dollar depreciates.
   b. An increase in U.S. net exports decreases the supply of dollars and the dollar depreciates.
   c. An increase in U.S. net exports decreases the demand for dollars and the dollar appreciates.
   d. An increase in U.S. net exports increases the demand for dollars and the dollar appreciates.

9. Which of the following statements regarding the market for foreign-currency exchange is true?
   a. An increase in U.S. net capital outflow increases the supply of dollars and the dollar appreciates.
   b. An increase in U.S. net capital outflow increases the supply of dollars and the dollar depreciates.
   c. An increase in U.S. net capital outflow increases the demand for dollars and the dollar appreciates.
   d. An increase in U.S. net capital outflow increases the demand for dollars and the dollar depreciates.

10. If the United States imposes a quota on the importing of apparel produced in China, which of the following is true regarding the market for foreign-currency exchange?
    a. The supply of dollars increases and the dollar depreciates.
    b. The supply of dollars decreases and the dollar appreciates.
    c. The demand for dollars increases and the dollar appreciates.
    d. The demand for dollars decreases and the dollar depreciates.

11. If the United States imposes a quota on the importing of apparel produced in China, which of the following is true regarding U.S. net exports?
    a. Net exports will rise.
    b. Net exports will fall.
    c. Net exports will remain unchanged.
    d. none of the above

12. Suppose, due to political instability, Mexicans suddenly choose to invest in U.S. assets as opposed to Mexican assets. Which of the following statements is true regarding U.S. net foreign investment?
    a. U.S. net foreign investment rises.
    b. U.S. net foreign investment falls.
    c. U.S. net foreign investment is unchanged because only U.S. residents can alter U.S. net foreign investment.
    d. none of the above

13. Suppose, due to political instability, Mexicans suddenly choose to purchase U.S. assets as opposed to Mexican assets. Which of the following statements is true regarding the value of the dollar and U.S. net exports?
    a. The dollar appreciates, and U.S. net exports fall.
    b. The dollar depreciates, and U.S. net exports fall.
    c. The dollar appreciates, and U.S. net exports rise.
    d. The dollar depreciates, and U.S. net exports rise.

14. An increase in U.S. private saving
    a. increases U.S. net exports and decreases U.S. net capital outflow.
    b. decreases U.S. net exports and increases U.S. net capital outflow.
    c. decreases U.S. net exports and U.S. net capital outflow the same amount.
    d. increases U.S. net exports and U.S. net capital outflow the same amount.

15. Which of the following statements about trade policy is true?
    a. A restrictive import quota increases a country's net exports.
    b. A restrictive import quota decreases a country's net exports.
    c. A country's trade policy has no impact on the size of its trade balance.
    d. none of the above

16. Which of the following groups would *not* benefit from a U.S. import quota on Japanese autos?
    a. stockholders of Ford Motor Company
    b. U.S. farmers who export grain
    c. members of the United Auto Workers union
    d. U.S. consumers who buy electronics from Japan

17. An example of a trade policy is
    a. an increase in the government budget deficit because it reduces a country's net exports.
    b. capital flight because it increases a country's net exports.
    c. a tariff on sugar.
    d. All are examples of trade policy.

18. An export subsidy should have the opposite effect of
    a. a tariff.
    b. capital flight.
    c. a government budget deficit.
    d. an increase in private saving.

19. Which of the following groups would be most harmed by a U.S. government budget deficit?
    a. U.S. residents wishing to buy foreign produced autos
    b. lenders of loanable funds
    c. foreigners who wish to buy assets in the United States
    d. Boeing Aircraft Manufacturing wishing to sell jets to Saudi Arabia

20. Capital flight
    a. decreases a country's net exports and increases its long-run growth path.
    b. decreases a country's net exports and decreases its long-run growth path.
    c. increases a country's net exports and decreases its long-run growth path.
    d. increases a country's net exports and increases its long-run growth path.

ADVANCED CRITICAL THINKING

Hong Kong has a capitalistic economic system. It was leased from China by Great Britain for 100 years. In 1997, it was returned to China, a socialist republic.

1. What do you think this event should do to the net capital outflow of Hong Kong? Why?

_____

_____

_____

_____

2. If the residents of Hong Kong chose Canada as a place to move some of their business activity, what impact do you suppose this will have on the value of the Canadian interest rate and exchange rate? Why?

_____

_____

_____

_____

3. Which Canadian industries, those engaged in importing or exporting, are likely to be pleased with Hong Kong's investment in Canada? Why?

_____

_____

_____

_____

4. What impact will Hong Kong's return to China have on the growth rate of Canada?

_____

_____

SOLUTIONS

Terms and Definitions

_4_ Twin deficits

_2_ Trade policy

_5_ Tariff

_1_ Import quota

_3_ Capital flight

Practice Problems

1. a. Panel (a), supply of loanable funds shifts right, real interest rate decreases. NCO increases, increasing the supply of dollars in the foreign-currency exchange market and causing the real exchange rate to depreciate. Saving and domestic investment have increased and the trade balance has moved toward surplus.
    b. Panel (c), NX fall at each exchange rate as imports increase causing the demand for dollars in the foreign-currency exchange market to shift left; the real exchange rate falls increasing NX to their original level. No change in trade balance, but a higher volume of trade (more imports and more exports).
    c. NCO falls as U.S. residents and foreigners buy U.S. assets. In panel (a), demand for loanable funds shifts left. Panel (b), NCO shifts left because of a decrease in NCO at each interest rate causing the supply of dollars in the foreign-currency exchange market to shift left and the exchange rate to rise. Result, real interest rate down, NCO and NX down, value of the dollar up, increase in domestic investment.

2. a. Panel (a), supply of loanable funds shifts right, real interest rate decreases. NCO increases, increasing the supply of dollars in the foreign-currency exchange market and causes the real exchange rate to depreciate. Saving and domestic investment have increased and the trade balance has moved toward surplus.
    b. No, because it doesn't matter why national saving increased. Either one will shift the supply of loanable funds to the right.
    c. Increase in the demand for loanable funds, raises real interest rate, lowers NCO and NX, decreases the supply of dollars in the foreign-currency exchange market which raises the value of the dollar. Domestic saving and investment have increased.
    d. Both increase domestic saving and investment, but an increase in saving moves the trade balance toward surplus while an increase in investment demand moves it toward deficit.

3. a. Shifts right.
    b. Real exchange rate rises so value of yen rises.
    c. NCO is unchanged therefore NX as a total is unchanged.
    d. If NX are constant, they must be importing more or exporting less of other items.
    e. NX as a total are determined by NCO so Japan's overall level of trade surplus is based on its saving behavior. However, the composition of its exports may be based on its relative quality of production.

4. a. The supply of Canadian dollars shifts right and the value of the Canadian dollar falls.
    b. The supply of U.S. dollars shifts left and the value of the U.S. dollar rises.

c. Yes. A rise in the value of the U.S. dollar relative to the Canadian dollar should correspond to the fall in the value of the Canadian dollar relative to the U.S. dollar.

d. The fall in the value of the Canadian dollar should improve its *NX* by a greater percentage than the fall in *NX* by the United States.

e. Canada is increasing its *NCO* in the United States and the United States is decreasing its *NCO* in Canada, so the United States will likely grow faster.

Short-Answer Questions

1. It is negatively sloped because a higher real interest rate reduces the desire to borrow funds to purchase capital domestically, and it discourages U.S. residents from buying foreign assets and encourages foreign residents to buy U.S. assets.

2. If *NCO* is positive, it adds to the demand for loanable funds. If *NCO* is negative, it subtracts.

3. It comes from dollars U.S. residents used for *NCO*.

4. It comes from the need for dollars from foreigners purchasing U.S. *NX*.

5. Because trade restrictions can improve the sales of some domestic companies facing competition from imports, but largely at the expense of other domestic companies producing for export.

6. No, it reduces the demand for dollars in the market for foreign-currency exchange and lowers the value of the dollar to keep *NX* unchanged.

7. It increases the supply of their currency in the market for foreign-currency exchange and lowers the exchange rate.

8. It decreases the U.S. real interest rate, increases *NCO* and *NX*, increases the supply of dollars on the foreign-currency exchange market, and lowers the dollar exchange rate.

9. Because a budget deficit tends to cause a trade deficit when it raises the domestic real interest rate, reducing *NCO* and *NX*.

10. Trade restrictions don't alter the total value of *NX* because *NX* = *NCO*. An increase in trade restrictions reduces both imports and exports by the same amount.

True/False Questions

1. F; *NCO* is the purchase of foreign assets by domestic residents minus the purchase of domestic assets by foreigners.

2. T

3. T

4. T

5. F; net exports are unchanged because *NCO* is unchanged.

6. T

7. F; an increase in the government's budget deficit shifts the supply of loanable funds to the left.

8. F; an increase in the government's budget deficit raises the real exchange rate.

9. T

10. F; net exports are unchanged because *NCO* is unchanged.

11. T

12. T

13. F; a country experiencing capital flight will experience an increase in its *NCO* and its net exports.

14. F; the dollar will depreciate.

15. T

Multiple-Choice Questions

1. b	5. e	9. b	13. a	17. c
2. a	6. c	10. c	14. d	18. a
3. d	7. a	11. c	15. c	19. d
4. b	8. d	12. b	16. b	20. c

Advanced Critical Thinking

1. It should increase the *NCO* of Hong Kong because foreigners are not buying assets in Hong Kong and Hong Kong residents are buying assets abroad—capital flight. Investors fear that China may nationalize much of Hong Kong's industry.

2. This will decrease Canada's *NCO*. This shifts the demand for loanable funds left and lowers the real interest rate. The reduced *NCO* reduces the supply of Canadian dollars in the foreign-currency exchange market, raises the exchange rate, and moves *NX* toward deficit.

3. The increase in the value of the Canadian dollar will make Canadian producers less competitive abroad, but will make imports cheaper.

4. The reduction in Canada's *NCO* (due to Hong Kong's increased *NCO*) increases the capital stock of Canada, causing it to grow.

20

AGGREGATE DEMAND AND AGGREGATE SUPPLY

CHAPTER OVERVIEW

Context and Purpose

To this point, our study of macroeconomic theory has concentrated on the behavior of the economy in the long run. Chapters 20 through 22 now focus on short-run fluctuations in the economy around its long-term trend. Chapter 20 introduces aggregate demand and aggregate supply and shows how shifts in these curves can cause recessions. Chapter 21 focuses on how policymakers use the tools of monetary and fiscal policy to influence aggregate demand. Chapter 22 addresses the relationship between inflation and unemployment.

The purpose of Chapter 20 is to develop the model economists use to analyze the economy's short-run fluctuations—the model of aggregate demand and aggregate supply. We will learn about some of the sources for shifts in the aggregate-demand curve and the aggregate-supply curve and how these shifts can cause recessions. We will also introduce actions policymakers might undertake to offset recessions.

CHAPTER REVIEW

Introduction

Over the last 50 years, U.S. real GDP has grown about 3 percent per year. However, in some years GDP has not grown at this normal rate. A period when output and incomes fall, and unemployment rises, is known as a **recession** when it is mild and a **depression** when it is severe. This chapter focuses on the economy's short-run fluctuations around its long-term trend. To do this, we employ the model of aggregate demand and aggregate supply.

Three Key Facts About Economic Fluctuations

- *Economic fluctuations are irregular and unpredictable:* Although economic fluctuations are often termed *the business cycle,* the term "business cycle" is misleading because it suggests that economic fluctuations follow a regular, predictable pattern. In reality, economic fluctuations are irregular and unpredictable.

- *Most macroeconomic quantities fluctuate together:* Although real GDP is usually used to monitor short-run changes in the economy, it really doesn't matter which measure of economic activity is used because most macroeconomic variables that measure income, spending, or production move in the same direction, though by different amounts. Investment is one type of expenditure that is particularly volatile across the business cycle.

- *As output falls, unemployment rises:* When real GDP declines, the rate of unemployment rises because when firms produce fewer goods and services, they lay off workers.

Explaining Short-Run Economic Fluctuations

Classical theory is based on the classical dichotomy and monetary neutrality. Recall, the classical dichotomy is the separation of economic variables into real and nominal while monetary neutrality is the property that changes in the money supply only affect nominal variables, not real variables. Most economists believe these classical assumptions are an accurate description of the economy in the long run, but not in the short run. That is, over a period of a number of years, changes in the money supply should affect prices but should have no impact on real variables such as real GDP, unemployment, real wages, and so on. However, in the short run, from year to year, changes in nominal variables such as money and prices are likely to have an impact on real variables. That is, in the short run, nominal and real variables are not independent.

We use the **model of aggregate supply and aggregate demand** to explain economic fluctuations. This model can be graphed with the price level, measured by the CPI or the GDP deflator on the vertical axis and real GDP on the horizontal axis. The **aggregate-demand curve** shows the quantity of goods and services households, firms, and government wish to buy at each price level. It slopes negatively. The **aggregate-supply curve** shows the quantity of goods and services that firms produce and sell at each price level. It slopes positively (in the short run). The price level and output adjust to balance aggregate supply and demand. This model looks like an ordinary microeconomic supply and demand model. However, the reasons for the slopes and the sources of the shifts in the aggregate supply and demand curves differ from those for the microeconomic model.

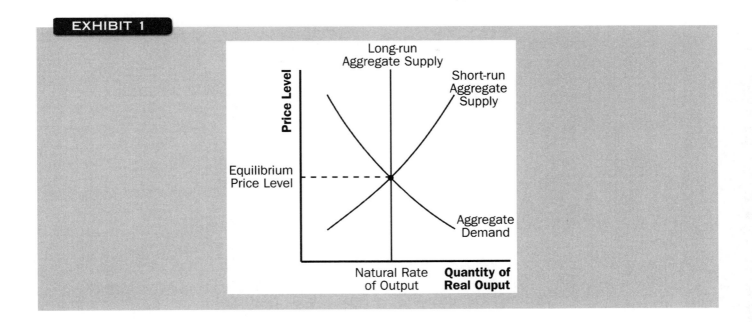

EXHIBIT 1

The Aggregate-Demand Curve

Exhibit 1 illustrates the model of aggregate supply and aggregate demand.

The aggregate-demand curve shows the quantity of goods and services demanded at each price level. Recall, GDP = $C + I + G + NX$. To address why aggregate demand slopes downward we address the impact of the price level on consumption (C), investment (I), and net exports (NX). (We ignore government spending (G) because it is a fixed policy variable.) A decrease in the price level increases consumption, investment, and net exports for the following reasons:

- The price level and consumption: *the wealth effect.* At a lower price level, the fixed amount of nominal money in consumer's pockets increases in value. Consumers feel wealthier and spend more, increasing the consumption component of aggregate demand.

- The price level and investment: *the interest-rate effect.* At a lower price level, households need to hold less money to buy the same products. They lend some money by buying bonds or depositing in banks, either of which lowers interest rates and stimulates the investment component of aggregate demand.

- The price level and net exports: *the exchange-rate effect.* Since, as described above, a lower price level causes lower interest rates, some U.S. investors will invest abroad, increasing the supply of dollars in the foreign currency-exchange market. This act causes the real exchange rate of the dollar to depreciate, reduces the relative price of domestic goods compared to foreign goods, and increases the net exports component of aggregate demand.

All three explanations of the downward slope of the aggregate-demand curve assume that the money supply is fixed.

When something causes a change in the quantity of output demanded at each price level, it causes a shift in the aggregate-demand curve. The following events and policies cause shifts in aggregate demand:

- *Shifts arising from changes in consumption:* If consumers save more, if stock prices fall so that consumers feel poorer, or if taxes are increased, consumers spend less and aggregate demand shifts left.

- *Shifts arising from changes in investment:* If firms become optimistic about the future and decide to buy new equipment, if an investment tax credit increases investment, if the Fed increases the money supply which reduces interest rates and increases investment, aggregate demand shifts right.

- *Shifts arising from changes in government purchases:* If federal, state, or local governments increase purchases, aggregate demand shifts right.

- *Shifts arising from changes in net exports:* If foreign countries have a recession and buy fewer goods from the U.S. or if the value of the dollar rises on foreign exchange markets, net exports are reduced and aggregate demand shifts left.

The Aggregate-Supply Curve

The aggregate-supply curve shows the quantity of goods and services firms produce and sell at each price level. In the long run, the aggregate-supply curve is vertical while in the short run it is upward (positively) sloping. Both can be seen in Exhibit 1.

The *long-run aggregate-supply curve* is vertical because, in the long run, the supply of goods and services depends on the supply of capital, labor, and natural resources, and on production technology. In the long run, the supply of goods and services is independent of the level of prices. It is the embodiment of the classical dichotomy and monetary neutrality. That is, if the price level rises and all prices rise together, there should be no impact on output or any other real variable.

The long-run aggregate-supply curve shows the level of production that is sometimes called *potential output* or *full-employment output*. Since in the short run output can be temporarily above or below this level, a better name is the *natural rate of output* because it is the amount of output produced when unemployment is at its natural, or normal, rate. Anything that alters the natural rate of output shifts the long-run aggregate-supply curve to the right or left. Since in the long run, output depends on labor, capital, natural resources, and technological knowledge, we group the sources of the shifts in long-run aggregate supply into these categories:

- *Shifts arising from labor:* If there is immigration from abroad or a reduction in the natural rate of unemployment from a reduction in the minimum wage, long-run aggregate supply shifts right.

- *Shifts arising from capital:* If there is an increase in physical or human capital, productivity rises and long-run aggregate supply shifts right.

- *Shifts arising from natural resources:* If there is a discovery of new resources, or a favorable change in weather patterns, long-run aggregate supply shifts right.

- *Shifts arising from technical knowledge:* If new inventions are employed, or international trade opens up, long-run aggregate supply shifts right.

Long-run growth and inflation may be depicted as a rightward shift in the long-run aggregate-supply curve (from the events described above) and an even larger rightward shift in the aggregate-demand curve due to increases in the money supply. Thus, over time, output grows and prices rise.

The short-run aggregate-supply curve slopes upward (positively) because a change in the price level causes output to deviate from its long run level for a short period of time, say, a year or two. There are three theories that explain why the short-run aggregate-supply curve slopes upward and they all share a common theme: output rises above the natural rate when the actual price level exceeds the expected price level. The three theories are:

- *The sticky-wage theory:* Suppose firms and workers agree on a nominal wage contract based on what they expect the price level to be. If the price level falls below what was expected, the real wage W/P rises, raising the cost of production and lowering profits, causing the firm to hire less labor and reduce the quantity of goods and services supplied.

- *The sticky-price theory:* Because there is a cost to firms for changing prices, termed *menu costs,* some firms will resist reducing their prices when the price level unexpectedly falls. Thus, their prices are "too high" and their sales decline, causing the quantity of goods and services supplied to fall.

- *The misperceptions theory:* When the price level unexpectedly falls, suppliers only notice that the price of their particular product has fallen. Hence, they mistakenly believe that there has been a fall in the *relative price* of their product, causing them to reduce the quantity of goods and services supplied.

Note two features of the explanations above: (1) in each case, the quantity of output supplied changed because actual prices deviated from expected prices and (2) the effect will be temporary because people will adjust their expectations over time. We can express aggregate supply mathematically with the following equation:

$$\begin{array}{ccccc} \text{Quantity} & & \text{Natural} & & \left(\begin{array}{cc} \text{Actual} & \text{Expected} \\ \end{array}\right) \\ \text{of Output} & = & \text{Rate of} & + & a\left(\begin{array}{cc} \text{Price} & - & \text{Price} \\ \end{array}\right) \\ \text{Supplied} & & \text{Output} & & \left(\begin{array}{cc} \text{Level} & \text{Level} \\ \end{array}\right) \end{array}$$

where a is a number that determines how much output responds to unexpected changes in the price level.

Events that shift the long-run aggregate-supply curve also tend to shift the short-run aggregate-supply curve in the same direction. However, the short-run aggregate-supply curve can shift while the long-run aggregate-supply curve remains stationary. In the short run, the quantity of goods and services supplied depends on perceptions, wages, and prices, all of which were set based on the expected price level. For example, if people and firms expect higher prices, they set wages higher, reducing the profitability of production and reducing the quantity supplied of goods and service at each price level. Thus, the short-run aggregate-supply curve shifts left. A lower expected price level shifts the short-run aggregate-supply curve to the right. In general, things that cause an increase in the cost of production (an increase in wages or oil prices) cause the short-run aggregate-supply curve to shift left while a decrease in the cost of production causes the short-run aggregate-supply curve to shift right.

Two Causes of Economic Fluctuations

Exhibit 1 shows the model of aggregate supply and aggregate demand in long-run equilibrium. That is, the level of output is at the long-run natural rate where aggregate demand and long-run aggregate supply intersect, and perceptions, wages, and prices have fully adjusted to the actual price level as demonstrated by short-run aggregate supply intersecting at the same point.

EXHIBIT 2

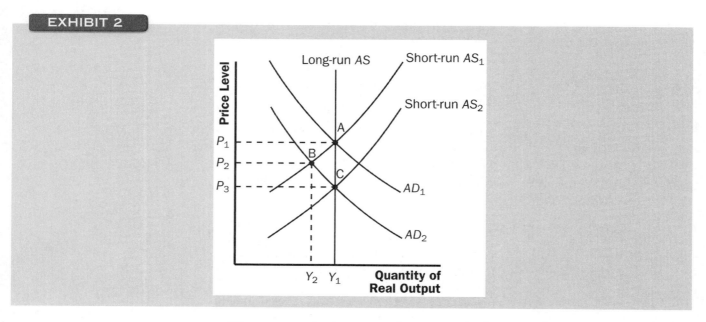

There are two basic causes of a recession: a leftward shift in aggregate demand and a leftward shift in aggregate supply.

A leftward shift in aggregate demand   Suppose households cut back on their spending because they are pessimistic or nervous about the future. Consumers spend less at each price level so aggregate demand shifts left in Exhibit 2. In the short run, the economy moves to point B because the drop in the price level was unexpected so some wages and some prices are too high. We can see that the economy is in a recession at P_2, Y_2 because output is below the natural rate. Policymakers could try to eliminate the recession by increasing aggregate demand with an increase in government spending or an increase in the money supply. If properly done, the government moves the economy back to point A. If the government does nothing, the recession will remedy itself or self-correct over time. Since actual prices are below prior expectations, price expectations will be reduced over time and wages and prices will fall to levels commensurate with P_3. The short-run aggregate-supply curve shifts right and the economy arrives at point C. To summarize, in the short run, shifts in aggregate demand cause fluctuations in output. In the long run, shifts in aggregate demand only cause changes in prices.

The two biggest shocks to aggregate demand in the United States were the leftward shift during the Great Depression and the rightward shift during World War II. During the recession in 2001, aggregate demand shifted left for three reasons: (1) the dot.com bubble in the stock market burst reducing both consumer and investment spending, (2) the terrorist attacks on September 11, 2001 caused uncertainty and reduced spending, and (3) a further reduction in the stock market due to the corporate accounting scandal further reduced aggregated demand.

A leftward shift in aggregate supply   Suppose OPEC raises the price of oil which raises the cost of production for many firms. This reduces profitability, firms produce less at each price level, and short-run aggregate supply shifts to the left in Exhibit 3. Prices rise, reducing the quantity demanded along the aggregate-demand curve and the economy arrives at point B. Since output has fallen (stagnation) and the price level has risen (inflation), the economy has experienced **stagflation.** If policymakers do nothing, the unemployment at Y_2 will, in time, put downward pressure on workers' wages, increase profitability, and shift

EXHIBIT 3

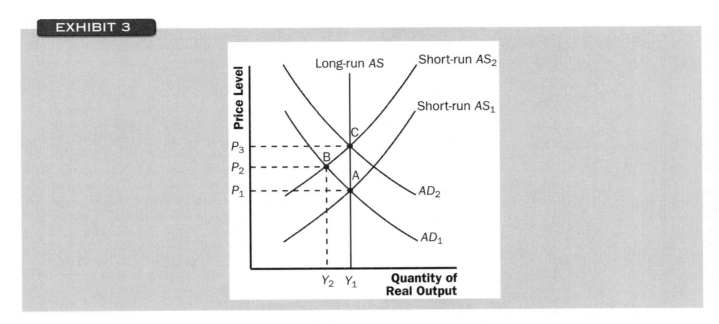

aggregate supply back to its original position and the economy returns to point A. Alternatively, policymakers could increase aggregate demand and move the economy to point C, avoiding point B altogether. Here, policymakers *accommodate* the shift in aggregate supply by allowing the increase in costs to raise prices permanently. Output is returned to long-run equilibrium but prices are higher. To summarize, a reduction in short-run aggregate supply causes stagflation. Policymakers cannot shift aggregate demand in a manner to offset both the increase in price and the decrease in output simultaneously.

HELPFUL HINTS

1. There are no changes in real variables along the long-run aggregate-supply curve. When all prices change equally, no real variables have changed. A vertical long-run aggregate-supply curve simply demonstrates this classical lesson. Pick any point on the long-run aggregate-supply curve. Now double the price level and all nominal values such as wages. Although the price level has doubled, relative prices have remained constant including the real wage, W/P. There has been no change in anyone's incentive to produce and, thus, no change in output. It follows that if the economy is temporarily producing a level of output other than the long-run natural rate, then at least some wages or prices have failed to adjust to the long-run equilibrium price level. This causes at least some relative prices to change, which stimulates or discourages production. This is, in fact, what is happening along a short-run aggregate-supply curve.

2. Output can fluctuate to levels both above and below the natural rate of output. The examples of economic fluctuations in the text tend to focus on recessions. That is, the examples deal with periods when output is less than the natural level. Note, however, that output can be above the natural rate temporarily because unemployment can be below its natural rate. This economic condition is known as a boom. A boom will occur when there is a positive aggregate demand shock—for example, if there is an increase in the

money supply, an increase in domestic investment, or an increase in government purchases. A boom will also occur if there is a positive aggregate supply shock—for example, if the price of oil were to fall or union wage demands were to decrease. To help you, these cases are addressed in the problems that follow.

3. You may shift the short-run aggregate-supply curve left and right or up and down. Suppose there is an increase in the wage of workers. We have suggested that the rise in the wage will increase the cost of production, decrease profitability at each price level and decrease production at each price level. That is, it will shift the short-run aggregate-supply curve to the left. However, we could have suggested that the increase in the wage will increase the cost of production, requiring firms to charge a higher price in order to continue the same level of production. That is, it shifts the short-run aggregate-supply curve upward on the graph. In the first case, we lowered the quantity supplied at each price. In the second case, we raised the price at each quantity supplied. The resulting shift is the same.

TERMS AND DEFINITIONS

Choose a definition for each key term.

Key terms:

4 __ Recession

8 __ Depression

2 __ The business cycle

10 __ Model of aggregate demand and aggregate supply

5 __ Aggregate-demand curve

9 __ Aggregate-supply curve

6 __ Natural rate of output

1 __ Menu costs

7 __ Stagflation

3 __ Accommodative policy

Definitions:

1. Costs associated with changing prices

2. Short-run economic fluctuations

3. A policy of increasing aggregate demand in response to a decrease in short-run aggregate supply

4. A period of mildly falling incomes and rising unemployment

5. The quantity of goods and services that households, firms, and the government want to buy at each price level

6. The amount of output produced when unemployment is at its natural rate, sometimes called potential output or full-employment output

7. A period of falling output and rising prices

8. A period of unusually severe falling incomes and rising unemployment

9. The quantity of goods and services that firms are willing to produce at each price level

10. The model most economists use to explain short-run fluctuations in the economy around its long-run trend

PROBLEMS AND SHORT-ANSWER QUESTIONS

When necessary, draw a graph of the model of aggregate demand and aggregate supply on scratch paper to help you answer the following problems and questions.

Practice Problems

1. For the following four cases, trace the impact of each shock in the aggregate demand and aggregate supply model by answering the following three questions for each: What happens to prices and output in the short run? What happens to prices and output in the long run if the economy is allowed to adjust to long-run equilibrium on its own? If policymakers had intervened to move output back to the natural rate instead of allowing the economy to self-correct, in which direction should they have moved aggregate demand?
   a. aggregate demand shifts left

   _____

   _____

   b. aggregate demand shifts right

   _____

   _____

   c. short-run aggregate supply shifts left

   _____

   _____

   d. short-run aggregate supply shifts right

   _____

   _____

2. The following events have their *initial impact* on which of the following: aggregate demand, short-run aggregate supply, long-run aggregate supply, or both short-run and long-run aggregate supply? Do the curves shift to the right or left?
   a. The government repairs aging roads and bridges.

   _____

   b. OPEC raises oil prices.

   _____

    c. The government raises unemployment benefits which raises the natural rate of unemployment.

_____

_____

    d. Americans feel more secure in their jobs and become more optimistic.

_____

_____

    e. A technological advance takes place in the application of computers to the manufacture of steel.

_____

_____

    f. The government increases the minimum wage.

_____

_____

    g. Because price expectations are reduced, wage demands of new college graduates fall.

_____

_____

    h. The Federal Reserve decreases the money supply.

_____

_____

    i. A drought destroys much of the midwest corn crop.

_____

_____

3. Suppose the economy is in long-run equilibrium. Then, suppose the Federal Reserve suddenly increases the money supply.
    a. Describe the initial impact of this event in the model of aggregate demand and aggregate supply by explaining which curve shifts which way.

_____

_____

    b. What happens to the price level and real output in the short run?

_____

_____

    c. If the economy is allowed to adjust to the increase in the money supply, what happens to the price level and real output in the long run? (compared to their original levels)

_____

_____

    d. Does an increase in the money supply move output above the natural rate indefinitely? Why?

_____

_____

4. Suppose the economy is in long-run equilibrium. Then, suppose workers and firms suddenly expect higher prices in the future and agree to an increase in wages.

    a. Describe the initial impact of this event in the model of aggregate demand and aggregate supply by explaining which curve shifts which way.

_____

_____

    b. What happens to the price level and real output in the short run?

_____

_____

    c. What name do we have for this combination of movements in output and prices?

_____

    d. If policymakers wanted to move output back to the natural rate of output, what should they do?

_____

_____

    e. If policymakers were able to move output back to the natural rate of output, what would the policy do to prices?

_____

_____

f. If policymakers had done nothing at all, what would have happened to the wage rate as the economy self-corrected or adjusted back to the natural rate of output on its own?

_____

_____

_____

g. Is it likely that an increase in price expectations and wages *alone* can cause a permanent increase in the price level? Why?

_____

_____

_____

5. Suppose the economy is at a point such as point B in Exhibit 2. That is, aggregate demand has decreased and the economy is in a recession. Describe the adjustment process necessary for the economy to adjust on its own to point C for each of the three theoretical short-run aggregate-supply curves.

a. the sticky-wage theory:

_____

_____

_____

_____

_____

_____

b. the sticky-price theory:

_____

_____

_____

_____

c. the misperceptions theory:

_____

_____

_____

_____

d. Do you think the type of adjustments described above would take place more quickly from a recession or from a period when output was above the long-run natural rate? Why?

_____

_____

_____

Short-Answer Questions

1. Name the three key facts about economic fluctuations.

_____

_____

2. What are the three reasons the aggregate-demand curve slopes downward? Explain them.

_____

_____

_____

_____

_____

_____

3. Suppose the economy is in long-run equilibrium. If we employ the sticky-wage theory of the short-run aggregate-supply curve, what initially happens to the real wage if there is a decrease in aggregate demand?

_____

_____

4. Referring to the previous question, if the economy is to adjust on its own back to the long-run equilibrium level of output, what must happen to the real wage?

_____

_____

_____

5. If the economy is in a recession, why might policymakers choose to adjust aggregate demand to eliminate the recession rather then let the economy adjust, or self-correct, on its own?

_____

_____

_____

6. Does a shift in aggregate demand alter output in the long run? Why?

_____

_____

_____

_____

7. Which component of aggregate demand is most volatile over the business cycle?

_____

8. Why is money unlikely to be neutral in the short-run?

_____

_____

_____

9. Suppose OPEC breaks apart and oil prices fall substantially. Initially, which curve shifts in the aggregate supply and aggregate demand model? In what direction does it shift? What happens to the price level and real output?

_____

_____

10. What causes both short-run and long-run aggregate supply to shift together. What causes only the short-run aggregate supply to shift while the long-run aggregate supply remains stationary?

_____

_____

_____

_____

SELF-TEST

True/False Questions

_T_ 1. Over the last 50 years, U.S. real GDP has grown at about 5 percent per year.

_T_ 2. Investment is a particularly volatile component of spending across the business cycle.

_T_ 3. An increase in price expectations shifts the long-run aggregate-supply curve to the left.

_F_ 4. If the classical dichotomy and monetary neutrality hold in the long run, then the long-run aggregate-supply curve should be vertical.

_F_ 5. Economists refer to fluctuations in output as the "business cycle" because movements in output are regular and predictable.

_T_ 6. One reason aggregate demand slopes downward is the wealth effect: a decrease in the price level increases the value of money holdings and consumer spending rises.

_____ 7. If the Federal Reserve increases the money supply, the aggregate-demand curve shifts to the left.

_____ 8. The misperceptions theory explains why the long-run aggregate-supply curve is downward sloping.

_____ 9. A rise in price expectations that causes wages to rise causes the short-run aggregate-supply curve to shift left.

_____10. If the economy is in a recession, the economy will adjust to long-run equilibrium on its own as wages and price expectations rise.

_____11. In the short run, if the government cuts back spending to balance its budget, it will likely cause a recession.

_____12. The short-run effect of an increase in aggregate demand is an increase in output and an increase in the price level.

_____13. A rise in the price of oil tends to cause stagflation.

_____14. In the long run, an increase in government spending tends to increase output and prices.

_____15. If policymakers choose to try to move the economy out of a recession, they should use their policy tools to decrease aggregate demand.

Multiple-Choice Questions

1. Which of the following statements about economic fluctuations is true?
   a. A recession is when output rises above the natural rate of output.
   b. A depression is a mild recession.
   c. Economic fluctuations have been termed the "business cycle" because the movements in output are regular and predictable.
   d. A variety of spending, income, and output measures can be used to measure economic fluctuations because most macroeconomic quantities tend to fluctuate together.
   e. none of the above

2. According to the interest rate effect, aggregate demand slopes downward (negatively) because
   a. lower prices increase the value of money holdings and consumer spending increases.
   b. lower prices decrease the value of money holdings and consumer spending decreases.
   c. lower prices reduce money holdings, increase lending, interest rates fall, and investment spending increases.
   d. lower prices increase money holdings, decrease lending, interest rates rise, and investment spending falls.

3. Which of the following would _not_ cause a shift in the long-run aggregate-supply curve?
   a. an increase in the available labor
   b. an increase in the available capital
   c. an increase in the available technology
   d. an increase in price expectations
   e. All of the above shift the long-run aggregate-supply curve.

4. Which of the following is _not_ a reason why the aggregate-demand curve slopes downward?
   a. the wealth effect
   b. the interest-rate effect
   c. the classical dichotomy/monetary neutrality effects
   d. the exchange-rate effect
   e. All of the above are reasons why the aggregate-demand curve slopes downward.

5. In the model of aggregate demand and aggregate supply, the initial impact of an increase in consumer optimism is to
   a. shift short-run aggregate supply to the right.
   b. shift short-run aggregate supply to the left.
   c. shift aggregate demand to the right.
   d. shift aggregate demand to the left.
   e. shift long-run aggregate supply to the left.

6. Which of the following statements is true regarding the long-run aggregate-supply curve? The long-run aggregate-supply curve
   a. shifts left when the natural rate of unemployment falls.
   b. is vertical because an equal change in all prices and wages leaves output unaffected.
   c. is positively sloped because price expectations and wages tend to be fixed in the long-run.
   d. shifts right when the government raises the minimum wage.

7. According to the wealth effect, aggregate demand slopes downward (negatively) because
   a. lower prices increase the value of money holdings and consumer spending increases.
   b. lower prices decrease the value of money holdings and consumer spending decreases.
   c. lower prices reduce money holdings, increase lending, interest rates fall, and investment spending increases.
   d. lower prices increase money holdings, decrease lending, interest rates rise, and investment spending falls.

8. The natural rate of output is the amount of real GDP produced
   a. when there is no unemployment.
   b. when the economy is at the natural rate of investment.
   c. when the economy is at the natural rate of aggregate demand.
   d. when the economy is at the natural rate of unemployment.

9. Suppose the price level falls but because of fixed nominal wage contracts, the real wage rises and firms cut back on production. This is a demonstration of the
   a. sticky-wage theory of the short-run aggregate-supply curve.
   b. sticky-price theory of the short-run aggregate-supply curve.
   c. misperceptions theory of the short-run aggregate-supply curve.
   d. classical dichotomy theory of the short-run aggregate-supply curve.

10. Suppose the price level falls but suppliers only notice that the price of their particular product has fallen. Thinking there has been a fall in the relative price of their product, they cut back on production. This is a demonstration of the
    a. sticky-wage theory of the short-run aggregate-supply curve.
    b. sticky-price theory of the short-run aggregate-supply curve.
    c. misperceptions theory of the short-run aggregate-supply curve.
    d. classical dichotomy theory of the short-run aggregate-supply curve.

11. Suppose the economy is initially in long-run equilibrium. Then suppose there is a reduction in military spending due to the end of the Cold War. According to the model of aggregate demand and aggregate supply, what happens to prices and output in the *short run?*
    a. Prices rise; output rises.
    b. Prices rise; output falls.
    c. Prices fall; output falls.
    d. Prices fall; output rises.

12. Suppose the economy is initially in long-run equilibrium. Then suppose there is a reduction in military spending due to the end of the Cold War. According to the model of aggregate demand and aggregate supply, what happens to prices and output in the *long run?*
    a. Prices rise; output is unchanged from its initial value.
    b. Prices fall; output is unchanged from its initial value.
    c. Output rises; prices are unchanged from the initial value.
    d. Output falls; prices are unchanged from the initial value.
    e. Output and the price level are unchanged from their initial values.

13. Suppose the economy is initially in long-run equilibrium. Then suppose there is a drought that destroys much of the wheat crop. According to the model of aggregate demand and aggregate supply, what happens to prices and output in the *short run?*
    a. Prices rise; output rises.
    b. Prices rise; output falls.
    c. Prices fall; output falls.
    d. Prices fall; output rises.

14. Suppose the economy is initially in long-run equilibrium. Then suppose there is a drought that destroys much of the wheat crop. If policymakers allow the economy to adjust to long-run equilibrium on its own, according to the model of aggregate demand and aggregate supply, what happens to prices and output in the *long run?*
    a. Prices rise; output is unchanged from its initial value.
    b. Prices fall; output is unchanged from its initial value.
    c. Output rises; prices are unchanged from the initial value.
    d. Output falls; prices are unchanged from the initial value.
    e. Output and the price level are unchanged from their initial values.

15. Stagflation occurs when the economy experiences
    a. falling prices and falling output.
    b. falling prices and rising output.
    c. rising prices and rising output.
    d. rising prices and falling output.

16. Which of the following events shifts the short-run aggregate-supply curve to the right?
    a. an increase in government spending on military equipment
    b. an increase in price expectations
    c. a drop in oil prices
    d. a decrease in the money supply
    e. none of the above

Use Exhibit 4 for the next two questions.

17. Suppose the economy is operating in a recession such as point B in Exhibit 4. If policymakers wished to move output to its long-run natural rate, they should attempt to
    a. shift aggregate demand to the right.
    b. shift aggregate demand to the left.
    c. shift short-run aggregate supply to the right.
    d. shift short-run aggregate supply to the left.

18. Suppose the economy is operating in a recession such as point B in Exhibit 4. If policymakers allow the economy to adjust to the long-run natural rate on its own,
    a. people will raise their price expectations and the short-run aggregate supply will shift left.
    b. people will reduce their price expectations and the short-run aggregate supply will shift right.
    c. people will raise their price expectations and aggregate demand will shift left.
    d. people will reduce their price expectations and aggregate demand will shift right.

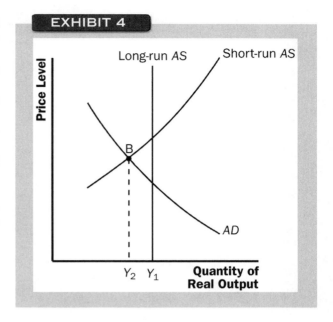

EXHIBIT 4

19. According to the model of aggregate supply and aggregate demand, in the long run, an increase in the money supply should cause
    a. prices to rise and output to rise.
    b. prices to fall and output to fall.
    c. prices to rise and output to remain unchanged.
    d. prices to fall and output to remain unchanged.

20. Policymakers are said to "accommodate" an adverse supply shock if they
    a. respond to the adverse supply shock by increasing aggregate demand, which further raises prices.
    b. respond to the adverse supply shock by decreasing aggregate demand, which lowers prices.
    c. respond to the adverse supply shock by decreasing short-run aggregate supply.
    d. fail to respond to the adverse supply shock and allow the economy to adjust on its own.

ADVANCED CRITICAL THINKING

You are watching the evening news on television. The news anchor reports that union wage demands are much higher this year because the workers anticipate an increase in the rate of inflation. Your roommate says, "Inflation is a self-fulfilling prophecy. If workers think there are going to be higher prices, they demand higher wages. This increases the cost of production and firms raise their prices. Expecting higher prices simply causes higher prices."

1. Is this true in the short run? Explain.

_____

_____

2. If policymakers do nothing and allow the economy to adjust to the natural rate of output on its own, does expecting higher prices cause higher prices in the long run? Explain.

_____

_____

3. If policymakers accommodate the adverse supply shock, does the expectation of higher prices cause higher prices in the long run? Explain.

_____

_____

_____

_____

SOLUTIONS

Terms and Definitions

_4_ Recession

_8_ Depression

_2_ The business cycle

_10_ Model of aggregate supply and demand

_5_ Aggregate-demand curve

_9_ Aggregate-supply curve

_6_ Natural rate of output

_1_ Menu costs

_7_ Stagflation

_3_ Accommodative policy

Practice Problems

1. a. Prices fall, output falls. Prices fall, output returns to the natural rate. Shift aggregate demand to the right.
   b. Prices rise, output rises. Prices rise, output returns to the natural rate. Shift aggregate demand to the left.
   c. Prices rise, output falls. Price level returns to original value, output returns to the natural rate. Shift aggregate demand to the right.
   d. Prices fall, output rises. Price level returns to original value, output returns to the natural rate. Shift aggregate demand to the left.

2. a. aggregate demand, right
   b. short-run aggregate supply, left
   c. both short-run and long-run aggregate supply, left
   d. aggregate demand, right
   e. both short-run and long-run aggregate supply, right
   f. both short-run and long-run aggregate supply, left
   g. short-run aggregate supply, right
   h. aggregate demand, left
   i. both short-run and long-run aggregate supply, left

3. a. Aggregate demand shifts to the right.
   b. Price level rises and real output rises.
   c. Price level rises and real output stays the same.
   d. No. Over time, people and firms adjust to the new higher amount of spending by raising their prices and wages.

4. a. Short-run aggregate supply shifts left.

  b. Prices rise and output falls.
  c. Stagflation.
  d. Shift aggregate demand to the right.
  e. Prices would rise more and remain there.
  f. The high unemployment at the low level of output would put pressure on the wage to fall back to its original value shifting short-run aggregate supply back to its original position.
  g. No. Increases in the cost of production need to be "accommodated" by government policy to permanently raise prices.

5. a. At point B, nominal wage contracts are based on the expectation of a higher price level so the real wage has risen and workers were laid off. As workers and firms recognize the fall in the price level (learn to expect P_3), new contracts will have a lower nominal wage, the real wage falls, and firms increase production at each price level shifting the short-run aggregate supply to the right.
  b. At point B, some firms have not reduced their prices because of menu costs. Their products are relatively more expensive and sales fall. When they realize the lower price level is permanent (learn to expect P_3), they lower their prices and output rises at each price level, shifting the short-run aggregate supply to the right.
  c. At point B, some firms mistakenly believe that only the price of their product has fallen and they have cut back on production. As they realize that all prices are falling (learn to expect P_3), they will increase production at each price, which will shift short-run aggregate supply to the right.
  d. More slowly from a recession because it requires prices to be reduced, and prices are usually more sticky downward. The adjustment when output is above normal requires prices and wages to rise.

Short-Answer Questions

1. Economic fluctuations are irregular and unpredictable, most macroeconomic quantities fluctuate together, and when output falls, unemployment rises.

2. Wealth effect: lower prices increase the value of money holdings and consumer spending increases. Interest-rate effect: Lower prices reduce the quantity of money held, some is loaned, interest rates fall, and investment spending increases. Exchange-rate effect: lower prices decrease interest rates, the dollar depreciates, and net exports increase.

3. Since the nominal wage is fixed for a period, the fall in the price level raises the real wage, W/P.

4. The nominal wage must fall so that the real wage can return to its initial level.

5. Because they think they can get the economy back to the long-run natural rate of output more quickly or, in the case of a negative supply shock, because they are more concerned with output than inflation.

6. No. In the long run, output is determined by factor supplies and technology (long-run aggregate supply). Changes in aggregate demand only affect output in the short-run because it temporarily alters relative prices.

7. Investment.

8. Because a shift in aggregate demand from a change in the money supply may change the price level unexpectedly. Some prices and wages adjust to the change more quickly than others causing changes in relative prices in the short run.

9. Short-run aggregate supply shifts right. Prices fall and output rises.

10. Changes in the available factors (labor, capital, natural resources) and technology shift both long-run and short-run aggregate supply. Changes in price expectations that may be associated with wage demands and oil prices only shift short-run aggregate supply.

True/False Questions

1. F; the U.S. economy has grown at about 3 percent per year.

2. T

3. F; changes in price expectations shift the short-run aggregate-supply curve.

4. T

5. F; fluctuations in output are irregular.

6. T

7. F; aggregate demand shifts to the right.

8. F; it explains why the short-run aggregate-supply curve is upward sloping.

9. T

10. F; in a recession, the economy adjusts to long-run equilibrium as wages and prices fall.

11. T

12. T

13. T

14. F; in the long run, it tends to increase prices, but it has no impact on output.

15. F; policymakers should increase aggregate demand.

Multiple-Choice Questions

1. d	5. c	9. a	13. b	17. a
2. c	6. b	10. c	14. e	18. b
3. d	7. a	11. c	15. d	19. c
4. c	8. d	12. b	16. c	20. a

Advanced Critical Thinking

1. Yes. An increase in price expectations shifts the short-run aggregate-supply curve to the left and prices rise.

2. No. In the long run, the increase in unemployment will cause wages and price expectations to fall back to their prior levels.

3. Yes. If policymakers accommodate the adverse supply shock with an increase in aggregate demand, the price level will rise permanently.

21

THE INFLUENCE OF MONETARY AND FISCAL POLICY ON AGGREGATE DEMAND

GOALS

⌈In this chapter you will

Learn the theory of liquidity preference as a short-run theory of the
interest rate

Analyze how monetary policy
affects interest rates and aggregate
demand

Analyze how fiscal policy affects
interest rates and aggregate
demand

Discuss the debate over whether
policymakers should try to stabilize the economy

OUTCOMES

⌈After accomplishing these
goals, you should be able to

Show what an increase in the
money supply does to the interest
rate in the short run

Illustrate what an increase in the
money supply does to aggregate
demand

Explain crowding out

Describe the lags in fiscal and
monetary policy

CHAPTER OVERVIEW

Context and Purpose

Chapter 21 is the second chapter in a three-chapter sequence that concentrates on short-run fluctuations in the economy around its long-term trend. In Chapter 20, we introduced the model of aggregate supply and aggregate demand. In Chapter 21, we see how the government's monetary and fiscal policies affect aggregate demand. In Chapter 22, we will see some of the tradeoffs between short-run and long-run objectives when we address the relationship between inflation and unemployment.

The purpose of Chapter 21 is to address the short-run effects of monetary and fiscal policies. In Chapter 20, we found that when aggregate demand or short-run aggregate supply shifts, it causes fluctuations in output. As a result, policymakers sometimes try to offset these shifts by shifting aggregate demand with monetary and fiscal policy. Chapter 21 addresses the theory behind these policies and some of the shortcomings of stabilization policy.

CHAPTER REVIEW

Introduction

Chapters 25 through 30 demonstrated the impact of fiscal and monetary policy on saving, investment, and long-term growth. Chapter 33 demonstrated that shifts in aggregate demand and short-run aggregate supply cause short-run fluctuations in the economy around its long-term trend and how monetary and fiscal policy-makers might shift aggregate demand to stabilize the economy. In this chapter, we address the theory behind stabilization policies and some of the shortcomings of stabilization policy.

How Monetary Policy Influences Aggregate Demand

The aggregate-demand curve shows the quantity of goods and services demanded at each price level. Recall from Chapter 33, aggregate demand slopes downward due to the wealth effect, the interest-rate effect, and the exchange-rate effect. Since money is a small part of total wealth and since the international sector is a small part of the U.S. economy, the most important reason for the downward slope of U.S. aggregate demand is the interest-rate effect.

The interest rate is a key determinant of aggregate demand. To see how monetary policy affects aggregate demand, we develop Keynes's theory of interest rate determination called the **theory of liquidity preference.** This theory suggests that the interest rate is determined by the supply and demand for money. Note that the interest rate being determined is both the nominal and the real interest rate because, in the short run, expected inflation is unchanging so changes in the nominal rate equal changes in the real rate.

Recall, the money supply is determined by the Fed and can be fixed at whatever level the Fed chooses. Therefore, the money supply is unaffected by the interest rate and is a vertical line in Exhibit 1. People have a demand for money because money, as the economy's most liquid asset, is a medium of exchange. Hence, people have a demand for it even though it has no rate of return because it can be used to buy things. The interest rate is the opportunity cost of holding

EXHIBIT 1

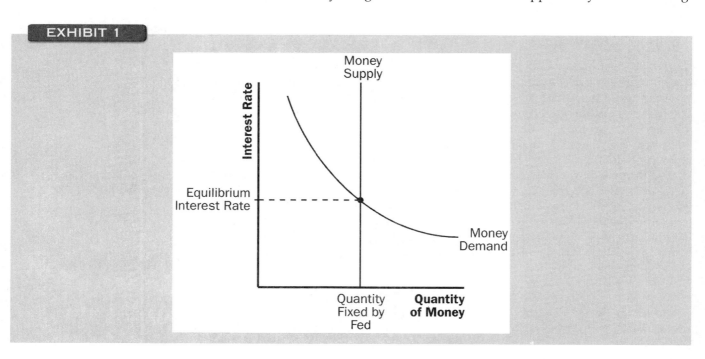

EXHIBIT 2

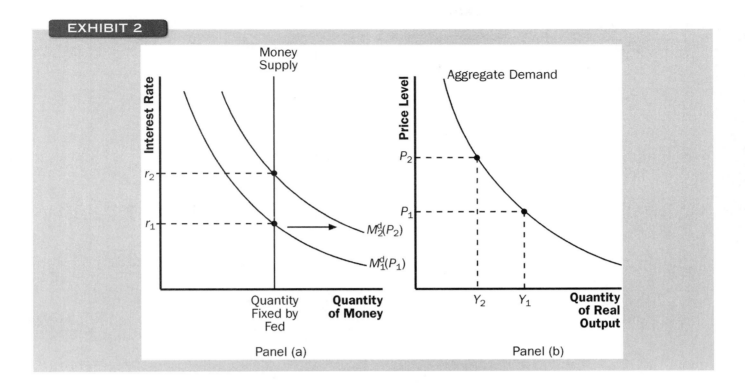

Panel (a)   Panel (b)

money. When the interest rate is high, people hold more wealth in interest-bearing bonds and economize on their money holdings. Thus, the quantity of money demanded is reduced. This is shown in Exhibit 1. The equilibrium interest rate is determined by the intersection of money supply and money demand.

Note that, in the long run, the interest rate is determined by the supply and demand for loanable funds. In the short run, the interest rate is determined by the supply and demand for money. This poses no conflict.

- In the long run, output is fixed by factor supplies and technology, the interest rate adjusts to balance the supply and demand for loanable funds, and the price level adjusts to balance the supply and demand for money.

- In the short run, the price level is sticky and cannot adjust. For any given price level, the interest rate adjusts to balance the supply and demand for money, and output responds to changes in aggregate demand and short-run aggregate supply.

Each theory highlights the behavior of interest rates over a different time horizon.

We can use the theory of liquidity preference to add precision to our explanation of the negative slope of the aggregate-demand curve. Recall from previous chapters, the demand for money is positively related to the price level because at higher prices, people need more money to buy the same quantity of goods. Thus, a higher price level shifts money demand to the right, as shown in Exhibit 2, panel (a). With a fixed money supply, a larger money demand raises the interest rate. A higher interest rate reduces investment expenditures and causes the quantity demanded of goods and services to fall in Exhibit 2, panel (b).

Returning to the point of this section: How does monetary policy influence aggregate demand? Suppose the Fed buys government bonds shifting the money

EXHIBIT 3

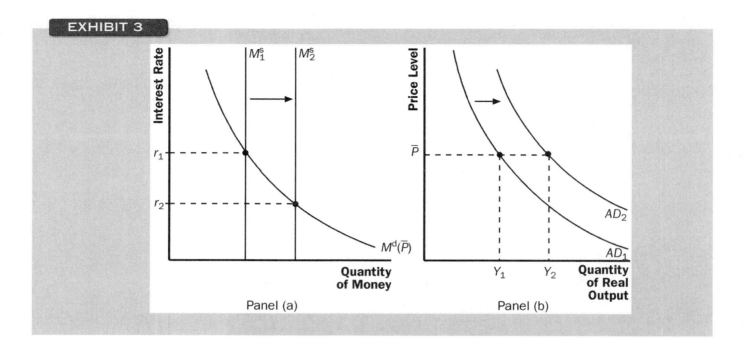

Panel (a)

Panel (b)

supply to the right, as in Exhibit 3, panel (a). The interest rate falls, reducing the cost of borrowing for investment. Hence, the quantity of goods and services demanded at each price level increases, shifting aggregate demand to the right in Exhibit 3, panel (b).

The Fed can implement monetary policy by targeting the money supply or interest rates. In recent years, the Fed has targeted the interest rate because the money supply is hard to measure. In particular, the Fed has targeted the *federal funds rate*—the interest rate banks charge each other for short-term loans. Whether the Fed targets the money supply or interest rates has little effect on our analysis because every monetary policy can be described in terms of the money supply or the interest rate. For example, the monetary policy expansion used to increase aggregate demand in the example above could be described as an increase in the targeted money supply or a decrease in the targeted interest rate.

How Fiscal Policy Influences Aggregate Demand

Fiscal policy refers to the government's choices of the levels of government purchases and taxes. While fiscal policy can influence growth in the long run, its primary impact in the short run is on aggregate demand.

An increase in government purchases of $20 billion to buy military aircraft is reflected in a rightward shift in the aggregate-demand curve. There are two reasons why the actual rightward shift may be greater than or less than $20 billion:

- *The multiplier effect:* When the government spends $20 billion on aircraft, incomes rise in the form of wages and profits of the aircraft manufacturer. The recipients of the new income raise their spending on consumer goods, which raises the incomes of people in other firms, which raises their consumption spending, and so on for many rounds. Since aggregate demand may rise by much more than the increase in government purchases, government purchases are said to have a **multiplier effect** on aggregate demand. There is a formula for the size of the multiplier effect. It says that for every dollar the government spends, aggregate demand shifts to the right by $1/(1 - MPC)$, where MPC

stands for the marginal propensity to consume—the fraction of extra income that a household spends on consumption. For example, if the *MPC* is 0.75, the multiplier is $1/(1-0.75) = 1/.25 = 4$ which means that $1 of government spending shifts aggregate demand to the right by a total of $4. An increase in the *MPC* increases the multiplier.

In addition to the multiplier, the increase in purchases may cause firms to increase their investment expenditures on new equipment, further increasing the response of aggregate demand to the initial increase in government purchases. This is known as the *investment accelerator*.

Thus, the aggregate demand curve may shift by more than the change in government purchases.

The logic of the multiplier effect applies to other changes in spending besides government purchases. For example, shocks to consumption, investment, and net exports may have a multiple effect on aggregate demand.

- *The crowding-out effect:* The **crowding-out effect** works in the opposite direction of the multiplier. An increase in government purchases (as in the case above) raises incomes, which shifts the demand for money to the right. This raises the interest rate, which lowers investment. Thus, an increase in government purchases increases the interest rate and reduces, or crowds out, private investment. Due to crowding out, the aggregate demand curve may shift right by less that the increase in government purchases.

Whether the final shift in the aggregate-demand curve is greater than or less than the original change in government spending depends on which is larger: the multiplier effect or the crowding-out effect.

The other half of fiscal policy is taxation. A reduction in taxes increases households' take-home pay and, hence, increases their consumption. Thus, a decrease in taxes shifts aggregate demand to the right while an increase shifts aggregate demand to the left. The size of the shift in aggregate demand depends on the relative size of the multiplier and crowding-out effects described above. In addition, a reduction in taxes that is perceived by households to be permanent improves the financial condition of the household a great amount and increases aggregate demand substantially. A change in taxes that is perceived to be temporary has a much smaller effect on aggregate demand.

Finally, fiscal policy might have an effect on aggregate supply for two reasons. First, a reduction in taxes might increase the incentive to work and cause aggregate supply to shift right. Supply-siders believe this effect is large. Second, government purchases of capital such as roads and bridges may increase the amount of goods supplied at each price level and shift the aggregate supply curve to the right. This effect is more likely to be important in the long run.

Using Policy to Stabilize the Economy

Keynes (and his followers) argued that the government should actively use monetary and fiscal policies to stabilize aggregate demand and, as a result, output and employment.

The Employment Act of 1946 holds the Federal Government responsible for promoting full employment and production. The act has two implications: (1) The government should not be the cause of fluctuations, so it should avoid sudden changes in fiscal and monetary policy, and (2) the government should respond changes in the private economy in order to stabilize it. For example, if consumer pessimism reduces aggregate demand, the proper amount of expansionary monetary or fiscal policy could stimulate aggregate demand to its original level, thereby avoiding a recession. Alternatively, if excessive optimism increases aggregate demand, contractionary monetary or fiscal policy could dampen aggregate demand to its original level, thereby avoiding inflationary pressures. Failure to actively stabilize the economy may allow for unnecessary fluctuations in output and employment.

Some economists argue that the government should not use monetary and fiscal policy to try to stabilize short-run fluctuations in the economy. While they agree that, in theory, activist policy can stabilize the economy, they feel that, in practice, monetary and fiscal policy affect the economy with a substantial lag. The lag for monetary policy is at least six months so it may be hard for the Fed to "fine tune" the economy. Fiscal policy has a long political lag because it takes months or years to pass spending and taxation legislation. These lags mean that activist policy could be destabilizing because expansionary policy could accidentally increase aggregate demand during periods of excessive private aggregate demand, and contractionary policy could accidentally decrease aggregate demand during periods of deficient private aggregate demand.

Automatic stabilizers are changes in fiscal policy that automatically stimulate aggregate demand in a recession so that policymakers do not have to take deliberate action. The tax system automatically lowers tax collections during a recession when incomes and profits fall. Government spending automatically rises during a recession because unemployment benefits and welfare payments rise. Hence, both the tax and government spending systems increase aggregate demand during a recession. A strict balanced budget rule would eliminate automatic stabilizers because the government would have to raise taxes or lower expenditures during a recession.

If there is to be activist monetary policy, most economists believe that the Federal Reserve will make better decisions if it continues to be politically independent. This is because it is politically difficult to increase interest rates and reduce aggregate demand when the economy is overheating (temporarily operating above the natural rate) but it may be necessary in order to avoid future inflation.

HELPFUL HINTS

1. The multiplier can be derived in a variety of different ways. Your text shows you that the value of the multiplier is $1/(1 - MPC)$. However, it doesn't show you how this number is generated. Below, you will find one of the many different ways that the value of the multiplier can be derived for the case of an increase in government spending:

$$\Delta \text{output demanded} = \Delta \text{spending on output,}$$

which says that the change in output demanded equals the change in spending on output. Denoting Y as output demanded, G as government spending, and noting that output equals income, then

$$\Delta Y = \Delta G + [(MPC) \times \Delta Y],$$

which says that the change in output demanded is equal to the change in total spending where total spending is composed of the change in government spending plus the change in consumption spending induced by the increase in income (say 0.75 of the change in income).

Solving for ΔY, we get

$$\Delta Y - [(MPC) \times \Delta Y] = \Delta G$$

$$\Delta Y \times (1 - MPC) = \Delta G$$

$$\Delta Y = 1/(1 - MPC) \times \Delta G,$$

which says that a $1 increase in government spending causes an increase in aggregate demand of $1/(1 - MPC) \times \$1$. If the MPC equals 0.75, then $1/(1 - 0.75) = 4$ and a $1 increase in government spending shifts aggregate demand to the right by $4.

2. An increase in the MPC increases the multiplier. If the MPC were 0.80, suggesting that people spend 80 percent of an increase in income on consumption goods, the multiplier would become $1/(1 - 0.80) = 5$. This is larger than the multiplier generated above from an MPC of 0.75. There is an intuitive appeal to this result. If people spend a higher percentage of an increase in income on consumption goods, any new government purchase will have an even larger multiplier effect and shift the aggregate-demand curve further to the right.

3. The multiplier works in both directions. If the government reduces purchases, the multiplier effect suggests that the aggregate-demand curve will shift to the left by a greater amount than the initial reduction in government purchases. When the government reduces purchases, wages and profits of people are reduced and they reduce their consumption expenditures, and so on, creating a multiple contraction in aggregate demand.

4. Activist stabilization policy has many descriptive names. Activist stabilization policy is the use of discretionary monetary and fiscal policies to manage aggregate demand in such a way as to minimize the fluctuations in output and to maintain output at the long-run natural rate. As such, activist stabilization policy is sometimes called *discretionary policy* to distinguish it from automatic stabilizers. It is also called *aggregate demand management* because monetary and fiscal policies are used to adjust or manage total spending in the economy. Finally, since policymakers attempt to counter the business cycle by reducing aggregate demand when it is too high and by increasing aggregate demand when it is too low, stabilization policy is sometimes referred to as *countercyclical policy*.

5. Activist stabilization policy can be used to move output toward the long-run natural rate from levels of output that are either above or below the natural rate of output. As in the previous chapter, most of the examples of stabilization policy in the text assume the economy is in a recession—a period when output is below the long-run natural rate. However, activist stabilization policy can be used to reduce aggregate demand and output in periods when output exceeds the long-run natural rate. When output exceeds the natural rate, we sometimes say that the economy is in a boom, an expansion, or that the economy is overheating. When the economy's output is above the natural rate, the economy is said to be overheating because, left alone, the economy will adjust to a higher level of expected prices and wages and output will fall to the natural rate (short-run aggregate supply shifts left).

Most economists believe that the Federal Reserve needs political independence to combat an overheating economy. This is because the activist policy prescription for an overheating economy is a reduction in aggregate demand, which usually faces political opposition. That is, "taking away the punch bowl just as the party gets going" is not likely to be politically popular.

TERMS AND DEFINITIONS

Choose a definition for each key term.

Key terms:

_____ Theory of liquidity preference

_____ Liquidity

_____ Federal funds rate

_____ Multiplier effect

_____ Investment accelerator

_____ Marginal propensity to consume, or MPC

_____ Crowding-out effect

_____ Stabilization policy

_____ Automatic stabilizers

Definitions:

1. The dampening of the shift in aggregate demand from expansionary fiscal policy, which raises the interest rate and reduces investment spending

2. The interest rate banks charge one another for short-term loans

3. The amplification of the shift in aggregate demand from expansionary fiscal policy, which raises investment expenditures

4. Keynes's theory that the interest rate is determined by the supply and demand for money in the short run

5. Changes in fiscal policy that do not require deliberate action on the part of policymakers

6. The use of fiscal and monetary policies to reduce fluctuations in the economy

7. The amplification of the shift in aggregate demand from expansionary fiscal policy, which raises incomes and further increases consumption expenditures

8. The ease with which an asset is converted into a medium of exchange

9. The fraction of extra income that a household spends on consumption

PROBLEMS AND SHORT-ANSWER QUESTIONS

Practice Problems

1. If the Federal Reserve were to engage in activist stabilization policy, in which direction should they move the *money supply* in response to the following events?

a. A wave of optimism boosts business investment and household consumption.

_____

b. To balance its budget, the federal government raises taxes and reduces expenditures.

_____

c. OPEC raises the price of crude oil.

_____

d. Foreigners experience a reduction in their taste for U.S.-produced Ford automobiles.

_____

e. The stock market falls.

_____

2. If the Federal Reserve were to engage in activist stabilization policy, in which direction should they move *interest rates* in response to the same events listed in the previous question?
   a. A wave of optimism boosts business investment and household consumption.

_____

   b. To balance its budget, the federal government raises taxes and reduces expenditures.

_____

   c. OPEC raises the price of crude oil.

_____

   d. Foreigners experience a reduction in their taste for U.S.-produced Ford automobiles.

_____

   e. The stock market falls.

_____

f. Explain the relationship between Fed policy in terms of the money supply and policy in terms of the interest rate.

_____

_____

_____

_____

3. If policymakers were to use fiscal policy to actively stabilize the economy, in which direction should they move government spending and taxes?
   a. A wave of pessimism reduces business investment and household consumption.

   _____

   b. An increase in price expectations causes unions to demand higher wages.

   _____

   c. Foreigners increase their taste for domestically produced Ford automobiles.

   _____

   d. OPEC raises the price of crude oil.

   _____

4. Suppose the economy is in a recession. Policymakers estimate that aggregate demand is $100 billion short of the amount necessary to generate the long-run natural rate of output. That is, if aggregate demand were shifted to the right by $100 billion, the economy would be in long-run equilibrium.
   a. If the federal government chooses to use fiscal policy to stabilize the economy, by how much should they increase government spending if the marginal propensity to consume (MPC) is 0.75 and there is no crowding out?

   _____

   _____

   b. If the federal government chooses to use fiscal policy to stabilize the economy, by how much should they increase government spending if the marginal propensity to consume (MPC) is 0.80 and there is no crowding out?

   _____

   _____

c. If there is crowding out, will the government need to spend more or less than the amounts you found in (a) and (b) above? Why?

_____

_____

_____

_____

d. If investment is very sensitive to changes in the interest rate, is crowding out more of a problem or less of a problem? Why?

_____

_____

_____

_____

e. If policymakers discover that the lag for fiscal policy is two years, should that make them more likely to employ fiscal policy as a stabilization tool or more likely to allow the economy to adjust on its own? Why?

_____

_____

_____

_____

5. a. What does an increase in the money supply do to interest rates in the short run? Explain.

_____

_____

_____

_____

b. What does an increase in the money supply do to interest rates in the long run? Explain.

_____

_____

_____

_____

c. Are these results inconsistent? Explain.

_____

_____

_____

Short-Answer Questions

1. Why is the money supply curve vertical when it is drawn on a graph with the interest rate on the vertical axis and the quantity of money on the horizontal axis?

_____

_____

_____

2. Why does the money demand curve slope negatively when it is drawn on a graph with the interest rate on the vertical axis and the quantity of money on the horizontal axis?

_____

_____

_____

_____

3. Why does an increase in the price level reduce the quantity demanded of real output? (Use the interest-rate effect to explain the slope of the aggregate demand curve.)

_____

_____

_____

_____

4. Explain how an increase in the money supply shifts the aggregate-demand curve.

_____

_____

_____

5. Explain the intuition of the multiplier effect resulting from an increase in government spending. Why should a bigger MPC make the multiplier effect larger?

_____

_____

_____

_____

6. Explain how an increase in government spending may lead to crowding out.

_____

_____

_____

7. Suppose the government spends $10 billion on a public works program, which is intended to stimulate aggregate demand. If the crowding-out effect exceeds the multiplier effect, will the aggregate demand curve shift to the right by more or less than $10 billion? Why?

_____

_____

_____

8. How does a cut in taxes affect aggregate supply?

_____

_____

9. Which is likely to have a greater impact on aggregate demand: A temporary reduction in taxes or a permanent reduction in taxes? Why?

_____

_____

10. Explain why taxes and government spending may act as automatic stabilizers. What would a strict balanced-budget rule cause policymakers to do during a recession? Would this make the recession more or less severe?

_____

_____

_____

_____

SELF-TEST

True/False Questions

_F_   1. An increase in the interest rate increases the quantity demanded of money because it increases the rate of return on money.

_T_   2. When money demand is drawn on a graph with the interest rate on the vertical axis and the quantity of money on the horizontal axis, an increase in the price level shifts money demand to the right.

_____ 3. Keynes's theory of liquidity preference suggests that the interest rate is determined by the supply and demand for money.

_____ 4. The interest-rate effect suggests that aggregate demand slopes downward because an increase in the price level shifts money demand to the right, increases the interest rate, and reduces investment.

_____ 5. An increase in the money supply shifts the money supply curve to the right, increases the interest rate, decreases investment, and shifts the aggregate demand curve to the left.

_____ 6. Suppose investors and consumers become pessimistic about the future and cut back on expenditures. If the Fed engages in activist stabilization policy, the policy response should be to decrease the money supply.

_____ 7. In the short run, a decision by the Fed to increase the targeted money supply is essentially the same as a decision to decrease the targeted interest rate.

_____ 8. Because of the multiplier effect, an increase in government spending of $40 billion will shift the aggregate demand curve to the right by more than $40 billion (assuming there is no crowding out).

_____ 9. If the MPC (marginal propensity to consume) is 0.80, then the value of the multiplier is 8.

_____10. Crowding out occurs when an increase in government spending increases incomes, shifts money demand to the right, raises the interest rate, and reduces private investment.

_____11. Suppose the government increases its expenditure by $10 billion. If the crowding-out effect exceeds the multiplier effect, then the aggregate-demand curve shifts to the right by more than $10 billion.

_____12. Suppose investors and consumers become pessimistic about the future and cut back on expenditures. If fiscal policymakers engage in activist stabilization policy, the policy response should be to decrease government spending and increase taxes.

_____13. Many economists prefer automatic stabilizers because they affect the economy with a shorter lag than activist stabilization policies.

_____14. In the short run, the interest rate is determined by the loanable funds market, while in the long run, the interest rate is determined by money demand and money supply.

_____15. Unemployment benefits are an example of an automatic stabilizer because when incomes fall, unemployment benefits rise.

Multiple-Choice Questions

1. Keynes's liquidity preference theory of the interest rate suggests that the interest rate is determined by
   a. the supply and demand for loanable funds.
   b. the supply and demand for money.
   c. the supply and demand for labor.
   d. aggregate supply and aggregate demand.

2. When money demand is expressed in a graph with the interest rate on the vertical axis and the quantity of money on the horizontal axis, an increase in the interest rate
   a. increases the quantity demanded of money.
   b. increases the demand for money.
   c. decreases the quantity demanded of money.
   d. decreases the demand for money.
   e. none of the above

3. When the supply and demand for money are expressed in a graph with the interest rate on the vertical axis and the quantity of money on the horizontal axis, an increase in the price level
   a. shifts money demand to the right and increases the interest rate.
   b. shifts money demand to the left and increases the interest rate.
   c. shifts money demand to the right and decreases the interest rate.
   d. shifts money demand to the left and decreases the interest rate.
   e. none of the above

4. For the United States, the most important source of the downward slope of the aggregate demand curve is
   a. the exchange-rate effect.
   b. the wealth effect.
   c. the fiscal effect.
   d. the interest-rate effect.
   e. none of the above

5. In the market for real output, the initial effect of an increase in the money supply is to
   a. shift aggregate demand to the right.
   b. shift aggregate demand to the left.
   c. shift aggregate supply to the right.
   d. shift aggregate supply to the right.

6. The initial effect of an increase in the money supply is to
   a. increase the price level.
   b. decrease the price level.
   c. increase the interest rate.
   d. decrease the interest rate.

7. The long-run effect of an increase in the money supply is to
   a. increase the price level.
   b. decrease the price level.
   c. increase the interest rate.
   d. decrease the interest rate.

8. Suppose a wave of investor and consumer pessimism causes a reduction in spending. If the Federal Reserve chooses to engage in activist stabilization policy, it should
   a. increase government spending and decrease taxes.
   b. decrease government spending and increase taxes.
   c. increase the money supply and decrease interest rates.
   d. decrease the money supply and increase interest rates.

9. The initial impact of an increase in government spending is to shift
   a. aggregate supply to the right.
   b. aggregate supply to the left.
   c. aggregate demand to the right.
   d. aggregate demand to the left.

10. If the marginal propensity to consume (MPC) is 0.75, the value of the multiplier is
    a. 0.75.
    b. 4.
    c. 5.
    d. 7.5.
    e. none of the above.

11. An increase in the marginal propensity to consume (MPC)
    a. raises the value of the multiplier.
    b. lowers the value of the multiplier.
    c. has no impact on the value of the multiplier.
    d. rarely occurs because the MPC is set by congressional legislation.

12. Suppose a wave of investor and consumer optimism has increased spending so that the current level of output exceeds the long-run natural rate. If policymakers choose to engage in activist stabilization policy, they should
    a. decrease taxes, which shifts aggregate demand to the right.
    b. decrease taxes, which shifts aggregate demand to the left.
    c. decrease government spending, which shifts aggregate demand to the right.
    d. decrease government spending, which shifts aggregate demand to the left.

13. When an increase in government purchases raises incomes, shifts money demand to the right, raises the interest rate, and lowers investment, we have seen a demonstration of
    a. the multiplier effect.
    b. the investment accelerator.
    c. the crowding-out effect.
    d. supply-side economics.
    e. none of the above.

14. Which of the following statements regarding taxes is correct?
    a. Most economists believe that, in the short run, the greatest impact of a change in taxes is on aggregate supply, not aggregate demand.
    b. A permanent change in taxes has a greater effect on aggregate demand than a temporary change in taxes.
    c. An increase in taxes shifts the aggregate-demand curve to the right.
    d. A decrease in taxes shifts the aggregate-supply curve to the left.

15. Suppose the government increases its purchases by $16 billion. If the multiplier effect exceeds the crowding-out effect, then
    a. the aggregate-supply curve shifts to the right by more than $16 billion.
    b. the aggregate-supply curve shifts to the left by more than $16 billion.
    c. the aggregate-demand curve shifts to the right by more than $16 billion.
    d. the aggregate-demand curve shifts to the left by more than $16 billion.

16. When an increase in government purchases increases the income of some people, and those people spend some of that increase in income on additional consumer goods, we have seen a demonstration of
    a. the multiplier effect.
    b. the investment accelerator.
    c. the crowding-out effect.
    d. supply-side economics.
    e. none of the above.

17. When an increase in government purchases causes firms to purchase additional plant and equipment, we have seen a demonstration of
    a. the multiplier effect.
    b. the investment accelerator.
    c. the crowding-out effect.
    d. supply-side economics.
    e. none of the above.

18. Which of the following is an automatic stabilizer?
    a. military spending
    b. spending on public schools
    c. unemployment benefits
    d. spending on the space shuttle
    e. All of the above are automatic stabilizers.

19. Which of the following statements about stabilization policy is true?
    a. In the short run, a decision by the Fed to increase the targeted money supply is essentially the same as a decision to increase the targeted interest rate.
    b. Congress has veto power over the monetary policy decisions of the Fed.
    c. Long lags enhance the ability of policymakers to "fine tune" the economy.
    d. Many economists prefer automatic stabilizers because they affect the economy with a shorter lag than activist stabilization policy.
    e. All of the above are true.

20. Which of the following best describes how an increase in the money supply shifts aggregate demand?
    a. The money supply shifts right, the interest rate rises, investment decreases, and aggregate demand shifts left.
    b. The money supply shifts right, the interest rate falls, investment increases, and aggregate demand shifts right.
    c. The money supply shifts right, prices rise, spending falls, and aggregate demand shifts left.
    d. The money supply shifts right, prices fall, spending increases, and aggregate demand shifts right.

ADVANCED CRITICAL THINKING

You are watching a nightly network news broadcast. The opening report is a story about today's meeting of the Fed's Federal Open Market Committee. The business correspondent reports that the Fed raised interest rates by a quarter of a percent today to head off future inflation. The report then moves to interviews with prominent politicians. The response of a member of Congress to the Fed's move is negative. She says, "The Consumer Price Index has not increased, yet the Fed is restricting growth in the economy, supposedly to fight inflation. My constituents will want to know why they are going to have to pay more when they get a loan, and I don't have a good answer. I think this is an outrage and I think Congress should have hearings on the Fed's policy-making powers."

1. What interest rate did the Fed raise?

2. State the Fed's policy in terms of the money supply.

3. Why might the Fed raise interest rates before the CPI starts to rise?

_____

_____

_____

_____

_____

4. Use the Congresswoman's statement to explain why most economists
    believe that the Fed needs to be independent of politics?

_____

_____

_____

_____

_____

SOLUTIONS

Terms and Definitions

_4_ Theory of liquidity preference

_8_ Liquidity

_2_ Federal funds rate

_7_ Multiplier effect

_3_ Investment accelerator

_9_ Marginal propensity to consume, or *MPC*

_1_ Crowding-out effect

_6_ Stabilization policy

_5_ Automatic stabilizers

Practice Problems

1. a. Decrease the money supply
    b. Increase the money supply
    c. Increase the money supply
    d. Increase the money supply
    e. Increase the money supply

2. a. Increase interest rates
    b. Decrease interest rates
    c. Decrease interest rates
    d. Decrease interest rates
    e. Decrease interest rates
    f. In the short run, with prices sticky or fixed, an increase in the money supply implies a reduction in interest rates and a decrease in the money supply implies an increase in interest rates.

3. a. Increase spending, decrease taxes
    b. Increase spending, decrease taxes
    c. Decrease spending, increase taxes
    d. Increase spending, decrease taxes

4. a. Multiplier $= 1/(1 - 0.75) = 4$; $100/4 = \$25$ billion.
    b. Multiplier $= 1/(1 - 0.80) = 5$; $100/5 = \$20$ billion.
    c. More, because as the government spends more, investors spend less so aggregate demand won't increase by as much as the multiplier suggests.
    d. More of a problem. Government spending raises interest rates. The more sensitive investment is to the interest rate—the more it is reduced or crowded out by government spending.
    e. More likely to allow the economy to adjust on its own because if the economy adjusts before the impact of the fiscal policy is felt, the fiscal policy will be destabilizing.

5. a. It lowers interest rates because, in the short run, with prices sticky or fixed, money demand is unchanging. Thus, an increase in the money supply requires a decrease in interest rates to induce people to hold the additional money.
   b. It has no effect because, in the long run, the increase in spending causes a proportional increase in prices, output is fixed at the natural rate, money is neutral, and interest rates are determined by the supply and demand for loanable funds which have not changed.
   c. No. Prices are likely to be sticky in the short run and flexible in the long run.

Short-Answer Questions

1. Because the quantity of money is fixed at whatever value the Fed chooses and this quantity is not dependent on the interest rate.

2. The interest rate is the opportunity cost of money since money earns no rate of return. Thus, an increase in the interest rate causes people to economize on cash balances and hold more wealth in interest bearing bonds.

3. An increase in the price level shifts money demand to the right, increases the interest rate, and decreases investment.

4. The money supply shifts right, the interest rate decreases, investment increases at each price level, which is a rightward shift in the aggregate-demand curve.

5. When the government purchases goods, it causes an increase in the incomes of the sellers. They spend some percent of their new higher income on goods and services, raising other's incomes, and so on. The higher the *MPC*, the greater the percent of new income spent in each round.

6. An increase in government spending raises incomes, shifts money demand right, raises the interest rate, and reduces investment.

7. By less than $10 billion because the crowding-out effect, which reduces the shift in aggregate demand, more than offsets the multiplier effect, which amplifies the shift.

8. It causes an increase in aggregate supply by increasing the incentive to work.

9. Permanent, because it improves the financial condition of the household more and, thus, they spend more.

10. Income tax collections fall during a recession and government spending on welfare and unemployment benefits rises. It would cause the government to raise other taxes and lower other spending. More severe.

True/False Questions

1. F; an increase in the interest rate decreases the quantity demanded of money because it raises the opportunity cost of holding money.

2. T

3. T

4. T

5. F; an increase in the money supply decreases the interest rate, and increases investment and shifts aggregate demand to the right.

6. F; the Fed should increase the money supply.

7. T

8. T

9. F; the value of the multiplier is 5.

10. T

11. F; the aggregate-demand curve shifts to the right by less than $10 billion.

12. F; policymakers should increase government spending and decrease taxes.

13. T

14. F; in the short run, the interest rate is determined by money demand and money supply, while in the long run, it is determined by the loanable funds market.

15. T

Multiple-Choice Questions

1. b	5. a	9. c	13. c	17. b
2. c	6. d	10. b	14. b	18. c
3. a	7. a	11. a	15. c	19. d
4. d	8. c	12. d	16. a	20. b

Advanced Critical Thinking

1. The federal funds rate.

2. They decreased the money supply (or lowered its growth rate).

3. Because monetary policy acts on the economy with a lag. If the Fed waits until inflation has arrived, the effect of its policy will arrive too late. Thus, the Fed may wish to respond to its forecast of inflation.

4. Politicians must be responsive to the short-term needs of voters. Monetary policy must take a long-term view and make politically painful decisions when the economy is overheating (when output is above the long-run natural rate) because the proper policy response is to contract aggregate demand.

THE SHORT-RUN TRADEOFF BETWEEN INFLATION AND UNEMPLOYMENT

CHAPTER OVERVIEW

Context and Purpose

Chapter 22 is the final chapter in a three-chapter sequence on the economy's short-run fluctuations around its long-term trend. Chapter 20 introduced aggregate supply and aggregate demand. Chapter 21 developed how monetary and fiscal policy affect aggregate demand. Both Chapters 20 and 21 addressed the relationship between the price level and output. Chapter 22 will concentrate on a similar relationship between inflation and unemployment.

The purpose of Chapter 22 is to trace the history of economists' thinking about the relationship between inflation and unemployment. You will see why there is a temporary tradeoff between inflation and unemployment, and why there is no permanent tradeoff. This result is an extension of the results produced by the model of aggregate supply and aggregate demand where a change in the price level induced by a change in aggregate demand temporarily alters output but has no permanent impact on output.

22

GOALS

In this chapter you will

Learn why policymakers face a short-run tradeoff between inflation and unemployment

Consider why the inflation-unemployment tradeoff disappears in the long run

See how supply shocks can shift the inflation-unemployment tradeoff

Consider the short-run cost of reducing the rate of inflation

See how policymakers' credibility affects the cost of reducing inflation

OUTCOMES

After accomplishing these goals, you should be able to

Draw a graph of a short-run Phillips curve

Draw a graph of a long-run Phillips curve

Show the relationship between a shift in the short-run aggregate-supply curve and a shift in the short-run Phillips curve

Explain the sacrifice ratio

Explain why more than rational expectations are needed to reduce inflation costlessly

CHAPTER REVIEW

Introduction

Since both inflation and unemployment are undesirable, the sum of inflation and unemployment has been termed the *misery index*. Inflation and unemployment are independent in the long run because unemployment is determined by features of the labor market while inflation is determined by money growth. However, in the short run, inflation and unemployment are related because an increase in aggregate demand temporarily increases inflation and output while it lowers unemployment. In this chapter, we trace the history of our understanding of the relationship between unemployment and inflation.

The Phillips Curve

In 1958, a British economist named A.W. Phillips found a negative relationship between inflation and unemployment. That is, years of high inflation are associated with low unemployment. This negative relationship has been found for other countries, including the United States, and has been termed the **Phillips curve.** The Phillips curve appears to offer policymakers a menu of inflation and unemployment choices. To have lower unemployment, one need only choose a higher rate of inflation.

The model of aggregate supply and aggregate demand can explain the relationship described by the Phillips curve. The Phillips curve shows the combinations of inflation and unemployment that arise in the short run as shifts in the aggregate-demand curve move along a short-run aggregate-supply curve. For example, an increase in aggregate demand moves the economy along a short-run aggregate-supply curve to a higher price level, a higher level of output, and a lower level of unemployment. Since prices in the previous period are now fixed, a higher price level in the current period implies a higher rate of inflation, which is now associated with a lower rate of unemployment. This can be seen in Exhibit 1. An increase in aggregate demand, which moves the economy from point A to

EXHIBIT 1

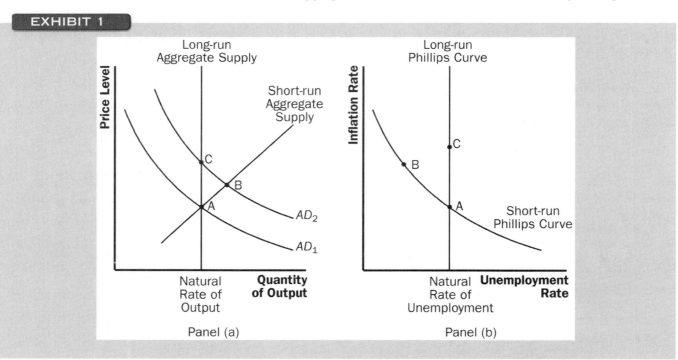

Panel (a)

Panel (b)

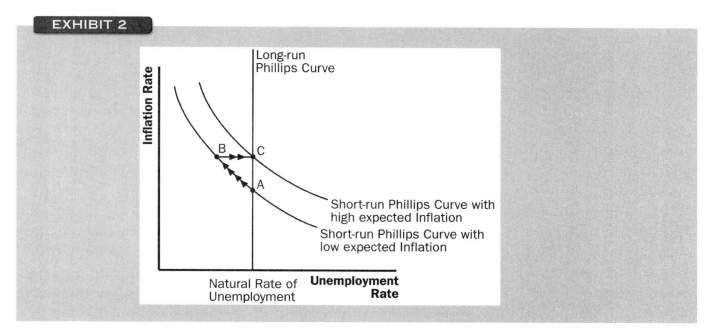

EXHIBIT 2

point B in panel (a), is associated with a movement along the short-run Phillips curve from point A to point B.

Shifts in the Phillips Curve: The Role of Expectations

In 1968, U.S. economists Friedman and Phelps argued that the Phillips curve is not a menu policymakers can exploit. This is because, in the long run, money is neutral and has no real effects. Money growth just causes proportional changes in prices and incomes, and should have no impact on unemployment. Therefore, the long-run Phillips curve should be vertical at the natural rate of unemployment— the rate of unemployment to which the economy naturally gravitates.

A vertical long-run Phillips curve corresponds to a vertical long-run aggregate-supply curve. As Exhibit 1 illustrates, in the long run, an increase in the money supply shifts aggregate demand to the right and moves the economy from point A to point C in panel (a). The corresponding Phillips curve is found in panel (b) where an increase in money growth increases inflation, but because money is neutral in the long run, prices and incomes move together and inflation fails to affect unemployment. Thus, the economy moves from point A to point C in panel (b) and traces out the long-run Phillips curve.

Friedman and Phelps used the phrase "natural" rate of unemployment, not because it is either desirable or constant, but because it is beyond the influence of monetary policy. Changes in labor market policies such as changes in minimum-wage laws and unemployment insurance that lower the natural rate of unemployment shift the long-run Phillips curve to the left and the long-run aggregate-supply curve to the right.

Even though Friedman and Phelps argued that the long-run Phillips curve is vertical, they argued that, in the short run, inflation could have a substantial impact on unemployment. Their reasoning is similar to that surrounding the short-run aggregate-supply curve in that they assume that, in the short run, *price expectations* are fixed. Just as with short-run aggregate supply, if price expectations are fixed in the short-run, an increase in inflation could temporarily increase output and lower unemployment below the natural rate. In Exhibit 2, this is a movement from point A to point B. However, *in the long-run, people adjust to the higher rate of inflation by raising their expectations of inflation and the short-run Phillips curve shifts upward.* The economy moves from point B to point C with higher inflation but no change in unemployment. Thus, policymakers face a short-run trade-off between inflation and unemployment, but if they attempt to exploit it, the relationship disappears and they arrive back on the vertical long-run Phillips curve.

The analysis of Friedman and Phelps can be summarized by the following equation:

$$\begin{array}{c} \text{Unemploy-} \\ \text{ment} \\ \text{Rate} \end{array} = \begin{array}{c} \text{Natural} \\ \text{Rate of} \\ \text{Unemployment} \end{array} + a \left(\begin{array}{c} \text{Actual} \\ \text{Inflation} \end{array} - \begin{array}{c} \text{Expected} \\ \text{Inflation} \end{array} \right)$$

This says that for any given expected inflation rate, if actual inflation exceeds expected inflation, unemployment will fall below the natural rate by an amount that depends on the parameter a. However, in the long run, people learn to expect the inflation that actually exists, and the unemployment rate will equal the natural rate.

Friedman and Phelps proposed the **natural rate hypothesis,** which states that unemployment eventually returns to its natural rate, regardless of inflation. While controversial, it proved to be true. During the 1960s, expansionary monetary and fiscal policies steadily increased the rate of inflation and unemployment fell. However, in the early 1970s, people raised their expectations of inflation and the unemployment rate returned to the natural rate—about five or six percent.

Shifts in the Phillips Curve: The Role of Supply Shocks

The short-run Phillips curve can also shift due to a supply shock. A **supply shock** is an event that directly alters firms' costs and prices, shifting the economy's aggregate-supply curve and Phillips curve. A supply shock occurred in 1974 when OPEC raised oil prices. This act raised the cost of production and shifted the U.S. short-run aggregate-supply curve to the left, causing prices to rise and output to fall, or *stagflation.* Since inflation has increased and unemployment has increased, this corresponds to a rightward (upward) shift in the short-run Phillips curve. Policymakers now face a less favorable tradeoff between inflation and unemployment. That is, policymakers must accept a higher inflation rate for each unemployment rate, or a higher unemployment rate for each inflation rate. Also, policymakers now have a difficult choice because if they reduce aggregate demand to fight inflation, they will further increase unemployment. If they increase aggregate demand to reduce unemployment, they further increase inflation.

If the supply shock raises expected inflation, the Phillips-curve shift is "permanent." If it does not raise expected inflation, the shift is temporary. In the United States during the 1970s, the Fed accommodated two adverse aggregate supply shocks by increasing aggregate demand. This caused expected inflation to rise and the rightward (upward) shift in the Phillips curve was "permanent." By 1980, inflation was 9 percent and unemployment was 7 percent.

The Cost of Reducing Inflation

In October 1979, Fed Chairman Paul Volcker chose to pursue a policy of *disinflation*—a reduction in the rate of inflation. A reduction in the money supply reduces aggregate demand, reduces production and increases unemployment. This is shown in Exhibit 3 as a movement from point A to point B. Over time, expected inflation falls and the short-run Phillips curve shifts downward and the economy moves from point B to point C.

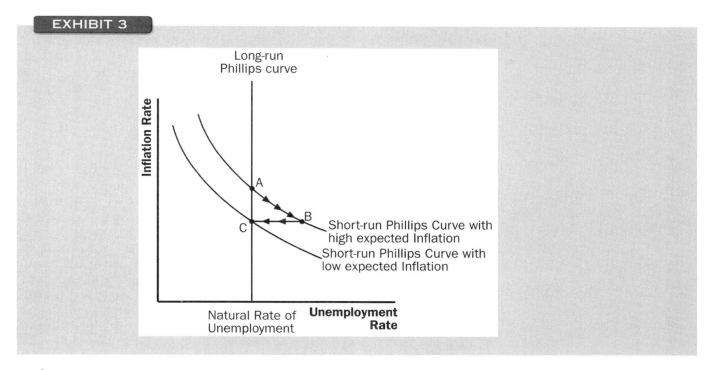

The cost of reducing inflation is a period of unemployment and lost output. The **sacrifice ratio** is the number of percentage points of annual output that is lost to reduce inflation one percentage point. The amount of output lost depends on the slope of the Phillips curve and how fast people lower their expectations of inflation.

Some economists estimated the sacrifice ratio to be about five, which is very large. Supporters of a theory called **rational expectations** suggested that the cost of disinflation could be much smaller and maybe zero. Rational expectations suggest that people optimally use all available information, including about government policies, when forecasting the future. Thus, an announced policy of disinflation *that is credible* could move the economy from point A to point C without traveling through point B. Volcker announced a disinflationary policy in late 1979 and reduced inflation from 10 percent to 4 percent by 1984, but at the cost of a substantial increase in unemployment. Note, however, that the increase in unemployment was less than that predicted by the estimated sacrifice ratio. The rational expectations theory may not be accurate, or people may not have believed the policy announcement.

Current monetary policy under Alan Greenspan has not repeated the mistakes of the 1960s when excessive aggregate demand pushed unemployment below the natural rate.

There are a variety of explanations regarding why the United States has experienced low unemployment and low inflation in the 1990s (i.e., explanations of why the Phillips curve has shifted left):

- Tight monetary policy has reduced inflation expectations

- Commodity prices declined (including oil prices)

- Labor markets include more older workers with lower unemployment rates

- Technological advances have increased productivity

Some economists argue that the Fed should publicly commit to an inflation target of about two percent. This policy would (1) institutionalize the successful anti-inflationary preferences of Volcker and Greenspan; (2) focus monetary policy on price stability—something it can influence; (3) reduce uncertainty about future Fed policy; and (4) prevent deflation.

HELPFUL HINTS

1. Short-run and long-run Phillips curves are almost a mirror image of short-run and long-run aggregate-supply curves. Look at the supply curves that appear in Exhibit 1. Notice the aggregate-supply curves in panel (a). Compare them to the Phillips curves in panel (b). They appear to be mirror images of each other. The long-run aggregate-supply curve is vertical because, in the long run, an increase in the price level is met by a proportionate increase in all prices and incomes so there is no incentive to alter production. Since an increase in prices has no effect on output in the long run, it has no effect on unemployment, and the long-run Phillips curve is vertical in panel (b). In the short run with price expectations fixed, an increase in the price level provides an incentive for firms to increase production, causing the short-run aggregate-supply curve to be positively sloped in panel (a). When output rises, unemployment tends to fall, so the short-run Phillips curve is negatively sloped in panel (b). In summary, since both graphs employ some measure of prices on the vertical axis, and since each graph uses real measures of economic activity that are negatively correlated on their respective horizontal axes (an increase in output is associated with a decrease in unemployment) then aggregate-supply curves and Phillips curves should "mirror" each other.

2. To understand the short-run Phillips curve, review short-run aggregate supply. To gain confidence deriving and shifting short-run Phillips curves, review the sources to the positive slope of the short-run aggregate-supply curve in Chapter 20.
   There you will be reminded that there are a number of reasons why a short-run aggregate supply-curve slopes positively—misperceptions about relative price, sticky wages, and sticky prices. Since short-run aggregate-supply curves and Phillips curves are mirror images of each other, the very same reasons that produce a positive slope in aggregate supply produce a negative slope in the Phillips curve. Also, recall that all three theories of the short-run aggregate-supply curve are based on the assumption of fixed price expectations. When price expectations rise, the short-run aggregate-supply curve shifts left. Correspondingly, since the short-run aggregate-supply curve and the Phillips curve are mirror images, a rise in price expectations shift the Phillips curve to the right.

3. The Phillips curve establishes a relationship between inflation and unemployment, but it does not establish causation. Reading the Phillips curve from the unemployment axis to the inflation axis suggests that when unemployment is unusually low, the labor market is tight and wages and prices start to rise more quickly.

4. Estimates of the natural rate of unemployment vary widely, causing policymakers to disagree on the appropriate monetary and fiscal policies. When

looking at a Phillips curve graph or the model of aggregate supply and aggregate demand, it appears as if policymakers should always know whether to expand or contract aggregate demand or whether to leave aggregate demand alone. This is because we can see whether the economy is operating above or below the long-run natural rate that we have chosen on the graph. In reality, however, the natural rate is very difficult to measure and policymakers are uncertain whether the economy is actually operating above or below the natural rate. For example, if the economy is currently operating at 6 percent unemployment, the economy is operating below capacity if the natural rate of unemployment is 5 percent, at capacity if the natural rate is 6 percent, and above capacity of the natural rate is 7 percent. Each situation might suggest a different stabilization policy, even though the actual rate of unemployment is unchanged at 6 percent.

TERMS AND DEFINITIONS

Choose a definition for each key term.

Key terms:

_____ Misery index

_____ Phillips curve

_____ Natural rate of unemployment

_____ Natural rate hypothesis

_____ Disinflation

_____ Supply shock

_____ Sacrifice ratio

_____ Rational expectations

Definitions:

1. A reduction in the rate of inflation

2. The normal rate of unemployment toward which the economy gravitates

3. The theory that suggests that people optimally use all available information, including about government policies, when forecasting the future

4. The sum of inflation and unemployment

5. The theory that unemployment returns to its natural rate, regardless of inflation

6. The short-run tradeoff between inflation and unemployment

7. The number of percentage points of annual output that is lost in order to reduce inflation one percentage point

8. An event that directly alters firms' costs and prices, shifting the economy's aggregate-supply curve and, thus, the Phillips curve

PROBLEMS AND SHORT-ANSWER QUESTIONS

Practice Problems

1. Describe the initial effect of the following events on the short-run and long-run Phillips curve. That is, describe the movements along a given curve or the direction of the shift in the curve.

   a. An increase in expected inflation

   _____

   _____

   b. An increase in the price of imported oil

   _____

   _____

   c. An increase in the money supply

   _____

   _____

   d. A decrease in government spending

   _____

   _____

   e. A decrease in the minimum wage, which lowers the natural rate

   _____

   _____

2. Use the Phillips curves in Exhibit 4 to answer the following questions.

   a. At what point is the economy located if people expect 10 percent inflation and inflation actually is 10 percent?

   _____

   b. Referring to (a) above, is unemployment above, below, or equal to the natural rate?

   _____

   c. At what point is the economy located if people expect 10 percent inflation and the actual rate of inflation is 15 percent?

   _____

EXHIBIT 4

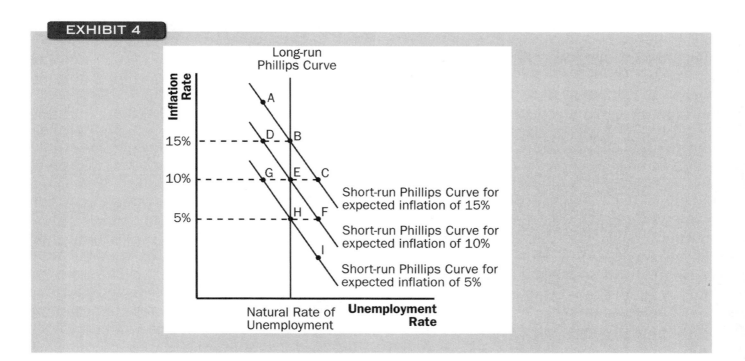

d. Suppose the economy is operating at point D. Over time, in which direction will people revise their expectations of inflation—up or down?

_____

e. Suppose the economy is operating at point D. As people revise their expectations of inflation, in which direction will the short-run Phillips curve shift—right or left?

_____

f. Suppose the economy is operating at point E. In the short run, a sudden decrease in aggregate demand will move the economy toward which point?

_____

g. Suppose the economy is operating at point E. In the long run, a decrease in government spending will tend to move the economy toward which point?

_____

h. Suppose people expect 5 percent inflation. If inflation actually ends up being 10 percent, in which direction will unemployment move—above or below the natural rate?

_____

3. Use a Phillips curve graph to answer the following questions. Assume the economy is initially in long-run equilibrium.
   a. What happens to unemployment and inflation in the short run if the Fed increases the growth rate of the money supply?

   _____

   _____

   _____

   b. What happens to unemployment and inflation in the long run if the Fed increases the growth rate of the money supply?

   _____

   _____

   c. Can printing money keep unemployment below the natural rate? Explain.

   _____

   _____

   _____

   d. What is the end result of a central bank repeatedly attempting to hold unemployment below the natural rate with expansionary monetary policy? Explain.

   _____

   _____

   _____

4. Suppose the economy is operating at the natural rate of unemployment with a high rate of inflation (point A in Exhibit 5). Suppose the Federal Reserve announces a sudden monetary contraction to reduce inflation. Shown below are two possible paths the economy might take to adjust to the new lower rate of money growth. Choose the path that best depicts what might happen in each of the following cases and explain your reasoning.
   a. The Fed's announcement is not believed.

   _____

   _____

EXHIBIT 5

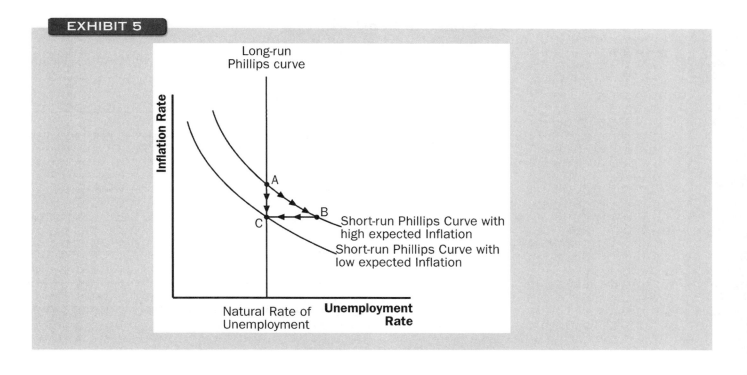

b. The Fed's announcement is believed and expectations of inflation are adjusted quickly.

_____

_____

c. The Fed's announcement is believed but all workers have long-term wage contracts that cannot be renegotiated.

_____

_____

_____

_____

d. Which of the above cases (a, b, or c) best describes what would happen if, in the past, the Fed had repeatedly announced that inflation is its number one priority, but it failed to actually engage in the threatened monetary contraction? Why?

_____

_____

_____

Short-Answer Questions

1. If unemployment is 6 percent and inflation is 5 percent, what is the value of the so-called misery index?

   _____

2. Use the model of aggregate demand and aggregate supply to describe why the short-run Phillips curve is negatively sloped.

   _____

   _____

   _____

   _____

3. Use the model of aggregate demand and aggregate supply to describe why the long-run Phillips curve is vertical.

   _____

   _____

   _____

   _____

4. Is the short-run Phillips curve actually a menu of inflation and unemployment combinations permanently available to the policymaker? Why or why not?

   _____

   _____

   _____

   _____

   _____

5. What is the natural rate hypothesis?

   _____

   _____

6. If actual inflation exceeds expected inflation, is the unemployment rate above or below the natural rate? Why?

_____

_____

_____

7. Which way does the short-run Phillips curve shift when there is an adverse aggregate supply shock such as an increase in the price of imported oil? Why?

_____

_____

_____

8. Referring to question 7 above, are the tradeoffs between unemployment and inflation that the economy now faces more favorable or less favorable than before the adverse supply shock? Explain.

_____

_____

_____

_____

9. Referring to question 8 above, if the Fed accommodates the adverse supply shock, what have they revealed about the weights they attach to the goals of low inflation and low unemployment?

_____

_____

10. If the sacrifice ratio is five, how much will output be reduced in order for inflation to be reduced four percentage points? If people have rational expectations, is the sacrifice ratio likely to be larger or smaller than five? Why?

_____

_____

_____

SELF-TEST

True/False Questions

_____ 1. The Phillips curve illustrates the positive relationship between inflation and unemployment.

_____ 2. If inflation is 4 percent and unemployment is 6 percent, the misery index is 2 percent.

_____ 3. In the short run, an increase in aggregate demand increases prices and output, and decreases unemployment.

_____ 4. When unemployment is below the natural rate, the labor market is unusually tight putting pressure on wages and prices to rise.

_____ 5. An increase in price expectations shifts the Phillips curve upward and makes the inflation unemployment tradeoff less favorable.

_____ 6. An increase in the money supply increases inflation and permanently decreases unemployment.

_____ 7. In the long run, the unemployment rate is independent of inflation and the Phillips curve is vertical at the natural rate of unemployment.

_____ 8. When actual inflation exceeds expected inflation, unemployment exceeds the natural rate.

_____ 9. The natural rate hypothesis suggests that, in the long run, unemployment returns to its natural rate, regardless of inflation.

_____10. An adverse supply shock, such as an increase in the price of imported oil, shifts the Phillips curve upward and makes the inflation unemployment tradeoff less favorable.

_____11. A decrease in unemployment benefits reduces the natural rate of unemployment and shifts the long-run Phillips curve to the right.

_____12. An increase in aggregate demand temporarily reduces unemployment, but after people raise their expectations of inflation, unemployment returns to the natural rate.

_____13. A sudden monetary contraction moves the economy up a short-run Phillips curve, reducing unemployment and increasing inflation.

_____14. If people have rational expectations, an announced monetary contraction by the Fed that is credible could reduce inflation with little or no increase in unemployment.

_____15. If the sacrifice ratio is four, a reduction of inflation from 9 percent to 5 percent requires a reduction in output of 8 percent.

Multiple-Choice Questions

1. The misery index, which some commentators suggest measures the health of the economy, is
   a. the sum of the growth rate of output and the inflation rate.
   b. the sum of the unemployment rate and the inflation rate.
   c. the sum of the Dow Jones Industrial Average and the federal funds rate.
   d. the sum of the natural rate of unemployment and the actual rate of unemployment.

2. The original Phillips curve illustrates
   a. the tradeoff between inflation and unemployment.
   b. the positive relationship between inflation and unemployment.
   c. the tradeoff between output and unemployment.
   d. the positive relationship between output and unemployment.

3. The Phillips curve is an extension of the model of aggregate supply and aggregate demand because, in the short run, an increase in aggregate demand increases prices and
   a. decreases growth.
   b. decreases inflation.
   c. increases unemployment.
   d. decreases unemployment.

4. Along a short-run Phillips curve,
   a. a higher rate of growth in output is associated with a lower unemployment rate.
   b. a higher rate of growth in output is associated with a higher unemployment rate.
   c. a higher rate of inflation is associated with a lower unemployment rate.
   d. a higher rate of inflation is associated with a higher unemployment rate.

5. If, in the long run, people adjust their price expectations so that all prices and incomes move proportionately to an increase in the price level, then the long-run Phillips curve
   a. is positively sloped.
   b. is negatively sloped.
   c. is vertical.
   d. has a slope that is determined by how fast people adjust their price expectations.

6. According to the Phillips curve, in the short run, if policymakers choose an expansionary policy to lower the rate of unemployment,
   a. the economy will experience a decrease in inflation.
   b. the economy will experience an increase in inflation.
   c. inflation will be unaffected if price expectations are unchanging.
   d. none of the above

7. An increase in expected inflation
   a. shifts the short-run Phillips curve upward and the unemployment inflation tradeoff is less favorable.
   b. shifts the short-run Phillips curve downward and the unemployment inflation tradeoff is more favorable.
   c. shifts the short-run Phillips curve upward and the unemployment inflation tradeoff is more favorable.
   d. shifts the short-run Phillips curve downward and the unemployment inflation tradeoff is less favorable.

8. Which of the following would shift the long-run Phillips curve to the right?
   a. an increase in the price of foreign oil
   b. an increase in expected inflation
   c. an increase in aggregate demand
   d. an increase in the minimum wage

9. When actual inflation exceeds expected inflation,
   a. unemployment is greater than the natural rate of unemployment.
   b. unemployment is less than the natural rate of unemployment.
   c. unemployment is equal to the natural rate of unemployment.
   d. people will reduce their expectations of inflation in the future.

10. A decrease the price of foreign oil
    a. shifts the short-run Phillips curve upward, and the unemployment inflation tradeoff is more favorable.
    b. shifts the short-run Phillips curve upward, and the unemployment inflation tradeoff is less favorable.
    c. shifts the short-run Phillips curve downward, and the unemployment inflation tradeoff is more favorable.
    d. shifts the short-run Phillips curve downward, and the unemployment inflation tradeoff is less favorable.

11. The natural rate hypothesis argues that
    a. unemployment is always above the natural rate.
    b. unemployment is always below the natural rate.
    c. unemployment is always equal to the natural rate.
    d. in the long run, the unemployment rate returns to the natural rate, regardless of inflation.

Use Exhibit 6 for questions 12 through 17

12. If people in the economy expect inflation to be 3 percent and inflation is 3 percent, the economy is operating at point
    a. A.
    b. B.
    c. C.
    d. D.
    e. E.
    f. F.
    g. G.
    h. H.
    i. I.

13. If people in the economy expect inflation to be 6 percent but inflation turns out to be 3 percent, the economy is operating at point
   a. A.
   b. B.
   c. C.
   d. D.
   e. E.
   f. F.
   g. G.
   h. H.
   i. I.

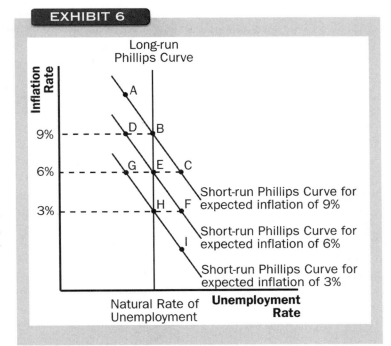

EXHIBIT 6

Long-run Phillips Curve

Inflation Rate

9%

6%

3%

A

D B

G E C

H F Short-run Phillips Curve for expected inflation of 9%

I Short-run Phillips Curve for expected inflation of 6%

Short-run Phillips Curve for expected inflation of 3%

Natural Rate of Unemployment

Unemployment Rate

14. Suppose the economy is in long-run equilibrium at point E. A sudden increase in government spending should move the economy in the direction of point
   a. A.
   b. B.
   c. C.
   d. D.
   e. E.
   f. F.
   g. G.
   h. H.
   i. I.

15. Suppose the economy is operating at point D. As people revise their price expectations,
   a. the short-run Phillips curve will shift in the direction of the short-run Phillips curve associated with an expectation of 3 percent inflation.
   b. the short-run Phillips curve will shift in the direction of the short-run Phillips curve associated with an expectation of 6 percent inflation.
   c. the short-run Phillips curve will shift in the direction of the short-run Phillips curve associated with an expectation of 9 percent inflation.
   d. the long-run Phillips curve will shift to the left.

16. Suppose the economy is operating in long-run equilibrium at point E. An unexpected monetary contraction will move the economy in the direction of point
   a. A.
   b. B.
   c. C.
   d. D.
   e. E.
   f. F.
   g. G.
   h. H.
   i. I.

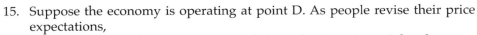

17. Suppose the economy is operating in long-run equilibrium at point E. *In the long run,* a monetary contraction will move the economy in the direction of point
   a. A.
   b. B.
   c. C.
   d. D.
   e. E.
   f. F.
   g. G.
   h. H.
   i. I.

18. If people have rational expectations, a monetary policy contraction that is announced and is credible could
   a. reduce inflation but it would increase unemployment by an unusually large amount.
   b. reduce inflation with little or no increase in unemployment.
   c. increase inflation but it would decrease unemployment by an unusually large amount.
   d. increase inflation with little or no decrease in unemployment.

19. If the sacrifice ratio is five, a reduction in inflation from 7 percent to 3 percent would require
   a. a reduction in output of 5 percent.
   b. a reduction in output of 15 percent.
   c. a reduction in output of 20 percent.
   d. a reduction in output of 35 percent.

20. If the Fed were to continuously use expansionary monetary policy in an attempt to hold unemployment below the natural rate, the long-run result would be
   a. an increase in the level of output.
   b. a decrease in the unemployment rate.
   c. an increase in the rate of inflation.
   d. all of the above.

ADVANCED CRITICAL THINKING

A worldwide drought has reduced food production. Inflation has increased, unemployment has risen above the natural rate. Americans are frustrated with their government. Your roommate says, "This economic mess has got to be somebody's fault—probably the president or Congress. A year ago, both inflation and unemployment were lower. We need to vote in some policymakers that know how to get rid of this inflation and unemployment."

1. Whose fault is the stagflation that is present in the economy?

_____

_____

2. Are the current inflation and unemployment choices facing the economy better or worse than before the supply shock? What has happened to the short-run Phillips curve?

_____

_____

3. If policymakers *increase* aggregate demand in response to the supply shock, in what direction will the economy move along the new short-run Phillips curve? What will happen to inflation and unemployment?

_____

_____

_____

4. If policymakers *decrease* aggregate demand in response to the supply shock, in what direction will the economy move along the new short-run Phillips curve? What will happen to inflation and unemployment?

_____

_____

_____

5. Is there a policy that can immediately reduce both inflation and unemployment? Explain.

_____

_____

SOLUTIONS

Terms and Definitions

_4_ Misery index

_6_ Phillips curve

_2_ Natural rate of unemployment

_5_ Natural rate hypothesis

_1_ Disinflation

_8_ Supply shock

_7_ Sacrifice ratio

_3_ Rational expectations

Practice Problems

1. a. Shifts short-run Phillips curve to the right (upward).
   b. Shifts short-run Phillips curve to the right (upward).
   c. Move up the short-run Phillips curve.
   d. Move down the short-run Phillips curve.
   e. Long-run and short-run Phillips curves shift left (downward).

2. a. E.
   b. Equal to the natural rate.
   c. D.
   d. Up.
   e. Right.
   f. F.
   g. H.
   h. Below the natural rate.

3. a. Inflation increases, unemployment decreases.
   b. Inflation increases, unemployment stays at the natural rate.
   c. No. Unemployment temporarily decreases, but as people grow to expect the higher inflation, unemployment returns to the natural rate.
   d. Continued attempts to move unemployment below the natural rate simply causes inflation.

4. a. Economy moves from A to B because people fail to reduce their price expectations and wage demands, so unemployment rises as inflation falls.
   b. Economy moves from A to C because people reduce their prices and wages proportionately.
   c. Economy moves from A to B because people are unable to actually reduce some of their wages and prices, so unemployment rises as inflation falls.
   d. Case (a), because people are rational to distrust a policymaker that has previously been untruthful.

Short-Answer Questions

1. 11 percent.

2. An increase in aggregate demand increases prices and output along the short-run aggregate-supply curve, which reduces unemployment. Prices have increased and unemployment has decreased.

3. An increase in aggregate demand increases prices, but output remains at the natural rate due to a vertical long-run aggregate-supply curve. Prices have increased but unemployment remains at the natural rate.

4. No. When inflation increases above expected inflation, unemployment temporarily decreases. However, after people revise their price expectations upward, the Phillips curve shifts upward (to the right).

5. Unemployment returns to the natural rate in the long run, regardless of inflation.

6. Below, because if prices are higher than expected additional output is produced and additional people are employed, reducing unemployment.

7. Aggregate supply shifts left showing lower production at each price. Thus, the Phillips curve shifts right (upward) showing more unemployment at each rate of inflation.

8. Less favorable. Now, at each level of unemployment, inflation is higher, or at each rate of inflation, unemployment is higher.

9. The Fed is more concerned with low unemployment.

10. 20 percent. Smaller because they will reduce their price expectations more quickly, shifting the Phillips curve to the left.

True/False Questions

1. F; the Phillips curve illustrates the negative relationship between inflation and unemployment.

2. F; the misery index is 10 percent.

3. T

4. T

5. T

6. F; an increase in the money supply may temporarily decrease unemployment.

7. T

8. F; when actual inflation exceeds expected inflation, unemployment is below the natural rate.

9. T

10. T

11. F; it shifts the long-run Phillips curve to the left.

12. T

13. F; a sudden monetary contraction moves the economy down a short-run Phillips curve, increasing unemployment and reducing inflation.

14. T

15. F; output must be reduced by $4 \times 4\% = 16\%$.

Multiple-Choice Questions

1. b	5. c	9. b	13. f	17. h
2. a	6. b	10. c	14. d	18. b
3. d	7. a	11. d	15. c	19. c
4. c	8. d	12. h	16. f	20. c

Advanced Critical Thinking

1. No one's. It was an act of nature.

2. Worse because the short-run Phillips curve has shifted upward.

3. The economy moves upward along the new short-run Phillips curve. Unemployment will be reduced but inflation will be increased.

4. The economy moves downward along the new short-run Phillips curve. Inflation will be reduced but unemployment will be increased.

5. No, the economy faces tradeoffs in the short run. A policy that reduces inflation increases unemployment. A policy that reduces unemployment increases inflation.

GOALS

⌈In this chapter you will

Consider whether policymakers should try to stabilize the economy

Consider whether monetary policy should be made by rule rather than by discretion

Consider whether the central bank should aim for zero inflation

Consider whether the government should balance its budget

Consider whether the tax laws should be reformed to encourage saving

FIVE DEBATES OVER MACROECONOMIC POLICY

CHAPTER OVERVIEW

Context and Purpose

Chapter 23 is the final chapter in the text. It addresses five unresolved issues in macroeconomics, each of which is central to current political debates. The chapter can be studied all at once, or portions of the chapter can be studied in conjunction with prior chapters that deal with the related material.

The purpose of Chapter 23 is to provide both sides of five leading debates over macroeconomic policy. It employs information and tools that you have accumulated in your study of this text. This chapter may help you take a position on the issues addressed or, at least, it may help you understand the reasoning of others who have taken a position.

OUTCOMES

⌈After accomplishing these goals, you should be able to

Give an example of a macroeconomic policy response that "leans against the wind"

Explain what is meant by the "time inconsistency of policy"

List the costs of inflation

Explain the benefits of reducing the budget deficit

Explain why a consumption tax encourages saving but enhances economic inequality

CHAPTER REVIEW

Introduction

This chapter presents both sides of five leading debates over macroeconomic policy. These issues are central to current political debates.

Should Monetary and Fiscal Policymakers Try to Stabilize the Economy?

Pro: Policymakers should try to stabilize the economy. Pessimism on the part of households and firms reduces aggregate demand and causes a recession. The resulting reduction in output and the increase in unemployment is a waste of resources. This waste of resources is unnecessary because the government has the power to "lean against the wind" and stabilize aggregate demand by, in this case, increasing government spending, reducing taxes, and increasing the money supply. If aggregate demand is excessive, these policies can be reversed.

Con: Policymakers should not try to stabilize the economy. Monetary and fiscal policy affect the economy with a substantial lag. Monetary policy affects interest rates, which may take six months or more to affect residential and business investment spending. A change in fiscal policy involves a long political process. Because forecasting is difficult and because many shocks are unpredictable, stabilization policy must be based on educated guesses about future economic conditions. Mistakes can make activist policy destabilizing. The first rule of policy should be to "do no harm" so policymakers should refrain from intervening often in the economy.

Should Monetary Policy Be Made by Rule Rather than by Discretion?

Recall, every six weeks the Federal Open Market Committee sets monetary policy by choosing an interest rate target and adjusting the money supply to reach that target. At present, the FOMC sets monetary policy with almost complete discretion.

Pro: Monetary policy should be made by rule. There are two problems with discretionary policy.

- First, discretionary policy does not limit incompetence and abuse of power. A central bank abuses its power when it manipulates monetary policy to favor a particular political candidate. It can increase the money supply prior to an election to benefit the incumbent and the resulting inflation doesn't show up until after the election. This creates what is known as the *political business cycle*.

- Second, discretionary policy might lead to more inflation than is desirable due to the *time inconsistency of policy*. This occurs because policymakers are tempted to announce a low inflation target but, once people have formed their inflation expectations, policymakers can raise inflation to lower unemployment by exploiting the short-run tradeoff between inflation and unemployment. As a result, people expect more inflation than policymakers say they are targeting, which shifts the Phillips curve upward to a less favorable position.

These problems can be avoided by committing the central bank to a policy rule. Congress could require the Fed to increase the money supply by a certain percent each year, say 3 percent, which is just enough to accommodate growth in real output. Alternatively, Congress could require a more active rule whereby the Fed would respond with a specific increase in the money supply if unemployment rose a certain percent above the natural rate. Some argue that the policy rule should be implemented by a computer.

Con: Monetary policy should not be made by rule.   Discretionary monetary policy is needed because monetary policy must be flexible enough to respond to unforeseen events such as a significant reduction in aggregate demand or a negative supply shock. Further, political business cycles may not exist and time inconsistency problems may be avoided if a central bank's announcements are credible. Finally, if monetary policy were to be guided by a rule, it is unclear what type of rule Congress should impose.

Should the Central Bank Aim for Zero Inflation?

Pro: The central bank should aim for zero inflation.   Inflation imposes the following costs on society:

- shoeleather costs associated with reduced money holdings,

- menu costs associated with frequent adjustment of prices,

- increased variability of relative prices,

- unintended changes in tax liabilities due to non-indexation of the tax code,

- confusion and inconvenience resulting from a changing unit of account,

- arbitrary redistributions of wealth associated with dollar-denominated debts.

The costs associated with reducing inflation to zero are temporary while the benefits of zero inflation are permanent. The costs can be reduced further if an announced policy of zero inflation is credible. The policy would be more credible if Congress made price stability the Fed's primary goal. Finally, zero inflation is the only non-arbitrary target for inflation. All other target levels can be incrementally revised upward.

Con: The central bank should not aim for zero inflation.   There are a number of reasons why the central bank should not aim for zero inflation:

- The benefits of zero inflation are small and uncertain, while the costs of achieving it are large. Recall, estimates of the sacrifice ratio are 5 percent of one year's output for a 1 percent reduction in inflation.

- The unemployment and social costs associated with the reduction in inflation are borne by the unskilled and inexperienced—those least able to afford it.

- People tend to dislike inflation because they mistakenly think it erodes their living standards but incomes tend to rise with inflation.

- Many of the costs of inflation can be eliminated without reducing inflation by indexing the tax system and issuing inflation-indexed bonds.

- Reducing inflation costlessly is unlikely to be possible.

- Disinflation leaves permanent scars on the economy because the capital stock is smaller and the unemployed workers have diminished skills.

Should the Government Balance Its Budget?

Pro: The government should balance its budget. Government debt places a burden on future generation of taxpayers who must choose to pay higher taxes, cut government spending, or both. Current taxpayers pass the bill for current spending to future taxpayers. Moreover, the macroeconomic effect of a deficit is to reduce national saving by making public saving negative. This increases interest rates, reduces capital investment, reduces productivity and real wages and, thus, reduces future output and income. As a result, deficits raise future taxes and lower future incomes. While deficits are justified during wars and recessions, the increase in the deficit from 1980 through 1995 occurred during peace and prosperity. The most recent deficits may be due to the recession of 2001 and the war on terrorism.

Con: The government should not balance its budget. The problem of government debt is exaggerated. The $13,000 of national debt per person is small compared to expected lifetime earnings of $1,000,000. Also, since some of government spending is on education, reducing the budget deficit by reducing spending on education may not improve the welfare of the next generation. Other government policies redistribute income across generations such as social security benefits. If people wish to reverse the intergenerational redistribution of income caused by budget deficits, they need only save more during their lifetime (due to their lower taxes) and leave bequests to their children so they can pay the higher taxes. Finally, government debt can continue to grow forever, yet not grow as a percent of GDP as long as the debt fails to grow more quickly than the nation's nominal income. In the United States, that would be a rate of about 5 percent, which equates to about a $175 billion sustainable deficit.

Should the Tax Laws Be Reformed to Encourage Saving?

Pro: The tax laws should be reformed to encourage saving. A nation's standard of living depends on its productive capability which, in turn, depends on how much it saves and invests. Since people respond to incentives, the government could encourage saving (or stop discouraging saving) by:

- Reducing taxes on the return to saving (interest income).

- Removing the double taxation of capital income from stocks. At present, corporations pay a corporate income tax. Then profits paid to stockholders in the form of dividends are subject to individual income tax.

- Reducing inheritance taxes so people will save and create bequests to the next generation.

- Reducing means tested government benefits such as welfare and Medicaid. These benefits are currently reduced for those that have been prudent enough to save which creates a disincentive to save.

- Increasing the availability of tax-advantaged savings accounts such as the Individual Retirement Account (IRA). In these accounts, income that is saved is not taxed until it is withdrawn at retirement.

- Replacing the income tax with a consumption tax. Income that is saved would not be taxed, making all saving equivalent to an IRA.

Con: The tax laws should not be reformed to encourage saving. One goal of taxation is to distribute the tax burden fairly. All of the proposals above will increase the incentive to save by reducing taxes on saving. Since high-income people save more than low-income people, this will increase the tax burden on the poor. Also, saving may not be sensitive to changes in the return to saving, so reducing taxes on saving will just enrich the wealthy. This is because a higher return to saving has both a *substitution effect* and an *income effect*. An increase in the return to saving will increase saving as people substitute saving for current consumption. However, the income effect suggests that an increase in the return to saving lowers the amount of saving needed to achieve any targeted level of future consumption.

A reduction in the deficit increases public saving and, thus, national saving. This could be accomplished by raising taxes on the wealthy. Indeed, reductions in taxes on saving might backfire by increasing the deficit and reducing national saving.

HELPFUL HINTS

1. A policy that destabilizes the economy moves the economy away from the natural rate of output. Stabilization policy is the use of monetary and fiscal policy to help move the economy toward the natural rate of output. However, if policy lags are long and unpredictable, the economy may have adjusted back to the natural rate (from an aggregate demand or aggregate supply shock) before the impact of the stabilization policy is felt. In this case, the stabilization policy would then move the economy away from the long-run natural rate and we would consider the policy to be destabilizing.

2. A political business cycle tends to involve both a monetary expansion prior to an election and a monetary contraction after an election. Political business cycles are discussed in the text with regard to the policymaker's behavior prior to elections.

    That is, prior to an election, a monetary expansion could increase output and decrease unemployment, enhancing the probability of the incumbent's re-election. Since this will tend to cause inflation after the election, however, this type of abuse of power usually involves a monetary contraction after the election to reduce inflationary pressures. Thus, the economy would tend to fluctuate between good economic performance prior to an election and poor economic performance after an election.

3. Zero money growth does not cause zero inflation if real output is growing. Recall from Chapter 17, the quantity equation states that $M \times V = P \times Y$, which says that money times velocity equals the price level times real output. If velocity is fixed, and if real output grows at about 3 percent per year, then the money supply would have to grow at 3 percent for prices to remain constant. Therefore, a monetary policy rule requiring the Fed to increase the money supply at 3 percent should generate zero inflation. If output is growing at 3 percent, money growth of 0 percent would actually create deflation.

TERMS AND DEFINITIONS

Choose a definition for each key term.

Key terms:

_____ "Leaning against the wind"

_____ Destabilizing policy

_____ Discretionary policy

_____ Political business cycle

_____ Time inconsistency of policy

Definitions:

1. Economic fluctuations caused by policymakers allying themselves with elected politicians

2. Policy which moves output away from the long-run natural rate

3. Engaging in a policy that stabilizes aggregate demand

4. The discrepancy between policy announcements and policy actions

5. A policy chosen by policymakers who have few guidelines

PROBLEMS AND SHORT-ANSWER QUESTIONS

Practice Problems

1. Suppose a wave of pessimism engulfs consumers and firms, causing them to reduce their expenditures.
   a. Demonstrate this event in Exhibit 1 using the model of aggregate demand and aggregate supply and assuming that the economy was originally in long-run equilibrium.
   b. What is the appropriate activist policy response for monetary and fiscal policy? In which direction would the activist policy shift aggregate demand?

   _____

   _____

   _____

EXHIBIT 1

Price Level

Quantity of
Real Ouput

c. Suppose the economy can adjust on its own in two years from the recession described in part (a). Suppose policymakers choose to use fiscal policy to stabilize the economy but the political battle over taxes and spending takes more than two years. Demonstrate these events in Exhibit 2 using the model of aggregate demand and aggregate supply.

d. Describe the sequence of events shown in the graph you created in part (c) above.

_____

_____

_____

_____

EXHIBIT 2

Price Level

Quantity of
Real Output

e. Did the activist fiscal policy stabilize or destabilize the economy? Explain.

_____

_____

_____

2. Suppose the Fed repeatedly announces that it desires price stability and that it is aiming for 0 inflation. However, it consistently generates 3 percent inflation.

a. Will this type of behavior on the part of the Fed reduce unemployment below the natural rate in the long run? Why?

_____

_____

_____

_____

b. Once people have formed expectations of 3 percent inflation, what would happen in the short-run if the Fed actually did target zero inflation?

_____

_____

_____

c. Would it help if Congress passed a law requiring the Fed to target zero inflation?

_____

_____

_____

Short-Answer Questions

1. Why would an improvement in our ability to forecast shocks to the macro-economy improve our use of activist stabilization policy?

_____

_____

_____

2. What three reasons are given in support of a monetary policy rule?

_____

_____

_____

3. Why are the costs of inflation permanent but the costs of reducing inflation temporary?

_____

_____

_____

_____

4. What could the government do to reduce the cost of continuous inflation?

_____

_____

_____

5. In what two ways does a government budget deficit harm future generations?

    _____

    _____

    _____

    _____

6. Does a balanced government budget guarantee the elimination of all redistributions of wealth across generations? Explain.

    _____

    _____

    _____

7. For an increase in the after-tax return to saving to cause an increase in saving, which effect must outweigh the other—the substitution effect or the income effect? Why?

    _____

    _____

    _____

    _____

    _____

    _____

8. Why will reforming our tax laws to encourage saving tend to increase the tax burden on the poor?

    _____

    _____

    _____

    _____

SELF-TEST

True/False Questions

_____ 1. Monetary policy affects the economy with a lag but fiscal policy has no lag.

_____ 2. Discretionary monetary policy suffers from time inconsistency because policymakers have an incentive to engage in a policy that differs from their policy announcements.

_____ 3. The political business cycle refers to a situation where corporate executives also hold political office.

_____ 4. Opponents of a monetary policy rule argue that a rule would make it more difficult for the Fed to respond to an unusual crisis.

_____ 5. Supporters of a zero inflation target for monetary policy argue that the cost of reducing inflation is temporary while the benefits of reducing inflation are permanent.

_____ 6. Those opposed to a zero inflation target for monetary policy argue that many of the costs of inflation can be eliminated by inflation-indexed taxes and bonds.

_____ 7. Government budget deficits tend to redistribute wealth from the current generation to future generations.

_____ 8. The United States has only incurred government budget deficits during wars and recessions.

_____ 9. Replacing the income tax with a consumption tax may increase saving, but it will tend to benefit the rich more than the poor.

_____10. A reduction in taxes on interest income will increase saving if the substitution effect from the increase in after-tax interest outweighs the income effect.

Multiple-Choice Questions

1. Suppose that the economy is suffering from pessimism on the part of consumers and firms. Which of the following is an activist stabilization policy that "leans against the wind?"
   a. Policymakers should decrease the money supply.
   b. Policymakers should increase taxes.
   c. Policymakers should decrease government spending.
   d. Policymakers should decrease interest rates.
   e. none of the above

2. Economists who argue that policymakers should *not* try to stabilize the economy make all of the following arguments *except:*
   a. Since stabilization policy affects the economy with a lag, well-intended policy could be destabilizing.
   b. Since forecasting shocks to the economy is difficult, well-intended policy could be destabilizing.
   c. Stabilization policy has no effect on the economy in the short run or the long run.
   d. The first rule of policymaking should be "do no harm."

3. Fluctuations in the economy caused by policymaker's manipulation of the economy for the purpose of affecting electoral outcomes is known as the
   a. political business cycle.
   b. time inconsistency of policy.
   c. discretionary effect.
   d. substitution effect.
   e. income effect.

4. The discrepancy between policy announcements and policy actions is known as the
   a. political business cycle.
   b. time inconsistency of policy.
   c. discretionary effect.
   d. substitution effect.
   e. income effect.

5. Economists who argue that monetary policy should be made by a rule make all of the following arguments *except:*
   a. A policy rule limits the incompetence of policymakers.
   b. A policy rule limits the abuse of power of policymakers.
   c. A policy rule is more flexible than discretionary policy.
   d. A policy rule eliminates the time inconsistency problem.

6. Which of the following is an example of a discretionary policy action that further destabilizes the economy?
   a. Investors become pessimistic, and the Fed responds with a reduction in interest rates.
   b. Consumers become pessimistic, and fiscal policymakers respond with a reduction in taxes.
   c. Investors become excessively optimistic, and the Fed responds with a reduction in the money supply.
   d. Consumers become pessimistic, and fiscal policymakers respond with a reduction in government spending.

7. Economists who support a zero inflation target for monetary policy make all of the following arguments *except:*
   a. Even small levels of inflation impose permanent costs on the economy such as shoe leather costs and menu costs.
   b. Inflation erodes peoples' incomes and zero inflation eliminates this problem.
   c. The cost of reducing inflation to zero is temporary while the benefits are permanent.
   d. The cost of reducing inflation to zero could be nearly eliminated if a zero inflation policy were credible.

8. A government budget deficit tends to
   a. redistribute wealth from future generations to the current generation.
   b. redistribute wealth from the current generation to future generations.
   c. have no redistributive effects.
   d. none of the above

9. Which of the following is *not* true with regard to government budget deficits?
   a. Budget deficits place the burden of current spending on future taxpayers.
   b. Budget deficits reduce national saving.
   c. Budget deficits should be scrutinized because they are the only way to transfer wealth across generations of taxpayers.
   d. Budget deficits reduce capital investment, future productivity and, therefore, future incomes.

10. Which of the following is a cost of inflation?
    a. shoeleather costs associated with reduced money holdings
    b. menu costs associated with frequent adjustment of prices
    c. confusion and inconvenience resulting from a changing unit of account
    d. all of the above

11. Economists who argue that the government need not balance its budget make all of the following arguments *except:*
    a. The national debt per person is actually quite small compared to a person's lifetime earnings.
    b. The effects of budget deficits can be somewhat offset if the current generation saves more and leaves bequests to the next generation.
    c. Budget deficits will not become an increasing burden as long as they do not grow more quickly than a nation's nominal income.
    d. Budget deficits increase future growth because they transfer wealth from the present generation to future generations.

12. Which of the following changes to tax laws would encourage more saving but also increase the tax burden on low-income people?
    a. reduce taxes on the return to saving
    b. remove the double taxation on capital income from stocks
    c. reduce inheritance taxes
    d. replace the income tax with a consumption tax
    e. all of the above

13. A reduction in taxes that increases the after-tax return to saving will increase the quantity of saving in the economy if the
    a. substitution effect from the increase in after-tax return to saving exceeds the income effect.
    b. income effect from the increase in after-tax return to saving exceeds the substitution effect.
    c. income effect from the increase in after-tax return to saving equals the substitution effect.
    d. policy is time inconsistent.

14. Tax reform that encourages saving tends to
    a. shift the tax burden toward high-income people away from low-income people.
    b. shift the tax burden toward low-income people away from high-income people.
    c. reduce the rate of growth of output.
    d. reduce the deficit.

15. If discretionary monetary policy is time inconsistent,
    a. the long-run Phillips curve shifts to the right.
    b. the long-run Phillips curve shifts to the left.
    c. the short-run Phillips curve shifts upward.
    d. the short-run Phillips curve shifts downward.

ADVANCED CRITICAL THINKING

Those opposed to government budget deficits argue, among other things, that budget deficits redistribute wealth across generations by allowing the current generation to enjoy the benefits of government spending while future generations must pay for it.

1. Under which of the following cases, (a) or (b), would you argue that there is a greater intergenerational transfer of wealth? Why?
   a. The government increases spending on social programs by buying apples and oranges for the poor but refuses to raise taxes and instead increases the budget deficit.
   b. The government increases spending on bridges, roads, and buildings but refuses to raise taxes and instead increases the budget deficit.

   _____

   _____

   _____

   _____

2. Does the preceding example provide a method by which we might judge when a government budget deficit is fair to each generation and when it is not? Explain.

   _____

   _____

   _____

3. Why might this method be difficult to enforce in practice?

   _____

   _____

   _____

SOLUTIONS

Terms and Definitions

<u>3</u> "Leaning against the wind"

<u>2</u> Destabilizing policy

<u>5</u> Discretionary policy

<u>1</u> Political business cycle

<u>4</u> Time inconsistency of policy

Practice Problems

1. a. See Exhibit 3.
   b. Increase the money supply, increase government spending, decrease taxes. Shift aggregate demand to the right.
   c. See Exhibit 4.
   d. As short-run aggregate supply shifts downward, the economy adjusts to the intersection of short-run AS_2 and AD_2. Then the expansionary aggregate demand policy shifts aggregate demand to AD_3 and the economy moves to the intersection of short-run AS_2 and AD_3.
   e. Destabilize, because the economy had already adjusted back to the long-run natural rate so the increase in aggregate demand caused output to rise above the natural rate.

2. a. No. In the long run, people will grow to expect 3 percent inflation and wages and prices will rise accordingly.
   b. We would move down a short-run Phillips curve and inflation would fall while unemployment would rise above the natural rate.
   c. Yes. The Fed's announcement of a zero inflation target would be more credible and the movement toward zero inflation would create a smaller increase in unemployment.

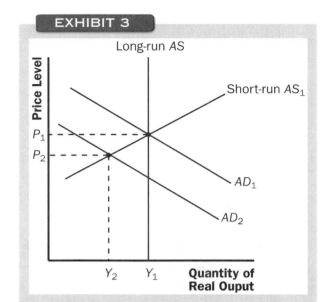

EXHIBIT 3

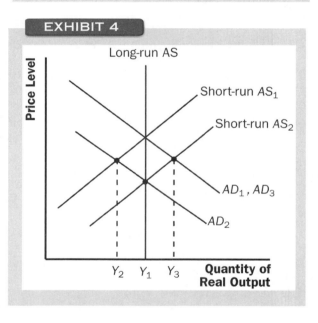

EXHIBIT 4

Short-Answer Questions

1. Macroeconomic shocks need to be forecast months or years into the future because there are lags in the implementation of activist stabilization policy.

2. A rule limits incompetence, abuse of power, and time inconsistency.

3. Inflation imposes continuous costs on the economy such as shoeleather costs and menu costs. Reducing inflation to zero will increase unemployment only temporarily but it will eliminate the continuous costs of inflation.

4. Index the tax system and issue inflation-indexed bonds.

5. It increases future taxes and lowers future incomes because it reduces the capital stock.

6. No. An increase in Social Security benefits paid for by an increase in the payroll tax moves income from working people to retired people, yet the budget deficit is unaffected.

7. The substitution effect must outweigh the income effect. An increase after-tax interest causes people to save more as people substitute saving for current consumption. However, the income effect of an increase in after-tax interest causes people to reduce the amount of saving necessary to reach a targeted amount of saving.

8. High-income people save more than low-income people so the tax relief would go disproportionately to the rich. Also, to maintain tax revenue, consumption taxes might have to be raised causing an additional burden on the poor.

True/False Questions

1. F; fiscal policy has a long decision lag due to the political process.

2. T

3. F; a political business cycle results when policymakers manipulate the economy to improve the incumbent's chance of re-election.

4. T

5. T

6. T

7. F; government budget deficits redistribute wealth to the current generation from future generations.

8. F; since the 1970s, the United States has incurred budget deficits during peace and prosperity.

9. T

10. T

Multiple-Choice Questions

1. d	4. b	7. b	10. d	13. a
2. c	5. c	8. a	11. d	14. b
3. a	6. d	9. c	12. e	15. c

Advanced Critical Thinking

1. Case (a), because the government purchased consumption goods that cannot be enjoyed by later generations, while in case (b) the government purchased capital which is durable and can be enjoyed by later generations.

2. It is more reasonable for the government to run a budget deficit and force future generations to pay for current expenditures if the expenditures are for capital goods.

3. Nearly every interest group can defend their spending as if it has a positive impact on future generations—military, education, etc.